Microsoft® .NET Development for Microsoft Office

Andrew Whitechapel

PUBLISHED BY
Microsoft Press
A Division of Microsoft Corporation
One Microsoft Way
Redmond, Washington 98052-6399

Library of Congress 2004113977

Printed and bound in the United States of America.

3 4 5 6 7 8 9   QWT   9 8 7 6 5

Distributed in Canada by H.B. Fenn and Company Ltd. A CIP catalogue record for this book is available from the British Library.

Microsoft Press books are available through booksellers and distributors worldwide. For further information about international editions, contact your local Microsoft Corporation office or contact Microsoft Press International directly at fax (425) 936-7329. Visit our Web site at www.microsoft.com/mspress. Send comments to mspinput@microsoft.com.

Microsoft, Active Accessibility, ActiveX, Authenticode, BizTalk, Encarta, IntelliSense, JScript, Microsoft Press, MSDN, MSN, Outlook, PowerPoint, SharePoint, Visio, Visual Basic, Visual C#, Visual C++, Visual Studio, Win32, Windows, Windows NT, and Wingdings are either registered trademarks or trademarks of Microsoft Corporation in the United States and/or other countries. Other product and company names mentioned herein may be the trademarks of their respective owners.

The example companies, organizations, products, domain names, e-mail addresses, logos, people, places, and events depicted herein are fictitious. No association with any real company, organization, product, domain name, e-mail address, logo, person, place, or event is intended or should be inferred.

This book expresses the author's views and opinions. The information contained in this book is provided without any express, statutory, or implied warranties. Neither the authors, Microsoft Corporation, nor its resellers, or distributors will be held liable for any damages caused or alleged to be caused either directly or indirectly by this book.

Acquisitions Editor: Ben Ryan
Project Editor: Devon Musgrave
Copy Editor: Ina Chang
Indexer: Seth Maislin

Body Part No. X10-94976

To Elisabeth and Darwin

Contents at a Glance

Table of Contents

What do you think of this book?
We want to hear from you!

Microsoft is interested in hearing your feedback about this publication so we can continually improve our books and learning resources for you. To participate in a brief online survey, please visit: *www.microsoft.com/learning/booksurvey/*

Introduction

A lot of people spend a lot of time in Microsoft Office. In some parts of the financial services industry, people spend their entire working days in Microsoft Excel. In many other industries, people spend their entire working days in Microsoft Word. Microsoft Outlook is another extremely popular productivity tool. A bad tool makes work frustrating; a good tool makes work satisfying. Office offers wide-ranging functionality but is still essentially generic. Everyone's daily workflow involves some generic aspects and some domain-specific aspects. Many people prefer to stay in Office, and developers support this by building extensions to Office or building custom applications that integrate with Office.

Office lends itself to such extension by exposing its native object model to automation and by supporting an increasing number of targeted protocols. Building domain-specific extensions to Office using the exposed object model and protocols fills in the gaps in the software support for user workflow.

All of this is good. But it can be challenging to figure out which protocol or technique to use for a given business requirement. Also, not all of the many possible techniques are well-known. Moreover, some techniques are feasible but make it extremely difficult to build robust or maintainable systems. Another question plaguing the industry is, "Whither VBA?" VBA will continue to be supported for a considerable amount of time. However, VBA comes with significant limitations—source control is difficult, the language lends itself to unstructured code, you face deployment and maintenance problems when the code is embedded in the document, the class library is limited, runtime performance is suboptimal, and so on.

When Microsoft .NET was introduced several years ago, it promised a brighter future. Now that .NET is rapidly maturing, this promise is clearly being borne out. From an infrastructure perspective, it offers features that combine the best behavior of older runtimes, such as the Microsoft Visual Basic runtime, the Java Virtual Machine, and the COM/OLE plumbing. From a development perspective, it offers languages that have the power of C and C++ with the RAD capabilities of Visual Basic or Delphi, and a library that's far more comprehensive and well-thought-out than the Microsoft Foundation Classes (MFC), Active Template Library (ATL), and Abstract Window Toolkit (AWT) put together.

Putting the development and runtime power of .NET together with the user experience richness of Office is a natural move. On the other hand, Office itself is not built with .NET managed code, so building managed solutions with Office offers some interesting technical challenges. Make no mistake: building managed solutions with Office is definitely the way forward, but developers and strategists need to take time to understand the issues and the options.

How This Book Is Organized

The atomic unit of this book is the section, each of which is numbered within the book's chapters. Each section in a chapter focuses on one or two specific techniques for interoperating between Office and managed code. Each section starts with an explanatory prologue and has one exercise or more illustrating the technique, presented in a step-by-step tutorial manner. The sections are grouped together into meaningful categories, which form the chapters of the book.

My original intention was to make each section completely self-contained. Indeed, the working title for the book was *The Office Interop Cookbook*. However, it soon became clear that this would mean a great deal of repetition, so I've put just enough ancillary information into each section not to distract from the main focus. But that means you must read some of the earlier sections before tackling some of the later ones. For example, many of the later examples explore the chosen technique in the context of add-ins, so you really need to understand how to build managed add-ins if you want to get the most out of those later sections. The most critical, "essential" sections that everyone should read first are sections 2.1, 2.2, 3.1, 4.2, 5.1, and 5.2.

Who This Book Is For

This book has two target audiences:

- Developers
- Architects and strategic IT decision makers

The book makes extensive use of practical exercises, which are aimed at developers. When I have my developer's hat on, I don't like just being told about techniques—I want to work through them, to understand them clearly, and to double-check what I'm being told. I never believe any theory about software unless I've checked it out for myself and tested it against real scenarios. Also, I want to know only the bare bones of the technique, without having to wade through a lot of arbitrary context. For these reasons, almost all the example solutions in this book are deliberately simple, so readers can internalize the technique and then apply it to their own domain-specific requirements. You get the critical information without a lot of window-dressing.

The prologue to each section is intended to fulfill the role of the "executive summary." My idea here is that if you read just the introductory part of the chapters, the summaries at the end, and the section prologues, you'll get a pretty good overall perspective on the entire landscape of .NET and Office interop. This is just the right level of detail to enable you to make strategic decisions and point your developers in the right direction.

System Requirements and Code Samples

For information on system requirements and code samples, see Section 1.2, "Notes on the Samples," in Chapter 1.

Microsoft Learning Technical Support

Every effort has been made to ensure the accuracy of this book. Microsoft Press provides corrections for books through the World Wide Web at the following address:

http://www.microsoft.com/learning/support/

To connect directly to the Microsoft Press Knowledge Base and enter a query regarding a question or issue that you may have, go to:

http://www.microsoft.com/learning/support/search.asp

If you have comments, questions, or ideas regarding this book, please send them to Microsoft Press using either of the following methods:

Postal Mail:

> *Microsoft Press Attn: Microsoft .NET Development for Microsoft Office Editor*
> *One Microsoft Way*
> *Redmond, WA 98052-6399*

E-mail:

> *mspinput@microsoft.com*

Acknowledgments

The list of people who contributed in various ways to this book is quite long. Many people saw value in it and gave freely of their time to comment and review. I'm truly grateful to all the wonderful people at Microsoft and elsewhere who helped me in this endeavor.

I was fortunate in having an army of seriously bright people to undertake technical reviews on topics that mapped to their area of expertise or interest. Without a doubt, the technical quality of the book has been improved immeasurably by their generous input. These people included: Jesse Bedford, Mark Boulter, Mark Bower, Paul Daley, Tristan Davis, Michael Herzfeld, Sonja Keserovic, Pat King, Jian Lee, Art Leonard, David Mortenson, Adam Nathan, Kelsey Pedersen, James Rivera, Chad Rothschiller, Alan Shi, Misha Shneerson, Christina Storm, Peter Torr, Lori Turner, and Junfeng Zhang. I tried to faithfully incorporate all their comments and corrections; any remaining errors are my own.

An extra-special word of thanks to Siew Moi Khor, who did a first-pass technical review of all the contents, including testing, identifying errors and omissions, pointing out additional resources, contributing content, and endless sanity checking. More than that, she "recruited" all the technical reviewers from among the good burghers of Redmond and managed the review process very conscientiously. I'm based in London, and Siew Moi did a tremendous job working countless hours into the night, looking after the book's interests across the Atlantic in Redmond. Many, many thanks.

Special thanks also must go to Joe Andreshak and Adam LeVasseur, who believed in the book and fought to get it published. All I wanted to do was get the book to my own customers. Joe and Adam had the vision to bring it to a wider audience. In the UK, Steve Leaback also fought on my behalf to overcome some significant logistical challenges to make sure the book made it into the light of day.

It might seem strange in a Microsoft Press book, but I must thank John Franklin, editorial director at APress, who also believed in the book.

My gratitude also to "Indefatigable" Chris Kunicki, Charles "Ice-Cream" Maxson, Jan Fransen, Julie Kremer, and the rest of the OfficeZealot gang for being supportive and kind to me when it mattered, and for running the best Office developer site in the alpha quadrant. Plus, Richard "PocketNerd" Stockley, from whom I admit I stole some ideas.

I also get tons of support on a day-to-day basis from my teammates in Microsoft Consulting Services UK: Dave Baker, Jon Bonnick, Graeme Buntin, Stefan Delmarco, Matt Helsby, John Hooper, Rob Jarratt, Ninad Kanthi, Eamon MacDermott, Maurice Magnier, Andy Reay, Michael Royster, Niroo Thaya-Paran, Ian Ticehurst, Ajith Vaithianathan, and Mark White.

Finally, this isn't my first book, so I'm familiar with the process, and I can also appreciate how very good my editorial team at Microsoft Press has been. So thanks to Devon Musgrave, Ina Chang, Dan Latimer, Joel Panchot, Bill Teel, Sandi Resnick, and Seth Maislin for such excellent, professional work.

Chapter 1
Overview

This book has two primary goals:

- To provide tactics and coding techniques that developers can quickly absorb
- To recommend strategic best practices for architects and business decision makers

The book covers the full range of options for interoperating between Microsoft Office applications and managed Microsoft .NET code and offers detailed, step-by-step tutorials. In addition to tactical guidelines, it offers a broad perspective on the approaches you can use to build managed solutions that are integrated with Office. All of the techniques presented here are at least reasonable and in many cases represent recommended best practice. I have been careful to exclude techniques that are unsupported or irresolvably flawed. In cases where a particular functional requirement can be met by using alternative strategies, the pros and cons of these strategies are compared.

A wide range of options are available for interoperating with Office applications, and one way to make sense of all the options—and to establish some perspective— is to distinguish between generic techniques and protocols. Generic techniques include automation, Platform Invoke (P/Invoke), Web services, and remoting— broad technologies that can be used in a wide variety of scenarios. Protocols, on the other hand, rely on a small number of interfaces or standards and are very focused in design. Office interop protocols include managed COM add-ins, RealTime Data components, Smart Tags, Smart Documents, and Microsoft Visual Studio Tools for Office (VSTO).

This book assumes a basic knowledge of the Microsoft .NET Framework, the C# language, and the .NET Framework class library. I've chosen to use C# for almost all the sample code because that's the language I'm most comfortable with. All the techniques shown will work equally well using Microsoft Visual Basic .NET or any other managed language. Section 2.6, "Visual Basic .NET vs. C#," highlights the differences between Visual Basic .NET and C# in the context of Office interop.

The primary applications used to illustrate Office interop are Microsoft Excel and Microsoft Word, and a few techniques are available only for Excel. It's a fact of life that Excel and Word have more programmability features than other Office applications. That said, the kinds of differences you can expect to deal with when you implement any particular technique with another Office application are pointed out. A few examples use Microsoft Outlook, Microsoft PowerPoint, or Microsoft Access.

This book contains a large number of practical examples, with step-by-step instructions that take you through a solution from beginning to end. For every technique, there is at least one sample solution (and often two or more). Full sample code is provided on the book's companion Web page (at *http://www.microsoft.com/learning/ books/products/7756*) for all the tutorials, including all solution files, database files, and Office documents. A couple of the sample solutions have evolved into quite useful little tools, and these are also supplied.

Many good articles are available on MSDN online, and I've relied on many of them to augment my own understanding of the various techniques. A number of sections in this book provide links to important sites but not to specific articles, because such links tend to change quickly. For a starting point, the major Microsoft sites to visit are *www.microsoft.com*, *msdn.microsoft.com*, and *office.microsoft.com*.

1.1 Version Variations

This book covers .NET interop with the following versions of Office:

- Office 97 (version 8)
- Office 2000 (version 9)
- Office XP (Office 2002, version 10)
- Office 2003 (version 11)

In most cases, the interop behavior is identical across versions, although some details of the code can vary slightly. Wherever the behavior or the code is different across versions, I have clearly documented this. Some of the newer techniques are available only with the newer versions of Office, and this is also clearly documented.

Note that whichever version of Office you're using, the latest available service pack is generally recommended. In particular, interop with Office 97 is problematic without SR-1 or, better, SR-2.

Each topic presented in its own section—for example, Section 2.1, "Managed Interop Assemblies," and all other numbered sections in the book—begins with a "version block" in the margin that indicates whether the specific technique under discussion is achievable under each version of Office. For example:

Office 97	⊗
Office 2000	?
Office XP	✓
Office 2003	✓

Here are the symbols used within the version blocks that appear throughout the book:

✓	This technique works with this version of Office.
⊗	This technique does not work with this version of Office.
?	This technique works partly with this version of Office or works completely, but the example used to illustrate the technique also uses other techniques that do not work with this version of Office.

The ? symbol might be a little confusing. In almost all cases where it is used, the specific technique works perfectly well with the associated version of Office but the sample solution also uses other version-specific techniques. Examples include Section 12.5, "Strong-Naming," and Section 12.6, "Authenticode Certificates." Both of these techniques apply 100 percent to all versions of Office, but the samples happen to use VSTO, which applies only to Office 2003.

The main techniques/topics described in this book are summarized in Table 1-1. In addition to the version information relevant to each numbered section, this table includes three additional columns. The IA? column indicates whether a technique uses application-specific interop assemblies (IAs). The VBA? column indicates whether this technique requires the additional use of Microsoft Visual Basic for Applications (VBA) in the Office document. The T/S column indicates whether the technique is generally more tactical or more strategic. The symbols used in these final three columns are summarized here:

✓	Uses application-specific IAs (e.g., Excel)
⊗	Does not use any IAs
▣	Uses only general Office IAs (e.g., Extensibility)
T	Tactical, narrowly focused, or solves a very specific problem, often combined with existing VBA scenarios
S	Strategic, broadly applicable, and continues to be relevant going forward

Table 1-1   Office Versions Mapped to Interop Techniques

Section	Technique	Office Version				Sample Solution	IA?	VBA?	T/S
		97	2K	XP	03				
2.1	Managed IAs	✓	✓	✓	✓		✓	✗	S
2.2	Basic interop projects	✓	✓	✓	✓	TestXXXPIA	✓	✗	S
2.3	Office interop wizards	✗	✗	✓	✓		✓	✗	S
2.4	Interface/class ambiguity	✓	✓	✓	✓	AmbiguousMember	✓	✗	S
2.5	Releasing COM objects	✓	✓	✓	✓	CleanRelease	✓	✗	S
2.6	Visual Basic .NET vs. C#	✓	✓	✓	✓	ManagedLanguages	✓	✗	S
2.7	Debugging interop solutions	✓	✓	✓	✓	SimpleBug	✓	✗	S
3.1	Platform Invoke	✓	✓	✓	✓	NativeDLL	✗	✗	S
3.2	Watching Excel quit	✗	?	✓	✓	ExcelQuitter	✓	✗	T
3.3	Using COM by reflection	✓	✓	✓	✓	ReflectCOM	✗	✗	T
3.4	Document properties	✓	✓	✓	✓	GetDocProps	✓	✗	T
3.5	Running instances	✓	✓	✓	✓	RunningInstances	✓	✗	T
3.6	Office accessible objects	✗	✓	✓	✓	AccessExcel	✓	✗	T
3.7	Monitoring Office applications	✗	✓	✓	✓	ExcelMonitor	✓	✗	T
4.1	Managed code from VBA	✓	✓	✓	✓	ManagedCallback	✓	✓	T
4.2	Managed CCW in VBA	✓	✓	✓	✓	ExtraStuff	✗	✓	T
4.3	Managed Office accelerators	✓	✓	✓	✓	ManagedOnKey	✓	✓	T
4.4	Programming the Visual Basic Editor	✓	✓	✓	✓	UseVBE	✓	✓	T
4.5	Office and managed windows	✓	✓	✓	✓	WinInterop	✓	✓	T
4.6	Office document browser	✓	✓	✓	✓	OfficeDocumentBrowser	✗	✗	S
4.7	COM drag-and-drop	✓	✓	✓	✓	OfficeDragDrop	✓	✗	S
5.1	Managed COM add-ins	✗	✓	✓	✓	MyOfficeAddin	◻	✗	S
5.2	Simple add-in projects	✗	✓	✓	✓	SimpleAddins	✓	✗	S

Table 1-1   Office Versions Mapped to Interop Techniques

Section	Technique	Office Version				Sample Solution	IA?	VBA?	T/S
		97	2K	XP	03				
5.3	Multiple host applications	✗	✓	✓	✓	OfficeHelper	✓	✗	T
5.4	Add-ins and user controls	✗	✓	✓	✓	OfficeCalendar	o	✗	S
5.5	Tactical add-in issues	✗	✓	✓	✓	ButtonImage	o	✗	S
5.6	COM add-ins as cell functions	✗	✓	✓	✓	TempConvAddin	o	✓	T
5.7	Excel Automation add-ins	✗	✗	✓	✓	AutomationAddin	o	✗	T
6.1	Managed smart tags	✗	✗	✓	✓	SmartTagDemo	o	✗	S
6.2	Smart tags and VSTO loader	✗	✗	✗	✓	SmartTagDemo_otkloadr	o	✗	S
6.3	*ISmartTagRecognizer2*	✗	✗	✗	✓	SmartTagDemo_otkloadr2	o	✗	S
6.4	MOSTL smart tags	✗	✗	✓	✓	FruitBar	✗	✗	T
6.5	MOSTL generator	✗	✗	✓	✓	MostlGenerator	o	✗	T
6.6	Troubleshooting smart tags	✗	✗	✓	✓		o	✗	S
7.1	Excel and SQL data	✓	✓	✓	✓	ExcelSQLDemo	✓	✗	S
7.2	Excel and XML	✗	?	✓	✓	ExcelXMLDemo	✓	✗	S
7.3	Excel and OLE DB	✓	✓	✓	✓	ExcelData	✓	✗	T
7.4	Managed data feed	✓	✓	✓	✓	LiveFeed	✓	✓	T
7.5	RealTime Data in Excel	✗	✗	✓	✓	MarketData	✓	✗	S
7.6	Sinking Office events	✓	✓	✓	✓	ExcelEvents	✓	✗	S
8.1	COM Shim Wizard	✗	?	✓	✓		o	✗	S
8.2	Add-in shim	✗	✓	✓	✓	MyOfficeAddin_Shimmed	o	✗	S
8.3	Smart tag shim	✗	✗	✓	✓	SmartTagDemo_Shimmed	o	✗	S
8.4	Shim Wizard internals	✗	?	✓	✓		o	✗	T
8.5	Config files	?	✓	✓	✓	ExtensionConfig	o	✗	S
9.1	SOAP Toolkit	✓	✓	✓	✓	OfficeWeb	✗	✓	T
9.2	Managed Web service proxies	?	?	✓	✓	WebAddin	o	✗	S
9.3	WSE security	?	✓	✓	✓	WseAddin	o	✗	S

Table 1-1   Office Versions Mapped to Interop Techniques

Section	Technique	Office Version				Sample Solution	IA?	VBA?	T/S
		97	2K	XP	03				
9.4	Research services	✗	✗	✗	✓	SimpleRascal	✗	✗	S
9.5	Remoting with Office	?	✓	✓	✓	Chat	[o]	✗	T
10.1	VSTO code-behind assemblies	✗	✗	✗	✓	ExcelProject1	✓	✗	S
10.2	Custom document properties	✗	✗	✗	✓	PersistenceControl	✓	✗	T
10.3	Debugging VSTO solutions	✗	✗	✗	✓	BugBehind	✓	✗	S
10.4	Word code-behind	✗	✗	✗	✓	WordProject1	✓	✗	S
10.5	XML lists	✗	✗	✗	✓	XmlList	✓	✗	S
10.6	XML data forms	✗	✗	✗	✓	XmlDataViewer	✓	✗	S
10.7	VSTO and Web services	✗	✗	✗	✓	VstoWeb	✓	✗	S
10.8	VSTO configs	✗	✗	✗	✓	TestConfigs	✓	✗	S
11.1	Smart documents core	✗	✗	✗	✓	BasicXlSmartDoc	✓	✗	S
11.2	Multiple target applications	✗	✗	✗	✓	BasicXlSmartDoc_Word	✓	✗	T
11.3	Smart documents and PIAs	✗	✗	✗	✓	BasicXlSmartDoc_ExcelInterop	✓	✗	S
11.4	Vertigo wrapper	✗	✗	✗	✓	SimpleVertigo	✓	✗	S
11.5	Smart documents and smart tags	✗	✗	✗	✓	SmartDocTags	✓	✗	T
11.6	MOSTL smart documents	✗	✗	✗	✓	CoffeeOnline	✓	✗	T
12.1	Office macro security	✓	✓	✓	✓		✗	✗	S
12.2	Code access security	✓	✓	✓	✓		✗	✗	S
12.3	VSTO security	✗	✗	✗	✓	vstoSecurity	✓	✗	S
12.4	Strong-naming	?	?	?	✓	TestSN	✓	✗	S
12.5	Authenticode certificates	?	?	?	✓	TestSigs	✓	✗	S
12.6	VSTO deployment options	✗	✗	✗	✓	vstoSecurity	✓	✗	S
12.7	Smart documents security	✗	✗	✗	✓	BasicXlSmartDoc_Secure	✓	✗	S

Clearly, the number of ways you can build solutions with managed code integrated with Office is increasing. This is both good and bad. It's good because we have increasing opportunities to meet business requirements. It's bad because it's often not clear which technique is the most appropriate for a given requirement or for a long-term strategy. A big part of the rationale for this book is to provide enough detail and perspective for developers and business decision makers to make informed technology decisions.

1.2 Notes on the Samples

To work with the sample code for this book, you need the following:

- The .NET Framework 1.0 or later (1.1 or later for the VSTO-based samples, including VSTO-loaded smart tags and smart documents)
- Microsoft Visual Studio .NET
- Microsoft Internet Information Services (IIS) 5.1 or later (for the Web services examples)
- Microsoft SQL Server 2000 Desktop Engine (MSDE 2000) or Microsoft SQL Server 2000 (for the database examples)
- Office 97, Office 2000, Office XP, or Office 2003
- Microsoft Internet Explorer 6.0 or later (for the Web browser examples)
- Microsoft Visual Studio Tools for Office 2003
- Primary interop assemblies (PIAs) for Office XP or Office 2003

The Office 2003 PIAs ship with the product itself, and installing them is an optional step in the Office 2003 setup. PIAs for Office XP are downloadable from Microsoft. For earlier versions of Office, you can generate your own IAs. Further details are given in Section 2.1, "Managed Interop Assemblies."

Several tools are supplied with the sample code, as listed in Table 1-2.

Table 1-2 **Sample Tools**

Tool	Description
ButtonFaces	Assembly and source code for the ButtonFaces managed COM add-in
MostlGenerator	Assembly and source code for the MOSTL XML Generator managed COM add-in
Office Interop Wizards	Installer for a set of Visual Studio wizards for generating starter solutions for interoperating with Office XP and Office 2003
GetSN	Simple command-line or Windows Explorer shell context menu tool to get the strong name from an assembly
SetSecurity.js	JavaScript file for setting wizard default VSTO CAS policy

The sample code is organized into folders named as per the instructions in the tutorial notes. There are subfolders for each version of Office, and each subfolder contains only the projects that are workable with that version of Office. Where a sample is workable with multiple versions of Office, you will find multiple versions of that sample in the various subfolders. Note that while a few of these samples might be identical across versions, most involve at least minor differences. Each version's projects reference that specific version's IAs—either ad hoc–generated IAs for Office 97 and 2000, or PIAs for Office XP and Office 2003.

All the VSTO samples are collected in a folder named VSTO. These can be used only with Office 2003. The sample Web services used in some of the examples are in a separate folder because their code is not specific to any version of Office.

In some cases, you might prefer to read through the instructions and follow along with the sample solution code. In other cases, you might want to work through an exercise from scratch. If you choose the second approach, you can use whatever names you like for your solution, project, classes, and so forth, but if you use the suggested names, your code will correspond with the sample solutions supplied. Of course, it is a good idea to put your own solutions in a different subdirectory from the sample code to avoid accidentally overwriting the samples. Some of the samples take shortcuts that are not realistic in production systems, and these are always pointed out so that you know how to do things the right way.

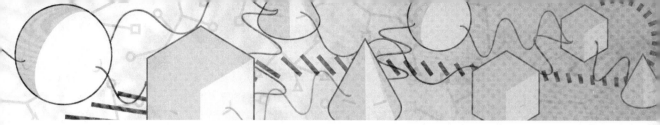

Chapter 2

Basics of Office Interoperability

In this chapter, we'll introduce all the basic concepts of interoperation between Microsoft .NET managed code and Microsoft Office applications. We'll also explore some practical examples that demonstrate how to develop managed applications using Office. The basic mechanics demonstrated in this chapter will form the basis of all later techniques presented in this book.

Office applications are COM servers, so the basis of the interoperation between Office applications and .NET code is COM Interop. The .NET Framework has good support for interaction with COM components, COM+ services, and native operating system services. Code executing under the control of the common language runtime (the CLR, or just "the runtime") is called *managed code*, while code that runs outside the CLR is called *unmanaged code*. All COM components and Win32 API functions are unmanaged code. As we'll see later, this doesn't prevent you from exposing managed .NET code in a way that is visible to, and consumable by, COM clients.

During development, you write your managed code against an interop assembly (IA). This is a managed .NET equivalent of the COM type library. There are several ways of getting an interop assembly, and there are some deployment issues that we need to consider. After you build your code, at run time the CLR places a proxy between your managed code and the Office component you're talking to. We'll see how this proxy behaves and what it does for us. In this chapter, we'll also consider some issues that arise with memory and object lifetime management when managed code interoperates with Office. Finally, we'll make a complete side-by-side comparison of Microsoft Visual Basic .NET and Microsoft C#, to examine their respective advantages and disadvantages for Office development.

At run time, when you make a call from managed code to an (unmanaged) Office function, the CLR performs a number of operations for you. One of the most important is marshaling. Marshaling takes the parameter values you've passed in your managed method call and hands them off to the underlying unmanaged method. Some data types have a common representation in both managed and unmanaged memory and therefore don't need any special handling by the interop marshaler: these types are called "blittable" types, and they include the integral types. All other types are nonblittable, including *char*, *string*, *array*, *struct*, *class*, and so forth. Therefore, as part of its marshaling functionality, the CLR packages up the parameter values and translates them in a way that makes them usable at the other end. The marshaler has a degree of built-in intelligence so it can make sensible decisions about how to translate from a managed data type to an unmanaged data type, and vice versa.

To support the framework's marshaling, you can use various tools that ship with Microsoft Visual Studio .NET to generate wrapper classes to make both managed and unmanaged clients think they are calling objects within their respective environment. The situation is summarized in Figure 2-1. During development, you get an IA that is a managed equivalent to a COM type library. Indeed, the IA is generated based on the type library of the COM server (in this context, an Office application). Then you write your custom .NET code against this IA. In this way, you can develop against the type information in the IA—that is, the enumerations, classes, and interfaces, along with their methods, properties, and events.

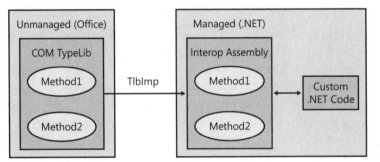

Figure 2-1   Using IAs during development.

Visual Studio .NET ships with a number of tools—which you can use from the command line or from within the IDE—for interoperating CLR and COM objects. They are described in Table 2-1.

Table 2-1   Visual Studio .NET Interop Tools

Tool	Description
AxImp	Creates a .NET proxy for an ActiveX control so the control can be used in a .NET Windows Forms application
TlbImp	Reads a COM type library to generate an IA that .NET clients can use with early binding
TlbExp	Exports a .NET component's type information into a type library file that COM components can use with early binding
RegAsm	Enters a .NET component into the system registry so it can be accessed by COM Services, which invokes it indirectly using the CLR execution engine

Many of the techniques described in this document involve the use of IAs for the Office applications. For Office 97 and Office 2000, you can autogenerate these IAs using TlbImp. Office XP includes pregenerated (and optimized) IAs that you should use instead of autogenerating IAs. An IA distributed by the owner of the original COM server is called a primary interop assembly (PIA). You should always use the specific version of the IA that matches the version of Office you're targeting.

In either case, the general pattern is to right-click the project in Solution Explorer and select Add Reference. Click the COM tab. Then select the appropriate type library—for example, for Excel you would select the following:

- Office 97: Microsoft Excel 8.0 Object Library
- Office 2000: Microsoft Excel 9.0 Object Library
- Office XP: Microsoft Excel 10.0 Object Library
- Office 2003: Microsoft Excel 11.0 Object Library

For Office 97 and Office 2000, this triggers TlbImp to generate a new IA based on the selected type library. For later versions (including Office XP and Office 2003), this simply adds a reference to the existing Microsoft-supplied PIA. You should also find that references have been added for the ancillary Office core and Visual Basic extensibility PIAs. Note that the minimum requirement is Office 97 with Service Release 1 (SR-1). The general behavior of the tools listed (as they are used from within Visual Studio .NET) is described in Table 2-2.

Table 2-2   Using Interop Tools from Visual Studio .NET

Operation	Behavior
Add Reference to COM component	If the PIA is registered, adds a reference to the PIA. Otherwise, runs TlbImp to generate a new IA.
Add Reference to ActiveX control	Runs AxImp.
Drag and drop an ActiveX control from the Tools palette	Runs AxImp.
Project Properties | Configuration Properties | Register for COM Interop	Runs Regasm /tlb /codebase.

At run time, whenever a managed client calls a method on a COM object, it uses a runtime callable wrapper (RCW). In the reverse situation, when a COM client calls into a .NET component, it uses a COM callable wrapper (CCW). This is summarized in Figure 2-2. The functionality provided by the CLR interop layer and the RCW includes translating between managed types (e.g., *string*) and their unmanaged equivalents (e.g., *char[]*). Similarly, return values are translated from their unmanaged type to managed equivalents.

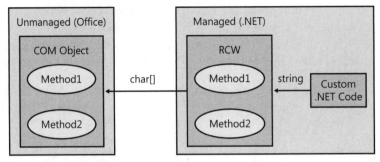

Figure 2-2   Runtime callable wrappers.

Section 2.1 looks at how to use Office IAs, how to launch Office applications, how to attach to running instances of Office applications, and basic use of the native object model of an Office application from managed code. In this way, we'll cover all the basic mechanics of interoperating between managed code and Office applications. Later chapters will build on these basic mechanics.

2.1 Managed Interop Assemblies

Office 97	✔
Office 2000	✔
Office XP	✔
Office 2003	✔

While anyone can create an IA for a COM server, only one IA is designated as the PIA for that server. The PIA contains the official description of the unmanaged types as defined by the publisher of those unmanaged types. The PIA usually also contains certain customizations that make the types easier to use from managed code. The PIA is always digitally signed by the publisher of the original unmanaged component.

Office XP PIAs

For Office XP, Microsoft has created several PIAs that contain the official description of commonly used Office XP type libraries for products such as Microsoft Access, Excel, Outlook, Word, and PowerPoint. These PIAs are known as the Office XP PIAs. Microsoft has customized these PIAs to make it easier for managed code to interoperate with the Office XP COM type libraries. Any Office XP COM IA that is not provided as part of the Office XP PIAs, or any Office XP COM IA that is generated by Visual Studio .NET at design time, should be considered unofficial, and you should avoid using it. The Office XP PIAs cover not only the primary type library for each application but also the dependent DLLs such as ADO, DAO, and MScomctl.

Note that for earlier versions of Office, you can use Visual Studio .NET (which uses TlbImp) to generate IAs from the type library. From that point on, using the Office application's object model will be very similar regardless of whether you're using the Office XP PIA or a TlbImp-generated IA. TlbImp is a tool that ships with Visual Studio .NET that imports a COM type library into a proxy .NET assembly that .NET clients can use with early binding.

You can download the Office XP PIAs from the Microsoft Downloads Web site (*http://msdn.microsoft.com/downloads/*), put them into the global assembly cache (GAC), and register them in the registry. This last step is to ensure that when you develop a .NET application to use Office and add a reference to the Office product of interest, the updated registry entry ensures that the PIA is picked up instead of generating a new IA.

When it comes to deploying a Visual Studio .NET solution that relies on the Office XP PIAs, you can deploy the relevant PIAs in the same folder as your application. But a better approach is to install the PIAs into the GAC on the target machine, using a Visual Studio .NET Setup project.

Office 2003 PIAs

The Office 2003 PIAs are deployed with Office 2003 and should be installed when Office is installed. (Note that the PIAs are not installed during a Typical install, although they are set to install on first use if the .NET Framework is already present.) The best approach is to use a Custom install of Office and select the .NET Programmability Support option for each Office application you want to develop against. Bear in mind that it is somewhat difficult to predict which applications you might want to develop against in the future. Also, there are some ancillary components, such as the Microsoft Forms 2.0 components, that you might not realize you need. For these reasons, it is simpler to select all the .NET Programmability Support options.

If you want to install the Office 2003 PIAs, .NET Framework 1.1 is required. If you don't have .NET Framework 1.1 installed when you install Office 2003, the PIAs will not be installed. Additionally, the option to install the PIAs doesn't show up in the Custom setup for Office. If you do have .NET Framework 1.1 installed, you'll see ".NET Programmability Support" in the list of options when you install Office.

If you install .NET Framework 1.1 only after you've installed Office 2003, to get the PIAs after that, you must rerun the Office setup. On the first page, be sure to select the Choose Advanced Customization Of Applications option.

On the second page, expand all the nodes in the tree to make sure you have identified all the .NET Programmability Support nodes. For instance, the Microsoft Graph PIA is a subnode of Microsoft Graph, which is itself a subnode of Office Tools. The following figure shows the very first PIA in the tree, the Access PIA:

Note that if you are doing development work, you shouldn't do a Typical install of Office 2003 if you want the PIAs. Because of a known bug in Visual Studio .NET and Visual Studio 2003, if PIAs are set to install on demand, as they are in a Typical install, when you reference an Office COM type library you might end up getting a Visual Studio–generated IA. To avoid this issue, do a Complete or Custom install to make sure the Office 2003 PIAs that you need to reference are already installed in the GAC before you start any development work.

Also note that PIA registrations get clobbered a lot. Sometimes a simple action such as installing some arbitrary independent software can clobber a PIA registration. If you know you have the Office 2003 PIAs in the GAC but somehow you keep getting an IA and not the PIA, some type library registration might have broken that specific PIA registration. To fix this, you can do any of the following:

- Do an Office repair: Control Panel || Add/Remove Programs || Office || Change | Repair.

- Reinstall the affected PIA. To do this, rerun Office setup.

- RegAsm that PIA from the GAC to reregister that PIA. For example, to RegAsm the Office PIA (substituting, say, C:\windows or C:\winnt for *%systemroot%*):

  %systemroot%\Microsoft.NET\Framework\v1.1.4322\RegAsm.exe %systemroot%\assembly\GAC\Office\11.0.0.0__71e9bce111e9429c\Office.dll

- Finally, note that when you deploy a solution that uses the Office 2003 PIAs, you should *not* deploy the PIAs themselves. Office setup should be the only mechanism for installing the Office 2003 PIAs.

2.2 Basic Interop Projects

Office 97	✓
Office 2000	✓
Office XP	✓
Office 2003	✓

In this section, we'll explore the use of IAs in a series of practical exercises. In each exercise, we'll create a simple managed Windows Forms application that will interoperate with a specific Office application. First we'll target Excel and demonstrate the basic mechanics of interoperating between Excel and managed code. We'll also look at the details that vary from one version of Excel to another. Then we'll work through similar projects that target Word, Outlook, and PowerPoint.

Throughout these exercises (and in all later exercises), you can use whatever name you like for your project, but if you use the suggested names your projects will correspond with the sample solutions supplied. Of course, it would be a good idea to put your own solutions in a different subdirectory from the sample code, to avoid accidentally overwriting the samples.

Basic Interop with Excel

In this first exercise, we'll create a managed Windows Forms application with a button on the form. When the user clicks the button, we'll launch Excel, add a new workbook to the collection of workbooks, get the ActiveSheet, and then put some dummy text into cell A1. Then we'll see how to quit Excel and make sure that we clean up all the Excel objects. Finally, we'll see where we need to modify our code to accommodate all versions of Excel.

Note The sample solution for this topic can be found in the sample code at <*install location*>\Code\Office<n>\TestExcelPIA.

1. In Visual Studio .NET, create a new Windows application called TestExcelPIA. Put a *Button* control on the form, and set its *Text* property to *Run Excel*. Add a handler for the *Click* event on this button.

2. In Solution Explorer, right-click and select Add Reference. Click the COM tab. For Office XP, select the Microsoft Excel 10.0 Object Library from the list. In the list this will appear as something like C:\Program Files\Microsoft Office\Office 10\Excel.exe, but once you've added the reference, if you look at its properties, you'll see that the path is set to something like this:

   C:\WINDOWS\assembly\GAC\Microsoft.Office.Interop.Excel\10.0.4504.0__ 31bf3856ad364e35\Microsoft.Office.Interop.Excel.dll

   This is the Excel PIA, not the Excel executable. Note that this will be a full path to the location of the PIA in the GAC—the exact path will depend on the version of Office you are developing against. You should also see that references have been added for the Office core and Visual Basic extensibility PIAs.

The procedure for Office 2003 is the same, except that you select the Microsoft Excel 11.0 Object Library from the Add Reference COM list. (For earlier versions of Office, see the following note.)

> **Note** When you select the referenced IA in Solution Explorer, if the *Copy Local* property in the Properties pane is set to *True*, you are referencing an auto-generated IA, not the PIA. You should remove this reference and add the correct one. If you correctly reference the Excel 2003 PIA, your Excel reference's *Copy Local* property will be *False* and the *Path* property, on a Windows XP machine, should look something like this:
>
> *C:\WINDOWS\assembly\GAC\Microsoft.Office.Interop.Excel\11.0.0.0_\
> 71e9bce111e9429c\Microsoft.Office.Interop.Excel.dll*

3. Once you have successfully set a reference to a specific Office IA, you can use it just like any other COM IA. At this point, it's worth running up the Object Browser, where you can see the IA equivalents for the Excel type library:

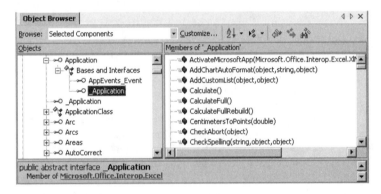

4. Add a *using* statement for the *Microsoft.Office.Interop.Excel* namespace. If you examine the Object Browser carefully, you'll realize that this will introduce an ambiguity: there's an *Application* interface in Excel and also an *Application* class in *System.Windows.Forms*. To fix this, you have a couple of choices. First, you can fully qualify the reference to *Application* in *Main*:

    ```
    System.Windows.Forms.Application.Run(new TestExcelPIAForm());
    ```

    Alternatively, you can reference the *Microsoft.Office.Interop.Excel* namespace through an alias, like so:

    ```
    using Excel = Microsoft.Office.Interop.Excel;
    ```

    Using this second approach, you would qualify each type in the *Microsoft.Office.Interop.Excel* namespace with this alias. For example:

    ```
    Excel.Application xl = new Excel.Application();
    ```

    Whichever approach you use for disambiguating the types, it's obviously a good idea to stick to that approach throughout.

5. In the button *Click* handler, we'll instantiate the Excel Application (not the *ApplicationClass*—see the "Interface/Class Ambiguity" section later) to launch Excel and make it visible:

```
Microsoft.Office.Interop.Excel.Application xl =
    new Microsoft.Office.Interop.Excel.Application();
xl.Visible = true;
```

6. Add a workbook to the collection of workbooks, and then get the active worksheet:

```
Workbook book = xl.Workbooks.Add(XlSheetType.xlWorksheet);
Worksheet sheet = (Worksheet)book.ActiveSheet;
```

7. Specify the cell Range A1 (that is, one cell) and set its value to some arbitrary text:

```
Range r = (Range)sheet.Cells[1,"A"];
r.Value2 = "Hello World";
```

8. Build and test. (Note: Because we set Excel to be visible, it is assumed to be under user control, so Excel doesn't shut down when our application does.)

9. It is quite likely that we want to automate Excel, not make it visible, and terminate it. If this is the required behavior, we should take responsibility for terminating Excel in our code. So add a second button to the form, labeled Quit Excel. Set its *Enabled* property to *false*. (We don't want the user trying to quit Excel before starting it.)

10. Move the declaration of the Excel *Application* object—make it a private field in the form class instead of a local variable in the button handler. We need to access this across two methods.

11. In the COM world, you have to be careful to manage the lifetime of COM objects and release them as soon as you're done with them. In the managed world, the CLR garbage collector cleans up memory for us, and the COM interop layer makes sure that any COM objects we use are eventually released. Sometimes, the nondeterministic release behavior of the CLR garbage collector can be problematic in COM interop situations. This is discussed further in a later section.

In the *Quit Excel* button handler, we'll explicitly quit Excel and set the reference to the *Application* object to *null*. Note that the memory associated with the reference (that is, the proxy to the Excel *Application* object, and therefore the interface pointer on the object itself) will be released according to the normal garbage collection mechanism. Therefore, the Excel process will remain in memory for some indeterminate time after we quit Excel. To clean up immediately, we can force a garbage collection. This is a somewhat heavyweight operation, and you don't want to do this often, but is useful if you want to make sure you're cleaning up completely. You should certainly consider doing this as a matter of course at key termination points, such as when a form or other significant managed object is being destroyed, and at the end of your application.

```
        if (xl != null)
        {
            xl.Quit();
            xl = null;
            GC.Collect();
            GC.WaitForPendingFinalizers();
            GC.Collect();
            GC.WaitForPendingFinalizers();
        }
```

Note that we're repeating the calls to *Collect* and *WaitForPendingFinalizers*. This is because the memory for the Excel reference might have survived the first pass, although it will then have been marked for collection on the next pass. So we will make a second pass to clean up anything that survived the first pass but was otherwise available for collection.

12. Build and test.

When you quit Excel, you'll get the usual prompt about saving your changes, and this message box might well be hidden behind the main Excel window. If you want to avoid this message box, you have several choices:

■ Save the workbook before you quit.

■ Turn off Excel's standard alerts.

■ Set the workbook's *Saved* status to *true*.

We'll look at saving workbooks in later sections because it introduces other issues. So, if you want to turn off Excel's standard alerts, just add this line of code–the sensible place to do this is just after you've instantiated the Excel *Application* object:

```
    xl.DisplayAlerts = false;
```

Alternatively, to set the workbook's *Saved* status to *true*, add this line of code instead (after making the code that actually changes the workbook's data):

```
book.Saved = true;
```

When you've done that, build and test the solution:

Interop with Office 97 and Office 2000

For Office 97 and Office 2000, don't install the Office XP/2003 PIAs. If you need to uninstall them, following the instructions in <Office XP PIA, install folder>\ ReadMe.htm. To save time, you can use the sample unregisterPIAs.bat file, which removes all the Office XP PIAs from the GAC. You must then remove the registry entries corresponding to the reg files in <Office XP PIA install folder>. The registry entries in these files will redirect most COM uses of Office to the Office XP PIAs. If necessary, reinstall Office 97 to restore the correct registry entries. Pay close attention to the gacutil output—if a GAC assembly is currently in use, it won't be deleted from the GAC.

Reinstalling Office 97 or Office 2000 will restore the Office 97 or Office 2000 registry entries, respectively, but it won't remove the additional entries added by the Office XP or Office 2003 PIAs. You particularly need to make sure that the additional typelib entries are removed because marshaling the COM interfaces is done on the basis of the application's type library. Registering the Office XP PIAs adds a typelib entry to the registry, as shown here (for Excel):

[HKEY_CLASSES_ROOT\TypeLib\{00020813-0000-0000-C000-000000000046}\1.4]

"PrimaryInteropAssemblyName"="Microsoft.Office.Interop.Excel, Version=10.0.4504.0, Culture=neutral, PublicKeyToken=31bf3856ad364e35"

So, using RegEdit, you can delete this 1.4 (Office XP) subkey or 1.5 (Office 2003) subkey, leaving the earlier 1.0 and 1.2 entries.

> **Warning** Editing the registry incorrectly can cause serious problems that might require you to reinstall Windows. There is no guarantee that problems resulting from the incorrect use of RegEdit (including the use of .reg files) can be solved. Use RegEdit at your own risk.

The Office XP and Office 2003 PIA registry entries include HKCR\CLSID InprocServer32 entries for the objects themselves. You can remove these or leave them in if you want, because the original LocalServer32 entries will be used instead.

In the project, don't reference the Office XP or Office 2003 PIAs. Instead, generate a new IA from the application's typelib—for example, from Excel8.olb in Office 97 or Excel9.olb in Office 2000. This will be listed on the COM tab of the Add References dialog box. When you add it, the ancillary interop assemblies (Office and VBIDE) will also be generated. The namespaces for these interop assemblies will be different from those in the PIAs. For example:

```
//using Microsoft.Office.Interop.Excel;    // Office XP version
using Excel;                    // Office 97/2000 version
```

Note that because the interop assembly for Excel that is generated by Visual Studio has Excel as its root namespace, you can't use the name Excel as an alias. You could use anything else, of course. Alternatively, and to avoid the ambiguity between the Excel.Application and the System.Windows.Forms.Application mentioned above, you can fully qualify the reference to the *Application* in *Main*:

```
System.Windows.Forms.Application.Run(new TestExcelPIAForm());
```

To launch the Excel application, you use the following changes:

```
// Microsoft.Office.Interop.Excel.Application xl =
//     new Microsoft.Office.Interop.Excel.Application();
Excel.Application xl  = new Excel.Application();
```

Subsequently, the bulk of the code will be the same for all versions of the application.

> **Note**   Instead of generating the IAs each time, you can generate them once, put them somewhere suitable, and thereafter reference them from that location.

Now that we've seen how to perform basic operations with Excel, we'll demonstrate how to perform equivalent functionality with Word, Outlook, and PowerPoint. You'll see that the basic interop mechanics are the same for all Office applications, even though the fine details differ according to each application's functionality. By the same token, you'll see that the basic mechanics are nearly identical across all versions of any particular application, with only minor changes to any of the project settings or code.

Basic Interop with Word

In this exercise, we'll create a simple Windows Forms application to launch Word, add a new document, and insert some dummy text.

> **Note**   The sample solution for this topic can be found in the sample code at <install location>\Code\Office<n>\TestWordPIA.

1. In Visual Studio .NET, create a new Windows application called TestWordPIA. Put a *Button* control on the form, and set its *Text* property to *Run Word*. Add a handler for the *Click* event on this button. Add a second *Button* control, set its *Text* property to *Quit Word*, and add a *Click* handler.

2. In Solution Explorer, right-click and select Add Reference. Click the COM tab. For Office 2003, select the Microsoft Word 11.0 Object Library from the list. This will appear in the list as something like C:\Program Files\Microsoft

Office\Office11\MSWord.olb, but once you've added the reference, if you look at its properties, you'll see that the path is set to something like this:

C:\WINDOWS\assembly\GAC\Microsoft.Office.Interop.Word
\11.0.0.0__71e9bce111e9429c\Microsoft.Office.Interop.Word.dll

This is the Word PIA, not the Word executable. Note that this will be a full path to the location of the PIA in the GAC–the exact path will depend on the version of Office you are developing against. You should also see that references have been added for the Office core and Visual Basic extensibility PIAs. All three of these should have their *Copy Local* property set to *False* by default.

3. Add a *using* statement for the *Microsoft.Office.Interop.Word* namespace. This intro-duces an ambiguity between the *Application* interface in Word and the *Application* class in *System.Windows.Forms*. To fix this, you can reference the *Microsoft.Office.Interop.Word* namespace through an alias:

```
using Word = Microsoft.Office.Interop.Word;
```

4. Qualify each type in the *Microsoft.Office.Interop.Word* namespace with this alias. For example, our first declaration should be for a *Word.Application* interface refer-ence. Declare this as a class field member:

```
private Word.Application word;
```

5. In the button *Click* handler for the Run Word button, set up a try block, instantiate the Word *Application* object to launch Word, and make it visible. Also, get hold of the *Documents* collection:

```
private void btnRunWord_Click(object sender, System.EventArgs e)
{
    try
    {
        word = new Word.Application();
        word.Visible = true;
        Word.Documents docs = (Word.Documents)word.Documents;
```

6. Add a *Document* to the collection of *Documents*. The *Documents.Add* method takes four parameters. All are optional; in this example, we only want to pass specific values for the last two. We can use the *System.Type.Missing* value for the first two. The third parameter specifies the type of document to add–in this case, a docu-ment (as opposed to a Web page or e-mail message). For the last parameter, we'll pass *true* to indicate that we want the document to be made visible:

```
object templateName = Type.Missing;
object openAsNewTemplate = Type.Missing;
object openVisible = true;
object documentType = Word.WdDocumentType.wdTypeDocument;
Word.Document doc = docs.Add(
    ref templateName, ref openAsNewTemplate,
    ref documentType, ref openVisible);
```

7. Next we need to get a *Range* object to insert some text. We'll use starting and ending positions of zero because we know there's no text in our new document yet. Call the *Range.InsertAfter* method, and then close off the *try/catch* block:

```
object startPosition = 0;
object endPosition = 0;
Word.Range r = (Word.Range)doc.Range(
    ref startPosition, ref endPosition);
r.InsertAfter("Hello TestWordPIAForm");
}
catch (Exception ex)
{
    Debug.WriteLine(ex.Message);
}
}
```

8. In the *Click* handler for the Quit Word button, first make a call to Word's *Application.Quit* method. Then be sure to clean up. In this simple example, the managed references we have used to access the *Documents* collection, and the *Document* and *Range* objects, will all go out of scope at the end of the *Click* handler and become available for collection, thereby releasing the underlying Word objects. However, the *Word.Application* reference was scoped to the form class and won't go out of scope until the form itself is destroyed. Because we are quitting Word in our *Quit Word* method, we can also clean up this reference at this point:

```
private void btnQuitWord_Click(object sender, System.EventArgs e)
{
    object missing = Type.Missing;
    word.Quit(ref missing, ref missing, ref missing);
    word = null;
    GC.Collect();
    GC.WaitForPendingFinalizers();
    GC.Collect();
    GC.WaitForPendingFinalizers();
}
```

9. Build and test. The run-time behavior should look like this:

> **Version Notes**   For each version of Word, the specific version of the PIA or IA should be referenced. The code as described above will work for both Word 2003 and Word XP. For Word 2000, the only change is to remove the aliased namespace using *statement*. For Word 97, remove the aliased namespace using *statement* and remove the last two parameters to the call to the *Documents.Add* method.

Basic Interop with Outlook

In this exercise, we'll create a simple Windows Forms application to launch Outlook and add a new *AppointmentItem*, including some dummy text and arbitrary properties. Consistency between the Office applications is good, but in terms of programmability they are by no means identical. Outlook probably differs most from the other Office applications. Outlook's object model is significantly different in many respects. This has a lot to do with the way Outlook integrates with Microsoft Exchange Server as well as with Outlook's wide-ranging functionality–support for e-mail, the address book, and calendaring are all significantly different in functionality. As a trivial example, we've seen that both Excel and Word offer an *Application* object, and that this object exposes a *Visible* property. Outlook does expose an *Application* object, but making Outlook visible is a somewhat more complicated proposition, as we will see.

> **Note**   The sample solution for this topic can be found in the sample code at <install location>\Code\Office<n>\TestOutlookPIA.

In Visual Studio .NET, create a new Windows application called TestOutlookPIA. Put two *Button* controls on the form, labeled Run Outlook and Quit Outlook. Add handlers for the *Click* events on these buttons.

In Solution Explorer, right-click and select Add Reference. Click the COM tab. For Office 2003, select the Microsoft Outlook 11.0 Object Library from the list. In the list this will appear as something like C:\Program Files\Microsoft Office\Office11\ MSOutl.olb, but once you've added the reference, if you look at its properties, you'll see that the path is set to something like this:

C:\WINDOWS\assembly\GAC\Microsoft.Office.Interop.Out-look\11.0.0.0__71e9bce111e9429c\Microsoft.Office.Interop.Outlook.dll

At the top of your code, add an aliased *using* statement for the Outlook namespace:

```
using Outlook = Microsoft.Office.Interop.Outlook;
```

Declare a reference to the *Outlook.Application* object as a field in your form class:

```
private Outlook.Application outlook;
```

In the Run Outlook button *Click* handler, set up a *try* block and launch Outlook through the Application reference. Then get hold of the MAPI *Namespace* object—we need this to make the calendar visible:

```
try
{
    outlook = new Outlook.Application();
    Outlook.NameSpace mapiNamespace = outlook.GetNamespace("MAPI");
    Outlook.MAPIFolder mapiFolder = mapiNamespace.GetDefaultFolder(
        Outlook.OlDefaultFolders.olFolderCalendar);
    mapiFolder.Display();
```

Use Outlook's *Application.CreateItem* method to create a new appointment and set some arbitrary properties. Save the appointment and finish off the *try/catch* block:

```
    Outlook.AppointmentItem appointment =
        (Outlook.AppointmentItem)outlook.CreateItem(
        Outlook.OlItemType.olAppointmentItem);
    appointment.Start = DateTime.Now.AddMinutes(1);
    appointment.Duration = 60;
    appointment.Subject = "Coffee";
    appointment.Body = "Go to cafe to get more coffee";
    appointment.Location = "London";
    appointment.Save();
}
catch (Exception ex)
{
    Debug.WriteLine(ex.Message);
}
```

Code the *Quit Outlook* handler to both quit Outlook and clean up the class-scoped *Application* reference:

```
    outlook.Quit();
    outlook = null;
    GC.Collect();
    GC.WaitForPendingFinalizers();
    GC.Collect();
    GC.WaitForPendingFinalizers();
```

Build and test. The run-time behavior should look like this:

Version Notes For each version of Outlook, the specific version of the PIA or IA should be referenced. The code as described above will work for both Outlook 2003 and Outlook XP. For Outlook 2000, the only change is to remove the aliased namespace *using* statement. For Outlook 97, remove the aliased namespace *using* statement and change the statement that calls *CreateItem* to use the older *OlItems* enumeration in place of the *OlItemType* enumeration:

```
Outlook.AppointmentItem appointment =
    (Outlook.AppointmentItem)outlook.CreateItem(
//      Outlook.OlItemType.olAppointmentItem);
    Outlook.OlItems.olAppointmentItem);
```

Basic Interop with PowerPoint

In this exercise, we'll create a simple Windows Forms application to launch Power-Point, add a new slide, and insert some dummy text. The PowerPoint object model is much closer in behavior to Excel and Word than Outlook's is. For example, Power-Point exposes an *Application* object with a *Visible* property. PowerPoint also exposes a *Presentations* collection, and each *Presentation* has a *Slides* collection. This is similar to Excel, which offers a *Workbooks* collection where each *Workbook* has a *Worksheets* collection. In much the same way, Word has a *Documents* collection.

Note The sample solution for this topic can be found in the sample code at <install location>\Code\Office<n>\TestPowerPointPIA.

1. In Visual Studio .NET, create a new Windows application called TestPowerPoint-PIA. Put two *Button* controls on the form, labeled Run PowerPoint and Quit PowerPoint. Add handlers for the *Click* events on these buttons.

2. In Solution Explorer, right-click and select Add Reference. Click the COM tab. For Office 2003, select the Microsoft PowerPoint 11.0 Object Library from the list. In the list this will appear as something like C:\Program Files\Microsoft Office\Office11\MSPpt.olb, but once you've added the reference, if you look at its properties, you'll see that the path is set to something like this:

   C:\WINDOWS\assembly\GAC\Microsoft.Office.Interop.Power-Point\11.0.0.0__71e9bce111e9429c\Microsoft.Office.Interop.PowerPoint.dll

3. At the top of your code, add an aliased *using* statement for the PowerPoint and core Office namespaces:

```
using PowerPoint = Microsoft.Office.Interop.PowerPoint;
using Office = Microsoft.Office.Core;
```

4. Declare a reference to the *PowerPoint.Application* object as a field in your form class:

```
private PowerPoint.Application powerPoint;
```

5. In the Run PowerPoint button *Click* handler, set up a *try* block, launch Power-Point through the *Application* reference, and make it visible. Then get hold of the *Presentations* collection and add a new *Presentation*:

```
try
{
    powerPoint = new PowerPoint.Application();
    powerPoint.Visible = Office.MsoTriState.msoTrue;
    PowerPoint.Presentations ppts = powerPoint.Presentations;
    PowerPoint.Presentation ppt = ppts.Add(
        Office.MsoTriState.msoTrue);
```

6. Get hold of the *Slides* collection, and add a new *Slide*:

```
PowerPoint.Slides slides = ppt.Slides;
PowerPoint.Slide slide = slides.Add(
    1, PowerPoint.PpSlideLayout.ppLayoutBlank);
```

7. Get hold of the *Shapes* collection, and add a text box shape. Put some dummy text into this text box. Finally, finish off the *try/catch* block.

```
PowerPoint.Shapes shapes = slide.Shapes;
PowerPoint.Shape shape =
    shapes.AddTextbox(
        Office.MsoTextOrientation.msoTextOrientationHorizontal,
        0, 0, 500, 50);
    shape.TextFrame.TextRange.InsertAfter(
        "Hello TestPowerPointPIAForm");
}
catch (Exception ex)
{
    Debug.WriteLine(ex.Message);
}
```

8. Code the *Quit PowerPoint* handler to both quit PowerPoint and clean up the class-scoped *Application* reference:

```
powerPoint.Quit();
powerPoint = null;
GC.Collect();
GC.WaitForPendingFinalizers();
GC.Collect();
GC.WaitForPendingFinalizers();
```

9. Build and test.

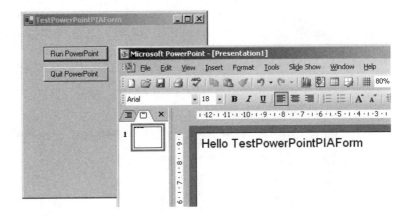

> **Version Notes**   For each version of PowerPoint, the specific version of the PIA or IA should be referenced. The code as described above will work for both PowerPoint 2003 and PowerPoint XP. For PowerPoint 2000 and PowerPoint 97, the only change is to remove the aliased namespace *using* statements.

From this section, it should now be clear that, while each Office application offers different functionality, there is some consistency across all the Office object models. More important, the basic mechanics for developing managed code against Office applications are essentially the same. There is also little variation across different versions of any one Office application. This means that throughout the rest of this book we can focus on the use of each technique without worrying unduly about the specific Office application or application version that we use to demonstrate the technique.

2.3 Visual Studio .NET Office Interop Wizards

Office 97	⊗
Office 2000	⊗
Office XP	✓
Office 2003	✓

The previous section demonstrated how to generate Visual Studio .NET projects that interoperate with Office, using either the PIAs that ship with Office XP and Office 2003 or Visual Studio–generated IAs for Office 97 and Office 2000.

Accompanying this book is a complete set of sample source projects for all the walk-through exercises (for each version of Office where workable). In addition, there is a set of simple tools that you can use to make managed Office development simpler and quicker. Among these tools is a Microsoft Installer file (MSI) for a set of Visual Studio .NET Office Interop Wizards. These are standard wizard extensions to Visual Studio .NET 2003 (Framework 1.1) that generate projects with predefined skeleton code and project properties. These properties include references to the Office 2003 or Office XP PIAs for the particular target Office application you're working with. The wizard-generated code includes a simple fragment that launches the target Office application and puts some simple data into it.

To install these wizards, first make sure you don't have any instances of Visual Studio currently running. Then simply run the MSI. Once you've installed the wizards, start Visual Studio and select File | New | Project. In the New Project dialog box, expand the Visual C# Projects node, and you will see a new child node labeled Office Interop. Expand this node, and you will see two further child nodes, for Office 2003 and Office XP, respectively:

As you can see, there are four different project types for each version of Office, covering Excel, Outlook, PowerPoint, and Word XP and Word 2003.

The default project name is based on the name of the target Office application and the version. As normal with Visual Studio projects, a numeric suffix is used, which is automatically incremented and allows for any other similarly named project that might already exist in the target location.

When you run one of the wizards, the code generated includes a simple test that launches the target Office application and inserts some dummy data. For example, the code generated for an Excel 2003 project includes code to launch Excel, add a *Workbook* to the *Workbooks* collection, and insert some dummy text into cell A1 in the *ActiveSheet*:

```
public Excel2003InteropApplication1Form()
{
    InitializeComponent();


    // TODO
    // This sample code demonstrates how to launch Excel.
    // After you have tested that this works, you can safely
    // remove all this code.
    try
```

```
    {
        Excel.Application xl = new Excel.Application();
        xl.Visible = true;

        Excel.Workbooks books = (Excel.Workbooks)xl.Workbooks;
        Excel.Workbook book = books.Add(Excel.XlSheetType.xlWorksheet);
        Excel.Worksheet sheet = (Excel.Worksheet)book.ActiveSheet;

        Excel.Range r = (Excel.Range)sheet.Cells[1,"A"];
        r.Value2 = "Hello Excel2003InteropApplication1Form";

        r = null;
        sheet = null;
        book = null;
        books = null;
        xl = null;
        GC.Collect();
        GC.WaitForPendingFinalizers();
        GC.Collect();
        GC.WaitForPendingFinalizers();
    }
    catch (Exception ex)
    {
        Debug.WriteLine(ex.Message);
    }
    // ODOT
}
```

Each of the eight wizards relies on the appropriate PIA for the target Office application being registered and deployed to the GAC. If you attempt to generate a project for an application for which the PIA is either not registered or not GAC-deployed, the wizard will fail with an explanatory message. You don't need all of the PIAs installed—just the one you're targeting.

When you've generated the skeleton project, it's a good idea to build it and execute it to make sure that the environment is set up correctly. Then you can safely delete the test code (or comment it out, if you want to use it for reference later).

The wizards were designed to work only with Office 2003 and Office XP because at the time of writing these are the only versions of Office for which Microsoft ships PIAs. While it would be easy enough to create wizards that cover Office 97 and Office 2000, the wizards do have to make certain assumptions about where the IAs are to be found. With Office 97 and 2000, it's not possible to make these assumptions. It would be possible, of course, to simply regenerate IAs based on the registered Office type library. However, regenerating IAs for each and every project is clearly inefficient. For these reasons, then, the wizards support only Office 2003 and Office XP. The wizards also generate only C# code. Again, it would be simple enough to generate Visual Basic .NET code, but the majority of the code in this book is written in C#, so I've kept things simple.

> **Note**   If you ever need to uninstall the wizards, you can do so either by running the MSI again (and choosing the Remove option) or by going to Control Panel | Add Or Remove Programs and clicking the Remove button for the Visual Studio .NET Office Interop Wizards in the normal way.

2.4 Interface/Class Ambiguity

Office 97	✓
Office 2000	✓
Office XP	✓
Office 2003	✓

The IAs, including the Office PIAs, include several types with the same root name, with or without the suffix "Class." You should use only objects that do not end with the suffix. For example, the *Excel.ApplicationClass* type is a class that implements the *Excel.Application, Excel._Application*, and *Excel.AppEvents_Event* interfaces. Confusion can arise because tools such as the Visual Studio Object Browser and ILDASM show the *_Application* and *AppEvents_Event* interfaces, but the only relevant class they show is *ApplicationClass*. In fact, there will also be an *Application* class. Therefore, the following statements, which declare instances of the Word and Excel *Application* classes, are correct, despite the listings in the Object Browser:

```
Word.Application wd = new Word.Application();
Excel.Application xl = new Excel.Application();
```

The (somewhat invisible) *Application* class gives us access to all the methods, events, and properties exposed by the "real" Excel Application COM object. So when we ask for a new *Application*, the real *Application* COM class object is actually instantiated on our behalf.

One reason why the exposed object services have been split into multiple interfaces is because .NET cannot resolve the difference between overloaded statements across member types. For example, the *Word.Application* object exposes both a *Quit* event and a *Quit* method, and the .NET CLR cannot resolve the ambiguity.

Another reason is an attempt to rationalize the behavior that is expected by developers who have a C/C++ background or a Visual Basic background. Traditional Visual Basic developers are used to dealing with classes, not interfaces. C/C++ developers are used to dealing with both classes and interfaces. Part of the behavior of traditional Visual Basic was to streamline development and effectively hide interfaces as classes. Now that many developers are transitioning from both traditional Visual Basic and C/C++ to Visual Basic .NET or C#, the distinction between classes and interfaces has to be more explicit.

In the following simple example, we'll develop a .NET Windows Forms application to interoperate with Word. We'll offer the user two buttons: one to launch Word, the other to quit Word. A common dilemma with Office interop is that if you make the application visible, you have to allow for the user to interact with it. So although we're launching Word, there is a possibility that the user will quit Word. We don't want to be in the situation where we try to quit an instance of Word that has already closed. Fortunately, Word fires a *Quit* event when it closes, so we can intercept this event and take appropriate action.

> **Note** The sample solution for this topic can be found in the sample code at <install location>\Code\Office<n>\AmbiguousMember.

C# Version

1. Create a new Windows Forms application called AmbiguousMember. Add a reference to the appropriate Word IAs for your target version of Office. Put two *Button* controls on the form, and get *Click* event handlers for each one. Set the *Enabled* property of the QuitWord button to *false*—there's no point letting users think they can quit Word if we haven't launched it yet:

2. Add a reference to the appropriate Word IAs for your target version of Office. Declare a class field for the *Word.Application* object.

   ```
   private Word.Application wd;
   ```

   Bear in mind that the runtime will instantiate a real Word *Application* object on our behalf, and this object will implement multiple interfaces. The COM-heads among you will realize that when we ask for a C# *Application* object, what's happening is that the runtime performs a *QueryInterface* on the COM *Application* class object to return us an *Application* interface pointer.

3. In the *Click* handler for the RunWord button, we'll instantiate the Word *Application* object and make it visible. For simplicity, we won't bother opening or adding any documents. Then we'll toggle the *Enabled* state of both buttons:

   ```
   private void btnRunWord_Click(object sender, System.EventArgs e)
   {
       wd = new Word.Application();
       wd.Visible = true;
       btnQuitWord.Enabled = true;
       btnRunWord.Enabled = false;
   }
   ```

4. In the *QuitWord* handler, we'll call the *Word.Quit* method, release the COM object, and force a garbage collection. Then we'll toggle the *Enabled* state of the buttons again:

```
private void btnQuitWord_Click(object sender, System.EventArgs e)
{
    if (wd != null)
    {
        object missing = Type.Missing;
        wd.Quit(ref missing, ref missing, ref missing);
        wd = null;
        GC.Collect();
        GC.WaitForPendingFinalizers();
        GC.Collect();
        GC.WaitForPendingFinalizers();
    }
    btnRunWord.Enabled = true;
    btnQuitWord.Enabled = false;
}
```

5. Build and test. So long as we do things in the right order and the user doesn't interfere, everything will be fine. However, see what happens if we launch Word, then the user quits Word interactively, and then we try to quit Word. Of course, the Word COM server will have stopped, so we'll get an RPC exception.

6. To allow for the user quitting Word from underneath us, we should hook up Word's *Quit* event. Now we have a slight problem: if you try to access the *Quit* event member from our existing *Application* object, you'll find that you can't. This is because the *Application* interface doesn't have a *Quit* method. However, remember that behind the scenes, we're really accessing a real COM Word *Application* class object, and that *Application* is only one of the interfaces it implements.

    If you look in the Object Browser, you'll see that the *ApplicationClass* class implements multiple interfaces, including several event interfaces:

So, should we have declared an *ApplicationClass* reference in the first place, instead of an *Application* reference? Well, you can try it, but it won't work. The *ApplicationClass* lists the *Quit* method, but it doesn't list the *Quit* event. If it did, the two *Quit* members would be ambiguous, and the runtime cannot resolve such ambiguity. In fact, the *Quit* event is listed in the event interfaces:

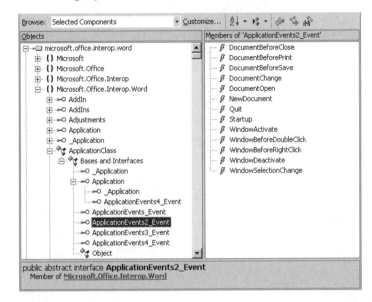

7. To hook up the *Quit* event using our existing reference, we'll need to cast to the appropriate interface. Remember that this is really doing a *QueryInterface* for us behind the scenes to switch from one interface pointer to another interface pointer on the same object. Add this code to the RunWord button *Click* handler:

```
Word.ApplicationEvents2_Event wdEvents2 =
    (Word.ApplicationEvents2_Event)wd;
wdEvents2.Quit +=
    new Word.ApplicationEvents2_QuitEventHandler(QuitHandler);
```

8. When you hook up an event handler in this way, what you're saying is that when Word fires the *Quit* event, the runtime should call into our custom method, where we can do whatever we think is appropriate. In the code above, we've specified a custom method called *QuitHandler*, which we now need to write. We'll implement it to simply set the *Application* reference to *null* and toggle the *Enabled* state of our buttons.

```
private void QuitHandler()
{
    wd = null;
    btnRunWord.Enabled = true;
    btnQuitWord.Enabled = false;
}
```

Note that, despite the somewhat confusing view we have of the *Application* class presented to us by the Object Browser and Visual Studio IntelliSense, we can quite happily instantiate classes using the *Application* type. We can also explicitly cast to any interface that this class implements. Although this seems confusing, we do end up coding correctly, using exactly the right type (class or interface) for each scenario.

9. If you're paying close attention, you'll notice that we've set up a race condition here. In our *QuitWord* button handler, there's a window of opportunity between calling *Quit* and releasing the object reference. If our *QuitHandler* is invoked at that precise point, the reference will be set to *null*, so when we try to release it we'll fail. One simple way to eliminate this possibility is to unhook the event handler before we call *Quit*:

```
if (wd != null)
{
    wdEvents2.Quit -=
        new Word.ApplicationEvents2_QuitEventHandler(QuitHandler);
    object missing = Type.Missing;
    wd.Quit(ref missing, ref missing, ref missing);
    wd = null;
    GC.Collect();
    GC.WaitForPendingFinalizers();
    GC.Collect();
    GC.WaitForPendingFinalizers();
}
```

10. Build and test again.

You should find that we have dealt cleanly with the situation in which we launch a particular instance of Word but the user has closed it. For completeness, a listing of all the significant code—that is, all the code apart from the wizard- and designer-generated code—follows. Don't forget that the material accompanying this book includes all the sample solutions in full for all versions of Office where that topic is feasible.

```
using System;
using System.Drawing;
using System.Collections;
using System.ComponentModel;
using System.Windows.Forms;
using System.Data;

using Word = Microsoft.Office.Interop.Word;
using System.Runtime.InteropServices;
using System.Diagnostics;


namespace AmbiguousMember
{
    public class AmbiguousMemberForm : System.Windows.Forms.Form
```

```csharp
{

    // Wizard/Designer code omitted here for brevity.
    private Word.Application wd;
    private Word.ApplicationEvents2_Event wdEvents2;


    private void btnRunWord_Click(object sender, System.EventArgs e)
    {
        wd = new Word.Application();
        wd.Visible = true;

        wdEvents2 = (Word.ApplicationEvents2_Event)wd;
        wdEvents2.Quit +=
            new Word.ApplicationEvents2_QuitEventHandler(QuitHandler);

        btnQuitWord.Enabled = true;
        btnRunWord.Enabled = false;
    }


    private void btnQuitWord_Click(object sender, System.EventArgs e)
    {
        if (wd != null)
        {
            wdEvents2.Quit -=
                new Word.ApplicationEvents2_QuitEventHandler(QuitHandler);

            object missing = Type.Missing;
            wd.Quit(ref missing, ref missing, ref missing);

            wd = null;
            GC.Collect();
            GC.WaitForPendingFinalizers();
            GC.Collect();
            GC.WaitForPendingFinalizers();
        }
        btnRunWord.Enabled = true;
        btnQuitWord.Enabled = false;
    }


    private void QuitHandler()
    {
        wd = null;
        btnRunWord.Enabled = true;
        btnQuitWord.Enabled = false;
    }

}
}
```

Visual Basic .NET Version

If we're working in Visual Basic .NET, we suffer the same problem of ambiguity and the same confusion about the *Application* class and the *Application* interface.

We need to declare the Word *Application* COM object reference to be an *Application* interface reference. We also need a reference to the Word *ApplicationEvents2_Event* interface, even though this interface does not show up in Microsoft IntelliSense nor in the Object Browser.

```
Public wd As Word.Application
Public wdEvents As Word.ApplicationEvents2_Event
```

Then, in our *RunWord* button handler, we instantiate the *Application* object and assign it to our *Application* reference. Then we can typecast from the *Application* interface to the *ApplicationEvents2_Event* interface (which, of course, performs a COM *QueryInterface* call behind the scenes). Then we can add a handler for the *Quit* event. We use the *AddHandler* statement instead of using the *Handles* keyword, because it allows us to dynamically remove the handler later. Note that IntelliSense does not offer the *ApplicationEvents2_Event* interface, nor the *Quit* member, so be careful with the spelling:

```
Private Sub btnRunWord_Click(ByVal sender As System.Object, _
ByVal e As System.EventArgs) Handles btnRunWord.Click
wd = New Word.ApplicationClass()
wd.Visible = True
wdEvents = CType(wd, Word.ApplicationEvents2_Event)
AddHandler wdEvents.Quit, _
AddressOf Me.wd_ApplicationEvents2_Event_Quit
btnQuitWord.Enabled = True
btnRunWord.Enabled = False
End Sub
```

In our *QuitWord* button handler, we'll unhook the event handler, call *Quit* on Word, and clean up as usual:

```
Private Sub btnQuitWord_Click(ByVal sender As System.Object, _
ByVal e As System.EventArgs) Handles btnQuitWord.Click
If Not wd Is Nothing Then
RemoveHandler wdEvents.Quit, _
AddressOf Me.wd_ApplicationEvents2_Event_Quit
wd.Quit()
wd = Nothing
GC.Collect()
GC.WaitForPendingFinalizers()
GC.Collect()
GC.WaitForPendingFinalizers()
End If
btnQuitWord.Enabled = False
btnRunWord.Enabled = True
End Sub
```

Finally, our handler for Word's *Quit* event:

```
Private Sub wd_ApplicationEvents2_Event_Quit()
wd = Nothing
btnQuitWord.Enabled = False
btnRunWord.Enabled = True
End Sub
```

Version Notes   Note that Word 97 exposes only one event interface on the *Application* object, and in the IA this will be named *ApplicationEvents_Event*. So the C# code should be modified slightly, as indicated here:

```
    private Word.ApplicationEvents_Event wdEvents;
...
        wdEvents = (Word.ApplicationEvents_Event)wd;
        wdEvents.Quit +=
            new Word.ApplicationEvents_QuitEventHandler(QuitHandler);
...
        wdEvents.Quit -=
            new Word.ApplicationEvents_QuitEventHandler(QuitHandler);
```

Version Notes   And the Visual Basic .NET equivalent:

```
Public wdEvents As Word.ApplicationEvents2_Event
...
wdEvents = CType(wd, Word.ApplicationEvents2_Event)
```

Version Notes   Also, Word 97 doesn't fire a *Quit* event unless at least one document is open. So for our exercise, we'll add some code to open a document when we open Word. The C# version is given here:

```
        object missing = Type.Missing;
        wd.Documents.Add(ref missing, ref missing);
```

Version Notes   And the Visual Basic .NET version:

```
wd.Documents.Add()
```

2.5 Releasing COM Objects

Office 97	✓
Office 2000	✓
Office XP	✓
Office 2003	✓

One area of interop between the managed world and the unmanaged world in which you need to be especially careful is in cleanly releasing COM objects when you're done with them. In the foregoing examples, we managed to achieve all the behavior we wanted using standard garbage collection. The only slight enhancement was to call

GC.Collect twice to ensure that any memory that was available for collection but survived the first sweep was collected on the second sweep.

In this section, we'll examine two other strategies for releasing COM objects that are being used by managed code:

- *ReleaseComObject*
- AppDomain unloading

Before we look at the specifics of these strategies, we need to understand why they might be useful. In the case of *ReleaseComObject*, we also need to understand the dangers of misusing the strategy.

The Office applications are all based on COM technology, which is what allows us to develop against them. However, a basic mismatch exists between the way COM expects memory to be managed and the way .NET manages memory. Memory management and object lifetime in COM are deterministic. That is, you explicitly allocate memory and explicitly deallocate it. Equally, when you get a pointer to a COM object interface, an internal reference count on the object is incremented. In the COM world, when you're done with an object, you explicitly release it, which decrements the reference count. When the reference counts goes to zero, the object is destroyed and its memory is released. The point is, you get to choose—to a fine degree of granularity—exactly when the object is destroyed and the memory is released.

In the .NET world, however, we have the luxury of a run-time garbage collector that deallocates memory for us in the background. We don't explicitly free the memory or the objects. Instead, we can set a reference to null, and if there are no other references to the same memory, that marks the memory as available for collection. Then, at some indeterminate time later, the garbage collector deallocates the memory. The point here is that we can never be entirely sure exactly when the object will be destroyed and the memory will be released.

In both the COM world and the .NET world, memory is eventually cleaned up, so does it matter that there's a difference? Well, maybe, sometimes. Consider the following scenarios:

- Your managed solution is referencing a COM object that's holding on to a lot of memory or other resource that you need to release eagerly (for performance or contention reasons).
- You believe a circular reference has deadlocked (say we're done with object A but object A holds a reference to object B, and object B can't be released until object A is released), and you want to break the cycle.
- If you leave everything to the CLR garbage collector, there is a very small window of opportunity where your managed object's cleanup code gets into a race with the CLR's shutdown. If your managed object holds a reference to a COM object, you might then be in danger of orphaning that COM object.

Recall that managed code does not make direct calls into COM objects. Instead, an RCW acts as a proxy between your managed code and the COM object. It's worth noting that when you have a .NET client talking through an RCW to a COM object, there is a reference count on the RCW, and this reference count is not the same as the COM object's internal reference count. The COM internal reference count is essentially a count of the number of clients. The RCW reference count is a count of the number of times the same interface pointer has entered the CLR—and this is almost always 1, regardless of the number of managed clients in the process.

If, in managed code, I declare a reference to a COM object (which will, of course, be a reference to an RCW at run time), what is the scope of the reference? Is it enough to declare the variable in, say, a *try* block, and force a garbage collection in the *finally* block? Well, that depends: in a debug build, the JIT compiler tracks local variables on a per-method basis. So even though an RCW reference might be nominally scoped to a *try* block, it's actually considered to be alive for the duration of the method. To complicate matters, this behavior is different in a release build. In a release build, forcing a garbage collection in the *finally* block cleans up all the RCWs and therefore all the COM objects. But in a debug build, you must force the garbage collection after the method returns.

So when we return from the method that's doing all this interop, we could force a garbage collection, and all our RCWs, including the implicit ones, should be cleaned up. But this approach has a couple of problems:

- How do you know you've returned from a method? Is this a foolish question? Well, not necessarily—if it's a simple method, it might be inlined by the JITer, which means that when the source code indicates you're returning, maybe at run time you're not.

- The CLR garbage collection is generational, so in some situations one or more of our RCWs might survive the first sweep and be promoted to generation 2.

Clearly, there is a basic mismatch between the COM world of deterministic object lifetime management and the .NET world of traced reference management. To reconcile this mismatch, the *System.Marshal* class exposes a *ReleaseComObject* method. You can call *Marshal.ReleaseComObject* on the RCW (that is, the managed proxy you have in your managed client) when you're done with it. *ReleaseComObject* will decrement the RCW reference count and return the updated reference count. There are a couple of points to note about this:

- If you have multiple .NET clients using the same RCW and any one of them calls *ReleaseComObject*, the object is released as far as the whole runtime is concerned. RCWs are created on a per-AppDomain basis. Therefore the RCW is no longer usable by any of the managed clients in the AppDomain.

■ *ReleaseComObject* returns the updated reference count after the call, which is almost always 0. The RCW reference count on a live object is almost always 1, but not always. Therefore, to be sure you're releasing the object, you can call *ReleaseComObject* in a loop until it returns 0.

It's worth repeating that *ReleaseComObject* decrements the reference count on an RCW and that the RCW is scoped to the AppDomain. The reason I want to emphasize this is that in any one AppDomain it is possible for there to be more than one "application." Your application might not be the only one in the AppDomain, and if you call *ReleaseComObject* in a reckless manner, you risk causing damage to other applications in the AppDomain. We'll revisit this point when we consider isolating managed extensions in Chapter 8. For now, a general rule of thumb is that you should consider using *ReleaseComObject* only if you can guarantee that you own all the code in the AppDomain. This applies, for example, if you have created a Windows Forms application that automates an Office application. Your Windows Forms application will be given a default AppDomain, and you are in control of all the code that runs in that AppDomain. Indeed, you might choose to create additional AppDomains in your code, and you will remain in control of all those AppDomains. This might not be true if you develop a managed COM add-in.

For completeness, the *Marshal* class also exposes a *Release* method, which decrements the internal COM refcount on the interface. You should never use this unless you also use *Marshal.AddRef* and you've got an *IntPtr* that represents the raw COM *IUnknown* pointer (by calling *Marshal.GetComInterfaceForObject* or one of its siblings).

Another common point of confusion is that you might inadvertently instantiate a COM object without knowing it. For example, consider the following code:

```
Excel.Application xl = new Excel.Application();
Excel.Workbook book = xl.Workbooks.Add(Excel.XlSheetType.xlWorksheet);
Excel.Worksheet sheet = (Excel.Worksheet)book.ActiveSheet;
```

How many COM objects have been instantiated? Answers generally range from three to five, and it depends on how much you know about the internal workings of the specific COM object model that you're interoperating with. In this case, we're likely instantiating these five objects:

■ the *Application* object

■ the *Workbooks* collection object

■ a *Workbook* object

■ the *Sheets* collection object

■ a *Worksheet* object

In the previous code we reference the *Workbooks* collection object and the *Worksheets* collection object. Both are COM objects that are implicitly created when we use the property. We don't keep any managed references to these objects ourselves, but that in itself confuses many developers. The CLR will have wrapped these objects for us, and because we don't have explicit references to them, we have no way of explicitly releasing them. Instead, we rely on the CLR to release them on our behalf.

In the following example, we'll explore a couple of ways of making our cleanup operations more deterministic—and more aggressive.

> **Note** The sample solution for this topic can be found in the sample code at <install location>\Code\Office<n>\CleanRelease. This solution includes three separate projects, corresponding to the three upcoming subsections.

Simple Garbage Collection

1. Create a new Windows Forms application called *SimpleCollection*. Add a reference to the appropriate Excel IAs for your target version of Office. Put three *Button* controls on the form, and get *Click* event handlers for each one:

2. Declare fields in the form class to hold references to an *Excel.Application* object and an *Excel.Workbook* object. We want to use these objects across multiple method calls, hence the need for them to be class fields. However, this is also the first step in making life difficult—now that our managed COM object references are no longer scoped to single method calls, they'll be much more difficult to track and clean up:

```
private Excel.Application xl;
private Excel.Workbook book;
```

3. In the *Click* handler for the Run Excel button, launch a new instance of Excel and cache the *Application* object reference in one of our class fields. We'll also create a new *Workbook* and cache that reference:

```
private void btnRunExcel_Click(object sender, System.EventArgs e)
{
    xl = new Excel.Application();
    xl.Visible = true;
    object missing = Type.Missing;
    book = xl.Workbooks.Add(missing);
}
```

4. In the *Click* handler for the New Sheet button, use the cached *Workbook* reference to create a new *Worksheet* object:

```
private void btnNewSheet_Click(object sender, System.EventArgs e)
{
    object missing = Type.Missing;
    book.Worksheets.Add(missing, missing, missing, missing);
}
```

Note that we're keeping things very simple here—for example, so as not to confuse the user, we should probably disable the NewSheet button until we've successfully instantiated the *Excel.Application* object.

5. In the CleanUp button handler, perform simple cleanup, as before, by nulling the references and forcing two garbage collections:

```
private void btnCleanUp_Click(object sender, System.EventArgs e)
{
    book = null;
    xl = null;
    GC.Collect();
    GC.WaitForPendingFinalizers();
    GC.Collect();
    GC.WaitForPendingFinalizers();
}
```

6. Build and test.

We've set up our code to release the Excel *Application* COM object—assuming the user clicks the buttons in the right order. On the other hand, we haven't invoked the *Excel.Quit* command, so even though we release our reference, Excel will continue to run. This is fine—if we're making Excel visible, presumably we want the user to interact with it, and we'll leave it up to them when to quit. We could do it either way, but in our simple example this is not important. What is more relevant is that we are relying on the user to click the CleanUp button at the end. What happens if the user doesn't? When you release the COM object, there's no visual feedback, of course. So to test this scenario, run the application and keep Task Manager open so that you can watch when the Excel process stops.

If the user runs Excel and then directly quits Excel, you'll see that the Excel process remains running—this is because we're holding a reference to one of Excel's COM objects in our managed application. Of course, the CLR will clean up this reference on our behalf when the application stops. However, a very long period of time might pass while Excel is still running after the user has quit it. This is good, because we're holding a reference to an Excel object and we presumably want to use it again at some later point.

Also, this application is being deliberately reckless with its managed references to COM objects. We only have one *Application* and one *Workbook* reference, but the user can keep clicking the buttons, and each time we'll overwrite our reference. For example, if you click the button to run Excel three times, you'll get three instances of Excel. If the user then independently quits those three Excel instances, all she's doing is hiding the three Excel main windows; the three Excel processes will continue to run. You can verify the behavior in Task Manager or Process Explorer (freeware from *www.sysinternals.com*).

If we did this (that is, overwrite our references to make them refer to new instances) in unmanaged COM code, we'd be leaking memory. However, in the .NET world, we're actually better off. Recall that we're using RCWs and that RCWs are scoped to the AppDomain. If we then click the button once to clean up our references, all three instances will be cleaned up at once because there's only one RCW in the AppDomain, so forcing that one RCW to be collected will terminate all three instances.

Using *ReleaseComObject*

In almost all situations, nulling the RCW reference and forcing a garbage collection will clean up properly. If you also call *GC.WaitForPendingFinalizers*, garbage collection will be as deterministic as you can make it. That is, you'll be pretty sure exactly *when* the object has been cleaned up—on the return from the second call to *WaitForPending-Finalizers*. As an alternative, you can use *Marshal.ReleaseComObject*. However, note that you are very unlikely to ever need to use this method. The following code shows our simple example modified to use *ReleaseComObject* instead of *GC.Collect*:

```
private void btnCleanUp_Click(object sender, System.EventArgs e)
{
    // book = null;
    // xl = null;
    // GC.Collect();
    // GC.WaitForPendingFinalizers();
    // GC.Collect();
    // GC.WaitForPendingFinalizers();

    if (book != null)
    {
        Marshal.ReleaseComObject(book);
        book = null;
    }
    if (xl != null)
    {
        Marshal.ReleaseComObject(xl);
        xl = null;
    }
}
```

If you try this code, you'll see that it behaves in essentially the same way as with the *GC.Collect* approach, in that the Excel *Workbook* and *Application* RCWs are released when the user clicks the button. However, *ReleaseComObject* relies on us passing a reference to the RCW we want to release, and we're then immediately nulling the reference.

Therefore, we can only do this once. Recall that we've allowed the user to run multiple instances of Excel and create multiple workbooks. Using the *ReleaseComObject* approach, with the code as it stands, we'd only ever release the last instance. If we wanted to use *ReleaseComObject*, we'd have to keep all the Excel *Application* and *Workbook* references in some kind of list or collection so we could later walk the list, releasing each one.

Note also that *ReleaseComObject* doesn't directly release the RCW—it only decrements the RCW reference count. Normally, the RCW reference count is 1, so calling *ReleaseComObject* normally decrements it to 0, which releases the underlying object. However, the count is not always 1, and if you need to be absolutely sure that you're releasing the RCW and its underlying COM object, you have to call *ReleaseComObject* repeatedly. So, in our sample code, we could simply keep calling *ReleaseComObject* until the reference count returned is 0:

```
if (book != null)
{
    //Marshal.ReleaseComObject(book);
    while (Marshal.ReleaseComObject(book) > 0) { }
    book = null;
}
if (xl != null)
{
    //Marshal.ReleaseComObject(xl);
    while (Marshal.ReleaseComObject(xl) > 0) { }
    xl = null;
}
```

Warning   If you call *ReleaseComObject* in a loop, the RCW will be unusable by any code in the AppDomain from that point on. Any attempt to use the released RCW will result in an *InvalidComObjectException* being thrown.

This risk is compounded when the COM component that is being used is a singleton because *CoCreateInstance* (which is how the CLR activates COM components under the covers) returns the same interface pointer every time it is called for singleton COM components. So separate and independent pieces of managed code in an AppDomain can be using the same RCW for a singleton COM component, and if either one calls *ReleaseComObject* on the COM component, the other will be broken.

As you can see, the standard .NET approach of relying on objects to go out of scope and be collected at some indeterminate point in the future is a little too relaxed when we're interoperating with COM objects. Fortunately, it takes little work to enhance this behavior by nulling the RCW references and forcing a double garbage collection sweep, coupled with waiting for the sweeps to complete. This approach gives us more deterministic behavior without running the risk of any unfortunate side effects. The only price we pay is a slight performance hit.

Best Practices   The option of using *ReleaseComObject* is safe only if you own all the code running in the AppDomain in which you call this method. It also has a couple of limitations that make it problematic to use. When we look at isolating managed extensions in Chapter 8, we'll examine the dangers more closely. For now, the best practice guideline is to not use *ReleaseComObject*.

AppDomain Unloading

An alternative strategy for ensuring that COM object references are properly released is to use AppDomains. A single .NET process can contain one or more AppDomains. By default, when a managed application starts, it is given an AppDomain by the runtime. Subsequently, the application can create as many new AppDomains as it likes. An AppDomain is programmatically represented by the *System.AppDomain* class. When you set up an AppDomain, you can load an assembly into it. If this assembly is an application, you can run it. This means that within a single Windows process, you can run multiple AppDomains, and each AppDomain can execute an application.

The ability to run multiple applications within a single process significantly increases scalability. Using AppDomains, you can stop individual applications without stopping the entire process—that is, you can unload a domain programmatically. Also, code running in one application cannot directly access code or resources from another application. The CLR enforces this isolation by preventing direct calls between objects in different AppDomains. Objects that pass between domains are either copied or accessed by proxy. Crucially, when an AppDomain is unloaded, the runtime releases all COM object references held in that domain.

The idea here is to create a new AppDomain and run all the COM-related code in it. Then we can unload the AppDomain. This ensures that any references to COM objects that we held in the AppDomain are cleaned up.

We'll implement this approach in a simple way—we'll create another application that creates a second thread. In the second thread, we'll create a second AppDomain. In the second AppDomain, we'll do all our Office interop. We need to run a second thread because otherwise, executing the second assembly on the same thread would block the first assembly.

1. Add another Windows application project to the solution. We don't need any references to Office IAs in this project because we won't be doing any interop directly. Put two *Button* controls on the form, and get *Click* event handlers for them. Set the *Enabled* property of the Unload button to *false* initially:

2. Declare three class fields—for the second *Thread*, the second *AppDomain*, and the *Form* for the second application:

```
private Thread excelThread;
private AppDomain excelDomain;
private Form appForm;
```

3. In the *Click* handler for the New App button, create the second thread, and then toggle the *Enabled* state of the two buttons:

```
private void btnNewApp_Click(object sender, System.EventArgs e)
{
    excelThread = new Thread(new ThreadStart(ThreadProc));
    excelThread.Start();
    btnNewApp.Enabled = false;
    btnUnload.Enabled = true;
}
```

4. When you create a thread, you must specify a controlling method for that thread, as an argument to the *ThreadStart* constructor. In our thread controlling method, create a second AppDomain, using the static method *AppDomain.CreateDomain*. Then, from this second domain, instantiate the second application's *Form* object using *CreateInstanceFromAndUnwrap*. This method creates an instance of the specified type in the second domain and returns a proxy for use in our (first) domain:

```
private void ThreadProc()
{
    string assemblyName =
        @"C:\Temp\SimpleRelease\bin\Debug\SimpleRelease.exe";
    string typeName = "SimpleRelease.SimpleReleaseForm";
    excelDomain = AppDomain.CreateDomain("ExcelDomain");
    appForm = (Form)excelDomain.CreateInstanceFromAndUnwrap(
        assemblyName, typeName);
    appForm.ShowDialog();
}
```

Note that in this code, you'll need to change the path for SimpleRelease.exe to wherever it actually is on your machine.

5. Because we've created a second thread, we should be careful not to exit from the main application until the second thread has stopped. We can do several things

to synchronize threads, some more sophisticated than others. In our simple example, we'll just wait for the second thread to terminate. (We're assuming here that the user will either unload the second assembly, or close it directly, before trying to close the first application.) So add this code to the *Dispose* method of the main application (that is, the new application that we're building to launch the original one):

```
if (excelThread != null)
{
    excelThread.Join();
}
```

6. In the *Unload* button handler, close the second application's window, and then unload the second AppDomain altogether:

```
private void btnUnload_Click(object sender, System.EventArgs e)
{
    if (appForm != null)
    {
        appForm.Close();
        appForm = null;
        AppDomain.Unload(excelDomain);
        excelDomain = null;
    }
    btnNewApp.Enabled = true;
    btnUnload.Enabled = false;
}
```

7. Build and test. Use Task Manager to check when the Excel process stops.

> **Best Practices**   To summarize this section, we have three basic choices for cleaning up COM objects:
>
> - **.NET garbage collection**   This is controlled in a deterministic manner by using *GC.Collect* and *GC.WaitForPendingFinalizers* (twice).
>
> - **ReleaseComObject**   This is highly deterministic but somewhat problematic to use, and it is potentially dangerous because it affects the target RCW for the entire AppDomain.
>
> - **AppDomain isolation**   This means isolating our interop functionality in a separate AppDomain, which we can later unload altogether, thereby releasing all RCWs in that AppDomain.
>
> We can also use either of the first two options in combination with the third. The general best practice guideline is to use .NET garbage collection wherever possible, to use AppDomain isolation in situations where you can (or must) cleanly isolate your interop code (such as in add-ins), and to avoid *ReleaseComObject* altogether if possible.

2.6 Visual Basic .NET vs. C#

Office 97	✓
Office 2000	✓
Office XP	✓
Office 2003	✓

All .NET languages are equal citizens, in the sense that they all conform to the Common Language Specification (CLS) and that all will compile to the same intermediate language code. However, each language might provide additional features over and above the CLS and might be optimized to suit a particular development scenario.

We have seen that the Office applications can interop with managed code to a very sophisticated degree. Nonetheless, they were historically never built with managed code and were designed to support programmability internally through Microsoft Visual Basic for Applications (VBA). Even unmanaged languages such as C and C++ that can be used to automate the Office applications (and for add-ins) are often less convenient for programming Office applications than VBA.

Consequently, while there are many advantages to developing for Office in managed code, it is worth noting that some VBA features do not correspond directly to features in managed languages. It is also worth noting that Visual Basic .NET as a language is closer to VBA than C# is.

This is not to suggest that Visual Basic .NET is better for Office interop than C# overall, just that in certain contexts it is slightly more convenient to code in Visual Basic .NET, as summarized here:

- Passing ref parameters to Word methods
- Optional parameters (all Office applications)
- Parameterized properties in Excel
- Hidden accessor methods in Word
- Accessing late-bound members

We will explore all these contexts by developing a managed application to automate both Word and Excel. The sample solution contains both Visual Basic .NET and C# versions, and relevant code snippets follow in both languages. Simple .xls and .doc files are supplied with the sample code for use in this exercise, although you can use any .xls and .doc files.

Note   The sample solution for this topic can be found in the sample code at <install location>\Code\Office<n>\ManagedLanguages.

1. Create a new Windows application (in Visual Basic .NET or C#, whichever you prefer) called InteropCSharp or InteropVB. Add references to the appropriate Excel and Word IAs for the version of Office you're targeting.

2. Put six buttons on the form, as shown in the following figure, and get a *Click* event handler for each one. Note that only the first Excel button and the first Word button are initially enabled—we don't want to try getting a range until we know we've opened a workbook or document. Similarly, a lot of Excel and Word dialog boxes are not available unless a workbook or document is open.

3. In the form class, declare field variables for the Excel and Word *Application* objects, and the *Document* and *Workbook* objects. The C# code is shown here:

```
private Excel.Application excelApp;
private Word.Application wordApp;
private Excel.Workbook book;
private Word.Document doc;
```

The Visual Basic .NET equivalent is shown here:

```
Private excelApp As Excel.Application
Private wordApp As Word.Application
Private book As Excel.Workbook
Private doc As Word.Document
```

Optional Parameters and Word Reference Parameters

Now to implement the button *Click* handlers. Our example will illustrate the use of optional parameters and Word's insistence on passing parameters by reference instead of value. We'll start with the button to open an Excel workbook. Excel's *Open* method takes a number of parameters, only the first of which is mandatory—the others are optional, but we still need to pass a parameter. In this situation, we can use either a *System.Type.Missing* or a *System.Reflection.Missing.Value*, as shown in the following C# code. Note that you'll need to change the path for Products.xls to wherever it actually is on your machine.

```
private void btnOpenXls_Click(object sender, System.EventArgs e)
{
    excelApp = new Excel.ApplicationClass();
    excelApp.Visible = true;
    string fileName = @"C:\Temp\ManagedLanguages\Products.xls";
    //object missing = System.Type.Missing;
    object missing = System.Reflection.Missing.Value;
    book = excelApp.Workbooks.Open(fileName,
        missing, missing, missing, missing, missing, missing, missing,
        missing, missing, missing, missing, missing, missing, missing);
```

```
            btnExcelRange.Enabled = true;
            btnExcelDialog.Enabled = true;
    }
```

Note that when we've successfully opened a workbook, we'll enable the remaining Excel-specific buttons. Also note that the code listed here is correct for Office 2003. For earlier versions, there are very slight differences—specifically in the number of parameters to Excel and Word's *Open* methods.

The Visual Basic .NET equivalent follows. As you can see, we don't need to pass any of the optional parameters that we're not interested in:

```
Private Sub btnOpenXls_Click(ByVal sender As System.Object, _
ByVal e As System.EventArgs) Handles btnOpenXls.Click
excelApp = New Excel.ApplicationClass()
excelApp.Visible = True
Dim fileName As String
fileName = "C:\Temp\ManagedLanguages\Products.xls"
book = excelApp.Workbooks.Open(fileName)
btnExcelRange.Enabled = True
btnExcelDialog.Enabled = True
End Sub
```

In this example, we can omit all parameters after the first one. If we want to pass some parameters at arbitrary positions in the parameter list, we can do so by specifying the parameter name. For example, the third parameter governs whether we open the file as read-only; we can specify this (using ":="), omitting the second parameter and all parameters after the third:

```
book = excelApp.Workbooks.Open(fileName, ReadOnly:=True)
```

As an aside, note that in this line of code, the *ReadOnly* parameter is a parameter identifier for the *Open* function. It's also a keyword in Visual Basic .NET, which is why it is in blue. However, the Visual Basic .NET compiler is smart enough to parse this correctly, so despite the editor's coloring, this line does in fact compile correctly.

To open a Word document, the *Open* method also takes optional parameters, but the additional point here is that Word requires all these parameters to be passed by reference, not by value:

```
    private void btnOpenDoc_Click(object sender, System.EventArgs e)
    {
        wordApp = new Word.ApplicationClass();
        wordApp.Visible = true;
        object fileName = @"C:\Temp\ManagedLanguages\Jabberwocky.doc";
        object missing = Missing.Value;
        doc = wordApp.Documents.Open(ref fileName,
            ref missing, ref missing, ref missing, ref missing, ref missing,
            ref missing, ref missing, ref missing, ref missing, ref missing,
            ref missing, ref missing, ref missing, ref missing, ref missing);
        btnWordRange.Enabled = true;
        btnWordDialog.Enabled = true;
    }
```

In Visual Basic .NET, we don't need to specify pass by reference because the compiler will do the extra work and silently translate for us. So, to implement the first Word-specific button on our form to open a document, the Visual Basic .NET equivalent is more streamlined:

```
Private Sub btnOpenDoc_Click(ByVal sender As System.Object, _
ByVal e As System.EventArgs) Handles btnOpenDoc.Click
wordApp = New Word.ApplicationClass()
wordApp.Visible = True
Dim fileName As String
fileName = "C:\Temp\oic\ManagedLanguages\Jabberwocky.doc"
doc = wordApp.Documents.Open(fileName)
btnWordRange.Enabled = True
btnWordDialog.Enabled = True
End Sub
```

Excel Parameterized Properties and Word Accessors

Excel exposes several parameterized properties—that is, properties that allow you to pass more than one parameter to them. Visual Basic .NET supports passing multiple parameters to properties, but C# does not. The Excel PIA provides a workaround for this limitation by providing *get_* and *set_* accessor methods as an alternative means of working with the properties.

For example, we'll implement the second Excel button to get an arbitrary range of cells and format them in bold. Note that while the *Range* object is exposed as a property of the *Worksheet* object, it is not accessible directly in C#. In the Object Browser, *Range* is not listed. However, the *get_Range* and *set_Range* methods are listed and also show up in IntelliSense because we need to specify more than one value to define a range (such as C2 to C13):

```
private void btnExcelRange_Click(object sender, System.EventArgs e)
{
    Excel.Range range = ((Excel.Worksheet)book.ActiveSheet).get_Range("C2",
        "C13");
    range.Font.Bold = true;
}
```

Visual Basic .NET supports passing multiple parameters to properties, so we can implement our second Excel button in Visual Basic .NET to pass both delimiters of the range to the *Range* property directly:

```
Private Sub btnExcelRange_Click(ByVal sender As System.Object, _
ByVal e As System.EventArgs) Handles btnExcelRange.Click
Dim range As Excel.Range
range = CType(book.ActiveSheet, Excel.Worksheet).Range("C2", "C13")
range.Font.Bold = True
End Sub
```

Note that C# developers generally know that properties are actually implemented by the compiler as *get_* and *set_* accessor methods behind the scenes, so this explicit use of *get_* and *set_* methods won't come as a huge surprise.

Word does not expose parameterized properties. On the other hand, it does still expose accessor methods because many properties in Word are defined to use *Variant* values. Visual Basic .NET supports *Variant* values, but C# does not, so to work with a property that uses *Variant* values in C# you must use the accessor methods.

As an aside, if you were to examine one of these parameterized properties using ILDASM, you'd see that they're attributed with *MethodImpl(MethodImplOptions.InternalCall)*. This attribute can't be applied to a property in C#, but it can be applied to the *get_* and *set_* accessor methods that implement a property.

In our exercise, we'll implement the second Word button to set the style of the document content. Both the Object Browser and IntelliSense expose the *Style* property of the *Range* object in Word. However, if you try to use this property, you'll get a compiler error:

```
private void btnWordRange_Click(object sender, System.EventArgs e)
{
    Word.Range range = doc.Content;
    range.Style = Word.WdStyleType.wdStyleEmphasis;
}
```

Specifically, the compiler will complain with this error message: "Property 'Style' is not supported by the language; try directly calling accessor methods 'get_Style' or 'set_Style'."

It's fortunate that the compiler is so explicit here because these accessor methods are hidden. They are not shown in the Object Browser or in IntelliSense. Although this is a little inconvenient, if you change the code to use the appropriate accessor, all will be well:

```
private void btnWordRange_Click(object sender, System.EventArgs e)
{
    Word.Range range = doc.Content;
    //range.Style = Word.WdStyleType.wdStyleEmphasis;
    object style = Word.WdBuiltinStyle.wdStyleEmphasis;
    range.set_Style(ref style);
}
```

In Visual Basic .NET, which is aware of *Variant* values—we can access the property directly, without using hidden accessors:

```
Private Sub btnWordRange_Click(ByVal sender As System.Object, _
ByVal e As System.EventArgs) Handles btnWordRange.Click
Dim range As Word.Range
range = doc.Content
range.Style = Word.WdBuiltinStyle.wdStyleEmphasis
End Sub
```

Accessing Late-Bound Members

Visual Basic .NET supports late binding in a way that's almost transparent—much like in VBA. However, this only works if you disable *Option Strict*. If you don't disable *Option Strict* (and it is generally recommended that you keep it enabled), coding for late binding in Visual Basic .NET is the same as in C#. This requires you to use a technique that is essentially a subset of the reflection features of .NET. Now, you could use reflection to implement late binding for everything, as demonstrated in Section 3.3, "Using COM by Reflection." However, there's no point in using late binding unless you're forced to.

One situation in which you're forced to use late binding is for Word and Excel built-in dialog boxes. Both Word and Excel offer a large number of internal dialog boxes, none of which are strongly typed. That is, you must use a generic *Excel.Dialog* interface and a generic *Word.Dialog* interface for all built-in dialog boxes. There are a couple of reasons for this. First, internal dialog boxes are triggered by a specific sequence of operations (usually a user's menu selection), which can itself be programmed instead of trying to directly invoke the dialog box. Second, the Excel and Word object models have evolved over many years, and implementing operations that are largely internal through late binding is a good strategy for keeping changes to the object model to a minimum.

Excel and Word take different approaches to working with these dialog boxes. The *Excel.Dialog* interface and the *Word.Dialog* interface are not the same. The *Excel.Dialog* interface is very minimal, exposing only three properties and one method. The *Show* method takes 30 optional parameters, named *Arg1* through *Arg30*. Each specific dialog box takes zero or more actual parameters. So if you want to specify how an Excel dialog box should look and behave, you call the *Show* method with whatever parameters you can that will modify the dialog box. The full list is supplied in the Excel VBA help under the section "Built-In Dialog Box Argument Lists."

We'll implement our third Excel button to display the Style dialog box, and we'll specify that the Bold and Italic check boxes should be checked, by passing *true* for the first two parameters. This dialog box takes only two parameters, so you cannot modify the appearance of any of the other check boxes, lists, and so forth:

```
private void btnExcelDialog_Click(object sender, System.EventArgs e)
{
    Excel.Dialog dlg = excelApp.Dialogs[Excel.XlBuiltInDialog.xlDialogStyle];
    object missing = Missing.Value;
    dlg.Show(true, true, missing, missing, missing, missing, missing,
        missing, missing, missing, missing, missing, missing, missing,
        missing, missing, missing, missing, missing, missing, missing,
        missing, missing, missing, missing, missing, missing, missing,
        missing, missing);
}
```

Note that the *Dialogs* collections in Word introduced a default property (allowing the collection to be indexed directly) from Word 2002 (Word XP). Prior to that, you had to use the *Item* method:

```
Word.Dialog dlg = wordApp.Dialogs.Item(Word.WdWordDialog.wdDialogInsertSymbol);
```

Note also that there is no direct way to execute an Excel dialog box without displaying the dialog box to the user. That is, Excel doesn't encourage you to perform operations by programmatically invoking dialog boxes, making programmatic selections, and programmatically closing the dialog box. Having said that, there is a way you could do it—by using *SendKeys* to simulate user keyboard input to make choices in the dialog box and simulate the Return key to close the dialog box, and by turning the *ScreenUpdating* property to *false* so the dialog box is never visible to the user. This is mentioned for completeness, but it is strongly discouraged—simulating keystrokes leads to localization problems and version upgrade problems (not to mention timing, window focus, and user interface problems).

The Visual Basic .NET equivalent is simpler because, of course, we don't have to pass optional parameters that we don't need. However, regardless of language, we're still limited by the properties that Excel exposes for any given dialog box:

```
Private Sub btnExcelDialog_Click(ByVal sender As System.Object, _
ByVal e As System.EventArgs) Handles btnExcelDialog.Click
Dim dlg As Excel.Dialog
dlg = excelApp.Dialogs(Excel.XlBuiltInDialog.xlDialogStyle)
dlg.Show(True, True)
End Sub
```

The pre–Word 2002 access to a *Dialog* from the *Dialogs* collection in Visual Basic .NET is shown here:

```
dlg = wordApp.Dialogs.Item(Word.WdWordDialog.wdDialogInsertSymbol)
```

The Word *Dialog* interface is slightly more complex than Excel's—there are six properties and four methods. The *Show* method takes only one optional parameter—a timeout value in milliseconds for how long the dialog box should be displayed before closing. If this is omitted, the dialog box is displayed until the user closes it.

So, for example, if we just want to show a Word dialog box (in this example, the Insert Symbol dialog box), we can call the *Show* method:

```
private void btnWordDialog_Click(object sender, System.EventArgs e)
{
    Word.Dialog dlg = wordApp.Dialogs[Word.WdWordDialog.wdDialogInsertSymbol];
    object missing = Missing.Value;
    dlg.Show(ref missing);
}
```

To modify the behavior of a Word dialog box, you must set dialog-specific properties on the dialog box before calling the *Show* or *Execute* method. To set dialog-specific properties when all we have is a generic *Dialog* interface, we must use reflection—specifically, the *InvokeMember* method of the *Type* class. (For the COM-heads among you, this behaves pretty much like *IDispatch::Invoke*.) So we'll implement the third Word button on our form to specify a particular font, tab, and character number in the dialog box, and then we'll execute it. We'll factor out the repetitive code into a new private method.

```
private void btnWordDialog_Click(object sender, System.EventArgs e)
{
    Word.Dialog dlg =
            wordApp.Dialogs[Word.WdWordDialog.wdDialogInsertSymbol];
    object missing = Missing.Value;
    //dlg.Show(ref missing);
    InvokeDialog(dlg, "Font", "Wingdings");
    InvokeDialog(dlg, "Tab", "Symbols");
    InvokeDialog(dlg, "CharNum", 74);
    dlg.Execute();
}

private void InvokeDialog(Word.Dialog dlg, string memberName,
        object memberValue)
{
    Type dlgType = dlg.GetType();
    dlgType.InvokeMember(memberName,
        BindingFlags.SetProperty | BindingFlags.Public |
            BindingFlags.Instance,
        null, dlg, new object[]{memberValue});
}
```

The result at run time is that the dialog box is silently invoked (with our chosen property values), executed, and closed. We will get character 74 from the Wingdings font inserted into our document, and the user will never see the dialog box. (As with most of the code in this book, this should all be done wrapped in *try/catch* exception handling, which has generally been omitted for brevity. This is particularly important when you're using late binding—by definition you won't get any help from the compiler to ensure you're doing the right things.)

The Visual Basic .NET code required if *Option Strict* is left enabled is essentially the same as for the C# version, using *Type.InvokeMember*. However, if *Option Strict* is turned off, Visual Basic .NET allows us to access late-bound members directly:

```
Private Sub btnWordDialog_Click(ByVal sender As System.Object, _
ByVal e As System.EventArgs) Handles btnWordDialog.Click
Dim dlg As Word.Dialog
dlg = wordApp.Dialogs(Word.WdWordDialog.wdDialogInsertSymbol)
dlg.Font = "Wingdings"
dlg.Tab = "Symbols"
dlg.CharNum = 74
dlg.Execute()
End Sub
```

In conclusion, a few features of Visual Basic .NET make it superficially more convenient to develop for Office interop than C#. Most of these features involve the Visual Basic .NET compiler doing extra work for us. In the case of parameterized Excel properties, it actually involves the Visual Basic .NET compiler *not* doing something that the C# compiler does. This reliance on extra compiler work is a technique that's familiar to Visual Basic and VBA developers, but many developers insist on a finer degree of control over their code. It comes down to a question of personal taste. Of the five issues listed at the beginning of this section, only one—the ability to omit optional parameters—is really at all useful. C# developers tend to work around this by writing one-time wrapper methods that they can call and by passing only the parameters they're interested in.

To round out the picture here, it's worth noting that other differences exist between C# and Visual Basic .NET that are not directly related to Office interop. These are language differences and differences in usage. The language differences are listed in Table 2-3.

Table 2-3 Summary of Differences Between Visual Basic .NET and C#

Visual Basic .NET	C#
Fully CLS compliant:	Offers non-CLS-compliant extensions:
Case-insensitive	Case-sensitive
Unsigned integers only	Supports *signed byte, unsigned short, unsigned int, unsigned long*
No *unsafe* code; no pointers	*unsafe* code, pointers, *sizeof*
	Automatic documentation through XML comments
	readonly member variables
	static constructors
	checked/unchecked code
Exponentiation operator: ^	
Redim: allows you to reallocate an array	
	Pre/post inc/decrement operators: ++ --
	Compound modulus operator: %=
	Compound bitwise AND, XOR, OR operators:
	&= ^= |=
Visual Basic .NET 2003 does include bitshifts:	Bitwise shift and compound bitwise shift operators:
<< >>	<< >> <<= >>=
Structured exception handling (*try, catch*) and unstructured exception handling (*On Error GoTo, On Error Resume Next*)	Structured exception handling (*try, catch*) only
Extra parentheses to force passing parameters by value (including reference types)	

Table 2-3   Summary of Differences Between Visual Basic .NET and C#

Visual Basic .NET	C#
Optional parameters	
Late binding supported by both implicit reflection helper and explicit reflection	Late binding possible through explicit reflection
Handles: allows you to specify the events for which an event procedure may be called	
With: evaluates an object expression once to access multiple members	
Static: use *Static* for local variables and *Shared* for "static" class members	*static*: for class members only
	volatile: allows an object to be modified asynchronously

Planned changes (at time of writing, next release of Visual Studio .NET 2005):

Visual Basic .NET	C#
Generics: like C++ templates	Generics: like C++ templates
	Iterators: like STL iterators
	Anonymous methods: dynamically defined delegates
Partial types: allows you to split class code across multiple files	Partial types: allows you to split class code across multiple files

The main differences in terms of usage are as follows:

- There is an ECMA/ISO standard for C# but not for Visual Basic .NET. An open standard is likely to encourage wider use, more support from third-party tool and library vendors, and more cross-platform use.

- As the planned changes just shown seem to indicate, C# is likely to be the initial .NET target for any significant advancements in language design–from Microsoft, industry momentum, or ECMA/ISO contributors.

- For some developers (Visual Basic 6.0 developers, scripting language developers, and new developers), the Visual Basic .NET learning curve is generally simpler due to:

  - **.NET Framework Visual Basic compatibility "shortcuts"**   The .NET Framework provides "classic" Visual Basic façade classes that provide shortcuts to underlying .NET behavior.

  - **Additional support from the Visual Studio IDE**   More prevalent IntelliSense (such as for type browsing in variables or method declarations), default "hiding" of automatically generated code, and greater use of autocomplete.

  - **Verbose "English" grammar**   Limited use of control/escape characters, delimiters, and special processing instructions.

- For C/C++, Java, Perl, and other terse language developers, C# might be more immediately productive because of its structural similarity.

- Many Visual Basic 6.0 developers move to C# when moving to .NET. C# offers the ease of development of Visual Basic 6.0 combined with the power of C++. Visual Basic 6.0 developers who had previously resisted moving to C++ or Java because of the inherent pitfalls of these languages don't see the same pitfalls with C#.

2.7 Debugging Interop Solutions

Office 97	✓
Office 2000	✓
Office XP	✓
Office 2003	✓

For each of the specific technologies that you can use to develop Office solutions with managed code, there are specific debugging issues. Each of these will be discussed in the appropriate chapter throughout this book. That said, a few general debugging techniques—and debugging and code-analysis tools—can be applied across all technologies. These are discussed in this section.

Note   The sample solution for this topic can be found in the sample code at this location: <install location>\Code\Office<n>\SimpleBug.

Use Structured Exception Handling

To some developers, structured exception handling (SEH) comes naturally, but it depends on your background and the types of languages you are familiar with. In the context of Office development, many developers have a Visual Basic background, where the use of SEH may be relatively unfamiliar.

The SimpleBug solution is a copy of the TestExcelPIA project introduced as the first example in Section 2.2. The only modification is to the index into the Cells collection: we've deliberately used a column index of 257 (which is greater than the maximum number of columns supported by Excel):

```
private void runExcel_Click(object sender, System.EventArgs e)
{
    xl = new Microsoft.Office.Interop.Excel.Application();
    xl.Visible = true;
    xl.DisplayAlerts = false;
    Excel.Workbook book = xl.Workbooks.Add(
Excel.XlSheetType.xlWorksheet);
    Excel.Worksheet sheet = (Excel.Worksheet)book.ActiveSheet;

    Excel.Range r = (Excel.Range)sheet.Cells[1,257];
    r.Value2 = "Hello World";
    quitExcel.Enabled = true;
}
```

When you run this application and click the Run Excel button, Excel will return the error HRESULT, which will be translated into a COMException. The error details are reasonably informative in this case and should allow you to identify the bug in your code. However, another issue is that if the bug appears inconsistently or is determined by something in the environment, it's far better to catch exceptions in your own code so that you can deal with them yourself:

```
private void runExcel_Click(object sender, System.EventArgs e)
{
    try
    {
        xl = new Microsoft.Office.Interop.Excel.Application();
        xl.Visible = true;
        xl.DisplayAlerts = false;

        Excel.Workbook book = xl.Workbooks.Add(
Excel.XlSheetType.xlWorksheet);
        Excel.Worksheet sheet = (Excel.Worksheet)book.ActiveSheet;

        Excel.Range r = (Excel.Range)sheet.Cells[1,257];
        r.Value2 = "Hello World";
        quitExcel.Enabled = true;
    }
    catch (COMException ex)
    {
        MessageBox.Show(ex.StackTrace, ex.Message);
    }
}
```

Using SEH, you can structure your code to deal with multiple anticipated exception types. You can ensure that you clean up memory if an unexpected exception is thrown. You can handle runtime errors in a manner that is useful to users and to operations support. In the example above, we've merely caught the exception and presented a message. From the user's perspective, the net result is not very different from the previous behavior. However, a more useful strategy would be to catch the exception and write details to a log—perhaps the event log or an external file, or some other event logging system.

> **Note**   In many of the code snippets presented in this book, exception-handling code has been omitted. This is not an indication of recommended practice—quite the opposite. It is simply that I've tried to keep the code snippets focused on the main point of the technique under discussion, so exception-handling code has been removed for the sake of brevity.

Check Assembly Dependencies

A problem that often comes up during Office development is that your solution loads a managed assembly that is bound to the wrong dependent assemblies. This typically happens when porting between versions of Office. The interop assemblies (including the PIAs) for Office are version-specific. It is possible to use the IA from one version of Office with a different version, provided that the code is simple and doesn't involve anything that changed in the object model between versions. However, this usage is not supported—you should always use the interop assembly for the specific version of Office that you plan to use in production. An easy way to determine which assemblies any assembly is dependent on—and in fact to determine maximum information about the assembly itself—is to use ILDASM.

ILDASM, the Microsoft Intermediate Language Disassembler, is a tool that ships with Visual Studio .NET. ILDASM takes as input a portable executable (PE) file containing MSIL code (either a .NET module or a .NET assembly) and creates a text file as output. It also offers a GUI display of the assembly, showing the assembly manifest, the type metadata, and the intermediate language (IL) code.

When you're happy with the debugger, it would be worth your while to spend a few minutes getting familiar with ILDASM. You can run ILDASM from a Visual Studio .NET command window, like this:

ildasm SimpleBug.dll

The ILDASM main window displays a treelist of the assembly, like this:

Of particular interest is the manifest. The manifest contains a list of the dependencies (in this case, Microsoft.Office.Interop.Excel.dll, System.Windows.Forms.dll, System.dll, etc.), as well as a description of the *SimpleBug* assembly itself.

Among other things, you can use the manifest dump to double-check or troubleshoot to find out which version of the Office PIAs your assembly has linked to. This is particularly useful if you have multiple PIA versions installed and want to be doubly sure.

For example, the one below links to Office 2003 (that is, v11.0.0.0).

```
MANIFEST                                                    _ □ X
.assembly extern /*23000003*/ Microsoft.Office.Interop.Excel
{
  .publickeytoken = (71 E9 BC E1 11 E9 42 9C )              // q..
  .ver 11:0:0:0
}
.assembly /*20000001*/ SimpleBug
{
  .custom /*0C000001:0A000007*/ instance void [mscorlib/* 23000004 */]System
  .custom /*0C000002:0A000001*/ instance void [mscorlib/* 23000004 */]System
  .custom /*0C000003:0A000002*/ instance void [mscorlib/* 23000004 */]System
  .custom /*0C000004:0A000003*/ instance void [mscorlib/* 23000004 */]System
  .custom /*0C000005:0A000006*/ instance void [mscorlib/* 23000004 */]System
```

Many developers find it useful to add ILDASM to the Tools menu in Visual Studio .NET. To do this, from the Tools menu, select External Tools, click the Add button, and type ILDASM (this will be the text of the menu item). Click the Browse button at the end of the Command field to navigate to where ILDASM.exe resides (probably either C:\Program Files\Microsoft.Net\FrameworkSDK\Bin\ILDASM.exe or C:\Program Files\Microsoft.Net\FrameworkSDK\v1.1\Bin\ILDASM.exe). Finally, in the Arguments box, click the right-arrow to get a list of variables; select $(TargetPath) for the current executable.

The Reflector tool, developed by Lutz Roeder, and available for download from *www.aisto.com/roeder/dotnet*, is a powerful alternative to ILDASM for viewing assembly contents.

Another tool to use in debugging is PerfMon. This offers a number of .NET-specific counters, as well as all the expected operating system and process counters. For example, you can add counters to track the number of times arguments and return values have been marshaled from managed to unmanaged code and vice versa:

The ProcessExplorer tool from *www.sysinternals.com* is another excellent debugging aid. You can use it to check all dependent DLLs (and other files) loaded for a given process, counts for AppDomains and assemblies, window and resource handles, and other useful runtime data:

Summary

In this chapter, we've introduced the basic concepts of interoperability between managed .NET code and Office. The Office applications are COM servers, so the basic mechanics of interoperation between managed code and Office are actually the same for interoperating between managed code and any COM servers. We've seen that during development we work with interop assemblies or primary interop assemblies. These are managed representations of the COM server's type library, and they allow us to develop against strongly typed classes, interfaces, and method signatures.

At run time, the .NET CLR places an RCW between our managed code and the Office components. This RCW acts as a proxy to the Office component so that when we make calls into the RCW, they are passed on to the underlying Office component. As part of this proxying behavior, the CLR marshals the parameters (both outgoing and incoming) and return values. This marshaling includes translation of types between the managed and unmanaged worlds.

For memory management and object lifetime, a basic mismatch exists between the expectations of COM components such as the Office applications and the expectations of .NET code. Several strategies are available for dealing with this mismatch, some more elegant than others. This is a topic that we'll revisit in later chapters because how you choose to deal with object lifetime depends to an extent on the context of your solution.

We've looked closely at some of the anomalies in the interop assemblies, and we've compared Visual Basic .NET with C# in the context of Office development. Both languages are very good for developing Office solutions, and the differences really come down to the historical evolution of the two languages. Visual Basic .NET does a little more for you during development, which makes it slightly more convenient. On the other hand, C# allows you to remain firmly and precisely in control of your own code.

Now that we've covered all the basic mechanics, we can begin to explore other simple techniques that build upon these basics.

Chapter 3

Office Interop Techniques

Now that we've covered the basic mechanics of how to interoperate between managed code and Microsoft Office applications, we'll consider some techniques that build on the basic mechanics. In later chapters, we'll examine the more narrowly focused protocols, such as add-ins, smart tags, and Visual Studio Tools for Office. In this chapter, we'll explore less formalized techniques that are slightly outside the mainstream. Although some of these techniques are not commonly used, they do introduce important concepts such as late binding, reflection, and accessibility.

Specifically, the topics to be covered include:

- **Platform Invoke**   Using methods from unmanaged DLLs.

- **Reflection**   Instead of using the strong types provided by an interop assembly, you can discover the types to use at run time. Getting and setting Office document properties involves using late binding, which is closely associated with reflection.

- **Connecting to running instances**   Instead of launching an Office application through automation, as we have done so far, you can use Platform Invoke to connect to instances of Office applications that are running independently.

- **Accessible objects in Office**   The *IAccessible* interface implemented by Office applications makes them more accessible both to users and to independent code.

3.1 Platform Invoke

Office 97	✓
Office 2000	✓
Office XP	✓
Office 2003	✓

Managed code can call functions in native code (that is, code native to the operating system the application is currently running on) that resides in DLLs, through a common language runtime (CLR) feature called Platform Invoke (P/Invoke). This is a commonly used feature, not just in Office interop solutions but also in Microsoft .NET development generally. When you develop a managed Office solution, you will generally make extensive use of the Office components that are exposed through COM. In addition, you are likely to use P/Invoke to talk to other (non-COM) components housed in DLLs, including system DLLs and any non-COM DLLs that you develop yourself or that you obtain from third parties.

To use P/Invoke in your code, you simply import the DLL by using the *DllImport* attribute. The CLR's interop marshaler will perform the same basic marshaling functionality for both P/Invoke and COM interop situations. In both cases, data types need to be marshaled between managed and unmanaged code. The standard marshaling rules apply in both cases, and the mapping between managed and unmanaged types that we examined in Chapter 2, "Basics of Office Interoperability," also holds good for both cases. In this section, we'll take a little time to examine the basic mechanics of P/Invoke in isolation before applying the technique to Office interop solutions.

Functions with Simple Parameters

In the following example, we have a simple console application that imports a Windows DLL in order to use the native Win32 API function *MessageBoxA*. Of course, this is an artificial example because the .NET Framework class library provides a perfectly good managed equivalent in the *System.Windows.Forms.MessageBox* class.

```
using System.Runtime.InteropServices;     // for DllImport

public class Class1
{
    [DllImport ("user32.dll")]              // all the defaults are OK
    public static extern int MessageBoxA (
        int h, string m, string c, int type);

    public static void Main(string[] args)
    {
        MessageBox(0, "Hello World", "nativeDLL", 0);
    }
}
```

As you can see from the code listing, we simply specify the DLL that contains the method we want, and we specify the method signature. Clearly, we need to use managed types in the parameter list and return value. In this way, when we make calls to the method, the CLR will pass these calls on to the "real" native method in the specified DLL.

There are additional parameters to the *DllImport* attribute that you can use if you wish. Note that when we tell the CLR where to find the method, we have to use a real function such as *MessageBoxA* or *MessageBoxW* rather than the macro *MessageBox*. However, when we use this method within our managed code, we can use any name we like.

```
[DllImport("user32", EntryPoint="MessageBoxA", SetLastError=true,
    CharSet=CharSet.Ansi, ExactSpelling=true,
    CallingConvention=CallingConvention.StdCall)]
public static extern int MessageBoxA (int h, string m, string c, int type);
```

If we want the CLR to find the appropriate real function based on the *CharSet* we supply, we can specify *ExactSpelling=false* and supply the simple name of the function:

```
[DllImport("user32", EntryPoint="MessageBox", SetLastError=true,
    CharSet=CharSet.Ansi, ExactSpelling=false,
    CallingConvention=CallingConvention.StdCall)]
```

The .NET CLR silently marshals the parameters from the managed code across to the native DLL function. In the specific case of *MessageBox*, there is a fairly obvious mapping between managed and unmanaged types (string to LPCSTR). In other cases, you might need to specify the way parameters are marshaled:

```
public static extern int MessageBox (
    int h,
    [MarshalAs(UnmanagedType.LPStr)] string m,
    string c, int type);
```

In some cases, you'll have to adjust the type of a parameter according to its intended use. For example, the *GetUserNameEx* Win32 API function takes an *enum*, the address of a character buffer, and the address of a *long* (both to be filled in on return):

```
BOOLEAN GetUserNameEx(EXTENDED_NAME_FORMAT NameFormat, LPTSTR lpNameBuffer, PULONG n
    Size);
```

To call this from managed code, you would use an *int* instead of the *enum*, a *StringBuilder* for the *char* buffer, and a *ref int* for the *long* pointer:

```
[DllImport("secur32.dll", CharSet=CharSet.Auto)]
public static extern int GetUserNameEx (int nameFormat,
    StringBuilder userName, ref uint userNameSize);
```

You can then call this method like this:

```
StringBuilder userName = new StringBuilder(255);
uint userNameSize = (uint)userName.Capacity;
GetUserNameEx(2, userName, ref userNameSize);
MessageBox(0, userName.ToString(), "GetUserNameEx", 0);
```

Functions with Struct Parameters

If you want the CLR to correctly marshal structs from managed to unmanaged code (or vice versa), you need to declare additional attributes for the struct declaration. For example, consider the native Win32 API function *GetLocalTime*, which takes a *System-Time* struct as its parameter:

```
[DllImport ("kernel32.dll")]
public static extern void GetLocalTime(SystemTime st);
```

For the struct parameter to be correctly marshaled, it needs to be declared with the *StructLayout* attribute, specifying that the data is to be laid out exactly as listed in the declaration (i.e., *Sequential*). If you don't do it this way, the data won't be correctly marshaled and the application is likely to crash:

```
[StructLayout(LayoutKind.Sequential)]
public class SystemTime {
    public ushort wYear;
    public ushort wMonth;
    public ushort wDayOfWeek;
    public ushort wDay;
    public ushort wHour;
    public ushort wMinute;
    public ushort wSecond;
    public ushort wMilliseconds;
}
```

This function can then be called like this:

```
SystemTime st = new SystemTime();
GetLocalTime(st);
```

We can then use this information in a call to *MessageBox*. Alternatively, we can use the Framework Class Library (FCL) *MessageBox* class instead of the Win32 *MessageBoxA/W* API functions. To do this, add a reference to the System.WinForms.dll (right-click References in Solution Explorer, and select Add Reference) and an appropriate *using* statement. Then we can use this code (continuing with the *SystemTime* example):

```
string s = String.Format("date: {0}-{1}-{2}",
    st.wDay, st.wMonth, st.wYear);
string t = String.Format("time: {0}:{1}:{2}",
    st.wHour, st.wMinute, st.wSecond);
string u = s + ", " + t;
System.Windows.Forms.MessageBox.Show(
    u, "Foo", MessageBoxButtons.OK, MessageBoxIcon.Exclamation);
```

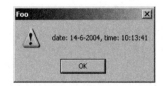

Now that we've seen the basic mechanics of P/Invoke, we are in a position to apply the technique to Office interop solutions.

3.2 Watching Excel Quit

Office 97	❌
Office 2000	❓
Office XP	✅
Office 2003	✅

In an earlier example, we demonstrated how to intercept the *Quit* event that Microsoft Word fires when it quits. Unfortunately, Microsoft Excel doesn't fire a *Quit* event. If we develop an application that interops with Excel, we remain in complete control as long as we don't make Excel visible to the user. As soon as we make Excel visible, we open the opportunity for the user to quit Excel, and there's no standard way of tracking if or when that has happened. In this section, we'll look at a way to work around this limitation.

You might think that we could watch the Excel process to see when it dies. Certainly, we could use Win32 API functions to do something like this:

1. We have an *Excel.Application* reference that exposes an *Hwnd* (window handle) property (from Excel XP), and using this window handle, we call the Win32 API *GetWindowThreadProcessId* to get hold of the Excel process ID.

2. Using the process ID, we call *OpenProcess* to get hold of Excel's process handle.

3. We then pass the process handle to *WaitForSingleObject*, which returns when the process handle is signaled (that is, when the process stops).

This will certainly tell us when the Excel process stops. Unfortunately, this isn't helpful because the Excel process won't stop so long as we're holding a managed reference to one of its objects. So even though the user might have quit Excel, we'll keep the Excel process alive.

This is a mixed blessing. If we're keeping a managed reference to an Excel object, presumably we want the Excel process to stay alive. On the other hand, if we've made Excel visible, presumably we're happy for the user to quit Excel. Furthermore, if we're happy for the user to quit Excel while we're holding managed references to Excel objects, the only scenario in which this makes any sense is if we're intending to release all our references as soon as Excel quits. Which brings us back to the main problem: how can we tell when Excel quits?

Can we track the thread that runs Excel's main window? Yes, we can—again, using *GetWindowThreadProcessId* and *OpenThread* to get hold of Excel's main window thread ID and thread handle. Unfortunately, we're assuming that when the user quits Excel, the thread that runs the main window stops. Well, it doesn't—not if we're holding references to Excel objects.

So, tracking the Excel process or threads is no use. Then what about the window handles? From Excel XP, the *Application* object in the interop assembly (IA) does give us access to Excel's main window handle. For Excel 97 and Excel 2000, we can use Win32 API functions such as *FindWindowEx* to get hold of Excel's main window handle. The basic technique described in this section will work with Excel 97 and Excel 2000 if we get our programmatic references from existing running instances (which can easily include running instances that we have started programmatically from our application). For further examination of the use of *FindWindowEx* and related API functions, see Section 3.7, "Monitoring Office Applications," later in this chapter.

You would think that when the user quits Excel, the main window closes (along with all child windows). Unfortunately, they don't: the main window is simply hidden. As long as we're holding the Excel process alive with a reference, Excel's main window also stays alive, albeit hidden.

That last point does give us a glimmer of hope. We can simply watch to see when Excel's main window is hidden. Note that hidden is not the same as minimized. If it's minimized to the taskbar, it's not hidden. If we've made it visible, or if the user launched Excel in the first place, he can't make it hidden—at most, he can minimize it. Just as we can programmatically make Excel visible, we can also programmatically make Excel hidden, and we can track when we're doing this. Therefore, the only other situation in which Excel's main window is hidden is when the user has quit it.

So, let's build an application to watch when the user quits Excel. Because we don't want to block the main user interface of our application, we'll do the Excel watching in a separate thread.

> **Note**   The sample solution for this topic can be found in the sample code at <install location>\Code\Office<n>\ExcelQuitter.

1. Create a new Windows Forms application called ExcelQuitter. Add a reference to the appropriate Excel IAs for your target version of Office. Put two *Button* controls on the form, and get *Click* event handlers for each one. Set the *Enabled* property of the QuitExcel button to *false* initially:

2. Declare a class field to cache our reference to the Excel *Application* object. Also declare a *Thread* reference.

    ```
    private Excel.Application xl;
    private Thread excelWatcherThread;
    ```

3. In the *Click* event handler for the RunExcel button, we'll launch Excel and make it visible. We'll also set up our second *Thread* object. We need to supply a method that will control this second thread, and we need to start the thread. We can optionally give it any arbitrary name (useful if we need to debug it). After all this important work, we'll toggle the *Enabled* stat of our buttons:

    ```
    private void btnRunExcel_Click(object sender, System.EventArgs e)
    {
        xl = new Excel.Application();
        xl.Visible = true;

        Thread excelWatcherThread = new Thread(new ThreadStart(ExcelWatcherProc
    ));
        excelWatcherThread.Name = "Excel Watcher";
        excelWatcherThread.Start();

        btnQuitExcel.Enabled = true;
        btnRunExcel.Enabled = false;
    }
    ```

4. Now that we're going to have another thread running, we really should wait for this thread to terminate before we close our application. If we don't, we run the risk of the thread trying to access our application's resources after they've been cleaned up. So, we'll enhance the wizard-supplied *Dispose* method to wait for the thread to stop:

    ```
    protected override void Dispose(bool disposing)
    {
        if (excelWatcherThread != null)
        {
            excelWatcherThread.Join();
        }
        ...
    ```

5. In the *Click* handler for our QuitExcel button, if the Excel *Application* reference is not null, we'll call *Excel.Quit* and clean up by forcing a garbage collection as normal. We'll also interrupt the second thread to tell it to stop watching Excel's window. Finally, we'll toggle the buttons:

    ```
    private void btnQuitExcel_Click(object sender, System.EventArgs e)
    {
        if (xl != null)
        {
            xl.Quit();
            xl = null;
    ```

```
        excelWatcherThread.Interrupt();

        GC.Collect();
        GC.WaitForPendingFinalizers();
        GC.Collect();
        GC.WaitForPendingFinalizers();
    }

    btnRunExcel.Enabled = true;
    btnQuitExcel.Enabled = false;
}
```

6. Before we can finally code the second thread's controlling method, we need to declare some Win32 API artifacts—the *ShowWindow* method and an *enum* for all the possible ways that a window can be shown. (We actually need only two of these values, but for completeness, and for any further experimentation, we'll declare them all here.)

```
[DllImport("user32")]
public static extern bool ShowWindow(int hwnd, int nCmdShow);

private enum SW
{
    HIDE            = 0,
    SHOWNORMAL      = 1,
    NORMAL          = 1,
    SHOWMINIMIZED   = 2,
    SHOWMAXIMIZED   = 3,
    MAXIMIZE        = 3,
    SHOWNOACTIVATE  = 4,
    SHOW            = 5,
    MINIMIZE        = 6,
    SHOWMINNOACTIVE = 7,
    SHOWNA          = 8,
    RESTORE         = 9,
    SHOWDEFAULT     = 10,
    FORCEMINIMIZE   = 11,
    MAX             = 11
}
```

7. Finally, our custom method needs to control our second thread. We need to put everything in a *try/catch* block because in one of our button *Click* handlers, we're calling *Thread.Interrupt*. This causes a *ThreadInterruptedException* to be thrown and is a simple technique for telling a thread to stop.

    We'll set up an infinite loop, pausing for 1000 milliseconds each time by calling *Thread.Sleep*. In the loop, we'll call *ShowWindow* with the least intrusive value, *SW.SHOWNA*. This means to show the window in its current size and position but not activate it. (If it were already activated, this would remain unchanged.) Now the crucial piece of information: if the Excel main window was not visible before we called *ShowWindow*, we can assume that the user quit Excel.

8. We still have a little work to do: if the Excel main window was not visible before we called *ShowWindow*, we've just made it visible even though the user quit it. So, we must make it hidden again. Then we can clean up as normal, toggle the buttons, and break out of the infinite loop:

```
private void ExcelWatcherProc()
{
    try
    {
        while (true)
        {
            bool wasVisible = ShowWindow(xl.Hwnd, (int)SW.SHOWNA);
            if (!wasVisible)
            {
                ShowWindow(xl.Hwnd, (int)SW.HIDE);

                xl = null;
                GC.Collect();
                GC.WaitForPendingFinalizers();
                GC.Collect();
                GC.WaitForPendingFinalizers();

                btnRunExcel.Enabled = true;
                btnQuitExcel.Enabled = false;

                break;
            }

            Thread.Sleep(1000);
        }
    }
    catch (ThreadInterruptedException) {}
}
```

9. Build and test. Regardless of whether we programmatically call *Excel.Quit* or whether the user interactively quits, we'll clean up properly. This will work even if Excel has been minimized to the taskbar.

10. Note that we've actually taken a slight shortcut in the second thread method. Strictly speaking, Windows Forms controls execute correctly only on the thread on which they are created: they are not thread-safe. If you want to get or set properties, or call methods, on a control from another thread, you should marshal the call to the thread that created the control. Five methods on a control are safe to call from any thread: *InvokeRequired*, *Invoke*, *BeginInvoke*, *EndInvoke*, and *CreateGraphics*. For all other method calls on a control, you should pass a delegate to that method as a parameter to the control's *Invoke* or *BeginInvoke* methods. These ensure that their delegate parameter's method is executed on the thread that owns this control's underlying window handle. We'll write a new custom method that will be called indirectly by our second thread, instead of accessing the button properties directly:

```
private void ResetButtons()
{
    btnRunExcel.Enabled = true;
    btnQuitExcel.Enabled = false;
}
```

11. Enhance the second thread method to invoke this method. We'll use *Begin-Invoke* to do this asynchronously. We can quickly set up a simple delegate using the *MethodInvoker* class. This works with simple methods with a void parameter list (such as our *ResetButtons* method):

```
// btnRunExcel.Enabled = true;
// btnQuitExcel.Enabled = false;
MethodInvoker invoker = new MethodInvoker(ResetButtons);
BeginInvoke(invoker);
```

We are relying here on Excel's behavior of not actually closing its main window or stopping its main window thread until after all objects are released. This is because the main window is associated with the main message pump.

This solution offers a workaround for a limitation in the Excel object model, in that Excel doesn't fire a *Quit* event. Be warned, however, that our sample application doesn't allow for any other code that might be associated with Excel at run time. For example, we haven't made any accommodation for COM add-ins, smart tags, smart docs, or indeed any VBA macro code that might have functionality that is dependent on the *Quit* behavior of Excel.

3.3 Using COM by Reflection

Office 97
Office 2000
Office XP
Office 2003

Instead of using TlbImp to import a COM type library for use in a .NET application, you can use run-time reflection in conjunction with the library classes *Type* and *Activator*. When you build a .NET assembly, the compiler embeds metadata in the assembly. This metadata is like a COM type library. It describes the assembly itself, in terms of its name, version, and other attributes, and any dependent assemblies. It also describes the types in the assembly—that is, the classes, structs, interfaces, and *enums*, including the signatures of the methods in these types.

The .NET Framework class library contains several types (mostly in the *System* and *System.Reflection* namespaces) that allow you to write code to reflect over (or parse) the metadata in an assembly. Reflection can also perform late binding, in which the application dynamically loads, instantiates, and uses a type at run time.

The *Type* class is the basis of all reflection operations: you use the members of *Type* to get information about a type declaration, such as the constructors, methods, fields, properties, and events of a class, as well as the module and the assembly in which the class is deployed—in other words, the whole metadata. The *Activator* class allows you to instantiate objects of any type, including COM objects, so long as you provide the *Type* information for the object.

In the following exercise, we'll use runtime reflection to instantiate a COM object (specifically, an automation object). We'll experiment with both Microsoft Internet Explorer and Excel.

> **Note**   The sample solution for this topic can be found in the sample code at <install location>\Code\Office<n>\ReflectCOM.

Using *GetTypeFromProgID*

1. In Visual Studio .NET, create a new Windows application called ReflectCOM. Don't add the Excel primary interop assembly (PIA)—we won't need it. Instead, add a *using* statement at the top for *System.Reflection*.

2. Put two buttons on the form, one to activate Internet Explorer, the other to activate Excel. Add *Click* handlers for both buttons.

3. In the Internet Explorer *click* handler, add code to get the type information based on the ProgID of the COM object. Then instantiate the object using the *CreateInstance* method of the *Activator* class:

```
Type t = Type.GetTypeFromProgID("InternetExplorer.Application");
object o = Activator.CreateInstance(t);
```

4. Use *InvokeMember* to set the *Visible* property of the Internet Explorer object:

```
t.InvokeMember(
    "Visible", BindingFlags.SetProperty,
    null, o, new object[]{true});
```

5. Use *InvokeMember* again to invoke the *Navigate* member of the Internet Explorer object (and note that the remaining four parameters are optional). Then build and test.

```
t.InvokeMember(
    "Navigate", BindingFlags.InvokeMethod,
    null, o, new object[] {"www.microsoft.com"});
```

Traversing a COM Object Model

This simple functionality is easy enough to achieve with reflection, but what about a more complex scenario? Specifically, can you navigate a COM server's object model to invoke methods and *get/set* properties on objects that cannot be directly created by reflection? For example, you can directly create an instance of the Excel *Application* object but not the Excel *Workbook* object—the latter is a COM object but is not independently creatable. To test this out, we'll add the following code to the second button *Click* handler.

1. As with Internet Explorer, declare a *Type* object and assign it from *GetTypeFromProgID*, and create an instance of this type of object.

```
Type excelType = Type.GetTypeFromProgID("Excel.Application");
object xl = Activator.CreateInstance(excelType);
```

Note: if you're interested, it would be worth putting in a few additional lines of code at this point, to list all the members of this type in the debug output window:

```
MemberInfo[] members = excelType.GetMembers(BindingFlags.Instance |
    BindingFlags.Static | BindingFlags.Public | BindingFlags.NonPublic);
foreach (MemberInfo mi in members)
{
    Debug.WriteLine(String.Format("{0} = {1}", mi.MemberType, mi));
}
```

For the Excel *Application* object, this will produce a lengthy listing.

2. To continue with the main functionality of our example, set the object's *Visible* property, as before:

```
excelType.InvokeMember(
    "Visible", BindingFlags.SetProperty,
    null, xl, new object[]{true});
```

3. Invoke a *GetProperty* member to get the *Workbooks* collection object:

```
object books = excelType.InvokeMember(
    "Workbooks", BindingFlags.GetProperty,
    null, xl, null);
```

4. Once we have the *Workbooks* object, we can add a new *Workbook*:

```
object book = books.GetType().InvokeMember(
    "Add", BindingFlags.InvokeMethod,
    null, books, new object[]{1});
```

5. Then we can get to the *ActiveSheet* property of the *Workbook*, which is a *Worksheet* object:

```
object sheet = book.GetType().InvokeMember(
    "ActiveSheet", BindingFlags.GetProperty,
    null, book, null);
```

6. From the *Worksheet* object, we can specify a *Range* object:

```
object range = sheet.GetType().InvokeMember(
    "Range", BindingFlags.GetProperty,
    null, sheet, new object[]{"a1"});
```

7. Finally, we can set the *Value2* property of the specified *Range* object:

```
range.GetType().InvokeMember(
    "Value2", BindingFlags.PutDispProperty,
    null, range, new object[]{"Hello World"});
```

8. Build and test.

We've seen that working with Office components via reflection is very powerful—so powerful that it even allows us to do things that the original designer of the component didn't anticipate. The result is that if you really need to, you can interoperate with Office and other COM servers without using an IA, and without using an RCW proxy. However, you still need knowledge of what's in the type library, so the situations in which this strategy might be useful are rare. Furthermore, there are obvious dangers if you use reflection to get access to functionality that you're not intended to access.

3.4 Document Properties

Office documents, such as Word documents and Excel workbooks, contain not only document data but also document metadata. This metadata consists of two types:

Office 97	✓
Office 2000	✓
Office XP	✓
Office 2003	✓

- **Built-in properties**   These are predefined properties, such as *Author*, *Title*, *Subject*, and statistics such as counts of *Lines*, *Words*, and *Paragraphs*.

- **Custom properties**   These are arbitrary custom properties, which might include items such as *Editor*, *Mailstop*, or *_AssemblyName0*. (See Chapter 10, "Visual Studio Tools for Office," to learn how this particular custom property is used.)

Just as you can use the exposed COM object model of each Office application to get and set the document data, you can also get and set the metadata. A couple of interesting things about document properties are worth mentioning here. The first is that they are late-bound. That is, they are not strongly typed. This is essentially the same model as pure *Dispatch* interfaces in the COM world. What this means is that the properties don't show up in the IA, nor in the Object Browser, because their types are not defined in the type library that is the basis of the IA. Instead, you must rely on documentation to work out the names of these properties, and discover at run time whether they actually exist. Clearly, you need to be especially careful to handle exceptions when working with late-bound members. As a general rule, you should avoid late binding if you can, but sometimes you have no choice.

The second interesting thing is that persisting the properties to the file on disk leads to behavior that often confuses developers. Two specific issues can be a little baffling at first. First, even reading the built-in properties marks the document as "dirty," so you need to take steps to either save the document or mark it as saved to avoid the "Do you want to save the changes?" dialog box. Second, if you make changes to the properties and want them persisted to disk, it's not enough to save the document. You must also call the *UpdateSummaryProperties* method.

In the following exercise, we'll create a simple Windows Forms application. In the application, we'll load a Word document and read some of the built-in properties, putting them into a list box in our form. Then we'll read a custom property—the test document has been set up with an arbitrary custom property in advance. Finally, we'll change the value of one of the built-in properties and create a new custom property, persisting both to the file on disk.

The only version variation in this example is in the number of parameters that need to be passed to the *Document.Open* method. This method takes the file name as its first parameter, followed by a number of optional parameters. Recall that we can use *System.Type.Missing* or *System.Reflection.Missing.Value* for these optional parameters. There are 9 missing parameters in Word 97, 11 in Word 2000, 14 in Word XP, and 15 in Word 2003.

> **Note**   The sample solution for this topic can be found in the sample code at <install location>\Code\Office<n>\GetDocProps.

1. Create a new Windows application called GetDocProps. Put a *ListBox* control on the form. Add a reference to the Word IA. (In Solution Explorer, right-click and select Add Reference, click the COM tab, and select the appropriate Microsoft Word Object Library from the list.) To use late binding, we need to use the classes in the *System.Reflection* namespace, so add a using statement for this at the top of the code.

2. At the top of the form class, declare some class fields for use across multiple methods. We'll be writing three methods: for opening the document, for getting the properties, and for setting the properties. We'll use the same document across all three methods. We will also use the two properties collections (built-in and custom) across methods, along with their types:

   ```
   private Word._Document doc;
   private object builtInProps;
   private Type typeBuiltInProps;
   private object customProps;
   private Type typeCustomProps;
   ```

3. Our first method will open the document—call this method *OpenDocument*. In the sample solutions, you'll find a simple test document called Jabberwocky.doc. This has been prepared with some arbitrary values for some of the built-in properties, and also an arbitrary custom property. You can, however, use any document you wish for this exercise. So, we'll first work out the path for the document file we want to use:

   ```
   string currentLocation = System.Environment.CurrentDirectory;
   string currentPath = currentLocation.Substring(
       0, currentLocation.IndexOf(@"bin\Debug"));
   string fileName = "Jabberwocky.doc";
   string filePath = Path.Combine(currentPath, fileName);
   ```

4. Launch Word and open the document, using the appropriate number of "missing" optional parameters according to the version of Word you're targeting:

```
try
{
    object missing = Type.Missing;
    Word.Application  = new Word.Application();
    word.Visible = true;

    object f = filePath;
    doc = word.Documents.Open(ref f,
        ref missing, ref missing, ref missing, ref missing, ref missing,
        ref missing, ref missing, ref missing, ref missing, ref missing,
        ref missing, ref missing, ref missing, ref missing, ref missing);
    bool wasSaved = doc.Saved;
}
catch (Exception ex)
{
    MessageBox.Show(ex.Message);
}
```

5. Make a call to this *OpenDocument* method at the end of the form constructor, after the call to *InitializeComponent*.

6. Our second method will read some of the built-in properties and the custom property—call it *GetProperties*. The first thing to do is to cache the current status of the *Saved* flag. This is because even reading the properties will set this flag to *false*. In this method, we won't make any changes—we'll only read the properties. Therefore, we'll cache the current status so that after we've read the properties (and the flag has been changed to *false*), we can restore it to its original value. Why don't we just set it to *true* at the end, regardless? Well, we're not making any changes programmatically, but we are opening the document and making it visible, so the user could make changes directly through the user interface. Ultimately, this is just a more flexible approach.

```
try
{
    bool wasSaved = doc.Saved;
```

7. Set up an array of strings for the built-in properties we want to read:

```
string[] propIndices = new string[]{
    "Title", "Subject", "Author", "Keywords", "Template",
    "Last Author", "Revision Number", "Application Name",
    "Creation Date", "Last Save Time", "Total Editing Time",
    "Number of Pages", "Number of Words", "Number of Characters",
    "Security", "Manager", "Company", "Number of Bytes",
    "Number of Lines"
    };
```

8. We'll read the values of built-in properties in the *BuiltInDocumentProperties* collection object that is a property of the *Document* object. What we'd like to do (if the collection is strongly typed) is something like this:

```
string propertyValue = doc.BuiltInDocumentProperties["Title"].Value;
```

However, the *BuiltInDocumentProperties* will be given to us as a simple object, so we can't just index into it in the way we'd like. We can get to the real type of the object by using the *GetType* method. This returns a *Type* reference. The *Type* class is the basis of all the reflection functionality for accessing type metadata, including getting and setting properties and invoking methods.

```
builtInProps = doc.BuiltInDocumentProperties;
typeBuiltInProps = builtInProps.GetType();
```

9. For each built-in document property, get its value and set it into our list box. We'll use the *Type.InvokeMember* to get the *Item* property from the collection, specified by its string name. We also have to specify the (late) binding behavior. In this case, we'll using *BindingFlags.Default* combined with *BindingFlags.GetProperty*. In this way, we'll get each invididual property from the collection. For each property, we then have to use late binding to get its *Value* property so that we can add this value to the list box as a string:

```
for (int i = 0; i < propIndices.Length; i++)
{
    string propValue;
    object builtInProp = typeBuiltInProps.InvokeMember("Item",
        BindingFlags.Default | BindingFlags.GetProperty,
        null, builtInProps, new object[] {propIndices[i]});
    if (builtInProp != null)
    {
        Type typeBuiltInProp = builtInProp.GetType();
        propValue = typeBuiltInProp.InvokeMember("Value",
            BindingFlags.Default | BindingFlags.GetProperty,
            null, builtInProp, new object[] {}).ToString();
        listBox1.Items.Add(string.Format(
            "{0} = {1}", propIndices[i], propValue));
    }
}
```

10. For the custom property, we'll use basically the same technique. Our sample document has a custom property called *MyCustomProperty*. This will be in the *CustomDocumentProperties* collection. We need to get this collection, get its *Type*, and use *InvokeMember* to get its *Item* property. This gets us the individual property, from which we can get its *Value* property. We'll add the string version of this *Value* to our list box.

```
string customPropString = "MyCustomProperty";
customProps = doc.CustomDocumentProperties;
typeCustomProps = customProps.GetType();
object customProp = typeCustomProps.InvokeMember("Item",
    BindingFlags.Default | BindingFlags.GetProperty,
    null, customProps, new object[]{customPropString});
string customPropValue;
if (customProp != null)
{
    Type typeCustomProp = customProp.GetType();
    customPropValue = typeCustomProp.InvokeMember("Value",
```

```
                    BindingFlags.Default | BindingFlags.GetProperty,
                    null, customProp, new object[]{}).ToString();
                listBox1.Items.Add(string.Format(
                    "{0} = {1}", customPropString, customPropValue));
        }
```

11. Reset the *Saved* status at the end of the method:

```
            doc.Saved = wasSaved;
    }
    catch (Exception ex)
    {
        MessageBox.Show(ex.Message);
    }
```

12. Make a call to this *GetProperties* method at the end of the form constructor, after the call to *OpenDocument*. It's probably a good idea to build and test the application at this point, before attempting to make any changes to the properties.

13. We'll call our third method *SetProperties*. First we'll change one of our built-in properties—say, the *Title*. We've previously cached a reference to the *Type* of the *BuiltInDocumentProperties* collection, so we just need to use this to set the *Item* property. *Item* is a parameterized property. This means that to set the value of this property, you can (and must) pass in more than one parameter. In this case, we need to pass in the string index name of the individual property we want to set, and the string value we want to set it to:

```
    try
    {
        // Set the value of the Built-In Title property.
        string propIndex = "Title";
        string propValue = "A true story of life in the north-west.";

        typeBuiltInProps.InvokeMember("Item",
            BindingFlags.Default | BindingFlags.SetProperty,
            null, builtInProps, new object[] {propIndex, propValue} );
```

14. Now we'll add a new custom property. Continue with the *SetProperties* method. Set up two strings: one for the index name of the new custom property and one for the string value of the property. You can use any strings you like here. So far, we've used late binding to get and set properties. Now, we'll use late binding to invoke a method—specifically, the *Add* method. We need to pass this method the custom property index name, a flag indicating whether this property is linked to the document contents, its type, and its value:

```
propIndex = "AnotherCustomProperty";
propValue = "Charles Lutwidge Dodgson";
object[] args = {propIndex, false,
    Office.MsoDocProperties.msoPropertyTypeString, propValue};

typeCustomProps.InvokeMember("Add",
    BindingFlags.Default | BindingFlags.InvokeMethod,
    null, customProps, args);
```

15. Make sure the changes are persisted by calling *UpdateSummaryProperties*, and also save the document. Make a call to *SetProperties* at the end of the form constructor, and then build and test again.

```
doc.UpdateSummaryProperties();
    doc.Save();
}
catch (Exception ex)
{
    MessageBox.Show(ex.Message);
}
```

> **Best Practices**   The considerable evolution of Office products over a long
> period of time has led to their object models having one or two little quirks. The
> way document properties are exposed as late-bound members is different from
> the way almost all other members are exposed (that is, through early-bindable,
> strongly typed COM interfaces). The designers did intend for us to work with
> these late-bound members, and the standard way to do this is by using the
> classes in the reflection namespace. This is one situation in which using late
> binding and reflection is acceptable and recommended. In all other situations,
> late binding and reflection should be avoided if at all possible.

3.5 Connecting to Running Instances

Office 97
Office 2000
Office XP
Office 2003

When you create an application to automate an Office application, you can either create a new instance of that Office application or get a reference to the instance that is already running. Microsoft generally recommends that you create a new instance instead of attaching to a running instance. The question then is, if you didn't start the application in the first place, how do you get hold of it to automate it?

Well, if the Automation server registered itself in the Running Object Table (ROT), you can connect to the application by querying the ROT. In the .NET Framework class library, a client can get a reference to a ROT-registered instance by calling *Marshal.GetActiveObject* or *Marshal.BindToMoniker*, depending on whether you know the object's ProgID or the moniker type—in other words, do you want to use, say, *"Excel.Application"* or *"Foo.xls"*?

Note that COM servers can be classified as multiuse (single instance) or single use (multiple instances), depending on the number of instances of that server that can run simultaneously on a single computer. Excel, Word, and Microsoft Access are single use (multiple instances) servers. Microsoft PowerPoint is a multiuse (single instance) server. Because potentially more than one instance of Word, Excel, or Access can be running, *GetActiveObject* on a particular server might return an instance that you did not expect—typically, the instance that was first registered in the ROT.

If you want to get an automation reference to a specific running instance of Word, Excel, or Access, use *BindToMoniker* with the name of the file that is opened in that instance. For a multiuse (single instance) server such as PowerPoint, it does not matter because the automation reference points to the same running instance.

In the following exercise, we'll specifically avoid launching Excel through direct automation. Instead, we'll create a simple Windows application with three buttons, and when the user clicks a button we'll connect to Excel in a different way. The purpose of each button is as follows:

■ **Start Excel Process**   Start a new instance of Excel using the FCL *Process.Start* method, and connect via *GetActiveObject*.

■ **Get Active Excel**   Call *GetActiveObject* to connect to an instance of Excel that's running independently.

■ **Excel Moniker**   Call *BindToMoniker* to connect to Excel.

> **Note**   The sample solution for this topic can be found in the sample code at
> <install location>\Code\Office<n>\RunningInstances.

1. Create a new Windows application called RunningInstances. Put three *Button* controls on the form, labeled as indicated above. Get *Click* event handlers for the buttons. Add a reference to the Excel IA. (In Solution Explorer, right-click and select Add Reference, click the COM tab, and select the appropriate Microsoft Excel Object Library from the list.)

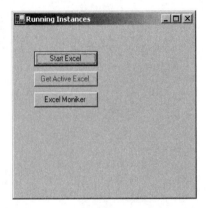

2. Add a using statement for the Excel namespace (with an alias to cut down on typing effort) and for the *System.IO* and *System.Runtime.InteropServices*. (We'll be working with filenames and the *Marshal* class.)

```
using System.IO;
using System.Runtime.InteropServices;
using Excel = Microsoft.Office.Interop.Excel;          // not for Office 97/2000
```

Starting Excel with *Process.Start*

In the first button handler, we'll start a new Excel process using *System.Diagnostics.Process.Start*. This strategy can be used to start any process, but it doesn't give you any direct reference to the application's object model. We can get a direct reference to the application's object model later by using *Marshal.GetActiveObject*.

1. Declare an *Excel.Application* reference, and call *Process.Start*. You must supply the appropriate path to the Excel.exe application. Note that Excel and other

Office applications register themselves in the ROT when their top-level window loses focus. For this reason, when we start Excel, we'll run up a message box to force Excel to lose focus. We can then get the reference to Excel from the ROT using *GetActiveObject*, display its name, and quit. Note that we force a garbage collection to maintain a degree of determinism when our COM objects are being released:

```
private void startExcel_Click(object sender, System.EventArgs e)
{
    Excel.Application xl;
    System.Diagnostics.Process.Start(
        @"C:\Program Files\Microsoft Office\Office11\Excel.exe");
    MessageBox.Show("Launched Excel");
```

2. Use *Marshal.GetActiveObject* to get the reference to Excel from the ROT. To prove we did get hold of it, do something simple like displaying its name:

```
xl = (Excel.Application)Marshal.GetActiveObject("Excel.Application");
MessageBox.Show(xl.Name);
```

3. Quit Excel and clean up:

```
xl.Quit();
xl = null;
GC.Collect();
GC.WaitForPendingFinalizers();
GC.Collect();
GC.WaitForPendingFinalizers();
}
```

Note the path variations for different versions of Office—prior to Office XP, the default installation folder was named simply Office rather than Office10, Office11, and so forth.

```
System.Diagnostics.Process.Start(
    //@"C:\Program Files\Microsoft Office\Office11\Excel.exe");
    //@"C:\Program Files\Microsoft Office\Office10\Excel.exe");
    @"C:\Program Files\Microsoft Office\Office\Excel.exe");
```

4. Build and test.

> **Note** Using *Process.Start* in the context of Office development is not generally recommended, for several reasons. First, it's not very flexible and therefore not very useful—you're simply launching another executable, and you have very little control over that executable from that point on. Second, there are significant security considerations. In fact, your code might not even be able to perform the *Process.Start* operation unless it has been granted appropriate security permissions. Third, it involves creating a new OS process, which is very expensive. In many scenarios you can achieve the same ends using automation or even using multiple AppDomains, without creating a separate process.

Using *GetActiveObject*

In the second handler, we'll use the ROT and *GetActiveObject* without programmatically starting the Excel process. We'll attempt to connect to Excel 10 times, with a half-second pause between each attempt. This is to allow for the race condition in which Excel starts at about the same time we click the button—*GetActiveObject* can fail if Excel has not yet registered its objects in the ROT.

1. Declare an *Excel.Application* reference, and start a 10-iteration *while* loop:

   ```
   private void getActive_Click(object sender, System.EventArgs e)
   {
       Excel.Application xl = null;
       int attempts = 0;

       while (attempts < 10)
       {
           try
           {
   ```

2. Set up a *try* block, and get the first running instance of Excel using *Marshal.GetActiveObject*. Just to prove we did get hold of it, display its name:

   ```
   xl = (Excel.Application)Marshal.GetActiveObject(
       "Excel.Application");
   MessageBox.Show(xl.Name);
   ```

3. Clean up the RCW. Note that we don't quit Excel because we didn't start it in the first place. Then finish off the *try* and *catch* blocks. Each time around the loop, we'll sleep for half a second.

   ```
   xl = null;
   GC.Collect();
   GC.WaitForPendingFinalizers();
   GC.Collect();
   GC.WaitForPendingFinalizers();
   break;
   }
   catch (Exception ex)
   {
       attempts++;
       if (attempts < 10)
       {
           System.Threading.Thread.Sleep(500);
       }
       else
       {
           MessageBox.Show(
               "GetActiveObject failed 10 times: "
   +ex.Message);
       }
   }
   }
   }
   ```

4. Build and test.

Using *BindToMoniker*

In the third handler, we'll use *Marshal.BindToMoniker* to get an instance of Excel for a given .xls file. (You'll need to create this, and the following code assumes you've put it into the current project folder.) This will work whether or not Excel is already running with the file open.

1. Get the full path to the test .xls file:

    ```csharp
    private void bindMoniker_Click(object sender, System.EventArgs e)
    {
        string currentLocation = System.Environment.CurrentDirectory;
        string currentPath = currentLocation.Substring(
            0, currentLocation.IndexOf(@"bin\Debug"));
        string fileName = "foo.xls";
        string filePath = Path.Combine(currentPath, fileName);
        bool weLaunchedExcel = false;
    ```

2. Set up a *try* block, and get a reference to the *Workbook* object by using a file moniker:

    ```csharp
    try
    {
        Excel.Workbook book = (Excel.Workbook)Marshal.BindToMoniker(filePath);
    ```

3. If Excel is up with this file open, it was already running; but if it isn't, we will have launched it, so we'd better make it visible:

    ```csharp
    Excel.Application xl =
                (Excel.Application)book.Application;
    if (xl.Visible == false)
    {
        xl.Visible = true;
        weLaunchedExcel = true;
    }
    ```

4. If Excel was already running, our *BindToMoniker* will load the workbook we want, but load it hidden. This state will also persist so that subsequent attempts to open the file will also open it hidden. So, we simply make sure it's visible here:

    ```csharp
    if (xl.Windows[fileName].Visible == false)
    {
        xl.Windows[fileName].Visible = true;
    }

    MessageBox.Show(xl.Name);
    ```

5. We quit Excel only if we started it in the first place:

    ```csharp
    if (weLaunchedExcel)
    {
        xl.Quit();
    }
    xl = null;
    ```

6. If we had to quit Excel, it will have come up with a Save Changes dialog box. This is enough to keep the Excel process alive until the application dies, unless we explicitly force a garbage collection.

```
        GC.Collect();
        GC.WaitForPendingFinalizers();
        GC.Collect();
        GC.WaitForPendingFinalizers();
    }
    catch (Exception ex)
    {
        MessageBox.Show(ex.Message);
    }
}
```

7. Build and test.

3.6 Office Accessible Objects

Office 97	❌
Office 2000	✅
Office XP	✅
Office 2003	✅

Microsoft Active Accessibility is a COM-based technology (available on Windows NT 4.0 SP6, Windows 98, and Windows XP and later) that improves the way accessibility aids work with applications running on Windows. By using Active Accessibility, developers can make applications running on Windows more accessible to many people with vision, hearing, or motion disabilities. While Office 97 applications have some support for accessibility, they do not support the *IAccessible* interface, and the interop technique described here cannot be used.

Programmatically, the Active Accessibility technology is represented by the *IAccessible* interface and a number of supporting APIs. The way this technology has been implemented actually serves a dual purpose. It makes software such as Office more accessible to a wider range of users, and it makes software such as Office more accessible to third-party applications that are designed to use it. From the perspective of interop, you can write a client application to connect to an accessible application via the Accessibility APIs. Once you've connected to the accessible object, you can get to its native object model (if the application supports this). To do this, you can use P/Invoke with some native APIs:

- *FindWindowEx* to find the main window of a running instance of Excel

- *EnumChildWindows* to find a child window of the Excel main window that supports *IAccessible*

- *GetClassName* to get the registered window class name of each window we find so we can check it against a known accessible window class name

- *AccessibleObjectFromWindow*, which gets a COM interface pointer into the COM object given the handle of an accessible window

In the following exercise, we'll use these APIs to connect to a running instance of Excel and get to its native object model. Let's be clear on what we're doing here: we're not launching Excel through automation, as we did in previous exercises. Rather, we're going to hook into instances of Excel that might already be running or might subsequently be started independently of our application.

> **Note**   The sample solution for this topic can be found in the sample code at <install location>\Code\Office<n>\AccessExcel.

1. Create a new Windows application called AccessExcel. Add a reference to the Excel IA. (In Solution Explorer, right-click and select Add Reference, click the COM tab, and select the appropriate Microsoft Excel Object Library from the list.) Put a *Button* control on the form, and get a *Click* event handler for it.

2. Add a *using* statement for the Excel namespace (with an alias to cut down on typing effort). Also add *using* statements for *System.Text* (we'll need *StringBuilder* later) and *System.Runtime.InteropServices* (for *DllImport*).

3. When we find an instance of the Excel main window, we have to walk its list of child windows to find one that supports accessibility. To do this, we call *Enum-ChildWindows*. This API expects a callback function as its third parameter. In .NET, a callback is represented as a delegate. So, declare a delegate type that takes a pair of incoming and outgoing integer parameters. The incoming *int* will be the HWND of a window to be examined, and the outgoing *int* will be the HWND of a window that we determine does support accessibility:

```
public delegate bool EnumChildCallback(int hwnd, ref int lParam);
```

4. We can now import the *EnumChildWindows* API, specifying our delegate type for the second parameter:

```
[DllImport("User32.dll")]
public static extern bool EnumChildwindows(
    int hwndParent, EnumChildCallback lpEnumFunc, ref int lParam);
```

5. To go with this delegate type, we also need a method that matches the signature. For each window handle we're passed, we call the Win32 API function *GetClass-Name* to match the class name of the window against the known class name of an Excel window that supports accessibility (*"EXCEL7"*)—note that this is the same for all versions from Office 2000 onward. So, import the *GetClassName* API:

```
[DllImport("User32.dll")]
public static extern int GetClassName(
    int hWnd, StringBuilder lpClassName, int nMaxCount);
```

...and define the callback method:

```
public bool EnumChildProc(int hwndChild, ref int lParam)
{
    StringBuilder buf = new StringBuilder(128);
    GetClassName(hwndChild, buf, 128);
    if (buf.ToString() == "EXCEL7")
    {
        lParam = hwndChild;
        return false;
    }
    return true;
}
```

6. Now we can code the button *Click* handler to find the HWND of a running instance of Excel, find its accessible child window, and then get to its native object model. First import the *FindWindowEx* API. Note that the last parameter to *FindWindowEx* is typed as a pointer to a null-terminated string that specifies the window name (the window's title). If this parameter is NULL, all window names match the search. In our example, we don't care about window captions, so we want to pass zero. However, that means we can't type the parameter as a string, so we must type it as an *int*:

```
[DllImport("User32.dll")]
public static extern int FindWindowEx(
    int hwndParent, int hwndChildAfter, string lpszClass,
    int missing); //string lpszWindow);
```

7. If we find an accessible child window, we can call *AccessibleObjectFromWindow* on it. So, import this API:

```
[DllImport("Oleacc.dll")]
public static extern int AccessibleObjectFromWindow(
    int hwnd, uint dwObjectID, byte[] riid,
    ref Microsoft.Office.Interop.Excel.Window ptr);
```

8. In the button *Click* handler, call *FindWindowEx* to find an instance of the Excel main window. This has the registered classname *"XlMain"*:

```
private void getExcel_Click(object sender, System.EventArgs e)
{
    int hwnd = FindWindowEx(0, 0, "XlMain", 0);
```

9. If we found an instance of Excel, we need to enumerate its child windows to find one that supports accessibility. To do this, instantiate the delegate and wrap the callback method in it, and then call *EnumChildWindows*, passing the delegate as the second parameter:

```
if (hwnd != 0)
{
    int hwndChild = 0;
    EnumChildCallback cb = new EnumChildCallback(EnumChildProc);
    EnumChildWindows(hwnd, cb, ref hwndChild);
```

> **Caution**   In this simple example, the code is quite safe. However, when you pass a managed delegate to unmanaged code, you should generally take steps to ensure that the managed delegate cannot be garbage-collected while the managed code has not finished using it.
>
> Using the example above, if the *EnumChildProc* callback method completes its work before the call to *EnumChildWindows* returns, there will be no problem. However, in a situation in which the callback method could continue beyond the method call that sets it up, you must be more circumspect. For example, we can declare the *EnumChildCallback* delegate as a class field so it will persist for the lifetime of the class. Alternatively, it might be enough to call the *GC.Keep-Alive* method at the end of the scope of the outermost method. (In this example, that would be the *getExcel_Click* method.)

10. If we found an accessible child window, call *AccessibleObjectFromWindow*, passing the constant *OBJID_NATIVEOM* (defined in winuser.h) and *IID_IDispatch*—we want an *IDispatch* pointer into the native object model:

```
if (hwndChild != 0)
{
    const uint OBJID_NATIVEOM = 0xFFFFFFF0;
    Guid IID_IDispatch =
    new Guid("{00020400-0000-0000-C000-000000000046}");
    Excel.Window ptr = null;

    int hr = AccessibleObjectFromWindow(
        hwndChild, OBJID_NATIVEOM,

                    IID_IDispatch.ToByteArray(), ref ptr);
```

11. If we successfully got a native object model *IDispatch* pointer, we can *QueryInterface* this for an Excel *Application* pointer (using the implicit cast operator supplied in the PIA). Using this, we can then display the application's name and clean up:

```
if (hr >= 0)
{
    Excel.Application xl = ptr.Application;
    if (xl != null)
    {
        MessageBox.Show(xl.Name);
        Marshal.ReleaseComObject(xl);
        xl = null;
    }
}
}
}
}
```

12. Build and test.

3.7 Monitoring Office Applications

Office 97	✖
Office 2000	✔
Office XP	✔
Office 2003	✔

The technique in the previous example is really just an enhancement of the technique that uses *IAccessible* to get hold of running instances of an Office application. Next we will build a managed Windows Forms application that searches for all running instances of Excel and displays them in a tree. The idea is based on users in financial services who frequently have dozens of instances of Excel running at the same time, each instance with potentially multiple workbooks and multiple worksheets. Keeping track of all these is a problem, and finding a particular worksheet among all the open windows is particularly difficult.

In our application, each workbook in each running instance will be listed in the tree, as well as each worksheet in each workbook. We will provide a button to allow the user to refresh the tree at any time and another button to make sure that all managed references to Excel objects are released. The final application is shown here. In the example, there are three running instances of Excel. The first instance has two open workbooks called Animals.xls and Fruit.xls, each with three worksheets. The second instance has one workbook called Product.xls with one worksheet. The third has one workbook called Sales.xls with three worksheets.

As a second-phase step, we will intercept the user double-clicking in the tree to bring the selected worksheet, workbook, or Excel instance to the foreground.

> **Note**   The sample solution for this topic can be found in the sample code at <install location>\Code\Office<n>\ExcelMonitor. There are two versions, for Phase 1 and for Phase 2.

Phase 1: Core Functionality

1. Create a new Windows application called ExcelMonitor. Add a reference for the appropriate Excel IA for your targeted version of Excel. Put two *Button* controls on the form, a *TreeView* control, and an *ImageList* control.

2. Select the *ImageList*, and click the *Images* property in the Property pane. Then add six images: a pair of images for each of the possible levels in our tree—Excel application, workbook, and worksheet. We need a pair because we'll have one image for normal display and a second image to show which node is currently selected. You can use any suitable images you like, and an appropriate set can be found in the solution folder for the sample code.

3. Get *Click* event handlers for the two buttons. Implement each one to call a custom method (which we will write later). The Refresh button will call a custom method called *GetExcelWindows*. The CleanUp button will call a custom method called *CleanReferences*.

4. Declare some simple class fields. We need two *ArrayList* objects—one for the collection of Excel windows, the other for the collection of Excel *Application* object instances. We need a root *TreeNode* for our *TreeView* and a label template for this root node:

```
private ArrayList excelWindows;
private ArrayList excelInstances;
public TreeNode rootNode;
private const string rootExcelNodeLabel = "Excels ({0})";
```

5. The code to find all Excel main windows, and from them to find all Excel child windows that support *IAccessible*, is essentially the same as in the previous example. As before, we will set up a callback (delegate) method to be invoked on each child window of each Excel main window. This delegate will use the API *GetClassName* to determine whether each child window is an *IAccessible* object: each accessible window that we find will be added to our *ArrayList* of child windows, for later use in building the tree.

```
private const string accessibleExcelChild = "EXCEL7";

[DllImport("User32")]
public static extern int GetClassName(
    int hWnd, StringBuilder lpClassName, int nMaxCount);

// Callback passed to EnumChildWindows to find any window
// with the registered classname "EXCEL7" - we need this to call
// AccessibleObjectFromWindow with OBJID_NATIVEOM later.
public bool EnumChildProc(int hWnd, ref int lParam)
{
    StringBuilder windowClass = new StringBuilder(128);
    GetClassName(hWnd, windowClass, 128);
    if (windowClass.ToString() == accessibleExcelChild)
```

```
        {
            lParam = hwnd;
            excelWindows.Add(hwnd);
        }
        return true;
    }
```

6. In our *GetExcelWindows* custom method, we will call the API *FindWindowEx* to
    find all Excel main windows running on the desktop, and *EnumChildWindows* to
    set up the delegate for each child. When we have gone through all Excel win-
    dows, we will have built our collection of accessible child windows. We'll then
    invoke another custom method, called *GetExcelOMs*, to walk this collection of
    windows in order to build our collection of *Excel.Application* instances:

```csharp
private const string registeredExcelClass = "XLMain";
public delegate bool EnumChildCallback(int hwnd, ref int lParam);

[DllImport("User32")]
public static extern int FindWindowEx(
    int hwndParent, int hwndChildAfter, string lpszClass,
    int missing);

[DllImport("User32")]
public static extern bool EnumChildWindows(
    int hwndParent, EnumChildCallback lpEnumFunc, ref int lParam);

// Get HWNDs of all running instances of Excel, and add them to
// our excelWindows collection.
public void GetExcelWindows()
{
    try
    {
        // Make sure the tree, the collection of Excel instances,
        // and the collection of Excel windows are all empty to start with.
        rootNode = new TreeNode(String.Format(rootExcelNodeLabel, 0));
        excelTree.Nodes.Clear();

        if (excelInstances != null)
        {
            CleanReferences();
        }
        excelInstances = new ArrayList();

        if (excelWindows != null)
        {
            excelWindows.Clear();
        }
        excelWindows = new ArrayList();

        // Walk the children of the desktop to find Excel main windows.
        int hwnd = FindWindowEx(0, 0, registeredExcelClass, 0);
        if (hwnd != 0)
        {
            // Walk the children of this window to see if any are IAccessible,
```

```
            // and if so, add them to the collection (via the callback).
            int hwndChild = 0;
            EnumChildCallback cb = new EnumChildCallback(EnumChildProc);
            EnumChildWindows(hwnd, cb, ref hwndChild);

            while (true)
            {
                // See if there are any more after the last one we found.
                hwnd = FindWindowEx(0, hwnd, registeredExcelClass, 0);
                if (hwnd != 0)
                {
                    hwndChild = 0;
                    cb = new EnumChildCallback(EnumChildProc);
                    EnumChildWindows(hwnd, cb, ref hwndChild);
                }
                else
                {
                    break;
                }
            }
        }
        GetExcelOMs();
    }
    catch (Exception ex)
    {
        Debug.WriteLine("GetExcelWindows: " +ex.Message);
    }
}
```

7. Our custom *GetExcelOMs* method will call *AccessibleObjectFromWindow* to get the Excel native object model from each Excel accessible window. From this, we'll cache the *Excel.Application* object reference in our second *ArrayList* collection. At the end of this operation, we'll invoke another custom method, *BuildExcelTree*, to create each *TreeNode* and add them all to the *TreeView*.

```
private const uint OBJID_NATIVEOM = 0xFFFFFFF0;
private Guid IID_IDispatch =
    new Guid("{00020400-0000-0000-C000-000000000046}");

// AccessibleObjectFromWindow gets the IDispatch pointer of an
// object that supports IAccessible, which allows us to get to the
// native object model.
[DllImport("Oleacc.dll")]
private static extern int AccessibleObjectFromWindow(
    int hwnd, uint dwObjectID,
    byte[] riid,
    ref Microsoft.Office.Interop.Excel.Window ptr);

// Walk the collection of IAccessible Excel child windows to cache
// the Excel OM Application object instances. Note that multiple
// child windows may share the same Application object.
private void GetExcelOMs()
{
    if (excelWindows != null)
    {
```

```
                      for (int i = 0; i < excelWindows.Count; i++)
                      {
                          int hwnd = (int)excelWindows[i];
                          if (hwnd != 0)
                          {
                              Excel.Window ptr = null;

                              // Get a pointer to the native object model.
                              int hr = AccessibleObjectFromWindow(
                                  hwnd, OBJID_NATIVEOM,
                                  IID_IDispatch.ToByteArray(), ref ptr);
                              if (hr >= 0)
                              {
                                  Excel.Application xl = ptr.Application;

                                  // See if this specific Excel Application instance has
                                  // already been added to our collection via a previous
                                  // IAccessible window. If not, add it now.
                                  int excelIndex = -1;
                                  for (int j = 0; j < excelInstances.Count; j++)
                                  {
                                      Excel.Application xlCached =
                                          (Excel.Application)excelInstances[j];
                                      if (xlCached == xl)
                                      {
                                          excelIndex = j;
                                          break;
                                      }
                                  }
                                  if (excelIndex == -1)
                                  {
                                      excelInstances.Add(xl);
                                  }
                              }
                          }
                      }

                      BuildExcelTree();
                      excelTree.Nodes.Add(rootNode);
                      excelTree.ExpandAll();
                  }
              }
```

8. Our *BuildExcelTree* method creates a *TreeNode* for each Excel *Application* object, each *Workbook*, and each *Worksheet*. Note that we specify appropriate index values into the *ImageList* collection of images for each node.

```
private void BuildExcelTree()
{
    foreach (Excel.Application xl in excelInstances)
    {
        // Create a new node for this Excel instance.
        TreeNode excelNode = new TreeNode(xl.Name, 0, 1);

        // Get each workbook in this instance of Excel.
        foreach (Excel.Workbook wb in xl.Workbooks)
```

```
        {
            // Create a new node for this workbook.
            TreeNode bookNode = new TreeNode(wb.Name, 2, 3);

            foreach (Excel.Worksheet ws in wb.Worksheets)
            {
                // Create a new node for this worksheet.
                TreeNode sheetNode = new TreeNode(ws.Name, 4, 5);
                bookNode.Nodes.Add(sheetNode);
            }

            // Add this book node to the current Excel node.
            excelNode.Nodes.Add(bookNode);
        }

        rootNode.Nodes.Add(excelNode);
    }
    rootNode.Text =
        String.Format(rootExcelNodeLabel, rootNode.Nodes.Count);
}
```

9. Our final custom method, *CleanReferences*, will make sure we're not holding any managed references to COM objects (otherwise, we run the risk of keeping Excel alive inadvertently even after the user has closed it):

```
private void CleanReferences()
{
    if (excelInstances != null)
    {
        for (int i = 0; i < excelInstances.Count; i++)
        {
            excelInstances[i] = null;
            excelInstances.RemoveAt(i);
        }
        excelInstances = null;
    }
    GC.Collect();
    GC.WaitForPendingFinalizers();
    GC.Collect();
    GC.WaitForPendingFinalizers();
}
```

10. Build and test.

Phase 2: Bringing Excel to the Front

Once we've got all the core functionality working, we'll handle the user double-clicking in the tree to bring the corresponding worksheet, workbook, or Excel instance to the foreground.

1. First we need to import some more Win32 API methods: *SetForegroundWindow* to bring a chosen Excel window to the front, and *ShowWindow*, which (among other things) will restore a window that was previously minimized to the task-

bar. For our call to *ShowWindow*, we need to pass the value 1 to indicate showing the window normally—that is, not maximized, not minimized, and not hidden. For completeness, we'll go a little over the top and declare an *enum* that corresponds directly to the list of *#define* constants for *ShowWindow* in the windows.h header file.

```
[DllImport("user32")]
public static extern bool SetForegroundWindow(int hWnd);

[DllImport("user32")]
public static extern bool ShowWindow(int hWnd, int nCmdShow);

public enum SW
{
    HIDE            = 0,
    SHOWNORMAL      = 1,
    NORMAL          = 1,
    SHOWMINIMIZED   = 2,
    SHOWMAXIMIZED   = 3,
    MAXIMIZE        = 3,
    SHOWNOACTIVATE  = 4,
    SHOW            = 5,
    MINIMIZE        = 6,
    SHOWMINNOACTIVE = 7,
    SHOWNA          = 8,
    RESTORE         = 9,
    SHOWDEFAULT     = 10,
    FORCEMINIMIZE   = 11,
    MAX             = 11
}
```

2. When the user clicks a particular node in the tree, we can easily work out which node she has clicked. We can also find out all the information about that node that has been set—which so far are the *Text*, *ImageIndex*, and *SelectedImageIndex* properties. It would be difficult to work out which specific worksheet or workbook this corresponds to, so our solution to this is to use custom *TreeNodes* instead of plain vanilla ones. We'll derive three custom classes from the *TreeNode* class to allow us to cache the corresponding *Excel.Worksheet*, *Excel.Workbook*, or *Excel.Application* object references within the node itself:

```
internal class SheetNode : TreeNode
{
    public Excel.Worksheet sheet;

    public SheetNode(Excel.Worksheet sheet)
    {
        this.sheet = sheet;
        this.Text = sheet.Name;
        this.ImageIndex = 4;
        this.SelectedImageIndex = 5;
    }
}

internal class BookNode : TreeNode
```

```
    {
        public Excel.Workbook book;

        public BookNode(Excel.Workbook book)
        {
            this.book = book;
            this.Text = book.Name;
            this.ImageIndex = 2;
            this.SelectedImageIndex = 3;
        }
    }

    internal class ExcelNode : TreeNode
    {
        public Excel.Application xl;
        public ExcelNode(Excel.Application xl)
        {
            this.xl = xl;
            this.Text = xl.Name;
            this.ImageIndex = 0;
            this.SelectedImageIndex = 1;
        }
    }
}
```

3. In accordance with this, we need to make some slight changes to our *Build-ExcelTree* method, replacing the vanilla *TreeNodes* with custom ones:

```
private void BuildExcelTree()
{
    foreach (Excel.Application xl in excelInstances)
    {
        // Create a new node for this Excel instance.
        //TreeNode excelNode = new TreeNode(xl.Name, 0, 1);
        ExcelNode excelNode = new ExcelNode(xl);

        // Get each workbook in this instance of Excel.
        foreach (Excel.Workbook wb in xl.Workbooks)
        {
            // Create a new node for this workbook.
            //TreeNode bookNode = new TreeNode(wb.Name, 2, 3);
            BookNode bookNode = new BookNode(wb);

            foreach (Excel.Worksheet ws in wb.Worksheets)
            {
                // Create a new node for this worksheet.
                //TreeNode sheetNode = new TreeNode(ws.Name, 4, 5);
                SheetNode sheetNode = new SheetNode(ws);
                bookNode.Nodes.Add(sheetNode);
            }

            // Add this book node to the current Excel node.
            excelNode.Nodes.Add(bookNode);
        }

        rootNode.Nodes.Add(excelNode);
```

```
        }
        rootNode.Text =
            String.Format(rootExcelNodeLabel, rootNode.Nodes.Count);
    }
```

4. Get a *DoubleClick* event handler for the *TreeView* control, and implement it to work out what kind of node has been clicked. If it's a *Worksheet* node, we need to activate the sheet and then bring the sheet's window to the foreground—we do this via the sheet's *Application* property. If it's a *Workbook* node, we activate the book and then bring the window to the foreground. If it's an *Application* node, we simply bring it to the foreground.

```
    private void excelTree_DoubleClick(object sender, System.EventArgs e)
    {
        if (excelTree.SelectedNode is SheetNode)
        {
            // Activate the selected worksheet, and bring the Excel
            // instance to the front.
            SheetNode node = (SheetNode)excelTree.SelectedNode;
            node.sheet.Activate();
            BringExcelToFront(node.sheet.Application);
        }
        else if (excelTree.SelectedNode is BookNode)
        {
            // Activate the selected workbook, and bring the Excel
            // instance to the front.
            BookNode node = (BookNode)excelTree.SelectedNode;
            node.book.Activate();
            BringExcelToFront(node.book.Application);
        }
        else if (excelTree.SelectedNode is ExcelNode)
        {
            // Bring the selected Excel instance to the front.
            ExcelNode node = (ExcelNode)excelTree.SelectedNode;
            BringExcelToFront(node.xl);
        }

        // else: Default behavior is to expand/collapse the node.
    }


    private void BringExcelToFront(Excel.Application xl)
    {
        // Bring the specified Excel instance (main window) to the foreground.
        SetForegroundWindow(xl.Hwnd);
        ShowWindow(xl.Hwnd, (int)SW.SHOWNORMAL);
    }
```

5. Build and test.

Phase 2: Excel 2000 Specifics

Excel XP was the first version of Excel to expose an *Hwnd* property from the *Application* object. So, for Excel 2000, we need to do a little extra work to get the window handle.

1. First we'll enhance our collection of Excel instances. With later versions, it is sufficient to cache the *Application* object because we can use that to get to the *Hwnd*. For Excel 2000, we need to cache both the *Application* object and the corresponding *Hwnd* in our collection. So we'll declare a simple new class that encapsulates both of these values:

```
internal class ExcelInstance
{
    public int hwnd;
    public Excel.Application xl;
    public ExcelInstance(Excel.Application xl, int hwnd)
    {
        this.xl = xl;
        this.hwnd = hwnd;
    }
}
```

2. In the *GetExcelOMs* method, where we build our collection of Excel instances, we'll change the code to add a new *ExcelInstance* object to the collection instead of just the *Excel.Application*:

```
for (int j = 0; j < excelInstances.Count; j++)
{
    Excel.Application xlCached =
        //(Excel.Application)excelInstances[j];
        ((ExcelInstance)excelInstances[j]).xl;
    if (xlCached == xl)
    {
        excelIndex = j;
        break;
    }
}
if (excelIndex == -1)
{
    //excelInstances.Add(xl);
    excelInstances.Add(new ExcelInstance(xl, hwnd));
}
```

3. We'll also enhance the *ExcelNode* class (including its constructor) to cache the window handle:

```
internal class ExcelNode : TreeNode
{
    // Extra field for Excel 2000.
    public int hwnd;

    public Excel.Application xl;
    public ExcelNode(Excel.Application xl, int hwnd)
    {
        this.xl = xl;
        this.Text = xl.Name;
        this.ImageIndex = 0;
        this.SelectedImageIndex = 1;
        this.hwnd = hwnd;
    }
}
```

4. We'll use this enhanced *ExcelNode* class when building the tree:

```
private void BuildExcelTree()
{
    //foreach (Excel.Application xl in excelInstances)
    foreach (ExcelInstance xlInstance in excelInstances)
    {
        Excel.Application xl = xlInstance.xl;

        // Create a new node for this Excel instance.
        //ExcelNode excelNode = new ExcelNode(xl);
        ExcelNode excelNode = new ExcelNode(xl, xlInstance.hwnd);
```

5. Next we need to use another Win32 API function, *GetParent*. This is because we want to set the Excel main window to the foreground, but the window handles we're dealing with are the *IAccessible* windows—that is, the *Workbook* windows. So, we'll use *GetParent* to walk up the hierarchy to the Excel main window:

```
[DllImport("user32")]
public static extern int GetParent(int hWnd);
```

6. Modify the method that we wrote to bring the chosen Excel window to the foreground, making use of *GetParent* to walk up two levels. The Excel main window is the parent of the Excel desktop (MDI container) window, which is the parent of the workbook windows. In our collection, we've cached handles to the workbook windows because they're the *IAccessible* windows.

```
private void BringExcelToFront(ExcelNode xlNode)
{
    //SetForegroundWindow(xl.Hwnd);
    //ShowWindow(xl.Hwnd, (int)SW.SHOWNORMAL);
    int hwndXlDesk = GetParent(xlNode.hwnd);
    int hwndXlMain = GetParent(hwndXlDesk);
    SetForegroundWindow(hwndXlMain);
    ShowWindow(hwndXlMain, (int)SW.SHOWNORMAL);
}
```

7. Change the code in the tree *DoubleClick* handler to use this modified method.

```
if (excelTree.SelectedNode is SheetNode)
{
    SheetNode node = (SheetNode)excelTree.SelectedNode;
    node.sheet.Activate();

    //BringExcelToFront(node.sheet.Application);
    ExcelNode xlNode = (ExcelNode)node.Parent.Parent;
    BringExcelToFront(xlNode);
}
else if (excelTree.SelectedNode is BookNode)
{
    BookNode node = (BookNode)excelTree.SelectedNode;
    node.book.Activate();

    //BringExcelToFront(node.book.Application);
    ExcelNode xlNode = (ExcelNode)node.Parent;
    BringExcelToFront(xlNode);
```

```
        }
        else if (excelTree.SelectedNode is ExcelNode)
        {
            ExcelNode node = (ExcelNode)excelTree.SelectedNode;

            //BringExcelToFront(node.xl);
            BringExcelToFront(node);
        }
```

8. Finally, we must change the code in the *CleanReferences* method to cast the list element to an *ExcelInstance* type before we can access the *Excel.Application* field:

```
        for (int i = 0; i < excelInstances.Count; i++)
        {
            //excelInstances[i] = null;
            ((ExcelInstance)excelInstances[i]).xl = null;
            excelInstances.RemoveAt(i);
        }
```

9. Build and test.

Summary

In this chapter, we've expanded on the basic mechanics of Office interop that we introduced in Chapter 2. P/Invoke is a very powerful technique and very commonly used—not just in Office interop solutions but generally in .NET development. The CLR's interop marshaler takes care of a lot of the details at run time to ensure that parameters and return values are correctly passed between managed and unmanaged code. This is just as true for P/Invoke as it is for COM interop. You would normally use COM interop to talk to Office components and P/Invoke to talk to other (non-COM) native DLLs, including system DLLs.

Most of the other techniques examined in this chapter are far less commonly used. Reflection is very powerful but also very cumbersome to use. It also imposes a performance penalty at run time. If used unwisely, reflection can also be dangerous. However, a small number of Office features are not exposed through COM and are accessible only through reflection. Document properties are the classic example of this.

The last technique we examined leverages the *IAccessible* interface. This interface is designed to make applications (including the Office applications from Office 2000 onward) more accessible to users. A little-known feature of this also happens to make the Office applications more accessible to external software. You can hook into an Office application from the outside by a combination of P/Invoke (using APIs such as *GetClassName* and *FindWindowEx*) and COM interop using *IAccessible*, and once you've hooked in you can use the Office object model as usual.

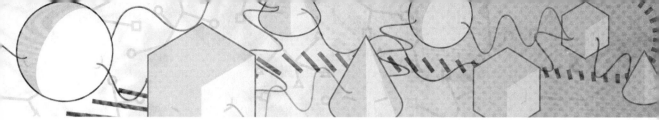

Chapter 4
Integrating Managed Code

The second and third chapters covered the basic mechanics and simple techniques for building solutions that combine managed code and Microsoft Office. We looked at all the possible low-level techniques for communicating with Office, and hopefully it is clear that the most important technique is automation using the primary interop assemblies (PIAs) or interop assemblies (IAs). IAs are crucial for enabling developers to build managed solutions that talk to Office applications in a predictable, strongly typed manner.

Now that we know how to talk to Office, the next question that arises is, To what extent can we integrate with Office? In later chapters, we'll look at all the specific protocols for integrating managed code with Office. These protocols—that is, Add-ins, Smart Tags, RealTime Data, Smart Documents, and Visual Studio Tools for Office—all rely on a very small number of interfaces or standards and are very focused in design. In this chapter, we'll look at more general, lower-level techniques for integration. Specifically, we'll look at integrating internal and external custom code, integrating managed and unmanaged windows, and integrating data via conventional drag-and-drop:

- **Integrating internal and external custom code**   Traditionally, Office development has made heavy use of custom internal code, in the form of VBA code that resides within an Office document. We'll consider the extent to which you can integrate code in an external managed assembly (typically written in Microsoft Visual Basic .NET or Microsoft C#) with VBA code that is internal to an Office document. VBA code can talk with managed code—in both directions—and there are two different strategies for supporting this. We'll also look at ways to manipulate VBA code from a managed solution.

- **Managed and unmanaged windows**   Office applications have a significant, sophisticated user interface. The .NET Framework class library has comprehensive support for user interface artifacts—windows, dialog boxes, toolbars, menus, and the like. Inevitably, you will want to develop solutions that leverage both the Office windows UI and also managed windows and controls. There are some significant issues with this that we must consider; it is important to clarify exactly where the constraints are and how to work around them. Again, alternative strategies are available to use in this context.

■ **Drag-and-drop**   This well-understood standard COM feature is supported by many applications, including all the Office applications. The .NET Framework class library also supports this technology and supplies standard events and event handlers for the messages sent when the user performs drag-and-drop operations. It's actually a simple matter to add drag-and-drop to your solution and to provide custom behavior during the operation. We'll work through some practical examples of developing drag-and-drop between managed code and Office, in both directions.

> **Caution**   Many of the examples in this chapter involve the use of VBA macro code. It is normally recommended that you set Office macro security to the highest possible level, not automatically trust installed add-ins and templates, and not trust access to the Visual Basic project. To check your settings, go to Tools | Macro | Security. If you run some of the sample applications with the highest security settings, they will fail because of their use of VBA macro code, unless you digitally sign them. For demonstration purposes on your own machine, you can choose to relax your security settings while you're testing the application. However, you should be sure to restore security to the settings approved by your organization immediately after testing.

4.1 Calling Managed Code from VBA

Office 97	✓
Office 2000	✓
Office XP	✓
Office 2003	✓

The Office applications offer rich functionality, but sometimes users require a little extra stuff—some extra functions in Excel, for instance. So, can you supply this extra functionality in a .NET managed component and incorporate it within an Office application? The answer, of course, is yes. You can extend Office applications with managed code in several ways. In this section, we'll consider the most lightweight approach—writing managed code that can be called back from unmanaged Office VBA.

To set up a managed component whose methods can be called from VBA, you can use two strategies:

■ A lightweight callback

■ A COM callable wrapper (CCW)

We'll first consider the lightweight callback. In the following section, we'll look at the CCW approach. The lightweight callback approach boils down to passing a managed object to VBA, where it can be cached and later its methods can be invoked. This technique can be useful in simple situations but might have unknown side effects if used in a complex or long-running context.

It's worth mentioning that because this technique involves both managed code calling into VBA and also VBA code calling into managed code, it can be used as part of a strategy for migrating VBA solutions to .NET solutions. During the transition period, .NET code can call back into legacy VBA code.

Another issue with this approach is that you have to have some way to start the operation. Somehow, you have to get the managed object into the VBA. If the managed object is not exposed through a CCW, you can't program against it in the Visual Basic Editor (VBE). You also can't initiate the creation of the object from VBA because there's no way for the Visual Basic runtime (or the COM runtime) to create the object. Consequently, you can use this technique only if you can start the operation from managed code.

Therefore, in the following exercise, we'll create a managed Windows Forms application that automates Excel and passes a managed object into a VBA method. As you will see, this involves late binding at both ends—an inherent weakness.

> **Note** The sample solution for this topic can be found in the sample code at <install location>\Code\Office<n>\ManagedCallback.

Managed Code

1. Create a new Windows Forms application called ManagedCallback. Put one button on the form, and get a *Click* event handler for it. Add references to the appropriate Excel IAs.

2. In the *Click* event handler, we'll launch Excel and make it visible:

   ```
   Excel.Application xl = new Excel.Application();
   xl.Visible = true;
   ```

3. Continue in the *Click* event handler, and open the dummy test workbook. (Note: This workbook will have to have our custom VBA code in it to cache the managed object that we're going to pass it.) Of course, you'll have to change the path to the .xls file to wherever it is on your machine:

   ```
   object missing = Missing.Value;
   xl.Workbooks.Open(@"C:\Temp\ManagedCallback\ManagedCallback.xls",
       missing, missing, missing, missing, missing, missing,
       missing, missing, missing, missing, missing, missing,
       missing, missing);
   ```

   Note that the *Workbooks.Open* method in Excel 97 and Excel 2000 takes fewer parameters than in Excel XP and Excel 2003, so this is the equivalent Office 97 and Office 2000 code:

   ```
   xl.Workbooks.Open(@"C:\Temp\ManagedCallback\ManagedCallback.xls",
       missing, missing, missing, missing, missing, missing,
       missing, missing, missing, missing, missing, missing);
       // , missing, missing);
   ```

4. Invoke Excel's *Application.Run* method to run our custom VBA method. Note that this relies on late binding—we can't tell during development whether this method will actually exist in this workbook:

```
xl.Run(CacheManagedObject", this,
    missing, missing, missing, missing, missing, missing,
    missing, missing, missing, missing, missing, missing,
    missing, missing, missing, missing, missing, missing,
    missing, missing, missing, missing, missing, missing,
    missing, missing, missing, missing, missing);
```

5. Expose our target method as a public member. This is the method we're hoping our VBA client will call. In this example, we'll perform a simple Fahrenheit-to-Celsius conversion:

```
public double F2C(double val)
{
    return ((5.0/9.0) * (val - 32.0));
}
```

Client VBA

1. In the dummy workbook, go to the VBE and add a new module. Add a global variable to cache the managed object, a method for our managed code to call to pass in the managed object, and a wrapper for the *F2C* method so it can be called from a cell:

```
Option Explicit

Dim managedObject As Object

Public Sub CacheManagedObject(mo As Object)
    Set managedObject = mo
End Sub

Public Function F2C(fVal As Double) As Double
    F2C = managedObject.F2C(fVal)
End Function
```

2. Back in the workbook, put a formula into one of the cells to invoke the VBA *F2C* method (which will, in turn, invoke the managed *F2C* method):

You can put this formula into a cell at any time, but it will produce an error unless the workbook has been loaded by our managed Windows application. So, test the whole thing by running the managed Windows application and clicking the button to load the workbook. If you enter the cell formula at this point, all will be well. If you previously entered the formula prior to running the managed code, you'll have to recalculate the worksheet to force it to use the managed object.

4.2 Managed CCW in VBA

Office 97 ✓
Office 2000 ✓
Office XP ✓
Office 2003 ✓

The previous section demonstrated the use of a lightweight technique for allowing managed code to be called from VBA. A more formalized, robust approach is to expose your managed code with a CCW. Using this approach, the Visual Basic Editor will give you a degree of IntelliSense support when you write VBA against the managed component. Also, because the object is COM-registered, you can initiate the creation of the object from VBA. The essence of this technique is to generate a COM type library from your managed assembly so that a COM-aware client can consume your managed code transparently as if it were a COM server. During development, you can use the tools RegAsm or TlbExp to generate a COM type library from your compiled managed assembly. These tools will be able to generate a type library because managed assemblies are fully self-describing. That is, they contain metadata that is the .NET equivalent to the COM typelib because it describes the enumerations, classes, and interfaces in the assembly, together with their methods, properties, and events. This development process is summarized in Figure 4-1.

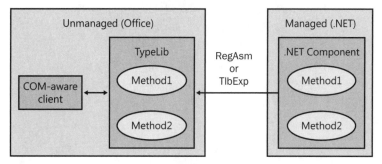

Figure 4-1   COM clients using .NET components at design time.

At run time, the unmanaged COM-aware client can instantiate the CCW proxy objects and makes calls that are then marshaled across to the real managed object. On the way, data types are converted as appropriate from unmanaged (such as *char[]*) to managed (such as *string*). The same is true for return values. This run-time behavior is summarized in Figure 4-2.

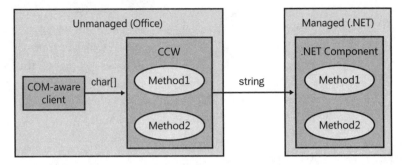

Figure 4-2   COM clients using .NET components at run time.

In the following exercise, we'll create a simple managed class library with one exposed interface with one method—a Fahrenheit-to-Celsius conversion method. We'll wrap this in a CCW and consume it from Excel VBA, calling the method from a cell function.

> **Note**   The sample solution for this topic can be found in the sample code at <install location>\Code\Office<n>\ExtraStuff.

Managed Component

1. Create a new class library project called ExtraStuff. In the project properties, set *Register* for COM Interop to *true*. Make sure the class has a default constructor (required for a COM interop). When you build an assembly and register it for COM interop, by default all the public types will be registered. You can impose finer-grained control by using the *[assembly: ComVisible(false)]* attribute on the whole assembly, and the *[ComVisible(true)]* attribute on each element that you want to make sure is visible to COM.

2. Use *GUIDGen* to generate a new GUID, and use this to attribute the whole assembly. Note: You'll have to add a *using* statement for *System.Runtime.Interop-Services* for the *GuidAttribute* to be recognized:

   ```
   [assembly: Guid("3EF68425-7F04-49a6-828C-5E79DDE59759")]
   ```

3. Write the interface to expose one method, and *GuidAttribute* the interface:

   ```
   [Guid("99B153AF-73D9-4b87-961D-9D6513641781")]
   [ComVisible(true)]
   public interface IExtraStuff
   {
       double F2C(double val);
   }
   ```

4. Implement the interface in a public class, also GUID attributed. This class should also be attributed with *ClassInterface(ClassInterfaceType.None)* so that *IExtraStuff* is the only interface that the class exposes. Otherwise, the process of

exposing a COM type library for this assembly will generate an unnecessary additional interface for the class called _ExtraStuffClass.

```
[Guid("0DB3ED7F-BCE5-4482-B9A0-EDD860EE8536")]
[ClassInterface(ClassInterfaceType.None)]
[ComVisible(true)]
public class ExtraStuffClass : IExtraStuff
{
    public double F2C(double val)
    {
        return ((5.0/9.0) * (val - 32.0));
    }
}
```

5. Use SN.EXE to generate a strong-name keyfile, and attach this by editing the *AssemblyKeyFile* attribute in assemblyinfo.cs. Also set the version number to something specific:

```
[assembly: AssemblyVersion("1.0.0.0")]
[assembly: AssemblyKeyFile(@"..\..\ExtraStuff.snk")]
```

6. That's it for the managed component. When you've built the project, you can check in the target folder to see that a type library was created—you can examine this in OLEVIEW if you like. You can also check in the registry to see that the component has been registered. You'll see that the registry entry specifies a *CodeBase* key, which in turn specifies the path to the assembly. An alternative that is often more useful is to put the assembly into the global assembly cache (GAC) and omit the *CodeBase* entry.

Managed Test Client

1. Create a simple managed console application to test our managed component. Add a reference to the ExtraStuff managed component. Code the *Main* method to instantiate the exposed class and call its *F2C* method:

```
static void Main(string[] args)
{
    ExtraStuffClass esc = new ExtraStuffClass();
    Console.WriteLine(esc.F2C(212));
}
```

2. Build and test.

VBA Client

1. Run Excel and open a new worksheet. Go to Tools | Macro to open the VBE. Go to Tools | References and add a reference to the managed ExtraStuff type library (that is, the CCW).

2. In the Project Explorer pane, right-click the project and insert a new module. Add code to the module to define a VBA function that wraps a call to the CCW for the managed component:

```
Option Explicit

Public Function F2C(val As Double) As Double
    Dim ccw As ExtraStuff.IExtraStuff
    Set ccw = New ExtraStuffClass
    F2C = ccw.F2C(val)
End Function
```

3. Back in the worksheet, put a call to this VBA function in one of the cells. (You can add the .xls file to the workspace if you like, for convenience.)

4.3 Managed Office Accelerators

Office 97
Office 2000
Office XP
Office 2003

Most applications, including all the Office products, ship with a set of predefined keystroke accelerators. For example, in Microsoft Word, Ctrl+O is the keystroke accelerator pair for File | Open. Ctrl+S is for File | Save, and Ctrl+P is for File | Print. Indeed, these particular accelerators are common across all Office applications and have been used for consistency with many other applications. When you're developing a custom solution with Office, you might want to add your own accelerators in addition to the standard ones. In some circumstances, you might even want to override one or more of the standard ones if you need to hook into a particular standard process to attach your own custom behavior.

You can access the accelerator keystrokes programmatically in Word and Microsoft Excel. Word exposes them through the *KeyBindings* collection of the *Document* object. With Excel, you can use the *OnKey* method of the *Application* object. In both cases, you can map a keystroke combination (either existing or new) to an arbitrary macro procedure. You can't, however, map to a managed method. On the other hand, bearing in mind the previous two sections, it would be feasible to map a keystroke combination to a VBA macro procedure that in turn wraps a managed method. This managed method can be hooked up with the VBA using either of the two techniques described at the beginning of this chapter—that is, using a lightweight callback or a CCW.

In the following exercise, we'll map a keystroke combination in Excel to a managed method, using the lightweight callback approach.

> **Note** The sample solution for this topic can be found in the sample code at <install location>\Code\Office<n>\ManagedOnKey.

Managed Code

This project starts off the same as the previous ManagedCallback project—so you might want to just modify a copy of that project (or use it to copy and paste into your new project) instead of typing everything from scratch.

1. Create a new Windows Forms application called ManagedOnKey. Add references to the appropriate Excel IAs. Put a button on the form and get a *Click* event handler for it. In the *Click* event handler, we'll launch Excel and make it visible:

   ```
   Excel.Application xl = new Excel.Application();
   xl.Visible = true;
   ```

2. Continue in the *Click* handler, and open the dummy test workbook. (Note: This workbook will have to have our custom VBA code in it to cache the managed object that we're going to pass it.) Of course, you'll have to change the path to the .xls to wherever it is on your machine:

   ```
   object missing = Missing.Value;
   xl.Workbooks.Open(@"C:\Temp\ManagedOnKey\Test.xls",
       missing, missing, missing, missing, missing, missing,
       missing, missing, missing, missing, missing, missing,
       missing, missing);
   ```

   The *Workbooks.Open* method in Excel 97 and Excel 2000 takes fewer parameters than in Excel XP and Excel 2003, so this is the equivalent Office 97 and Office 2000 code:

   ```
   xl.Workbooks.Open(@"C:\ Temp\ManagedOnKey\Test.xls ",
       missing, missing, missing, missing, missing, missing,
       missing, missing, missing, missing, missing, missing);
       // , missing, missing);
   ```

3. Invoke Excel's *Application.Run* method to run our custom VBA method. Recall that this relies on late binding—we can't tell during development whether this method will actually exist in this workbook:

   ```
   xl.Run("CacheManagedObject", this,
       missing, missing, missing, missing, missing, missing,
       missing, missing, missing, missing, missing, missing,
       missing, missing, missing, missing, missing, missing,
       missing, missing, missing, missing, missing, missing,
       missing, missing, missing, missing, missing);
   ```

4. Call the *Application.OnKey* method to map a keystroke combination to a VBA macro. Use any combination you like—the following example shows that we're overriding the Ctrl+S combination, which is a standard combination. Map the keystroke to a macro called *ManagedSetColor*—this doesn't exist yet, but we'll write it in VBA shortly:

```
xl.OnKey("^s", "ManagedSetColor");
```

5. The first parameter is the keystroke combination as a string, and the second is the name of the macro as a string. The keystroke parameter can specify any single key combined with Alt, Ctrl, or Shift, or any combination of these keys. Each key is represented by one or more characters, such as "a" for the character *a* or "{ENTER}" for the Enter key. If the macro parameter is "" (empty text), nothing happens when the keystroke combination is pressed. This form of *OnKey* changes the normal result of keystrokes in Excel. If you omit the macro name altogether (by using *Type.Missing*), the keystroke combination reverts to its normal result in Excel, and any special key assignments made with previous calls to *OnKey* are cleared.

6. Expose our target method as a public member. This is the method we're expecting our VBA client will call. In this example, we'll cycle through all 56 possible colors that Excel supports in a worksheet, to change the color of the currently active cell. This functionality is abitrary—for the purposes of this exercise, we could just as easily use something simple like a message box. However, one problem with using a message box in this scenario is that because the message box runs within the scope of a VBA method call, the Excel window will be brought to the front, thereby obscuring the message box. This makes it a little irritating to test, so I've chosen something else that is equally obvious visually while still being very simple.

```
public void SetColor()
{
    // We'll work with the Interior property of the current cell.
    Excel.Interior interior = xl.ActiveCell.Interior;
    int colorIndex = Convert.ToInt32(interior.ColorIndex);
    colorIndex++;

    // Make sure the ColorIndex value is within acceptable limits.
    // If it hasn't been explicitly set, it will be negative.
    if (colorIndex > 56 || colorIndex < 1)
    {
        interior.ColorIndex = 1;
    }
    else
    {
        interior.ColorIndex = colorIndex;
    }
    interior.Pattern = Excel.XlPattern.xlPatternSolid;
    interior.PatternColorIndex =
            Excel.XlPattern.xlPatternAutomatic;
}
```

7. Build the project.

Client VBA

1. In the dummy workbook, go to the VBE, and add a new module. Add a global variable to cache the managed object, a method for our managed code to call to pass in the managed object, and a wrapper for the managed *SetColor* method so it can be called from the macro:

```
Option Explicit

Dim managedObject As Object

Public Sub CacheManagedObject(mo As Object)
    Set managedObject = mo
End Sub

Public Sub ManagedSetColor()
    managedObject.SetColor
End Sub
```

2. Save the macro and the worksheet, and close Excel. To test the solution, run the Windows Forms application and click the button. This should launch Excel and set up the managed callback and the keystroke accelerator mapping. So, in Excel, you should be able to use Ctrl+S to cycle through the colors in the current cell:

4.4 Programming the Visual Basic Editor

Office 97
Office 2000
Office XP
Office 2003

The Office VBE, included with all of the Office core products, is the primary development environment in which you attach VBA code to an Office application. The VBE itself exposes a type library, which means you can programmatically control the VBE. For example, you can write code to programmatically:

- Create a new VBA code module
- Create a new command bar and wire up the buttons
- Create a new VBA class module

- Create a new VBA form component
- Add macro code to new or existing worksheets
- Get information about all current components (code modules, classes, forms)

You might wonder when you'd ever want to do this. Well, I know one large company that uses this approach to impose a source control system on its VBA codebase. They suck out the VBA from Excel workbooks and store it in a database. Later they can reconstitute any workbook solution by populating a fresh workbook from the VBA in the database.

In the following walkthrough, we'll create a managed Windows Forms application to program the VBE to perform all these tasks. With the security settings at their highest, when you run the following sample application, it will fail because it will be denied access to the Visual Basic Project (macro code). For the purposes of this exercise (and later exercises which involve VBA macro code), you may relax your security settings while you're testing the application. However, you should be sure to restore security to the settings approved by your organization immediately after testing.

 Note   The sample solution for this topic can be found in the sample code at <install location>\Code\Office<n>\UseVBE.

1. Create a new Windows Forms application called UseVBE. Add references to the appropriate IAs for Excel. Add a corresponding using statement for the Office, VBE, and Excel namespaces:

   ```
   using Office = Microsoft.Office.Core;
   using VBIDE = Microsoft.Vbe.Interop;
   using Excel = Microsoft.Office.Interop.Excel;
   ```

2. Declare references to the Excel *Application* and *Workbook* objects as fields in the *Form* class—we'll use these objects across multiple method calls:

   ```
   private Excel.Workbook book;
   private Excel.Application xl;
   ```

3. Put eight buttons on the form, one to launch Excel and seven more for each type of operation we want to perform. Set the *Enabled* property of each one apart from the first one to *False*—we don't want to try any operations until we've launched Excel. Get *Click* event handlers for all the buttons.

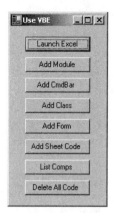

4. Code the button handler to launch Excel: we'll cache the Excel *Application* and *Workbook* references, make Excel visible, and enable all the other buttons:

```
private void launchExcel_Click(object sender, System.EventArgs e)
{
    object missing = Type.Missing;
    xl = new Excel.Application();
    book = xl.Workbooks.Add(missing);
    xl.Visible = true;
    xl.UserControl = true;

    addModule.Enabled = true;
    addCmdBar.Enabled = true;
    addClass.Enabled = true;
    addForm.Enabled = true;
    addDoc.Enabled = true;
    listComponents.Enabled = true;
    deleteAllCode.Enabled = true;
}
```

5. Before we forget, let's also enhance the form's *Dispose* method to clean up, to make sure we don't leave any COM objects alive when we go:

```
protected override void Dispose( bool disposing )
{
    book = null;
    xl = null;
    GC.Collect();
    GC.WaitForPendingFinalizers();
    GC.Collect();
    GC.WaitForPendingFinalizers();
    if( disposing )
    {
        if (components != null)
        {
            components.Dispose();
        }
    }
    base.Dispose( disposing );
}
```

6. It's not a bad idea to build the solution to check that this works before proceeding, and to do this after implementing each of the button click handlers. (Note: If you relax the macro security for this exercise, be sure to reset it afterwards.)

7. For the second button click handler, we'll add a standard macro code module to the workbook, with a simple subroutine:

```
private void addModule_Click(object sender, System.EventArgs e)
{
    VBIDE.VBComponent module;
    String sCode;

    // Create a new VBA code module.
    module = book.VBProject.VBComponents.Add(
        VBIDE.vbext_ComponentType.vbext_ct_StdModule);
    sCode =
        "sub VBAMacro()\r\n" +
        "   msgbox \"VBA Macro called\"\r\n" +
        "end sub";

    // Add the VBA macro to the new code module.
    module.CodeModule.AddFromString(sCode);
}
```

8. When you test this code so far, in Excel, go to Tools | Macro | Visual Basic Editor. You should find that a code module has been added:

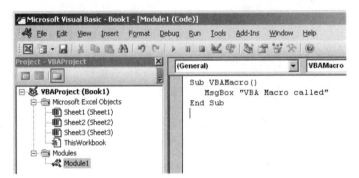

9. For the third button, we'll add a command bar with a single button to Excel's collection, and we'll wire up the button to the macro we created above. Note that this command bar is added to Excel, not just the current workbook.

```
private void addCmdBar_Click(object sender, System.EventArgs e)
{
    Office.CommandBar bar;
    Office.CommandBarButton barButton;
    Object missing = System.Reflection.Missing.Value;

    try
    {
        // Create a new toolbar and show it to the user.
        bar = xl.CommandBars.Add(
            "VBAMacrobar",missing, missing, missing);
        bar.Visible = true;
```

```
                     // Create a new button on the toolbar.
                     barButton =
                         (Office.CommandBarButton) bar.Controls.Add(
                         Office.MsoControlType.msoControlButton,
                         missing, missing, missing, missing);

                     // Assign a macro to the button.
                     barButton.OnAction = "VBAMacro";

                     // Set the caption of the button.
                     barButton.Caption = "Call VBAMacro";

                     // Set the icon on the button to a picture.
                     barButton.FaceId = 2151;
                 }
                 catch(Exception)
                 {
                     MessageBox.Show("VBAMacrobar already exists.","Error");
                 }
             }
```

Note   The values for the *FaceId* property range from zero (no image) to the total number of button images used in the host application (typically a few thousand).

Note   If you want to remove a (custom) command bar from Excel's collection, go to Tools | Customize | Toolbars tab. Find the command bar in the list, and click Delete.

10. The run-time behavior of button 3 should be to add a new command bar with one button with the specified button image. When the user clicks the button, we'll get a message box:

![Excel window screenshot showing a custom toolbar button and a "Microsoft Excel" message box with the text "VBA Macro called" and an OK button]

11. For button 4, we'll create a new VBA Class Module component:

```
private void addClass_Click(object sender, System.EventArgs e)
{
    try
    {
        VBIDE.VBComponent module =
book.VBProject.VBComponents.Add(
            VBIDE.vbext_ComponentType.vbext_ct_ClassModule);
    }
    catch (Exception ex)
    {
        MessageBox.Show(ex.Message);
    }
}
```

12. When you test button 4, in Excel, go to Tools | Macro | Visual Basic Editor. You should find that an empty class module, called Class1, has been added.

13. Button 5 creates a new VBA Form component:

```
private void addForm_Click(object sender, System.EventArgs e)
{
    try
    {
        VBIDE.VBComponent module =
book.VBProject.VBComponents.Add(
            VBIDE.vbext_ComponentType.vbext_ct_MSForm);
    }
    catch (Exception ex)
    {
        MessageBox.Show(ex.Message);
    }
}
```

14. With button 6, we'll add macro code to a worksheet—this is slightly different from adding a completely separate code module. Note that you can't use the same technique as for buttons 2, 4, and 5 above because you can't add a *vbext_ct_Document*. Nor can you add a *vbext_ct_ActiveXDesigner*. However, you can add a new work-

sheet by using the Excel object model, or you can work with an existing work-sheet. Either way, you can get a VBE representation of the worksheet you want by looking for a unique property (such as its *Name* property). In this approach, you treat the worksheet just like any other VBE component, and you can add VBA code to it. In our example, we'll stay focused on the VBE aspects and just access an existing worksheet, which we'll assume is called Sheet1.

```csharp
private void addDoc_Click(object sender, System.EventArgs e)
{
    VBIDE.VBComponent module;
    string sCode;

    int compCount = book.VBProject.VBComponents.Count;
    for (int i = 1; i <= compCount; i++)
    {
        module = book.VBProject.VBComponents.Item(i);
        if (module.Type ==
            VBIDE.vbext_ComponentType.vbext_ct_Document
            && module.Name == "Sheet1")
        {
            sCode =
                "sub SheetMacro()\r\n" +
                "   msgbox \"Sheet Macro called\"\r\n" +
                "end sub";
            module.CodeModule.AddFromString(sCode);
        }
    }
}
```

15. For button 7, we'll iterate the collection of components and print out all their names in a message box. (Note: Excel 97 doesn't support the *vbext_ct_ActiveXDesigner* type, so test for this only in later versions.)

```csharp
private void listComponents_Click(object sender, System.EventArgs e)
{
    StringBuilder sb = new StringBuilder();

    foreach (VBIDE.VBComponent vbComp in
        book.VBProject.VBComponents)
```

```
        {
            switch (vbComp.Type)
            {
            case VBIDE.vbext_ComponentType.vbext_ct_ActiveXDesigner :
                sb.Append("vbext_ct_ActiveXDesigner: "
                    +vbComp.Name + Environment.NewLine);
                break;
            case VBIDE.vbext_ComponentType.vbext_ct_ClassModule :
                sb.Append("vbext_ct_ClassModule: "
                    +vbComp.Name + Environment.NewLine);
                break;
            case VBIDE.vbext_ComponentType.vbext_ct_Document :
                sb.Append("vbext_ct_Document: "
                    +vbComp.Name + Environment.NewLine);
                break;
            case VBIDE.vbext_ComponentType.vbext_ct_MSForm :
                sb.Append("vbext_ct_MSForm: "
                    +vbComp.Name + Environment.NewLine);
                break;
            case VBIDE.vbext_ComponentType.vbext_ct_StdModule :
                sb.Append("vbext_ct_StdModule: "
                    +vbComp.Name + Environment.NewLine);
                break;
            }
        }
        MessageBox.Show(sb.ToString());
    }
```

16. For button 8, we'll iterate the collection of components and remove them. (Note: Excel 97 doesn't support the *vbext_ct_ActiveXDesigner* type, so test for this only in later versions.) While we're at it, we'll also remove all project references (apart from the built-in ones), Excel4 macro sheets, and dialog sheets:

```
private void deleteAllCode_Click(object sender, System.EventArgs e)
{
    foreach (VBIDE.VBComponent vbComp in
        book.VBProject.VBComponents)
    {
        switch (vbComp.Type)
        {
        case VBIDE.vbext_ComponentType.vbext_ct_StdModule :
        case VBIDE.vbext_ComponentType.vbext_ct_ClassModule :
        case VBIDE.vbext_ComponentType.vbext_ct_MSForm :
        case VBIDE.vbext_ComponentType.vbext_ct_ActiveXDesigner:
            book.VBProject.VBComponents.Remove(vbComp);
            break;
        case VBIDE.vbext_ComponentType.vbext_ct_Document :
```

```
                              vbComp.CodeModule.DeleteLines(1,
            vbComp.CodeModule.CountOfLines);
                    break;
                }
            }

            // Remove all references.
            foreach (VBIDE.Reference reference in
                    book.VBProject.References)
            {
                if (!reference.BuiltIn)
                {
                    book.VBProject.References.Remove(reference);
                }
            }

            // Remove all Excel4Macros
            foreach (Excel.Worksheet sheet in book.Excel4IntlMacroSheets)
            {
                sheet.Delete();
            }

            // Remove all DialogSheets.
            foreach (Excel.DialogSheet dialogSheet in book.DialogSheets)
            {
                dialogSheet.Delete();
            }
    }
```

4.5 Office and Managed Windows

Office 97	✓
Office 2000	✓
Office XP	✓
Office 2003	✓

Can you run .NET managed Windows Forms from unmanaged code? Well, if you try to invoke a form from an unmanaged app, you will hit issues because it is likely that the unmanaged message is not compatible with the Windows Forms message pump: if you call *Form.Show*, the form will display, but keyboard and focus handling on the form will not work.

That said, it's perfectly possible to use managed Windows Forms with Office. There are two possible approaches you can use to work around the message pump issue:

- Use *Form.ShowDialog*, which starts a Windows Forms message pump for the form.

- Put the form on a separate thread and call *Application.Run(new FormXXX)* to start a Windows Forms message pump on that thread (where *FormXXX* is the name of your form class).

If you use the second thread approach, you will need to marshal any calls to the form from the unmanaged application using *Control.Invoke* or one of its cousins. In the following exercise, we'll explore the first approach: we'll create a managed class library that exposes methods to create and display managed Windows Forms. We'll then use this library in an unmanaged client—a VBA client running from Excel.

> **Note** The sample solution for this topic can be found in the sample code at <install location>\Code\Office<n>\WinInterop.

Managed Windows Form

1. Create a new Windows application called WinInterop. We really want a class library project, but it's just easier if we get the wizard to generate all the Windows Forms standard stuff for us. You'll need to set the project properties to class library and OK it before you can set the property to register the assembly for COM interop. Use SN.EXE to generate a strong name keyfile and apply this keyfile in the assemblyinfo.cs. Also set a specific version number.

   Note that while the Office XP and Office 2003 PIAs are strongly named and GAC-deployed, if you autogenerate IAs using TlbImp (for Office 97 or Office 2000, for example), these will not be strongly named and so cannot be GAC-deployed. For the scenario described here, this is not a problem. So if you're not using the Office XP or Office 2003 PIAs, you should also not strongly name your *WinInterop* assembly; otherwise, it will fail to build because it depends on non–strongly named IAs.

2. Make sure the class has a default constructor (required for COM interop). Generate a GUID and attribute the assembly with this GUID:

   ```
   [assembly: Guid("709F00FB-637F-4e67-B9A4-5DCF1CC01718")]
   ```

3. We'll need to use Excel *Worksheet* and *Range* types, so add a reference to the Excel PIA. Add a using statement for the Excel namespace:

   ```
   using Excel = Microsoft.Office.Interop.Excel;    // not Office 97/2000
   ```

4. Put a *TextBox* control and a *Button* control on the form, as indicated here–the plan is that when the unmanaged client shows the form, we'll extract the value from a cell in the spreadsheet and put it into the form. Then, when the user clicks the Set Value button, we'll put the new value back into the cell.

5. Declare a private field to cache the Excel range and a public property to provide access to it:

```
private Excel.Range range;

public Excel.Range ExcelRange
{
    get { return range; }
    set
    {
        range = value;
        cell.Text = range.Value2.ToString();
    }
}
```

6. We should make sure we release any COM interface pointers we might be holding when the form is destroyed, so enhance the wizard-generated *Dispose* method accordingly:

```
protected override void Dispose( bool disposing )
{
    range = null;
    GC.Collect();
    GC.WaitForPendingFinalizers();
    GC.Collect();
    GC.WaitForPendingFinalizers();
    if (disposing)
    {
        if (components != null)
        {
            components.Dispose();
        }
    }
    base.Dispose(disposing);
}
```

7. Get a *Click* handler for the *Button* control, and code it to set the value of the *Text-Box* back into the Excel spreadsheet cell:

```
private void setValue_Click(object sender, System.EventArgs e)
{
    range.Value2 = cell.Text;
}
```

Interop Interface

1. Define an interface to be used by the client, with a new GUID attribute. This interface needs only one method—to show the form. When the client calls this method, it must specify a *Worksheet* object and a cell reference (in the conventional alphanumeric form, as in A1).

```
[Guid("0001DE68-0FF0-4798-B4E9-A424A0F8396A")]
public interface IWinInterop
{
    void ShowForm(Excel.Worksheet sheet, string cellRef);
}
```

2. Define a class to implement this interface. Again, use a new GUID attribute. In the *ShowForm* method, use the *get_Range* accessor method to get a *Range* object that corresponds to the supplied cell reference. Then create a form, assign the *Range* reference, and show the form:

```
[Guid("789828D5-7E45-41e5-A61B-033B2CCE63C7")]
public class FormShower: IWinInterop
{
    public void ShowForm(Excel.Worksheet sheet, string cellRef)
    {
        Excel.Range range = sheet.get_Range(cellRef, Type.Missing);
        WinInteropForm f = new WinInteropForm();
        f.ExcelRange = range;
        f.ShowDialog();
        f.Dispose();
    }
}
```

> **Note** *ShowDialog* will show the form as a modal dialog box. The *Form.Show* method is used to show a form as a modeless window. However, managed modeless forms do not work with Office applications because they run on a thread other than the main thread, and the Office object model is not designed to be used with multiple threads. All of the user interface operations in Office must reside on the main UI thread.

3. Build the library project.

Excel VBA Client

1. Run Excel, and open a new worksheet. Put some arbitrary values in the first few cells, as shown here. Then put a button control on the sheet.

2. Double-click the button to go to the VBE. Go to Tools | References and add a reference to the managed WinInterop type library (that is, the CCW). Add code to

Sheet1 to define a VBA function that wraps a call to the CCW for the managed component:

```
Option Explicit

Private Sub cmdShowForm_Click()
    Dim ccw As WinInterop.IWinInterop
    Set ccw = New WinInterop.FormShower
    Call ccw.ShowForm(Sheet1, "a2")
    Set ccw = Nothing
End Sub
```

3. Close the VBE and save the worksheet. Then click the button to test the use of the managed form.

> **Warning**   Customers often ask if you can take this technique a step further and make the Office application host the managed window in a more integrated manner, by setting up a child-parent relationship or an owner-owned relationship. My answer is, "Yes, you could, but no, you shouldn't."
>
> There are significant differences in the way the .NET Framework class library supports managed windows and controls compared with the Win32 API support for windows or even the MFC/ATL class libraries. Notwithstanding, a managed window will ultimately map to a native OS window and can therefore be manipulated in a similar way. Technically, this includes windows created by Office applications. There are two basic approaches to this:
>
> ❑ Connect an appropriate Office application window with your managed window through a parent-child relationship, perhaps using the Win32 API *SetParent*.
>
> ❑ Keep the unmanaged and managed windows disconnected but synchronized, by hooking all appropriate events on the one and relaying executing parallel behavior in the other. For example, hook the *Move*, *Size*, *Maximize*, *Minimize*, *Show*, *Destroy*, and other such messages/events for one window and trigger equivalent events on the other window.
>
> Both approaches are problematic. It is generally not a good idea to interfere with the management of an application's windows from outside the application. The scope for conflict and unexpected behavior is significant. Parenting windows across threads is not supported. Synchronizing messages and events is a maintenance nightmare. The bottom line: don't even think about it.

4.6 Office Document Browser

Office 97	✓
Office 2000	✓
Office XP	✓
Office 2003	✓

When a Web server returns a file to a browser, it tells the browser what type of content is contained in the file. This enables the browser to determine whether it can display the file itself or whether it has to call another application. For example, if the Web server returns an Excel worksheet, the browser will start a copy of Excel to display the page. The Web server recognizes file types by mapping the file name extension to a list of Multipurpose Internet Mail Extensions (MIME) types. For example, to start Excel, the browser needs to recognize the application/vnd.ms-excel MIME type.

Using this information, we can create a managed Windows Forms application that hosts a Web browser control and thus allow the user to open any Office document.

> **Note**   The sample solution for this topic can be found in the sample code at <install location>\Code\Office<n>\OfficeDocumentBrowser.

1.   Create a new Windows application called OfficeDocumentBrowser. Put two buttons on the form, labeled Get Doc and Clear. We'll use these to open a new Office document and close the document, respectively.

2.   Import a *WebBrowser* control. To do this, open the form in Design view. Then right-click any tab in the Toolbox and select Customize Toolbox (in Visual Studio .NET 2002) or Add/Remove Items (in Visual Studio .NET 2003). Switch to the COM tab and scroll down the list to find the *Microsoft Web Browser* control. Select it, check the check box, and click OK:

Customize Toolbox		

.NET Framework Components	COM Components

Name	Path	Library
☐ Microsoft Visio 11.0 Drawing Control	C:\PROGRA~1\MI699F~1\Visio11\VI...	Microsoft Visio 1...
☑ Microsoft Web Browser	C:\WINDOWS\System32\shdocvw.dll	Microsoft Intern...
☐ Microsoft WinSock Control, version ...	C:\WINDOWS\system32\mswinsck.ocx	Microsoft Winso...
☐ Migration Wizard OOBE Automation...	C:\WINDOWS\System32\SHELL32.dll	Microsoft Shell ...
☐ MMC IconControl class	C:\WINDOWS\System32\mmcndmgr.dll	NodeMgr 1.0 Ty...
☐ MMCCtrl class	C:\WINDOWS\System32\cic.dll	cic 1.0 Type Libr...
☐ MODWorkflowState Class	C:\Program Files\Microsoft Office De...	
☐ MoveBvr Class	C:\WINDOWS\System32\lmrt.dll	
☐ MS TV Video Control	C:\WINDOWS\System32\msvidctl.dll	MS Video Contr...
☐ MSASCIILog Control	C:\WINDOWS\System32\inetsrv\iislo...	

Microsoft Web Browser

Language: Language Neutral

Version: 1.1

[Browse...]

[OK]   [Cancel]   [Reset]   [Help]

3.   This will add an Explorer icon to the Toolbox. Drag and drop this icon onto your form. This will generate runtime callable wrapper (RCW) proxy code for the Web browser control. In your references list, you should see new entries for the interop proxy (SHDocVw) and the new .NET control (AxSHDocVw):

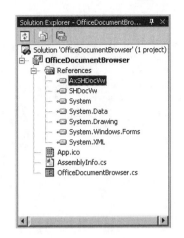

The wizard will also have generated the corresponding code, including this declaration (and later initialization) of the browser control:

```
private AxSHDocVw.AxWebBrowser axWebBrowser1;
…
this.axWebBrowser1 = new AxSHDocVw.AxWebBrowser();
```

4. Now drag and drop an *OpenFileDialog* onto the form. This will appear in the nonvisual controls panel at the bottom. We could set some of its properties statically in the design-time Properties pane, but we'll set the *InitialDirectory* property to correspond with the run-time current directory. So set all the properties in the form constructor, after the call to *InitializeComponent*. For example, work out the path to the project directory (we'll put a sample Excel file in there), set up the dialog filter to allow the user to open any Office document (.doc, .xls, .ppt, and so forth), and set the initial *FileName* to our sample test file:

```
string currentLocation = System.Environment.CurrentDirectory;
string currentPath = currentLocation.Substring(
    0, currentLocation.IndexOf(@"bin\Debug"));
openFile.Filter =
    "Office Documents(*.doc, *.xls, *.ppt)|*.doc;*.xls;*.ppt" ;
openFile.InitialDirectory = currentPath;
openFile.RestoreDirectory = true;
openFile.Title = "Open Office Document";
openFile.FilterIndex = 1;
openFile.FileName = Path.Combine(
    currentPath, "OfficeDocumentBrowser.xls");
```

Note: You can use any Office document or use a copy of the sample test .xls from the sample code folder.

5. Generate a *Click* event handler for the Get Doc button. In this handler, we'll show the OpenFile dialog box, to allow the user to select an Office document to open. We'll pass the selected filename to the Web browser control:

```
        if (openFile.ShowDialog() == DialogResult.OK)
        {
            // If the user didn't cancel, we'll open the document.
            if (openFile.FileName.Length != 0)
            {
                object missing = Missing.Value;
                axWebBrowser1.Navigate(openFile.FileName,
                ref missing, ref missing, ref missing, ref missing);
            }
        }
```

6. Get a *Click* event handler for the Clear button, and implement it to clear the browser window by navigating to the standard blank page:

```
object missing = Missing.Value;
axWebBrowser1.Navigate("about:blank",
    ref missing, ref missing, ref missing, ref missing);
```

At this point, you could build and test the application, although there are a few more things we should do.

7. As well as viewing the selected Office document, we might want to automate the document object in some way. To do this, we need to retrieve the automation object that represents the document. So, first declare an object field in the form class to hold a reference to this object:

```
private object officeDoc;
```

8. Before we can automate the document, we should make sure the document has been fully loaded. The best way to ensure this is to hook up the event that the browser fires when a page load has completed. We can do this in the form constructor after the call to *InitializeComponent*:

```
this.axWebBrowser1.NavigateComplete2 +=
    new AxSHDocVw.DWebBrowserEvents2_NavigateComplete2EventHandler(
    this.axWebBrowser1_NavigateComplete2);
```

9. The *axWebBrowser1_NavigateComplete2* method is a custom delegate method that we must implement to handle this event. First we'll show the docked toolbars. (Note: This is a toggle option, so you call it once to show the toolbars, and again to hide them—this works with Internet Explorer 5.0 and later.) Then we'll get the automation object for the Office document we've just opened. We can also get the corresponding Office application:

```
public void axWebBrowser1_NavigateComplete2(
    object sender,
AxSHDocVw.DWebBrowserEvents2_NavigateComplete2Event e)
    {
        object missing = Missing.Value;
        axWebBrowser1.ExecWB(
        SHDocVw.OLECMDID.OLECMDID_HIDETOOLBARS,
        SHDocVw.OLECMDEXECOPT.OLECMDEXECOPT_DONTPROMPTUSER,
        ref missing, ref missing);
```

```
    object o = e.pDisp;
    officeDoc = o.GetType().InvokeMember(
        "Document", BindingFlags.GetProperty, null, o, null);
    object officeApp = o.GetType().InvokeMember(
        "Application", BindingFlags.GetProperty, null, officeDoc, null);
}
```

10. We must be sure to clean up Office document RCW when we're done with it. So, write a new method to perform this cleanup:

```
private void ReleaseOfficeDoc()
{
    officeDoc = null;
    GC.Collect();
    GC.WaitForPendingFinalizers();
    GC.Collect();
    GC.WaitForPendingFinalizers();
}
```

11. We can then call this method in all the appropriate places:

   ❑ At the beginning of the click handler for the Get Doc button, before opening a new document

   ❑ At the beginning of the *Dispose* method

   ❑ At the beginning of the click handler for the Clear button, before navigating to a blank page

12. Build and test:

Additional Step for Office 97

For Office 97, although the document will be opened in the browser window, the host application (such as Excel) will open its main window separately as well. So, in the *NavigateComplete* event handler, we can get the application automation object for the document and use it to hide the parent window:

```
officeApp.GetType().InvokeMember("Visible",
    BindingFlags.SetProperty, null, officeApp,
new object[]{false});
```

4.7 COM Drag-And-Drop

Office 97	✓
Office 2000	✓
Office XP	✓
Office 2003	✓

Drag-and-drop is a COM feature that relies on the *IDataObject*, *IDropSource*, and *IDropTarget* interfaces. The *System.Windows.Forms.Control* class supports these interfaces and supplies standard events and event handlers for the messages sent when the user performs drag-and-drop operations. It's a simple matter to add custom event handlers for specific purposes.

In the following exercise, we'll develop a managed application to receive drag-and-drop data from external applications. We'll start by dragging and dropping simple text data from Word into a Windows Forms text box. Next we'll extend this to drag-and-drop from Excel. Then we'll use one of the alternative data formats that Excel supports when dragging and dropping and drop some Excel data into a *DataGrid* control. Finally, we'll build in support for dragging and dropping in the other direction. That is, we'll drag and drop from our Windows Forms application to Office (and to any other target that supports drag-and-drop).

Note   The sample solution for this topic can be found in the sample code at <install location>\Code\Office<n>\OfficeDragDrop. This solution contains three versions of the project, corresponding to the three main phases described next (dropping Word text, dropping Excel text and cells, and dropping into Office).

Dropping Word Text

1. Create a new Windows application called OfficeDragDrop. Put a *Button* control on the form, label it Run Word, and get a *Click* handler. Add a reference to the Word IA. (In Solution Explorer, right-click and select Add Reference, click the COM tab, and select the appropriate Microsoft Word Object Library from the list.)

2. Add a *using* statement for the *Word* namespace (with an alias to cut down on typing effort) and for the *System.IO namespace*. (We'll be working with files.)

```
using System.IO;
using Word = Microsoft.Office.Interop.Word;      // not Office 97/2000
```

3. Put a *TextBox* control on the form, with the name *txtData*. Set its properties to include *Multiline*, both *Scrollbar* properties, and *AllowDrop*. In the Properties window, switch to Events view and add event handlers for the *DragEnter* and *DragDrop* events. The wizard will add event handlers to these events on the *TextBox*:

```
txtData.DragDrop += new DragEventHandler(txtData_DragDrop);
txtData.DragEnter += new DragEventHandler(txtData_DragEnter);
```

4. The wizard also generates skeleton handler methods. Implement the *DragEnter* handler to test the data being dragged to see if it contains text. If so, set the *Effect* of the drag-and-drop operation to *Copy*. Note that Word data that is encapsulated via *IDataObject* actually supports multiple formats, including text metafiles and bitmaps.

```
private void txtData_DragEnter(object sender, DragEventArgs e)
{
    if (e.Data.GetDataPresent("Text"))
    {
        e.Effect = DragDropEffects.Copy;
    }
}
```

5. In the *DragDrop* event handler, extract the data as a string and set it into the *TextBox* control:

```
private void txtData_DragDrop(object sender, DragEventArgs e)
{
    txtData.Text = (string)e.Data.GetData(typeof(string));
}
```

6. We could run any external application that supports drag-and-drop to test our application. However, we'll use interop to automate Word. Code the button *Click* event handler to automate Word and open a sample document. (Note that the *Documents.Open* method call shown here is for Word 2003; alternatives are shown in the following paragraphs for other versions.)

```
private void runWord_Click(object sender, System.EventArgs e)
{
    // Work out the path for the Doc file we want.
    // This assumes we're running the application from
    // Visual Studio.
    string currentLocation = System.Environment.CurrentDirectory;
    string currentPath = currentLocation.Substring(
        0, currentLocation.IndexOf(@"bin\Debug"));
    string fileName = "Jabberwocky.doc";
    object filePath = Path.Combine(currentPath, fileName);

    // Launch Word and open the sample Doc file.
    Word.Application word = new Word.Application();
    word.Visible = true;
    object missing = Type.Missing;
```

```
Word.Document doc = word.Documents.Open(ref filePath,
    ref missing, ref missing, ref missing, ref missing,
    ref missing, ref missing, ref missing, ref missing,
    ref missing, ref missing, ref missing, ref missing,
    ref missing, ref missing, ref missing);
}
```

Calling the *Documents.Open* method in Word XP:

```
Word.Document doc = word.Documents.Open(ref filePath,
    ref missing, ref missing, ref missing, ref missing,
    ref missing, ref missing, ref missing, ref missing,
    ref missing, ref missing, ref missing, ref missing,
    ref missing, ref missing);
    //, ref missing);
```

Calling the *Documents.Open* method in Word 2000:

```
Word.Document doc = word.Documents.Open(ref filePath,
    ref missing, ref missing, ref missing, ref missing,
    ref missing, ref missing, ref missing, ref missing,
    ref missing, ref missing, ref missing);
    //, ref missing, ref missing, ref missing);
```

Calling the *Documents.Open* method in Word 97:

```
Word.Document doc = word.Documents.Open(ref filePath,
    ref missing, ref missing, ref missing, ref missing,
    ref missing, ref missing, ref missing, ref missing,
    ref missing); //, ref missing,
    // ref missing, ref missing, ref missing, ref missing);
```

7. Build and test:

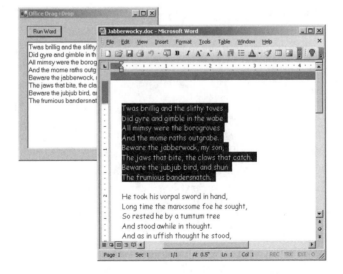

Dropping Excel Text

Excel also supports drag-and-drop, and just like Word, the operation supports multiple data formats. If we want only the text from Excel, the operation is almost identical to the Word operation. We'll test this first, and then we'll enhance the application to work with the structure of the data being dropped from Excel.

1. Add a reference to the Excel IA, and a *using* statement for the *Excel* namespace. Add a second button, label it Run Excel, and get a *Click* event handler. Code the second *Click* handler to automate Excel and open a sample workbook:

```csharp
private void runExcel_Click(object sender, System.EventArgs e)
{
    // Work out the path for the XLS file we want.
    string currentLocation = System.Environment.CurrentDirectory;
    string currentPath = currentLocation.Substring(
        0, currentLocation.IndexOf(@"bin\Debug"));
    string fileName = "Products.xls";
    string filePath = Path.Combine(currentPath, fileName);

    // Launch Excel and open the sample XLS file.
    Excel.Application xl = new Excel.Application();
    xl.Visible = true;
    object missing = Type.Missing;
    Excel.Workbook book = xl.Workbooks.Open(filePath,
        missing, missing, missing, missing, missing,
        missing, missing, missing, missing, missing,
        missing, missing, missing, missing);
}
```

Note that the *Workbooks.Open* method in Excel 97 and Excel 2000 takes fewer parameters than in Excel XP and Excel 2003, so this is the equivalent Office 97 and Office 2000 code:

```csharp
Excel.Workbook book = xl.Workbooks.Open(filePath,
    missing, missing, missing, missing, missing,
    missing, missing, missing, missing, missing,
    missing, missing);    //, missing, missing);
```

2. Build and test. Note that in Excel XP and Excel 2003, to perform a drag-and-drop operation on a multicell selection, you must first select the range of cells and then move the mouse to the border of the selection. (The cursor shape will change to an arrowed cross.) In Excel 97 and Excel 2000, you must first select the range of cells, and also hold down the Ctrl key and move the mouse to the border of the selection to get a cursor with a + sign.

Dropping Excel Cells

As you can see, when we code the drag-and-drop functionality into the drop target, it makes little difference what the drop source is. So, as far as our *TextBox* drop target is concerned, it doesn't matter whether the data came originally from Word or Excel (or, indeed, anywhere else). All it cares about is whether the data object being dropped contains data in a format that it can handle. Up until now, we've been interested only in simple string data—which is one of the formats supported by both Word and Excel when they parcel up data to be dropped elsewhere. In fact, both Word and Excel support multiple formats. In the continuation exercise, we'll drag some data from Excel and drop it using its comma separated variable (CSV) format. This format separates each cell value with a comma, and each row of data with a newline. In this way, we can easily parse the data and retain some aspects of its original structure. What we'll do with it is to put it into a *DataGrid*, which has a row-column structure similar to that of Excel.

1. Parsing the dropped data and using it to populate a *DataGrid* will take a little more work. First put a *DataGrid* control on the form. Set its *AllowDrop* property to *true*. Get *DragEnter* and *DragDrop* event handlers for the *DataGrid*:

```
gridData.DragDrop += new DragEventHandler(gridData _DragDrop);
gridData.DragEnter += new DragEventHandler(gridData _DragEnter);
```

2. Of all the formats used in Excel drag-and-drop, probably the most useful in this scenario is the CSV format. So, code the *DragEnter* handler to query for "CSV." (Note that this is not case-sensitive.)

```
private void dg_DragEnter(object sender, DragEventArgs e)
{
    if (e.Data.GetDataPresent("CSV"))
    {
        e.Effect = DragDropEffects.Copy;
    }
}
```

3. In the *DragDrop* handler, set up a *try* block and get the data from the drag-and-drop operation into a memory stream:

```
private void gridData_DragDrop(object sender, DragEventArgs e)
{
    try
    {
        MemoryStream stream = (MemoryStream)e.Data.GetData("Csv");
        StreamReader reader = new StreamReader(stream);
```

4. Again, we'll assume that the first row contains header information (an arbitrary assumption). Read the first line from the stream, split it into separate strings (using the comma separators), and use each string for the column header of a new *DataTable*:

```
DataTable table = new DataTable();
string firstRow = reader.ReadLine();
string[] headers = firstRow.Split(',');
for (int col = 0; col < headers.Length; col++)
{
    table.Columns.Add(headers[col]);
}
```

5. Read the remaining lines for use as the grid cell values, again splitting on the commas, and adding each *DataRow* to the *DataTable*:

```
while (true)
{
    string row = reader.ReadLine();
    if (row == null)
    {
        break;
    }
    string[] cells = row.Split(',');
    DataRow dataRow = table.NewRow();
    for (int col = 0; col < cells.Length; col++)
    {
        dataRow[col] = cells[col];
    }
    table.Rows.Add(dataRow);
}
```

6. Attach the *DataTable* to the *DataGrid*, and close off the *try/catch* block:

```
    gridData.DataSource = table;
}
catch (Exception ex)
{
    MessageBox.Show(ex.Message);
}
}
```

7. Build and test:

Dropping into Office

In the final phase of this solution, we'll build in further code to our Windows Forms application to allow the user to drag data from the *DataGrid* and drop it elsewhere. We'll parcel up the data in a simple tab-delimited string format so that it can be dropped onto Office applications, including Excel.

1. Declare a *bool* field in the form class—we'll use this to determine whether the user is attempting a drag-and-drop operation.

    ```
    private bool isDragging;
    ```

2. In the Forms Designer, select the *DataGrid*, and in the Properties window, select the Events panel. Get event handlers for the *MouseDown*, *MouseUp*, and *Mouse-Move* events.

3. In the *MouseDown* event handler, we'll use the incoming *MouseEventArgs* parameter to determine whether the button that's down is the left button. To be consistent with standard UI practice, we want to perform the drag-and-drop operation only if the left mouse button is down. If it is, we'll toggle our *bool* flag on.

    ```
    private void gridData_MouseDown(object sender,
        System.Windows.Forms.MouseEventArgs e)
    {
        if ((e.Button & MouseButtons.Left) == MouseButtons.Left)
        {
            isDragging = true;
        }
    }
    ```

4. In the *MouseUp* event handler, we'll turn our toggle back to *false*:

    ```
    private void gridData_MouseUp(object sender,
        System.Windows.Forms.MouseEventArgs e)
    {
        isDragging = false;
    }
    ```

5. In the *MouseMove* handler, we'll first test to see if our toggle is on. If it isn't, we'll simply do nothing and return. If it is on, we can start the drag-and-drop operation. The first thing to do is to set up a *MemoryStream* and an associated *Stream-Writer*. This is so we can gather all the data from the *DataGrid* and put it into a single data stream. The data is not directly held in the *DataGrid* but in its *Data-Source* property—and we know that in this case the *DataSource* is a *DataTable*.

    ```
    private void gridData_MouseMove(object sender,
        System.Windows.Forms.MouseEventArgs e)
    {
        if (isDragging)
    ```

```
    {
        MemoryStream stream = new MemoryStream();
        StreamWriter writer = new StreamWriter(stream);

        DataTable dt = (DataTable)gridData.DataSource;
```

6. Walk through the collection of columns in the *DataTable*, and write out each column's *Caption* to the stream, separated by tabs, and with a new line at the end:

```
    int columnCount = dt.Columns.Count;
    for (int i = 0; i < columnCount; i++)
    {
        DataColumn dc = dt.Columns[i];
        writer.Write(dc.Caption.ToString());
        if (i+1 < columnCount)
        {
            writer.Write("\t");
        }
    }
    writer.WriteLine();
```

7. Iterate the collection of *DataRow* objects in the *DataTable*, and write out the data for each one, column by column, with a tab separating each one and a new line at the end of each row:

```
    foreach (DataRow dr in dt.Rows)
    {
        for (int i = 0; i < columnCount; i++)
        {
            DataColumn dc = dt.Columns[i];
            writer.Write(dr[dc]);
            if (i+1 < columnCount)
            {
                writer.Write("\t");
            }
        }
        writer.WriteLine();
    }
```

8. Make sure all the data has been written to the stream, and close the writer. Then get the stream into a byte array, and convert it to a string:

```
    writer.Flush();
    writer.Close();

    byte[] buffer = stream.GetBuffer();
    stream.Close();
    System.Text.Encoding _encoding =
new System.Text.UTF8Encoding();
    string tabData = _encoding.GetString(buffer, 0, buffer.Length);
```

9. Pass the string as the data to be dragged and dropped, by calling *DoDragDrop*. This method takes two parameters. The first parameter is the data to be dropped (which must be a base-managed class [*String, Bitmap,* or *Metafile*] or an object

that implements *ISerializable* or *IDataObject*. In our case, it's a *String*. The second parameter determines which drag operations are allowed on this call. In our case, we're allowing the data to be copied (not moved or linked).

```
gridData.DoDragDrop(tabData, DragDropEffects.Copy);
        }
    }
```

10. Build and test. You should find that you can drag and drop from the *DataGrid* not only into the *TextBox* in the same application, but also into Excel or Word, and any other application that accepts tab-delimited text.

Summary

In this chapter, we've looked at some general, low-level techniques for integrating managed code with Office: integration with VBA, windowing support, and drag-and-drop.

We've seen that you can integrate code in an external managed assembly, written in Visual Basic .NET or C#, with VBA code that is internal to an Office document. VBA code can talk with managed code—in both directions—and we considered both a lightweight callback strategy and a more sophisticated CCW-based strategy. We've also seen that you can write managed code to manipulate VBA code within a document—to insert, delete, and modify that code.

Both Office and .NET have extensive windowing and UI capability, and you will want to develop solutions that leverage both the Office windows UI and managed windows and controls. We've seen that using managed windows with an Office solution is perfectly feasible, but that there are some constraints. We've also addressed the question of setting up host or parent-child relationships between managed and unmanaged windows. The bottom line here is that some things you just shouldn't do. It's a credit to the developers of the common language runtime (CLR) that interoperating between managed and unmanaged code is relatively painless and offers rich functionality. Pushing this to extremes by manipulating windows programmatically is always going to be risky, and my feeling is that clear guidelines on what you shouldn't do are just as important as guidelines on what you should do.

Finally, we saw that .NET supports the COM drag-and-drop technology as standard for control-based classes. Therefore, implementing drag-and-drop within a managed application and across managed and unmanaged applications is almost trivial. Once you've built in drag-and-drop support, that aspect of your solution will work with anything else that supports drag-and-drop, including (but not limited to) Office applications.

Chapter 5
Add-Ins

Add-ins enable you to extend the capabilities of Office applications by adding custom commands and specialized features that meet a specific business requirement. Over time, the term "add-in" has been used to cover a wide range of different technologies, as described in Table 5-1.

Table 5-1   Add-In Types

Technique	Description	Advantages	Disadvantages
VBA add-ins (Excel XLAs, Word DOTs)	Office applications support VBA add-ins that you can create with the VBA Editor included in each application.	Easy to develop.	Not compiled, run slowly, are susceptible to user corruption, lead to unstructured, unmaintainable code, and can pose a security risk.
Excel XLLs, Word WLLs, and Visio VSLs	Compiled, application-specific DLLs, developed in languages such as C++ and Visual Basic.	Closely integrated with the host, and therefore usually very performant.	Application-specific, have very limited support, and a very small developer pool.
COM add-ins	COM-based add-ins that conform to a well-known interface used by Office 2000 and later.	Fast, fully encapsulated. Can be tailored to a specific application or designed to work in multiple Office applications.	Requires skills in developing with COM. Available for Office 2000 and later only. Functions in COM add-ins cannot be called from formulas in Excel worksheets.
Automation add-ins	Extended from COM add-ins.	Functions in Automation add-ins can be called from formulas in Excel worksheets.	Requires skills in developing with COM. Available for Excel XP and later only.

> **Note** From the information in Table 5-1, it looks like you can't create a COM add-in where you can call the functions from an Excel cell, but as we'll see later, you can overcome this constraint in a couple of ways.

Since we're interested in .NET managed interop, this chapter will focus on the last two options: COM add-ins and Automation add-ins. Section 5.7, "Excel Automation Add-Ins," will explain the differences in detail.

COM add-ins can be set to load when the targeted Office application(s) starts up, and they can also be loaded and unloaded through the UI, using the COM Add-Ins toolbar option. This option is not visible by default, but you can add it to any toolbar using View | Toolbars | Customize. Then you can select it to display the COM Add-ins dialog box, which lists all COM add-ins that are installed on your system and are available on a per-user basis. The dialog box doesn't list any COM add-ins installed for all users on the machine—this ensures that an individual user cannot uninstall an add-in that is intended for all users on the machine. In the list of available (per-user) add-ins, the ones that are currently loaded are indicated by a check in the box.

The COM Add-ins dialog box does not list the Automation add-ins. Automation add-ins are set up using a different dialog box, which is available from Tools | Add-ins:

5.1 Managed COM Add-Ins

<table>
<tr><td>Office 97</td><td>✖</td></tr>
<tr><td>Office 2000</td><td>✔</td></tr>
<tr><td>Office XP</td><td>✔</td></tr>
<tr><td>Office 2003</td><td>✔</td></tr>
</table>

Office 2000 and later support a design architecture for building application add-ins to enhance and control Office applications. These add-ins are called COM add-ins. A COM add-in is an in-process COM server that implements the *IDTExensibility2* interface as defined in the Add-in Designer type library (Msaddndr.dll). All COM add-ins must implement this interface, which exposes the five methods described in Table 5-2.

Table 5-2   *IDTExtensibility2* Methods

Method	Description
OnConnection	Called whenever the add-in is connected. The add-in might be connected on startup, by the end user, or through Automation.
OnDisconnection	Called when the add-in is disconnected and just before it unloads from memory. The add-in should perform any cleanup of resources in this event and restore any changes made to the host application.
OnAddInsUpdate	Called when the set of registered COM add-ins changes. In other words, whenever a COM add-in is installed or removed from the host application, this event fires.
OnStartupComplete	Called if the add-in was connected during startup. At the point when this method is called, the host application's UI is fully active.
OnBeginShutdown	Called if the host disconnects the add-in during shutdown. This is the last point at which the host application's UI is fully active.

Note that the table details the standard behavior across all Office applications. There are variations of this behavior in some versions of Outlook. The Microsoft support site has further information on these variations.

In the following exercise, we'll create an Office COM add-in with one custom button on the toolbar and minimal behavior. Note that while you're developing the add-in, you should not have any Office applications running until you're ready to test the add-in. This is because the set of add-ins available will be loaded by Office for the first Office application to run, so subsequent changes might not be picked up even if you run a different Office application.

> **Note** The sample solution for this topic can be found in the sample code at <install location>\Code\Office<n>\MyOfficeAddin.

Basic Add-In

1. Create a new Extensibility Project, a Shared Add-in. Type MyOfficeAddin as the name of the add-in. This starts the Visual Studio Add-in Wizard, which offers a choice of C#, Visual Basic .NET, or C++. In this exercise, we'll use C#.

2. On page 2 of the wizard, select the Office applications you want this add-in to work with. For simplicity, we'll select just one application in this exercise: Excel. Note, however, that apart from the fact that we're registering this add-in for use with Excel only, there is actually nothing Excel-specific in any of the code.

3. On page 3, provide a suitable FriendlyName and Description for the add-in—these will be presented in the COM Add-Ins dialog box in the Office applications.

4. On page 4, select the first option but not the second. That is, the add-in should load when the host application loads. If you don't select this option, the add-in will be registered with a flag that tells Office to put it into the list in the COM Add-Ins dialog box but not to actually load it until the user requests it. We want the add-in to load automatically when the Office application (Excel, in this case) starts—the user will always have the option to unload it using the COM Add-Ins dialog box.

   We're leaving the second option deselected because we want this add-in to be available only to the user who installs it. This ensures that the add-in will be listed in the COM Add-Ins dialog box. It therefore means that the user has the option to load or unload it, and even to completely unregister it. If, instead, we were to check the second option, this would register the add-in for all users on the machine. That is, it would be registered under HKEY_LOCAL_MACHINE instead of HKEY_CURRENT_USER. If you register on a per-machine basis instead of a per-user basis, no user will be able to control the loading, unloading, or unregistering of the add-in.

   Which option you choose will be determined by your operational environment. In practice, however, per-machine registration is often more effort than it's worth—special cases inevitably arise that require you to change the administrative deployment. Also, users might be hot-desking and need the software stack on the machine to reflect their profile based on their logon. There might even be security/permission issues here in which certain add-ins must be made available only on a per-user basis. If you change your mind about this registration detail after running the wizard, you can always change the setup project at any time subsequently (as detailed later).

5. The wizard adds references for the Extensibility PIA that ships with Visual Studio .NET as well as for a version of the core Office PIA that ships with both Office and Visual Studio .NET.

   If you're wondering why these two PIAs ship with Visual Studio .NET, remember that you can build Visual Studio add-ins (hence the Extensibility PIA) and that Visual Studio itself uses the Office command bars (hence the Office PIA). The properties for these two assemblies specify Copy Local to be False because they will be used directly from their original locations. This is not the GAC; it is a well-known location that varies according to the version of the .NET Framework deployed. The Extensibility.dll is normally somewhere like C:\Program Files\Microsoft Visual Studio .NET\Common7\IDE\Public Assemblies. The Office.dll is normally somewhere like C:\Windows\Microsoft .NET\Framework\v1.1.4.322.

The setup project does not exclude these two assemblies, so they will be deployed as part of the setup on the client machine. This makes sense for the Extensibility.dll, because the client machine is unlikely to have Visual Studio .NET installed. On the other hand, if they have the .NET Framework installed, and they have Office installed, they will have the Office.dll installed.

6. The wizard creates a C# class library project containing a *Connect* class that implements the *IDTExtensibility2* interface. The build settings of the project have Register For COM Interop selected. The assembly key (.snk) file is generated and is referenced in the *AssemblyKeyfile* attribute in Assemblyinfo.cs. Along with the class library project, the wizard generates a setup project that you can use to deploy the COM add-in on other computers.

7. In addition to generating code, the wizard makes entries in the registry that correspond to the choices you made in the wizard pages. The wizard makes these entries simply to make it easier to develop and test the add-in. When you deploy the add-in, you must duplicate these registry entries. To do that, you should build and run the wizard-generated setup (MSI) project. Even during development, some developers find it more convenient to build and run the MSI. That way, they have an easy means of installing and uninstalling the add-in on the development machine, which they might need to do for testing purposes. When you build the setup project, you can install it by running the resultant MSI directly. Alternatively, you can right-click the setup project in the Solution Explorer window and select the Install option.

    Similarly, to uninstall, you can either run the MSI again (and select Remove), or right-click the setup project and select Uninstall. You can also run the uninstaller by going to the Windows Start menu and choosing Settings | Control Panel | Add/Remove Programs.

    In addition to normal COM registration, a COM add-in needs to register itself with each Office application in which it runs, by creating a subkey, using its ProgID as the name for the key, under HKCU or HKLM:

    \Software\Microsoft\Office\<OfficeApp>\Addins\ProgID

8. Note that the LoadBehavior value of 3 indicates that the add-in should be loaded on application startup and is shown as being connected in the COM Add-Ins dialog box (or programmatically). If we want it loaded only when the

user asks for it, we can set LoadBehavior to 9. If we don't want it loaded, we can set it to 0. The possible values of LoadBehavior are described in Table 5-3.

Table 5-3   The Meaning Of LoadBehavior Values

LB	Meaning	Status in COM Add-Ins Dialog Box	Behavior Description
0		Disconnected	The add-in is not loaded when the application starts. It can be loaded through the COM Add-Ins dialog box or programmatically, which sets the status to 1.
1		Connected	The add-in is not loaded when the application starts. It can be loaded through the COM Add-Ins dialog box or programmatically.
2	BootLoaded	Disconnected	The add-in is loaded when the application starts, changing the status from 2 to 3. Once the add-in is loaded, it remains loaded until it is explicitly unloaded.
3	Bootloaded	Connected	The add-in is loaded when the application starts. Once the add-in is loaded, it remains loaded until it is explicitly unloaded.
8	DemandLoaded	Disconnected	The add-in is loaded and connected when the host application requires it, e.g., when a user clicks on a button that uses functionality in the add-in, which sets the status to 9.
9	DemandLoaded	Connected	The add-in is loaded and connected when the host application requires it, e.g., when a user clicks on a button that uses functionality in the add-in.
16	ConnectFirstTime	Disconnected	The add-in loads when the user runs the host application for the first time, and it creates a button or menu item for itself. The next time the user starts the application, the add-in is loaded on demand—that is, it doesn't load until the user clicks the button or menu item associated with the add-in. This sets the status to 9.

9. Using RegEdit, you can see how our initial choices in the wizard pages are eventually mapped to registry entries. Because we chose not to make this add-in available for all users on the machine, the entries will be under HKEY_CURRENT_USER.

Then navigate to Software\Microsoft\Office\Excel\Addins. Our new add-in will be listed under its ProgId—that is, MyOfficeAddin.Connect:

10. Have a quick look at the generated code. It includes a *Connect* class that implements *IDTExtensibility2* (and is attributed with a GUID and ProgId), as shown here. This GUID and ProgId are registered when the project is built. Note that we're given a reference to our host application in the *OnConnection* method:

```
[GuidAttribute("CF5C2EE3-8896-4729-9CCE-C34A842B5CE4"),
ProgId("MyOfficeAddin.Connect")]
public class Connect : Object, Extensibility.IDTExtensibility2
{
    private object applicationObject;
    private object addInInstance;
    public void OnConnection(object application,
        Extensibility.ext_ConnectMode connectMode,
        object addInInst, ref System.Array custom)
    {
        applicationObject = application;
        addInInstance = addInInst;
    }
...
```

Add-In Connection/Disconnection

1. Now we'll enhance the implementation of the *OnConnection* method. You'll notice that this is passed an *Extensibility.ext_ConnectMode* parameter. This is an *enum* value that indicates how the add-in was loaded.

   If something failed during *OnConnection*, Office resets the LoadBehavior. If, for example, you initially set the LoadBehavior to 3 but then the add-in fails to load, Office will reset the 3 in the registry to 2. This means your add-in was actually loaded but not connected. If this happens, the user can still attempt to load the add-in manually, using the COM Add-Ins dialog box. If the error persists, of course, the load will still fail, and the registry entry will still to be set to 2. To track down what caused the failure, you would need to add some error handling to *OnConnection* to trap the exception.

2. In *OnStartupComplete*, we'll set up our custom button. In *OnBeginShutdown*, we'll delete the button. If you want to modify the UI–for example, to create new command bars or add custom buttons–you should do this in *OnStartupComplete* because then you'll know the host application's UI (including standard command bars) is fully loaded.

3. Recall that we specified that the add-in should be started by the host application at startup, so if *OnConnection* is being called for any other reason, we need to duplicate the behavior that happens at startup. For example, *OnConnection* is called if the user disconnects the add-in using the COM Add-Ins dialog box and then reconnects it using the COM Add-Ins dialog box. The behavior at startup is to call *OnStartupComplete*, so what we have to do is check whether *OnConnection* is being called for anything other than *ext_cm_Startup*, and if so, we must call *OnStartupComplete* ourselves:

```
applicationObject = application;
addInInstance = addInInst;
if(connectMode !=
    Extensibility.ext_ConnectMode.ext_cm_Startup)
{
    OnStartupComplete(ref custom);
}
```

4. Similarly, in *OnDisconnection*, if we're being disconnected for any other reason than because the host is being shut down, we can simply call into our *OnBegin-Shutdown* method (and set our application reference to null):

```
if(disconnectMode !=
    Extensibility.ext_DisconnectMode.ext_dm_HostShutdown)
{
    OnBeginShutdown(ref custom);
}
applicationObject = null;
```

Note that *OnDisconnection* is called when the user deselects our add-in in the COM Add-Ins dialog box. This removes the add-in from the Office application but does not unregister it from the registry, so the user can go back at a later time and reselect it.

5. In this exercise, we're not interested in the event that fires when the set of registered COM add-ins changes, so we can leave *OnAddInsUpdate* as an empty implementation. It has to be said that in practice this is the normal case–that is, it is unusual to provide any custom implementation in this method.

Custom Button

In our add-in, we'll add a button to the host application's command bar and display a message box in all the key methods. First we'll add a reference to the System.Windows.Forms.dll, and add a using statement for the *System.Windows.Forms* namespace—this is so we can use the *MessageBox* class. Add a field in the *Connect* class for the command bar button:

```
private CommandBarButton myButton;
```

OnStartupComplete is where we'll set up our button. First we'll declare local variables for the *CommandBars* collection and the individual *CommandBar* we want to modify:

```
CommandBars bars;
CommandBar bar = null;
```

Then we'll work out which of the host application's command bars to attach our custom button to. We have several approaches to choose from. For example, we could create a new command bar, specify one that we know to be in use (such as Standard), or find one with enough space on the end. In our example, we'll walk the collection to find the first visible one. (Note: This is likely to be the menu bar, not a toolbar, but both are *CommandBar* objects, and we can add our button to either type of *Command-Bar*.)

```
Type applicationType = applicationObject.GetType();
bars = (CommandBars)applicationType.InvokeMember(
    "CommandBars", BindingFlags.GetProperty, null,
    applicationObject, null);
//bar = bars["Standard"];
foreach (CommandBar b in bars)
{
    if (b.Visible == true)
    {
        bar = b;
        break;
    }
}
```

Now we'll add our button to the command bar. We'll call the *Add* method of the *Controls* collection. This method takes a number of optional parameters, and in this case we don't need to specify anything because we're happy with the defaults. As in earlier sections, we'll pass a "missing" value, using either *System.Reflection.Missing.Value* or *System.Type.Missing*.

```
object missing = Type.Missing;
myButton = (CommandBarButton) bar.Controls.Add(
    1, missing, missing, missing, missing);
myButton.Caption = "My Button";
myButton.Style = MsoButtonStyle.msoButtonCaption;
```

Hook up an event handler for the *Click* event on the button.

```
myButton.Click +=
    new _CommandBarButtonEvents_ClickEventHandler(
    this.myButton_Click);
```

Write the corresponding *Click* event handler to just display a simple message:

```
private void myButton_Click(
    CommandBarButton cmdBarbutton,ref bool cancel)
{
    MessageBox.Show("MyButton was Clicked", "MyOfficeAddin");
}
```

Finally, we'll implement *OnBeginShutdown* to ensure that the add-in cleans itself up. When we added our new button to the command bar, we passed a "missing" value as the last parameter. This last parameter indicates whether the button should be temporary or permanent. By default, it is set to be permanent. In this exercise, we will remove it when our add-in is unloaded. You could argue that it would have been simpler to make the button temporary in the first place. However, the purpose of this exercise is to demonstrate enough of the mechanics and infrastructure of managed COM add-ins so the developer can apply these techniques generally. For that reason, we've taken a slightly longer route to get to the same place.

```
object missing = Type.Missing;
myButton.Delete(missing);
```

To test our example add-in, we need to run Excel. You can trigger it from Visual Studio by changing the project properties. You select the project in Solution Explorer, and then select Properties | Configuration Properties| Debugging. The wizard sets the Start Application by default to Visual Studio. (Don't forget, the wizard also creates Visual Studio add-ins.) We need to change this to Excel.

Build and test. You should see our new button in the first visible command bar in Excel:

When the user clicks this button, we get a simple message box.

> **Note** If you want to unregister the add-in, you can remove the registry keys indicated above and also the COM registration—including the ProgID in HKCR and the CLSID in HKCR. If you installed the add-in with the MSI, you can remove both sets of registry settings by running the uninstaller from Control Panel | Add/Remove Programs or by right-clicking the setup project in Visual Studio and selecting Uninstall. It's a good idea to build the setup project and install it—you have to test it anyway, and doing this allows you to install/uninstall at will, instead of manually editing the registry (which is always dangerous and not generally recommended).

Working with the Setup Project

For completeness, we'll now spend a little time looking at the setup project that the wizard generated when you first created the add-in project.

1. If you select the setup project in Solution Explorer, you'll see that the collection of buttons at the top of the window changes. You'll see buttons for a set of editors for manipulating the setup project: File System, Registry, File Types, User Interface, Custom Actions, Launch Conditions, and Properties.

2. With the setup project selected in Solution Explorer, you can view the general properties:

Properties	
MyOfficeAddinSetup Deployment Project Properties	
AddRemoveProgramsIcon	(None)
Author	Microsoft
Description	
DetectNewerInstalledVersion	True
Keywords	
Localization	English (United States)
Manufacturer	Microsoft
ManufacturerUrl	
ProductCode	{4F2D0ADA-17A1-4EA6-8B27-C54139693D7D}
ProductName	MyOfficeAddinSetup
RemovePreviousVersions	False
SearchPath	
Subject	
SupportPhone	
SupportUrl	
Title	MyOfficeAddinSetup
UpgradeCode	{51C37D07-BD8E-42F6-8488-8CFCB23710F3}
Version	1.0.0

The Author and Manufacturer properties will be set to whatever name you registered Visual Studio to when you installed it. This is typically your company name. The ProductName and Title will be set to the name you chose for your add-in project, with *Setup* appended. Normally, you'll want to remove *Setup* and just leave the name of your add-in as the name to be used during setup. This will be used in the Setup Wizard pages when you install the add-in.

3. The Manufacturer and ProductName properties are also used to determine the file system location where the add-in will be installed. If you click the File System Editor button and select Application Folder, you can see how these are used:

4. In the list of Detected Dependencies, you can see the merge module (MSM) for the .NET Framework redistributable. If you look at the properties for this, you'll see that it has the Exclude property set to *True*. This is an example of a dependency that will not be deployed as part of the installation of the add-in. Compare this with the properties for the Extensibility.dll, which has Exclude set to *False*. This is because the user will have the Extensibility.dll present only if Visual Studio .NET is installed—which is not usually the case for end users. You should carefully examine the Exclude setting for each of the dependencies to make sure it is appropriate for your target users.

5. Also, using Extensibility.dll as an example, you can see that the Register property is set to *vsdraDoNotRegister*. Compare this with the value for the Primary Output (that is, the add-in assembly itself), which is set to *vsdrpCOM*. This means the add-in will be registered for COM interop. This will effectively have the same behavior as using the Register For COM Interop setting within the add-in project itself—except that that setting is used during build on the development machine, not on the deployment target machine.

6. Click the Registry Editor button, and you will see the corresponding registry entries that the installer will make. These will match the choices you made when creating the project in the first place. In our example, you should see that only HKEY_CURRENT_USER has any entries. We're registering this add-in for use with Excel, using the add-in ProgId. Under that node, you can see the Description and FriendlyName that you chose. You can also see the LoadBehavior set to 3. You can edit any of these values in this editor. For instance, if you change your mind and want to register this add-in for all users on the machine, you can simply drag and drop the entire Software node from HKCU to HKLM.

The string values can't be edited in place. Instead, you select the item and edit it in the Properties window.

5.2 Simple Add-In Projects

Office 97	✗
Office 2000	✓
Office XP	✓
Office 2003	✓

The intention of the Shared Add-in Extensibility Project type is to allow you to develop add-ins for applications that support *IDTExtensibility2*–which includes Office applications. The skeleton code generated is suitable for an add-in that works with only one Office application or an add-in that works with multiple Office applications. When you select this project type, the wizard lets you choose which Office applications you want your new add-in to support.

Recall that the wizard generates a *Connect* class with two fields:

```
private object applicationObject;
private object addInInstance;
```

These are both generic objects. The *applicationObject* is a reference to the hosting Office application and has not been typed to any specific application object. The wizard asks you which application or applications you want your add-in to be hosted by, but this information is used only to generate the registry keys. The information does not affect the C# (or Visual Basic .NET) code that is generated.

Furthermore, in our first add-in project, we registered the add-in for use with Excel, but there was nothing Excel-specific in any of the code. We used late binding to get the runtime type of the application and then invoke its members, so that we could add a button to a command bar:

```
Type applicationType = applicationObject.GetType();
    CommandBars bars = (CommandBars)applicationType.InvokeMember(
        "CommandBars", BindingFlags.GetProperty, null,
        applicationObject, null);
    CommandBar bar = bars["Tools"];
```

The early-bound equivalent (for Excel) looks like this:

```
CommandBar bar = applicationObject.CommandBars["Tools"];
```

It is certainly feasible to create an add-in that will be used across multiple Office applications, and we'll explore this scenario in a later section. However, most add-ins are designed to operate within the context of one specific Office application and use the object model for that application.

In this section, we'll work through a set of add-ins, each of which will target one specific Office application. For each one, we'll incorporate the PIA or interop assembly (IA) for that application. This means we can streamline our code by developing against the strongly typed object model for each application. This will also be faster at run time. As you work through these examples, you'll notice that many of the steps are the same, regardless of the specific target host application. Fundamentally, this is because the *IDTExtensibility2* interface is defined in a DLL that is shared across all Office applications. In the same way, all Office applications use a common DLL for their command UI.

The sample solution for this topic can be found in the sample code at <install location>\Code\Office<n>\SimpleAddins. This solution contains four projects—for the Excel, Word, Outlook, and PowerPoint add-ins.

Excel Add-In

Our Excel add-in will offer a new button on the Tools menu. When the user clicks this button, we'll calculate the maximum value of all the cells in the selected range and display the result in a message box.

1. First create a new Shared Add-in project called ExcelMax. Deselect all application hosts except Excel. Specify that the add-in should load when the host application loads. When the wizard has generated the initial project, add a reference to the System.Windows.Forms.dll and a *using* statement for the *System.Windows.Forms* namespace—this is so that we can use the *MessageBox* class.

2. Add a reference to the appropriate Excel PIA or IA for the version you're targeting. This results in the duplication of references to the Office.dll. As we previously noted, you can remove one of these.

3. When you add a dependency to the add-in project, such as the Excel IAs, these dependencies are also added to the setup project. For Visual Studio–generated

IAs for Office versions before XP and for the Office XP PIAs, this is fine because it is acceptable to distribute these IAs as part of your solution. However, your target organization might already have versions of these IAs deployed—possibly to the GAC—and you need to make sure that it is appropriate to bundle them with your setup. For Office 2003, it is not acceptable to deploy the PIAs because they are installed as part of the installation of Office itself.

Therefore, if you need to ensure that the IAs are not deployed, you should go to the properties for your setup project and change the value of the *Exclude* property for each affected dependency to *True*.

4. Now to the code changes. Change the declaration of the *applicationObject* field from a generic object to a specific *Excel.Application* reference:

    ```
    //private object applicationObject;
    private Excel.Application applicationObject;
    ```

5. Also change the corresponding initialization in the *OnConnection* method. Continue with this method, and add the additional code to call into the *OnStartupComplete* method, as before:

    ```
    public void OnConnection(object application,
        Extensibility.ext_ConnectMode connectMode,
        object addInInst, ref System.Array custom)
    {
        //applicationObject = application;
        applicationObject = (Excel.Application)application;
        addInInstance = addInInst;

        if (connectMode !=
    Extensibility.ext_ConnectMode.ext_cm_Startup)
        {
            OnStartupComplete(ref custom);
        }
    }
    ```

6. Code *OnDisconnection* in the same way as before:

    ```
    public void OnDisconnection(
        Extensibility.ext_DisconnectMode disconnectMode,
        ref System.Array custom)
    {
        if (disconnectMode !=
            Extensibility.ext_DisconnectMode.ext_dm_HostShutdown)
        {
            OnBeginShutdown(ref custom);
        }
        applicationObject = null;
    }
    ```

7. Declare a *CommandBarButton* reference as a new class field:

    ```
    private CommandBarButton button;
    ```

8. In *OnStartupComplete*, we'll create a new command bar button. First start a *try* block and find the Tools menu. Previously, we used late binding to do this. In this application-specific add-in, we can early-bind to the Excel object model. Specifically, we can get the *CommandBars* collection, which is exposed as a property of the *Application* object.

```
public void OnStartupComplete(ref System.Array custom)
{
    string buttonName = "Get Max Value";

    try
    {
        CommandBar bar = applicationObject.CommandBars["Tools"];
```

9. As before, we can use *FindControl* to see if our button is already on the command bar. If we don't find it, we'll add it. If we do find it, we'll simply cache the reference to it.

```
object missing = Type.Missing;
CommandBarButton tmp = (CommandBarButton)
    bar.FindControl(MsoControlType.msoControlButton,
    missing, buttonName, true, true);
if (tmp == null)
{
    button = (CommandBarButton) bar.Controls.Add(
        MsoControlType.msoControlButton, 1, missing,
        missing, true);
    button.FaceId = 304;
    button.Caption = buttonName;
    button.Tag = buttonName;
}
else
{
    button = tmp;
}
```

10. Hook up an event handler for the button's *Click* event, and finish off the *try/catch* block:

```
button.Click += new
    _CommandBarButtonEvents_ClickEventHandler(button_Click);
    }
    catch (Exception ex)
    {
        MessageBox.Show(ex.Message);
    }
}
```

Note that we're using very simple exception handling here—just catching a generic *Exception*. Strictly speaking, its always better to catch the specific type of exception that you're expecting in each situation. So in this situation, we could catch a *COMException* instead. I've often left the *catch* blocks in the sample code to catch generic exceptions just to keep things simple and to focus on other aspects of the code rather than the exception handling. However, in a production system, you should always use standard best practices for exception handling.

11. Finally, code the button *Click* handler. We can get the currently selected range of cells directly from the *Application* object. Then we can use the *Max* worksheet function to calculate the maximum value in this range:

```
private void button_Click(
    CommandBarButton cmdBarbutton, ref bool cancelButton)
{
    try
    {
        Excel.Range selection =
            (Excel.Range)applicationObject.Selection;
        object missing = Type.Missing;
        object maxValue =
            applicationObject.WorksheetFunction.Max(selection,
            missing, missing, missing, missing, missing,
            missing, missing, missing, missing, missing,
            missing, missing, missing, missing, missing,
            missing, missing, missing, missing, missing,
            missing, missing, missing, missing, missing,
            missing, missing, missing, missing);
        MessageBox.Show(maxValue.ToString());
    }
    catch (Exception ex)
    {
        MessageBox.Show(ex.Message);
    }
}
```

12. Adjust the project properties to run Excel when you debug. Build and test. The new button should be at the bottom of the Tools menu.

Type in some dummy values into a small number of cells, select that range of cells, and click the Get Max Value button:

Word Add-In

If you spend any amount of time working with text documents, you'll often cut and paste text from Notepad to Word or from an e-mail or a Web site to Word. Depending on your WordWrap setting in Notepad or on the formatting of the source text, the text might come across into Word with a paragraph mark at the end of every line—that is, with hard line wraps. We'll write a Word add-in that removes all paragraph marks at the end of a line when that line is within a paragraph. To do this, we'll use the Word *Find* object, which takes regular expressions as parameters to the *Execute* method.

Our Word add-in will offer a new button on the Tools menu. When the user clicks this button, we'll replace all the unwanted paragraph marks in the current document. We'll honor any paragraph marks that truly delimit paragraphs.

1. First we'll create a new Shared Add-in project called UnWordWrap. Deselect all application hosts except Word. Specify that the add-in should load when the host application loads. When the wizard has generated the initial project, add a reference to the System.Windows.Forms.dll and a *using* statement for the *System.Windows.Forms* namespace.

2. Add a reference to the appropriate Word PIA or IA for the version you're targeting. This results in the duplication of references to the Office.dll. As we previously noted, you can remove one of these. If you need to ensure that the IAs are not deployed, you should go to the properties for your setup project and change the value of the Exclude property for each affected dependency to *True*. See the previous Excel add-in exercise for more details.

3. Now change the declaration of the *applicationObject* field from a generic object to a specific *Word.Application* reference:

    ```
    //private object applicationObject;
    private Word.Application applicationObject;
    ```

4. Also change the corresponding initialization in the *OnConnection* method.

    ```
    //applicationObject = application;
    applicationObject = (Word.Application)application;
    ```

5. Continue with the *OnConnection* method, and add the additional code to call into the *OnStartupComplete* method, as before. Then, code the *OnDisconnection* method to call *OnBeginShutdown* in the same way as before.

6. Declare a *CommandBarButton* reference as a new class field:

    ```
    private CommandBarButton button;
    ```

7. In *OnStartupComplete*, we'll create a new command bar button. First start a *try* block and find the Tools menu. In this application-specific add-in, we can early-

bind to the Word object model. Specifically, we can get the *CommandBars* collection, which is exposed as a property of the *Application* object.

```
public void OnStartupComplete(ref System.Array custom)
{
    string buttonName = " Un-WordWrap";

    try
    {
        CommandBar bar = applicationObject.CommandBars["Tools"];
```

8. As before, we can use *FindControl* to see if our button is already on the command bar. If we don't find it, we'll add it. If we do find it, we'll simply cache the reference to it. See the Excel project for an example of how to do this–the code will be identical, except you might want to use a different *FaceId* value (say, 6). Then hook up an event handler for the button's *Click* event, and finish off the *try/catch* block.

9. Finally, code the button *Click* handler. Get the currently active document from the *Application* object, and then use the *Execute* method of the *Find* object that is exposed by the *Content* property of the *Document*. Find all paragraph marks that are at the end of a line but within a paragraph–when we concatenate the lines, be sure to keep a space between them.

```
private void button_Click(
    CommandBarButton cmdBarbutton, ref bool cancelButton)
{
    try
    {
        Word.Document doc = applicationObject.ActiveDocument;
        object missing = Type.Missing;
        object findText = @"([!^13])(^13)([!^13])";
        object replaceText = @"\1 \3";
        object wildCards = true;
        object replace = Word.WdReplace.wdReplaceAll;
        doc.Content.Find.Execute(ref findText,
            ref missing, ref missing, ref wildCards,
            ref missing, ref missing, ref missing, ref missing,
            ref missing, ref replaceText, ref replace,
            ref missing, ref missing, ref missing, ref missing);
    }
    catch (Exception ex)
    {
        MessageBox.Show(ex.Message);
    }
}
```

10. Adjust the project properties to run Word when you debug. Build and test. The new button should be at the bottom of the Tools menu.

You can use the Jabberwocky.doc test document from the sample code or use any document with hard returns at the end of each line:

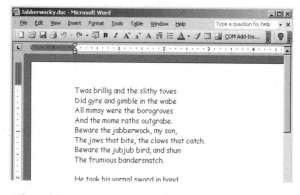

When the user clicks the Un-WordWrap button, the text is reformatted:

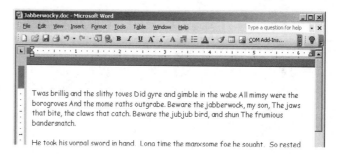

Outlook Add-In

Our Outlook add-in will offer a new button on the Tools menu. When the user clicks this button, we'll walk through the collection of contacts, extract some of the fields, and write them out to a text file.

> **Note** A COM add-in must be able to detect when the host application is shutting down so the add-in can release its references. If it didn't do this, the host application could be forced to remain in memory (because at least one of its COM objects is still unreleased). The following add-in behaves correctly with Outlook XP and Outlook 2003 but not with Outlook 2000. Therefore, this solution cannot be used with Outlook 2000.

1. First create a new Shared Add-in project called ExportContacts. Deselect all application hosts except Outlook. Specify that the add-in should load when the host application loads. When the wizard has generated the initial project, add a reference to the System.Windows.Forms.dll and a *using* statement for the *System.Windows.Forms* namespace.

2. Add a reference to the appropriate Outlook PIA or IA for the version you are targeting. This results in the duplication of references to the Office.dll. As we previously noted, you can remove one of these. If you need to ensure that the IAs are not

deployed, you should go to the properties for your setup project and change the value of the Exclude property for each affected dependency to *True*. See the earlier Excel add-in exercise for more details. Now change the declaration of the *applicationObject* field from a generic object to a specific *Outlook.Application* reference:

```
//private object applicationObject;
private Outlook.Application applicationObject;
```

3. Also change the corresponding initialization in the *OnConnection* method:

```
//applicationObject = application;
applicationObject = (Outlook.Application)application;
```

4. Continue with this method, and add the additional code to call into the *OnStartupComplete* method, as before. Then, code the *OnDisconnection* method to call *OnBeginShutdown* in the same way as before.

5. Declare a *CommandBarButton* reference as a new class field:

```
private CommandBarButton button;
```

6. In *OnStartupComplete*, we'll create a new command bar button. First find the Tools menu. We have added a reference to the Outlook IA, so we can early-bind to the Outlook object model. Specifically, we can get the *CommandBars* collection, which is exposed as a property of the *Outlook.Explorer* objects. An Outlook *Explorer* is an object model representation of Outlook's main window. As before, we can use *FindControl* to see if our button is already on the command bar. If we don't find it, we'll add it. If we do find it, we'll simply cache the reference to it. Either way, hook up an event handler for the button's *Click* event:

```
public void OnStartupComplete(ref System.Array custom)
{
    string buttonName = "Export Contacts";

    try
    {
        CommandBar bar =
applicationObject.ActiveExplorer().CommandBars["Tools"];
        object missing = Type.Missing;
        CommandBarButton tmp = (CommandBarButton)
            bar.FindControl(MsoControlType.msoControlButton,
            missing, buttonName, true, true);
        if (tmp == null)
        {
            button = (CommandBarButton) bar.Controls.Add(
                MsoControlType.msoControlButton, 1, missing,
                missing, true);
            button.Caption = buttonName;
            button.Tag = buttonName;
        }
        else
        {
            button = tmp;
        }
```

```
                    button.Click += new
_CommandBarButtonEvents_ClickEventHandler(button_Click);
        }
        catch (Exception ex)
        {
            MessageBox.Show(ex.Message);
        }
    }
```

7. Finally, code the button *Click* handler to create a new text file, using the *Stream-Writer* class. Put this in a *using* block to make sure it gets disposed of properly when execution leaves the scope of the *using* block. Get hold of the *Contacts* folder and the collection of *ContactItems*. Iterate all the contacts, and write out the *LastName*, *FirstName*, and *BusinessTelephoneNumber* to the file. When we're done, we'll confirm this to the user with a message box:

```
private void button_Click(
    CommandBarButton cmdBarButton, ref bool cancelButton)
{
    using (StreamWriter writer =
      new StreamWriter(@"C:\Temp\ExportContacts\Contacts.txt"))
    {
        Outlook.NameSpace mapiNamespace =
            applicationObject.GetNamespace("MAPI");
        Outlook.MAPIFolder contactsFolder =
            mapiNamespace.GetDefaultFolder(
            Outlook.OlDefaultFolders.olFolderContacts);
        foreach (Outlook.ContactItem contact in contactsFolder.Items)
        {
            string s = String.Format("{0}, {1} - {2}",
                contact.LastName, contact.FirstName,
                contact.BusinessTelephoneNumber);
            writer.WriteLine(s);
        }
        MessageBox.Show("Contacts successfully written to file");
    }
}
```

8. Adjust the project properties to run Outlook when you debug. Build and test. The new button should appear at the bottom of the Tools menu.

When the user clicks the Export Contacts button, the add-in writes the chosen fields for all the contacts to a text file:

PowerPoint Add-In

Our PowerPoint add-in will offer a new button on the Tools menu. When the user clicks this button, we'll extract all the notes from the slides in the current presentation, and write them out to a text file.

1. First create a new Shared Add-in project called SlideNotes. Deselect all application hosts except PowerPoint. Specify that the add-in should load when the host application loads. When the wizard has generated the initial project, add a reference to the System.Windows.Forms.dll and a *using* statement for the *System.Windows.Forms* namespace.

2. Add a reference to the appropriate PowerPoint PIA or IA for the version you're targeting. This results in the duplication of references to the Office.dll. As we previously noted, you can remove one of these. If you need to ensure that the IAs are not deployed, you should go to the properties for your setup project and change the value of the Exclude property for each affected dependency to *True*. See the earlier Excel add-in exercise for more details.

3. Now change the declaration of the *applicationObject* field from a generic object to a specific *PowerPoint.Application* reference:

    ```
    //private object applicationObject;
    private PowerPoint.Application applicationObject;
    ```

4. Also change the corresponding initialization in the *OnConnection* method.

    ```
    //applicationObject = application;
    applicationObject = (PowerPoint.Application)application;
    ```

5. Continue with this method, and add the additional code to call into the *OnStartupComplete* method, as before. Then, code the *OnDisconnection* method to call *OnBeginShutdown* in the same way as before.

6. Declare a *CommandBarButton* reference as a new class field:

    ```
    private CommandBarButton button;
    ```

7. In *OnStartupComplete*, we'll create a new command bar button. First find the Tools menu. In this application-specific add-in, we can early-bind to the PowerPoint object model. Specifically, we can get the *CommandBars* collection, which is exposed as a property of the *Application* object. As before, we can use *FindControl* to see if our button is already on the command bar. If we don't find it, we'll add it. If we do find it, we'll simply cache the reference to it. See the Excel project for an example of how to do this—the code will be identical, except you might want to use a different *FaceId* value (say, *244*). Then hook up an event handler for the button's *Click* event.

8. Finally, code the button *Click* handler. First get the currently active *Presentation* from the *Application* object. Then set up a scoped *StreamWriter* for the text file

that we'll be writing to. Of course, in a real production system, we'd probably ask the user for the pathname of the file. Loop through each slide in the deck, and write out its name to the file. Then find the body of the notes page for each slide, and write out the whole text to the file. At the end, notify the user that we've written the file.

```csharp
private void button_Click(
    CommandBarButton cmdBarButton, ref bool cancelButton)
{
    try
    {
        object missing = Type.Missing;
        PowerPoint.Presentation ppt =
            applicationObject.ActivePresentation;
        using (StreamWriter writer =
            new StreamWriter(@"C:\Temp\SlideNotes\SlideNotes.txt"))
        {
            foreach (PowerPoint.Slide slide in ppt.Slides)
            {
                writer.WriteLine(slide.Name);
                foreach (PowerPoint.Shape shape in
                    slide.NotesPage.Shapes)
                {
                    if (shape.PlaceholderFormat.Type ==
                    PowerPoint.PpPlaceholderType.ppPlaceholderBody)
                    {
                        writer.WriteLine(
                            shape.TextFrame.TextRange.Text);
                    }
                }
            }
        }
        MessageBox.Show("Slide Notes successfully written to file");
    }
    catch (Exception ex)
    {
        MessageBox.Show(ex.Message);
    }
}
```

9. Adjust the project properties to run PowerPoint when you debug. Build and test. The new button should be at the bottom of the Tools menu.

   You can use the dummy presentation Jabberwocky.ppt from the sample code. When the user clicks the Slide Notes button, the add-in writes out the slide notes to a text file:

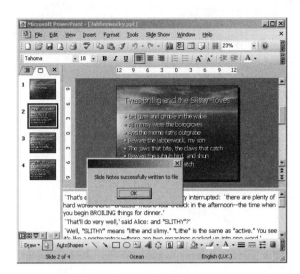

5.3 Multiple Host Applications

Office 97	✖
Office 2000	✔
Office XP	✔
Office 2003	✔

There is a degree of consistency across the range of Office applications in the way they work with add-ins. The basic mechanics are the same. However, even with the basic mechanics, the implementation details differ slightly. In this section, we'll explore some of these differences.

Recall that the Shared Add-in Wizard generates code based around a generic application object, and that we can use this object to make late-bound calls to the underlying Office application object. You might think that if we want to implement generic functionality across multiple Office applications, we would need to retain the use of late binding. Certainly, many properties and methods exposed by the application objects in the Office products are identical. However, even more properties and methods are not the same across any two Office applications. Furthermore, once you navigate the object model beyond the application object, there are even fewer commonalities. For this reason, even for an add-in that is designed to work with multiple host applications, it is generally more convenient (and more performant at run time) to use early binding.

Another issue that any serious Office developer should consider is the design of reusable libraries. Because of the commonalities across Office applications and across add-in solutions, it's only sensible to design a set of reusable components that encapsulate these commonalities. This can be done at various levels, and reusable components often accrete over a period of time in an organic fashion. This is actually a perfectly valid way to achieve such components. Designing them all in a vacuum up front is difficult and error-prone. It's better by far to work on a number of real projects and then to stand back and take stock, to see what refactoring can be done to build reusable components.

In the following exercise, we'll create an add-in that is designed to be used in both Word and Excel. Our add-in will create a custom toolbar with four buttons. These buttons will get the name of the current document or workbook, get the path of the current document or workbook, put some arbitrary text in the status bar, and invoke help on the current application.

> **Note**   The sample solution for this topic can be found in the sample code at <install location>\Code\Office<n>\ OfficeHelper.

1. First create a new Shared Add-in project called OfficeHelper. Deselect all application hosts except Word and Excel. Specify that the add-in should load when the host application loads.

2. Add a reference to the appropriate Excel and Word PIAs or IAs for the version you're targeting. This results in the duplication of references to the Office.dll. As we previously noted, you can remove one of these. Also determine whether you need to exclude the IAs from your setup project.

3. The first major enhancement is to add a new class, called *OfficeHost*. This will serve a dual purpose: it will encapsulate as much of the common code as possible, and it will wrap the Word and Excel application object passed in by the host application. Of course, there will only ever be one such object—although the add-in can be used by multiple hosts, each instance of the add-in can run in only one host at a time. By encapsulating the host application, the wrapper class can take care of the mundane details of working out which host is in use. In this way, our calling code doesn't have to worry about which host it's running in.

4. Declare an *Excel.Application* and a *Word.Application* reference as fields in the *OfficeHost* class. Also, make the *OfficeHost* class implement the *IDisposable* interface. In this way, we have a convenient mechanism for cleaning up our COM object references in a timely fashion:

```
public class OfficeHost : IDisposable
{

    private Excel.Application xl;
    private Word.Application wd;

    public void Dispose()
    {
        xl = null;
        wd = null;
    }
}
```

5. Write a constructor for the *OfficeHost* class. This should take in as a parameter the generic application object that the host application passes on to the *Connect*

class in the first instance. From this generic application object, we can use late binding (actually we don't have any choice here) to find the name of the host application. With that information, we can cast the generic application object to the specific Office *Application* type that it represents.

```
public OfficeHost(object application)
{
    Type applicationType = application.GetType();
    string appName = (string)applicationType.InvokeMember(
        "Name", BindingFlags.GetProperty, null,
        application, null);
    switch (appName)
    {
        case "Microsoft Excel":
            xl = (Excel.Application)application;
            break;
        case "Microsoft Word":
            wd = (Word.Application)application;
            break;
        default:
            break;
    }
}
```

Clearly, because we'll only ever be running in one host at a time, only one of the two *Application* references will ever be used and the other will always be null. We can rely on this information later on when we have to distinguish which host we're running in.

6. Continue with the *OfficeHost* class. The first example of how we'll encapsulate functionality that's conditional upon the specific host application type is the *CommandBars* collection. In this case, Word and Excel both expose a *Command-Bars* property from their *Application* object, so the code is virtually identical. Of course, we've saved ourselves the effort of using late binding, at the expense of conditional code statements. This code will run faster than if we'd used late binding, and it will obviously be more maintainable. So, we'll write a read-only *CommandBars* property:

```
public CommandBars Bars
{
    get
    {
        if (xl != null)
        {
            return xl.CommandBars;
        }
        else if (wd != null)
        {
            return wd.CommandBars;
        }
        else
```

```
                {
                    return null;
                }
            }
        }
```

7. Next we'll write a new method for adding a new *CommandBarButton* to a given *CommandBar*. We won't encapsulate the *CommandBar* itself because we want to keep this component as reusable as we can, and in that context we can't predict which bar any particular solution will want to use. We can, however, compromise by making some reasonable assumptions about the new button. Specifically, we can assume:

   ❑ It is a control button.

   ❑ We'll always add the button as blank at first (and specify the *FaceId* later).

   ❑ We don't want to interoperate with VBA macros.

   ❑ We're happy for the new button to be placed at the end of the bar.

   ❑ The button is permanent on this bar.

   With these assumptions, we can write the method to take in only an *int* value for the *FaceId* that will be used, a string for both the ToolTip text and the *Tag*, and a *Click* handler delegate.

```csharp
public CommandBarButton AddBarButton(CommandBar bar,
    int faceId, string tooltipText,
    _CommandBarButtonEvents_ClickEventHandler clickHandler)
{
    object missing = Type.Missing;
    CommandBarButton button = (CommandBarButton)
        bar.Controls.Add(
        MsoControlType.msoControlButton, 1,
        missing, missing, missing);
    button.FaceId = faceId;
    button.TooltipText = tooltipText;
    button.Click += clickHandler;
    button.Tag = tooltipText;
    return button;
}
```

   Note that the *Tag* property must be set because we'll be using this add-in with Word, which identifies individual controls by their *Tag*. Excel doesn't care about the *Tag*.

8. We'll come back to the reusable *OfficeHost* class later on, to complete the functionality of the four buttons on our toolbar. For now, let's turn our attention back to the main *Connect* class. First remove the declaration of the generic *applicationObject* reference and replace it with a reference to our new *OfficeHost* class. Also declare fields for the *CommandBar* and four *CommandBarButtons*.

```
//private object applicationObject;
private OfficeHost officeHost;
private object addInInstance;
private CommandBar bar;
private CommandBarButton docButton;
private CommandBarButton pathButton;
private CommandBarButton statusButton;
private CommandBarButton helpButton;
```

9. Code the *OnConnection* method to convert the incoming generic application reference to a strongly typed *Application* reference (by wrapping it in our *OfficeHost* class). Also call the *OnStartupComplete* method in the normal way:

```
public void OnConnection(object application,
    Extensibility.ext_ConnectMode connectMode,
    object addInInst, ref System.Array custom)
{
    //applicationObject = application;
    officeHost = new OfficeHost(application);
    addInInstance = addInInst;
    if(connectMode !=
Extensibility.ext_ConnectMode.ext_cm_Startup)
    {
        OnStartupComplete(ref custom);
    }
}
```

10. Code the *OnDisconnection* to clean up our *OfficeHost*, by calling its *Dispose* method. Also call into the *OnBeginShutdown* method in the normal way:

```
public void OnDisconnection(
    Extensibility.ext_DisconnectMode disconnectMode,
    ref System.Array custom)
{
    if (disconnectMode !=
        Extensibility.ext_DisconnectMode.ext_dm_HostShutdown)
    {
        OnBeginShutdown(ref custom);
    }
    officeHost.Dispose();
}
```

11. In the *OnStartupComplete*, we'll make use of our *OfficeHost* class by getting the *CommandBars* collection. Recall that this will in turn get the *CommandBars* collection from the specific Word or Excel host application. With this collection object, we can then add a new *CommandBar* directly. We specify in the *Add* method a caption for the new bar, its position, whether it's a menu bar (false), and whether it's temporary (true). We can use the *OfficeHost* to create four new buttons, specifying their ID, ToolTip, and *Tag* name, and the delegate for the *Click* events:

```
public void OnStartupComplete(ref System.Array custom)
{
    try
```

```
        {
            CommandBars bars = officeHost.Bars;
            bar = bars.Add("Office Helper",
                MsoBarPosition.msoBarTop, false, true);
            docButton = officeHost.AddBarButton(bar, 139, "Name",
                new
                _CommandBarButtonEvents_ClickEventHandler(docButton_Click));
            pathButton = officeHost.AddBarButton(bar, 140, "Path",
                new
                _CommandBarButtonEvents_ClickEventHandler(pathButton_Click));
            statusButton = officeHost.AddBarButton(bar, 172, "Status",
                new
                _CommandBarButtonEvents_ClickEventHandler(statusButton_Click));
            helpButton = officeHost.AddBarButton(bar, 49, "Help",
                new
                _CommandBarButtonEvents_ClickEventHandler(helpButton_Click));
            bar.Visible = true;
        }
        catch(Exception ex)
        {
            MessageBox.Show(ex.StackTrace, ex.Message);
        }
    }
```

12. For good housekeeping, we should also unhook the *Click* event handlers in the *OnBeginShutdown*. Recall that this will be called either because the host application is shutting down or because the user is connecting/disconnecting the add-in via the COM Add-Ins dialog box. If we don't unhook the event handlers during a shutdown, it doesn't really matter because the entire runtime will be unloaded very soon after. On the other hand, if we don't unhook the event handlers during a disconnect, we run the risk that the add-in will remain in memory, and if the user subsequently reconnects it, we'll end up with multiple invocations to our event handlers.

```
public void OnBeginShutdown(ref System.Array custom)
{
    docButton.Click -=
        new
        _CommandBarButtonEvents_ClickEventHandler(docButton_Click);
    pathButton.Click -=
        new
        _CommandBarButtonEvents_ClickEventHandler(pathButton_Click);
    statusButton.Click -=
        new
        _CommandBarButtonEvents_ClickEventHandler(statusButton_Click);
    helpButton.Click -=
        new
        _CommandBarButtonEvents_ClickEventHandler(helpButton_Click);
    bar.Delete();
}
```

We created our bar as a temporary bar, but we still want to delete it in the *OnBeginShutdown*. If this seems like an unnecessary step, let me explain. We've created a temporary bar that will be destroyed when the host application shuts down. However, at any time prior to application shutdown the user might choose to disconnect or remove the add-in using the COM Add-Ins dialog box. When this happens, we route the code path to our *OnBeginShutdown* method, and then we can delete the bar. Otherwise, the bar would be deleted only when the host application shuts down, and not when the user disconnects the add-in.

13. Now let's go back to our *OfficeHost* to finish off the functionality behind the buttons. When the user clicks the first button, we'll return a string that corresponds to the name of the currently active Excel *Workbook* or Word *Document*. Similarly, when the user clicks the second button, we'll return the *Path*. We can implement this behavior through properties, which will be very similar in construct to the *CommandBars* property that we implemented earlier.

```csharp
public string DocumentName
{
    get
    {
        if (xl != null)
        {
            return xl.ActiveWorkbook.Name;
        }
        else if (wd != null)
        {
            return wd.ActiveDocument.Name;
        }
        else
        {
            return "";
        }
    }
}


public string DocumentPath
{
    get
    {
        if (xl != null)
        {
            return xl.ActiveWorkbook.Path;
        }
        else if (wd != null)
        {
            return wd.ActiveDocument.Path;
        }
        else
        {
            return "";
        }
    }
}
```

14. For button 3, we'll put some arbitrary text into the status bar. Word and Excel both expose a *StatusBar* property from their respective *Application* objects, but they're not quite the same.

   For Excel, we first need to find out if the status bar is in fact visible. Whatever its current visibility, we must cache this so we can reset it after we're done putting text into it. This behavior is exposed through the *DisplayStatusBar* property. Next we'll set the text into the *StatusBar* property itself. We'll pause for 3 seconds to simulate some operation before restoring the default status bar text—by setting the *StatusBar* property to *false*. It might come as a surprise that even a strongly typed property can be assigned either a *string* or a *bool* value, but don't forget that these values are converted to VARIANT values and handed on to the underlying COM object by the CLR marshaler.

   ```
   public void SetStatusText(string text)
   {
       try
       {
           if (xl != null)
           {
               bool oldStatus = xl.DisplayStatusBar;
               xl.DisplayStatusBar = true;
               xl.StatusBar = text;
               System.Threading.Thread.Sleep(3000);
               xl.StatusBar = false;
               xl.DisplayStatusBar = oldStatus;
           }
           else if (wd != null)
           {
               wd.StatusBar = text;
           }
       }
       catch (Exception ex)
       {
           MessageBox.Show(ex.StackTrace, ex.Message);
       }
   }
   ```

   For Word, we don't need to restore the default text, and we also don't need to simulate any operation. In Word, the status bar text remains until something else happens that overwrites it. Word also doesn't use the concept of restoring the default text, and it doesn't support assigning anything except a string. If you look carefully at the Word and Excel versions of the *StatusBar* property in the Object Browser, you'll see that the Excel version is typed as an object, while the Word version is typed as a string.

15. Finally, we'll implement the functionality behind the fourth button. When the user clicks this button, we'll run up the Help system for this application. Again, both the *Word.Application* and *Excel.Application* objects expose a *Help* method, and again the method is different for each. With Excel, you can pass the name of

the online help file you want to use and the ID number of the topic within that file that you want to display. If you omit the Help file parameter, you'll get the default Excel help. If you omit the ID number, you'll get the default (front page).

```
public void GetHelp()
{
    if (xl != null)
    {
        object missing = Type.Missing;
        xl.Help(missing, missing);
    }
    else if (wd != null)
    {
        object helpType = Word.WdHelpType.wdHelp;
        wd.Help(ref helpType);
    }
}
```

Word's *Help* method, on the other hand, takes only a single parameter–a predefined constant that indicates the type of help you want to display (general help topics, the About box, context-sensitive help for the currently active document, help on help, etc.).

16. The very last operation to code is to hook up the button *Click* handlers back in the *Connect* class to the new functionality in the *OfficeHost* class. These will be completely trivial because all the real work is done in the *OfficeHost* class. This is one of the purposes of building such a reusable component–the calling solution can concentrate on domain specifics instead of common plumbing:

```
private void docButton_Click(
    CommandBarButton cmdBarbutton, ref bool cancelButton)
{
    MessageBox.Show(officeHost.DocumentName);
}

private void pathButton_Click(
    CommandBarButton cmdBarbutton, ref bool cancelButton)
{
    MessageBox.Show(officeHost.DocumentPath);
}

private void statusButton_Click(
    CommandBarButton cmdBarbutton, ref bool cancelButton)
{
    officeHost.SetStatusText("Doing something...");
}

private void helpButton_Click(
    CommandBarButton cmdBarbutton, ref bool cancelButton)
{
    officeHost.GetHelp();
}
```

17. Build and test. This is how the solution should look at run time:

5.4 Add-Ins and User Controls

Office 97	✕
Office 2000	✓
Office XP	✓
Office 2003	✓

As demonstrated in Section 4.5, "Office and Managed Windows," you can develop managed windows that can be exposed as COM objects to unmanaged code, including VBA code in Office. As an alternative strategy, you can develop a managed add-in that itself makes use of managed windows. In this case, you don't have to expose the managed windows as COM objects, and life is much simpler.

The *System.Windows.Forms.UserControl* class is designed to allow developers to build reusable custom controls of their own. These custom or "user" controls can be used from Office add-ins in much the same way as the standard controls that ship with the Framework library.

In the following exercise, we'll create a managed add-in that includes two user controls. The add-in will offer the user a new command bar with two buttons. One button will display a calendar; the other will display a digital clock. Note that we will make no attempt to provide any deep integration between the Office application and the managed windows, for all the reasons discussed in Section 4.5. Instead, we'll simply display our managed windows as modal dialog boxes, which means the user will have to dismiss them before continuing to work in the application. Given the functionality of our add-in (displaying a simple calendar and clock), this is a reasonable strategy from the perspective of user experience.

For this add-in, we'll draw together a couple of the threads running through this chapter. In addition to offering managed windows, we'll also target multiple Office applications–specifically, Word and Excel. This time, however, we won't use the specific Word and Excel IAs because we won't have any functionality that is specific to either application.

> **Note**   The sample solution for this topic can be found in the sample code at <install location>\Code\Office<n>\OfficeCalendar.

Core Add-In

1. Create a new Shared Add-in project called OfficeCalendar. As you go through the wizard pages, deselect all applications except Word and Excel, enter a suitable name and description, and check the Load When The Host Application Loads check box.

2. Leave the existing declarations of the generic *applicationObject* and *addInInstance* fields as they are, and add some new class fields for the application's collection of command bars, a new custom command bar, and the buttons we'll put on it. Also add fields for the application's *System.Type* and a couple of *int* fields for caching the position of the application's main window:

```
private Office.CommandBars bars;
private Office.CommandBar calendarBar;
private Office.CommandBarButton calendarButton;
private Office.CommandBarButton clockButton;
private Type applicationType;
private int appTop;
private int appLeft;
```

3. As described in Section 5.1, "Managed COM Add-Ins," in the *OnConnection* method, conditionally call the *OnStartupComplete* method. In *OnDisconnection*, conditionally call the *OnBeginShutdown* method, and code the *OnBeginShutdown* method to delete our custom command bar.

4. In *OnStartupComplete*, we'll set up our custom command button. Declare a string for the name (used in *CommandBars* as a window caption). Then get the host application's type, and cache it. We want to cache this in a class-scoped (field) variable because we'll be using it across multiple methods—first to set up the command bar, and later to get the window position.

5. Get the host application's collection of *CommandBars*, cache it so that we can add to the collection later, and add a new command bar. Add two new buttons to the bar, and assign values to the *FaceId* and *TooltipText* properties. Also, hook up *Click* event handlers, and make the bar visible. In a previous exercise, we set up a reusable component that abstracted this behavior, and you can reuse that component here if you wish.

6. When we display our calendar and clock, we want to position them according to where the host application's window is. So we'll write a custom method to find the host application's window position and use it later in the button *Click* handlers. Call this method *GetAppPosition*. Start a *try* block, and use the previously cached application *Type* to find out which host application we're running in.

   Switch on the application's name, and use late binding to get the *Top* and *Left* properties. We have to distinguish between Word and Excel here because, although they both expose *Top* and *Left* properties, they're typed differently. For both properties, for both Word and Excel, the return type is a *variant*. However, Excel returns the *variant* set up as a *double*, and Word returns the *variant* set up as an *int*. Therefore, for Word, we can cast the return to an *int*, and assign the result to our *int* field. For Excel, we still want to assign the result to our *int* field, but we must first cast it to a *double* and then cast again to an *int*:

```csharp
private void GetAppPostion()
{
    try
    {
        string appName = (string)applicationType.InvokeMember(
            "Name", BindingFlags.GetProperty, null,
            applicationObject, null);
        switch (appName)
        {
            case "Microsoft Excel":
                appTop = (int)(double)applicationType.InvokeMember(
                    "Top", BindingFlags.GetProperty, null,
                    applicationObject, null);
                appLeft = (int)(double)applicationType.InvokeMember(
                    "Left", BindingFlags.GetProperty, null,
                    applicationObject, null);
                break;
            case "Microsoft Word":
                appTop = (int)applicationType.InvokeMember(
                    "Top", BindingFlags.GetProperty, null,
                    applicationObject, null);
                appLeft = (int)applicationType.InvokeMember(
                    "Left", BindingFlags.GetProperty, null,
                    applicationObject, null);
                break;
            default:
                break;
        }
    }
    catch (Exception ex)
    {
        MessageBox.Show(ex.StackTrace, ex.Message);
    }
}
```

7. The two *Click* event handlers will be very similar. For this first phase, just display a message box. When we've tested the main behavior of the add-in, we'll come back to these methods to add the target functionality. The *Click* handler for one of the buttons is shown here:

```csharp
private void calendarButton_Click(
    Office.CommandBarButton cmdBarbutton, ref bool cancelButton)
{
    MessageBox.Show("calendarButton_Click");
}
```

8. Build and test. The new "menu item" should appear on the Tools menu, for both Word and Excel. When you click this button, it should display the new *CommandBar* with two *CommandBarButtons*:

When you click either button, you should get a message box.

Calendar and Clock Controls

Once the main add-in functionality is tested, we'll add a calendar control and a clock control. The calendar control is very simple because there is an existing calendar control in the Visual Studio .NET Toolbox, but we need to do a bit more work for the clock control:

1. Add a new Windows Form to the project, calling it CalendarForm. In Design view, set the form's *FormBorderStyle* property to *FixedToolWindow*. (We don't want the user to be able to resize the window, and it's a small tool window, not a main form.) Recall that we want to control the position of the form, so we must set its *StartPosition* property to *Manual*.

2. Drag and drop a *MonthCalendar* control from the Toolbox onto the form. Adjust the form's size to exactly fit the control—you can do this simply by setting the *Dock* property to *Fill*.

3. In the *Click* handler for the calendar button, remove the *MessageBox* code, and instead instantiate the new *CalendarForm* and display it, offset from the host application's window position. Note that modal dialog boxes (those displayed with *ShowDialog*) need to be explicitly disposed to make sure all resources are cleaned up. When you've finished this piece, build and test.

```
private void calendarButton_Click(
    Office.CommandBarButton cmdBarbutton, ref bool cancelButton)
{
    GetAppPostion();
    CalendarForm form = new CalendarForm();
    form.Top = appTop +150;
    form.Left = appLeft +200;
    form.ShowDialog();
    form.Dispose();
}
```

4. The last piece of the puzzle is the clock control. There isn't a suitable clock control in the Toolbox by default, so we can add one of our own. Right-click the project in Solution Explorer, and select Add | Add User Control, calling the control *Clock*.

5. In Design view, change the *BackColor* property of the *Clock* control to some color of your choice. Your design guidelines probably indicate what your choice of color should be here (probably something standard like the control background), but it doesn't really matter in this exercise. To get the display updated every second, we can make use of a *Timer* control from the Toolbox. Put one of these on the *Clock* control form. (It will be invisible on the form and added to the panel for non-visual controls at the bottom of the Forms Designer window.) In the Properties window, make sure the timer is *Enabled*, and set the *Interval* property to 1000 milliseconds. This will trigger a *Tick* event every second.

6. To handle the *Tick* event, switch to the Events pane in the Properties window, and double-click the *Tick* event: this will generate code for the event handler. We'll implement this to force a repaint:

```
private void timer1_Tick(object sender, System.EventArgs e)
{
    Invalidate(this.Region);
    Update();
}
```

7. We've set up our control to repaint itself every second, so we can now code the paint behavior to display a simple digital clock. Override the *OnPaint* method, and make a call to the base *OnPaint*. Then format a string based on the current time, and draw it using an appropriate font:

```
protected override void OnPaint(PaintEventArgs e)
{
    base.OnPaint(e);
    Rectangle r = this.ClientRectangle;
    Font f = new Font("Arial", 24);
    SolidBrush b = new SolidBrush(Color.AliceBlue);
```

```
        DateTime dt = DateTime.Now;
        string s = String.Format("{0:00}:{1:00}:{2:00}",
            dt.Hour, dt.Minute, dt.Second);
        e.Graphics.DrawString(s, f, b, r);
    }
```

8. To make use of this *Clock* control in our add-in, we need to add another Windows Form. Call this one *ClockForm*. Size it appropriately, and set its *StartPosition* property to *Manual*. You should find that the *Clock* control has been added to the Toolbox, so you can drag and drop it onto the new form. As before, set its *Dock* property to *Fill*.

9. In the *Click* handler for the calendar button, remove the *MessageBox* code, and instead instantiate the new *ClockForm* and display it, offset from the host application's window position.

```
private void clockButton_Click(
    Office.CommandBarButton cmdBarbutton, ref bool cancelButton)
{
    GetAppPostion();
    ClockForm form = new ClockForm();
    form.Top = appTop +150;
    form.Left = appLeft +200;
    form.ShowDialog();
    form.Dispose();
}
```

10. Build and test. This is how the solution should look at run time:

You can extend the behavior in many ways to offer useful additional functionality. For instance, you can copy the current date and/or time to the clipboard or to the current Excel cell or Word range.

Note that the Tools folder includes a Visual Studio .NET solution with full source code for a managed COM Office add-in that creates a custom *CommandBar* to display all the available button faces in the currently running version of Office (ButtonFaces.sln). The design of this tool is an extension of this Office-Calendar project:

5.5 Tactical Add-In Issues

Office 97	✗
Office 2000	✓
Office XP	✓
Office 2003	✓

In Chapter 2, "Basics of Office Interoperability," we saw how the mismatch between COM deterministic object lifetime management and .NET garbage collection can give rise to some interesting problems. We also saw how we could resolve these problems through the judicious use of standard .NET class methods such as *GC.Collect* and *Marshal.ReleaseComObject*.

In the context of COM add-ins, a number of other issues arise from the combination of managed and unmanaged code. These issues can be divided into two broad categories: tactical and strategic. We'll be looking in depth at the strategic issues in Chapter 8, "Isolating Managed Extensions," because the same issues apply to managed COM add-ins, managed smart tags, and managed RealTime Data components. Here we'll focus on some tactical issues. These are essentially implementation details rather than design issues:

- Scoping of command UI artifacts such as command bar buttons and the resultant effect on *Click* event handlers
- Custom button images
- Soft and hard disabling of managed COM add-ins

In the following exercise, we'll create a simple managed COM add-in that offers two custom command bar buttons. We'll create the images for these two buttons in two different ways and explain the pros and cons of each. We'll also identify the scoping issue and use our simple add-in to explore the "soft" and "hard" disabling scenarios.

 Note The sample solution for this topic can be found in the sample code at <install location>\Code\Office<n>\ButtonImage.

Command UI Object Scoping

In this first phase, we'll concentrate on setting up a custom command bar and custom command bar buttons correctly. We'll use predefined images from the Office DLLs. In the second phase, we'll change these using custom images.

1. Create a new Shared Add-in project called ButtonImage. As you go through the wizard pages, deselect all applications except one—it doesn't really matter which one because we won't be doing anything specific to any host application. Enter a suitable name and description, and check the Load When The Host Application Loads check box.

2. Leave the existing declarations of the generic *applicationObject* and *addInInstance* fields as they are—we won't do anything that requires the use of the host application's object model. We'll create a custom command bar and put two buttons on it. Declare class fields for the references to all three of these objects. We need the buttons to have class scope so the *Click* event handlers function correctly. We need the bar to have class scope so we can delete it in the *OnBeginShutdown* method. After we've set this up correctly, we can experiment with the declarations to confirm that we do indeed need this level of scoping, but for now let's just get everything working correctly.

   ```
   private CommandBar customBar;
   private CommandBarButton customButton1;
   private CommandBarButton customButton2;
   ```

3. As described in Section 5.1, in the *OnConnection* method, after the initialization of the two standard fields, conditionally call the *OnStartupComplete* method. In *OnDisconnection*, conditionally call *OnBeginShutdown* method, and code *OnBeginShutdown* to clean up our custom command bar.

4. In *OnStartupComplete*, we'll set up our custom command bar and buttons. Declare three strings for the names. Get the host application's collection of bars, and add a new bar. Add two new buttons to the bar, specifying arbitrary *FaceId* values to use predefined Office button images. As always, specify a *Caption* and *Tag*, and hook up corresponding *Click* event handlers:

   ```
   public void OnStartupComplete(ref System.Array custom)
   {
       string barName = "MyBar";
       string buttonName1 = "MyButton1";
       string buttonName2 = "MyButton2";

       try
       {
           Type applicationType = applicationObject.GetType();
           CommandBars bars = (CommandBars)applicationType.InvokeMember(
               "CommandBars", System.Reflection.BindingFlags.GetProperty,
               null, applicationObject, null);
           customBar = bars.Add(barName,
   ```

```
                            MsoBarPosition.msoBarTop, false, true);
                        object missing = Type.Missing;
                        customButton1 = (CommandBarButton) customBar.Controls.Add(
                            MsoControlType.msoControlButton, 1, missing,
                            missing, true);
                        customButton1.FaceId = 59;
                        customButton1.Caption = buttonName1;
                        customButton1.Tag = buttonName1;
                        customButton1.Click +=
                            new _CommandBarButtonEvents_ClickEventHandler(button1_Click);

                        customButton2 = (CommandBarButton) customBar.Controls.Add(
                            MsoControlType.msoControlButton, 1, missing,
                            missing, true);
                        customButton2.FaceId = 330;
                        customButton2.Caption = buttonName2;
                        customButton2.Tag = buttonName2;
                        customButton2.Click +=
                            new _CommandBarButtonEvents_ClickEventHandler(button2_Click);
                        customBar.Visible = true;
                    }
                    catch (Exception ex)
                    {
                        MessageBox.Show(ex.Message);
                    }
                }
```

5. Code both *Click* event handlers to do something simple like displaying a message:

```
private void button1_Click(
    CommandBarButton cmdBarbutton, ref bool cancelButton)
{
    MessageBox.Show("button1_Click");
}
```

6. Build and test. We've been careful to scope the references to the command bar and buttons at class level. In this way, these references will stay alive as long as the *Connect* class itself stays alive. In the case of the bar, the reasoning is obvious—we need to be able to work with the bar across both the *OnStartupComplete* method and the *OnBeginShutdown* method. The case for making the buttons class-scoped is less obvious because we're using them directly only in *OnStartupComplete*.

    In the interests of experimentation, you can comment out the field declarations for the button references and declare variables local to the *OnStartupComplete* method instead. When you build and test again, you should find that the button *Click* events are handled the first few times and then no more. Exactly how many times will vary. The button object will stay alive as long as there is at least one live reference to it. If we have only a method-scoped reference, it will go out of scope and be available for garbage collection at the end of the method. This means that at some indeterminate point after *OnStartupComplete* returns, the button object will be garbage collected. At any time after that, when the user clicks the button, our event handler will no longer be hooked up. When you're satisfied that this is indeed the behavior, you should change the code back again so that the event handlers function correctly.

Button Images

Now we'll turn our attention to the button images. We'll replace the standard predefined images with custom images. You can actually set up custom button images in two ways. The first approach is the simpler of the two but offers a less-than-perfect user experience. The second approach takes a little more work but is a more complete solution.

Before we can write the code to work with the images, we need to have some images. The best way to work with images is to build them into the assembly as embedded resources. When you develop a Windows Forms application, the wizard generates all the necessary resource files for you, making it relatively easy to embed image resources—whether they're icons, bitmaps, or images in image lists. Because we're developing a COM add-in, not a Windows Forms application, we have to do a little more work.

We need to create a resource file, insert some graphical images into it, add the resource file to the project, and embed it when we build the assembly. This will allow us to work with the images programmatically at run time. The most convenient way to create a resource file is to use the ResEditor tool, which ships with Visual Studio .NET as a tutorial sample. You'll find the source code in the install location for Visual Studio, which will be somewhere like this:

C:\Program Files\Microsoft Visual Studio .NET 2003\SDK\v1.1\Samples\ Tutorials\resourcesandlocalization\reseditor

You need to build the ResEditor sample so that we can use it as a tool in the ongoing ButtonImage project. When you've built it, launch ResEditor. This starts with an empty list ready for you to add resources. In the Add drop-down list box, select System.Drawing.Icon. Type **Icon1**, and click the Add button. This adds a blank icon to the resource file. Click the Browse button next to this, and navigate to an external .ico file. This can be any .ico file—the data from the file is copied into the resource file, and the original .ico file is not affected in any way, nor is any path information stored. Repeat this process for a second icon:

1. Go to File | Save As, navigate to the project folder for the ButtonImage project (where the .cs source files are). Type the name **IconImages**, and select the ResX type to save the file.

2. Now that we've created a resources file, we need to incorporate it into our project. Back in the ButtonImage project, in Solution Explorer, right-click the project, select Add | Add Existing Item, and select the IconImages.resX file. In the Properties window, you can see that by default the Build Action for this is set to Embedded Resource. This will build the resources—including the icon images—into the assembly.

3. Now back to the code. Change the code that sets the *FaceId* for both buttons to assign 0 in both cases. Then add a call to the custom method that we'll write to set up the custom image. We'll have two methods, one for each approach. The first uses the clipboard and the second uses the *AxHost* class, so name the methods accordingly:

```
    //customButton1.FaceId = 59;
    customButton1.FaceId = 0;
SetButtonImageFromClipboard();
    ...
    //customButton2.FaceId = 330;
    customButton2.FaceId = 0;
SetButtonImageFromAxHost();
```

4. For the first approach, we'll use the clipboard, an icon resource, and the *Icon* class. To use the *Icon* class, you must add a reference to the System.Drawing.dll and a namespace *using* statement. You also need a *using* statement for the *System.Resources* namespace because we'll be using the *ResourceManager* class. In

the new method, create a *ResourceManager* object—this is used to work with the embedded resources. In the constructor, we need to specify the name of the embedded resources, prefixed with the name of the current assembly.

Use the *ResourceManager* to extract the first icon image, specified by name. Then add the icon to an *ImageList*. We need to do this because we want to put the image into the clipboard, which supports many formats, including the graphical format represented by the *Image* class. Then we can paste the contents of the clipboard into the button by using the *PasteFace* method:

```
private void SetButtonImageFromClipboard()
{
    ResourceManager resourceManager = new ResourceManager(
        "ButtonImage.IconImages", this.GetType().Assembly);
    Icon iconResource = (Icon)resourceManager.GetObject("Icon1");
    ImageList imageList = new ImageList();
    imageList.Images.Add(iconResource);
    Clipboard.SetDataObject(imageList.Images[0], true);
    customButton1.PasteFace();
}
```

Note that while this approach is simple, we're overwriting the contents of the clipboard to transfer our icon image from the resources part of the assembly into the button. This is not ideal—if you want to use this approach, you should first check to see if there's anything in the clipboard before overwriting it.

5. You can build and test at this point. You should find that the first button has our custom image (and the second button has a blank image). Of course, both buttons should still be operational.

6. For the second approach, we won't use the clipboard. Instead, we'll present a more sophisticated technique that uses the *AxHost* class. We'll also use the *Picture* property of the *CommandBarButton* class. Note that although this property exists in the Office 2000 IAs, it was not fully supported until Office XP, so it will not work with Office 2000.

   The *AxHost* class is used by the AxImp tool to wrap ActiveX controls and expose them as Windows Forms controls. Crucially, for our purposes, it offers a method called *GetIPictureDispFromPicture*. This method takes in an *Image* and converts it to an *IPictureDisp*. We need an *IPictureDisp* because that's the type of the *Picture* property exposed by the *CommandBarButton* class. So we'll use *AxHost* to convert our icon resource into an *IPictureDisp* so that we can assign it to the button.

   IPictureDisp is an interface defined in the stdole type library and IA. Therefore, we need to add a reference to it. You'll find the stdole IA listed on the .NET tab in the Add Reference dialog box.

7. So far, so good. The next issue is that the *GetIPictureDispFromPicture* method is a protected static in the *AxHost* class. Being static is not a problem, but because

it is protected we can access it only from a class derived from *AxHost*. What we have to do is write a class that derives from *AxHost*—we can then write a custom method that internally calls *GetIPictureDispFromPicture*. We can make this class either public or internal to the *Connect* class. Be sure to initialize the base class (that is, *AxHost*) with null—this is where you'd specify the ActiveX control if you were using *AxHost* to wrap an ActiveX control.

```
internal class ImageConverter : System.Windows.Forms.AxHost
{
    private ImageConverter() : base(null)
    {
    }

    public static stdole.IPictureDisp Convert(Image image)
    {
        return (stdole.IPictureDisp)
            AxHost.GetIPictureDispFromPicture(image);
    }
}
```

8. Now that we've set up our image-converter class, we can go ahead and write the new method to extract the icon resource and set the converted image into the button. We start off in the same way as with our previous method—that is, we create a *ResourceManager* to get the icon from the resources. As before, we'll add the icon to an *ImageList*. In this way, we can pass it as an *Image* to our *ImageConverter*. Finally, assign the converted image to the *Picture* property of the button:

```
private void SetButtonImageFromAxHost()
{
    ResourceManager resourceManager = new ResourceManager(
        "ButtonImage.IconImages", this.GetType().Assembly);
    Icon iconResource = (Icon)resourceManager.GetObject("Icon2");
    ImageList imageList = new ImageList();
    imageList.Images.Add(iconResource);
    customButton2.Picture = ImageConverter.Convert(imageList.Images[0]);
}
```

9. Build and test. This is how the solution should look at run time:

Add-In Disabling

A COM add-in can become disabled in two ways. You can think of these as "soft" and "hard" disabling, as described in Table 5-4.

Table 5-4   Add-In Disabling Scenarios

Disabling	Scenario	Description
Soft	User selection in the COM Add-Ins dialog box.	The user can disable a COM add-in by deselecting the check box for that add-in. This doesn't remove the add-in; it merely disables it. This is translated and persisted as the *LoadBehavior* registry value.
	A COM add-in returns a failure HRESULT from its constructor or from the *OnConnection* method.	The Office host resets the *LoadBehavior* bit to Disconnected. For example, if the *LoadBehavior* value was originally 3 (load on startup, and connected), under these failure conditions it is reset to 2 (load on startup, but disconnected). Unhandled managed exceptions are considered "soft" failures because they are converted into E_EXCEPTION return codes by the .NET runtime's COM interop layer.
Hard	A COM add-in causes the host to crash.	This can happen if the host application crashes during the initialization of an add-in.
	During add-in development, the developer resets the debuggee while execution is in the add-in's constructor or in the *OnConnection* method.	Office applications interpret this as a crash.

Before an add-in is called into, its associated file name is added to a blacklist. If the add-in crashes before returning to the host Office application code, that entry isn't removed. In the case of a managed add-in, the only file name that Office knows about is mscoree.dll. So if one managed add-in dies and gets blacklisted, on next startup every managed add-in is flagged as being blacklisted, and even though the information is still in the registry, the add-in is not loaded.

Each application's disabled list is separate. If an add-in crashes in Word, this doesn't automatically disable the add-in in Excel (although, of course, the same add-in might well crash in Excel also). Different registry keys are used for each application. They are all under HKEY_CURRENT_USER–that is, the disabled list is a per-user setting. You'll find them in a location such as:

HKCU\Software\Microsoft\Office\<version>\<App>\Resiliency\DisabledItems

For example:

HKCU\Software\Microsoft\Office\11.0\Excel\Resiliency\DisabledItems

This is where all disabled item entries are stored, not just add-ins. The name of the registry entry is determined at the time the entry is created (it actually uses *GetTickCount*)—that is, the name is unpredictable. Furthermore, the entry is of type REG_BINARY because the data is actually a dumped memory type. For an add-in, this entry will contain in Unicode "mscoree.dll" as well as the *FriendlyName* (present in the registry) of the blacklisted component. This data is at the end of the entry—it also contains other values to tell the host application what kind of component it is, whether the user needs to be prompted about it at next startup, and so on.

"Hard" disabling overrides "soft" disabling. That is, if an add-in has been hard-disabled, it will be listed as disconnected in the COM Add-Ins dialog box. If you attempt to reconnect it using this dialog box, this will have no effect. You can re-enable hard-disabled add-ins from the Disabled Items dialog box (or by manually editing the registry, although this approach is generally discouraged).

Recall that when you register a managed add-in, the primary entry in the registry points to mscoree.dll (the .NET runtime). Therefore, if a managed add-in crashes its host application (for example, Excel), mscoree.dll is disabled for that particular application (in this example, Excel). This means that *all* managed add-ins are disabled for Excel for this user. Let's experiment a little with these concepts by deliberately causing our add-in to fail:

1. First we'll cause a soft disable. We can easily do this by throwing an uncaught exception in the *Connect* constructor or in the *OnConnection* method:

   ```
   public Connect()
   {
       throw new Exception("foo");
   }
   ```

2. Build and test. Although we're not catching the exception in our code, it will get caught and swallowed up by the host application. The result will be that the add-in is disabled. You can confirm this in the COM Add-Ins dialog box.

3. When you're satisfied with the soft-disabling behavior, remove the exception code and re-enable the add-in (via the COM Add-Ins dialog box). Test again to make sure everything is back to normal working order.

4. Next we'll cause the host to crash during startup. Rather than deliberately entering code that will cause the host to crash, we'll display a message box in the *Connect* constructor (or in the *OnConnection* method), and while the application is paused we'll terminate the debug session.

   ```
   public Connect()
   {
       //throw new Exception("foo");
       MessageBox.Show("foo");
   }
   ```

5. If you terminate the debug session while the host application is blocked, displaying the message box, the host will interpret this as a crash. The add-in that was executing at the time will be entered in the list of add-ins that failed to start correctly for this host application in the registry. This will be under HKCU\Software\Microsoft\Office\11.0\<app>\Resiliency\StartupItems:

6. Next time you start the host application, you'll see a dialog box prompting you to disable the add-in.

7. If you choose not to disable the add-in, the entry will be cleared from the *StartupItems* list in the registry, and the host application will attempt to load the add-in again. On the other hand, if you choose to disable the add-in, it will be entered in the *DisabledItems* key in the registry for this host and will not be loaded. This will be under HKCU\Software\Microsoft\Office\11.0\<app>\Resiliency\DisabledItems.

8. To re-enable a disabled add-in, you can go to the Help menu, select About, and then click the Disabled Items button:

As you can see, the disabled add-in is listed with the name used to register it and the path to the registered binary. Of course, for managed add-ins this binary will be mscoree.dll. This explains why disabling one managed add-in disables all managed add-ins for that host application, for the current user. To re-enable the add-in, select it from the list and click Enable.

5.6 COM Add-Ins as Cell Functions

Office 97	✗
Office 2000	✓
Office XP	✓
Office 2003	✓

Excel XP cannot call a function directly in a COM add-in from a worksheet cell formula. However, you can create a VBA wrapper for the COM add-in function so that the function may be called indirectly. By setting the Object property of your COM add-in, you can enable VBA code in Office applications to access the public functions of the COM add-in by way of the *COMAddins* collection of the application. The Office object model exposes the *COMAddins* collection of *COMAddin* objects, each of which exposes an *Object* property.

In the following exercise, we'll explore how to call a function in a managed COM add-in from a cell in an Excel worksheet.

Note   The sample solution for this topic can be found in the sample code at: <install location>\Code\Office<n>\TempConvAddin.

Managed COM Add-In

1. First create a new Extensibility Project, a Shared Add-in. Type TempConvAddin as the name of the add-in. In the Extensibility Wizard, select a C# project. On page 2, deselect all the boxes except the one for Excel. On page 3, provide a suitable FriendlyName and Description for the add-in. On page 4, select all of the

available options—that is, the add-in should load when the host application loads, and it should be available to all users of this machine.

2. In the *OnConnection* method, we're passed an object called *addInInst* that represents this instance of the add-in. Although typed as a *System.Object*, this is in fact a *Microsoft.Office.Core.COMAddin* object. We must set the *Object* property of this parameter to the current object so we can later retrieve it in another COM add-in or directly from VBA code. Although it might seem strange to set the value of a property in an incoming parameter, don't forget that this parameter is actually a reference type.

```
((Microsoft.Office.Core.COMAddIn)addInInst).Object = this;
```

3. Also expose a custom interface called *ITemperatureConversion*, and *Guid* attribute it:

```
[Guid("AA244A6A-E4F5-4ae1-8094-193B467330B6")]
public interface ITemperatureConversion
{
    double F2C(double val);
    double C2F(double val);
}
```

4. For simplicity, we'll make our wizard-generated *Connect* class double up to implement our custom *ITemperatureConversion* interface as well as the standard *IDTExtensibility2* interface:

```
[GuidAttribute("41A4EF7C-77D1-4368-8981-C521C072E6A5"),
    ProgId("TempConvAddin.Connect")]
public class Connect :
    Object, Extensibility.IDTExtensibility2,
    ITemperatureConversion
{
```

5. Code the interface methods appropriately:

```
public double F2C(double val)
{
    return ((5.0/9.0) * (val - 32.0));
}

public double C2F(double val)
{
    return ((val * (9.0/5.0)) + 32.0);
}
```

6. Build the managed COM add-in project.

Excel Client

1. Run Excel and open a new worksheet. Go to Tools | Macro to open the Visual Basic Editor. Go to Tools | References, and add a reference to the managed *TempConvAddin* type library (that is, the CCW). We don't need to instantiate any

objects from this CCW because it will be loaded for us as any other (startup-loaded) COM add-in. However, we do need to declare variables of types defined in the type library.

2. In the Project Explorer pane, right-click the project and insert a new module. Add code to the module to define VBA functions that wrap calls to the CCW for the managed component:

```
Option Explicit

Public Function F2CWrapper(val As Double) As Double
    Dim c As TempConvAddin.ITemperatureConversion
    Set c = Application.COMAddIns.Item( _
        "TempConvAddin.Connect").Object
    F2CWrapper = c.F2C(val)
    Set c = Nothing
End Function

Public Function C2FWrapper(val As Double) As Double
    Dim c As TempConvAddin.ITemperatureConversion
    Set c = Application.COMAddIns.Item( _
        "TempConvAddin.Connect").Object
    C2FWrapper = c.C2F(val)
    Set c = Nothing
End Function
```

3. In the worksheet, put some arbitrary values in two of the cells (cells A2 and C4 in the following screenshots). We'll convert one of these from Fahrenheit to Celsius, and the other from Celsius to Fahrenheit. In the adjacent cells (A4 and C2), put cell formulas to call the two VBA wrapper functions:

4. Note that there is a slight issue with our choice of names for our methods. While Excel is perfectly happy to resolve the name *F2CWrapper* to our VBA method, it gets confused about the name *C2FWrapper*. Specifically, it tries to interpret this as a cell reference instead of a method name. To help Excel resolve this correctly, we can specify the fully qualified name of the method, that is, *Module1.C2FWrapper*.

5.7 Excel Automation Add-Ins

Office 97	✖
Office 2000	✖
Office XP	✔
Office 2003	✔

Automation add-ins were introduced for Excel starting with Excel XP. They are not available for other Office products because the whole point of Automation add-ins is to allow you to develop custom functions that can be called directly from cells in Excel worksheets.

Some confusion exists about what COM add-ins and Automation add-ins are. Many people know that Automation is a technology that is essentially an extension of COM. All Automation servers are, by definition, also COM servers (although the reverse is not true). In the context of Office add-ins, the terms "Automation" and "COM" have more tightly constrained meanings. An Excel Automation add-in can also be an Office COM add-in, but it doesn't have to be.

COM add-ins must be in-process COM servers that support the *IDTExtensibility2* interface; however, Automation add-ins can be in-process or out-of-process COM servers, and implementation of *IDTExtensibility2* is optional. An Automation add-in that implements *IDTExtensibility2* can be loaded in the Excel user interface through both the COM Add-Ins dialog box and the Add-Ins dialog box. Table 5-5 describes the behavior of an Automation add-in based on whether it is loaded in one or both of these dialog boxes:

Table 5-5   Automation Add-In and COM Add-In Load Behavior

When Loaded	Behavior
Loaded only in the Add-Ins dialog box	The add-in is loaded on demand. Functions in the add-in might be called from formulas in a worksheet.
Loaded only in the COM Add-Ins dialog box	The add-in is loaded as a COM add-in, and its load behavior is determined from settings in the registry. Functions in the add-in cannot be called from formulas in a worksheet.
Loaded in both the COM Add-Ins dialog box and the Add-Ins dialog box	Two separate instances of the add-in are loaded. One instance is loaded as a COM add-in, and the other instance is loaded as an Automation add-in. The COM add-in instance uses the load behavior indicated in the registry; the Automation add-in instance loads on demand. The two instances work independently of one another and do not share global variables.

In the following exercise, we will use the Shared Add-ins Wizard to generate a managed COM add-in project and then enhance it so the add-in works as an Automation add-in. We will expose a couple of useful methods that can then be called from cells within a worksheet. Converting a COM add-in into an Automation add-in is almost trivial—only two enhancements need to be made.

> **Note** The sample solution for this topic can be found in the sample code at <install location>\Code\Office<n>\AutomationAddin.

1. First create a Shared Add-In project called AutomationAddin. Select only Excel as the application host, and supply a suitable name and description. Don't select either of the final check boxes—we don't want this add-in to load when the host application loads because that would load it as a COM add-in, not as an Automation add-in.

2. Once the wizard has generated the add-in project, select the setup project, and click the registry editor button. In the registry editor, create an additional subkey of HKEY_CLASSES_ROOT named CLSID, and leave all properties at their defaults. Create another new key as a child of CLSID, with the GUID of the *Connect* class, delimited with braces—for example, {883C1BBA-F8B8-4B85-B7BF-51DB55773A6C}. Set the *AlwaysCreate* property to *True*. Create a final key as a child of this GUID key, named Programmable. This needs no value. Set the *AlwaysCreate* property to *True* for this key also.

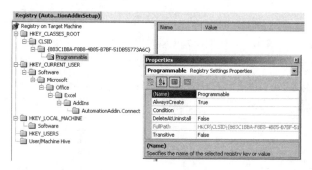

3. The *Connect* class is already attributed with a *Guid* and *ProgId*. Add a third attribute for *ClassInterface*, specifying *AutoDual* as the type. Using *AutoDual* class interfaces is normally discouraged because such interfaces allow clients to bind to a specific interface layout that might change as the class evolves, thereby breaking the client. Instead of using class interfaces, you should normally define a custom interface explicitly. This is the approach we took in Section 4.2, "Managed CCW in VBA."

   You should use class interfaces only if you understand the limitation. One crucial result of using an *AutoDual* class interface is that type information is produced for the interface and published in a type library, and the type library is registered. This is essential for an Automation add-in.

```
[GuidAttribute("883C1BBA-F8B8-4B85-B7BF-51DB55773A6C"),
ProgId("AutomationAddin.Connect"),
ClassInterface(ClassInterfaceType.AutoDual)]
public class Connect : Object, Extensibility.IDTExtensibility2
{
```

4. Add some arbitrary public methods that will be used as worksheet cell functions in Excel. For example, add methods for converting between Fahrenheit and Celsius:

```
public double F2C(double val)
{
    return ((5.0/9.0) * (val - 32.0));
}

public double C2F(double val)
{
    return ((val * (9.0/5.0)) + 32.0);
}
```

Note that these method names are reasonable (although somewhat curt), and they have been chosen for a reason, which will be explained shortly.

5. Change the add-in project properties—*Configuration Properties, Debugging, Start Application*—to launch Excel instead of Visual Studio. Then build the add-in project.

6. Recall that when you generate a Shared Add-in project, two sets of registry entries are made. The entries that register the add-in as an add-in are made when the project is first created—but only on the development machine, of course. The standard COM registration entries are made when you build the project because the build runs RegAsm. However, neither of these operations will add the CLSID registry entry that we need under HKEY_CLASSES_ROOT. We've added this information to the setup project so that it will be registered when you run the setup MSI. Therefore, to properly test this add-in on the development machine, you have to build the setup project and install it. The only alternative is to manually edit the registry, but that's generally discouraged, and you have to test the setup anyway.

7. When you've built the add-in, built the setup, and installed it, you can test it. In Excel, go to Tools | Add-ins to get the list of Automation add-ins. Click the Automation button to get a list of all programmable Automation servers registered on the machine. Select your add-in component from the list, and click OK. If you get the message "Cannot find add-in 'mscoree.dll'. Delete from list?," click No.

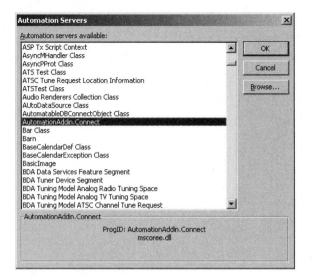

8. Back in the Add-Ins dialog box, the new Automation add-in should be listed. Close the dialog box.

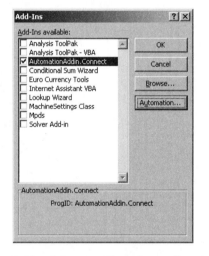

9. In Excel, in any cell, make a call to the *F2C* method exposed by our Automation add-in to convert from Fahrenheit to Celsius:

Recall that the *F2C* and *C2F* method names were carefully chosen to highlight an issue that arises with any custom cell function that you build, whether or not it is implemented through a managed Automation add-in. You should find no problems using the *F2C* method. However, when you try to use the *C2F* method, Excel will decide that you really intended to type in the cell reference *CF2*.

10. To avoid this situation, you need to enter the fully qualified method name—that is, the name of the class that implements the method (including the namespace), followed by the method name, with dot separators. In this case, we need to use the name *AutomationAddin.Connect.C2F*.

11. When you press Enter, Excel renders the function call in single quotes. Note, however, that you can't enter it using this syntax—you have to use the fully qualified name.

Of course, you can avoid all this by simply choosing a method name that doesn't confuse Excel in the first place. The problem is that cell function names are traditionally very short—for good reason, because the user doesn't want to spend a long time typing a cell function name. Another issue, of course, is being careful not to choose a name for your custom method that conflicts with an existing in-built function name (or indeed, the name of any XLL add-in function).

Summary

In this chapter, we considered the range of technologies loosely labeled as add-ins, and then rapidly focused on developing managed COM add-ins. Visual Studio .NET supports the creation of managed COM add-ins through a standard Shared Add-ins project type. This generates skeleton code for the required implementation of the *IDTExtensibility2* interface, which the Office applications talk to when an add-in is hosted.

We've worked through a number of simple managed add-in projects, targeting the range of Office host applications. Not surprisingly, the basic mechanics of getting your code to talk to an Office host are essentially the same across all hosts. This is because the *IDTExtensibility2* interface and the command UI (command bars, buttons, and controls) are shared across Office applications. There's clearly scope for abstracting out this commonality into a set of reusable components, and indeed for establishing an Office add-in service layer.

When working generically in a host-agnostic manner, the standard approach is to use the common IAs (Extensibility and Office) in a strongly typed manner. You can combine this with the use of late binding to access the native object model of the host application, while at the same time retaining the host-agnostic nature of the code. The classes in the *System.Reflection* namespace are used for this purpose.

A common requirement for Office-based solutions is to provide additional windows, dialog boxes, and controls to enrich the user experience and to customize the host application for use in a specific business workflow. You can achieve this easily with managed COM add-ins because the add-in itself can run up whatever managed controls and windows you choose to build into it. Limitations exist, however, in the degree of user interaction supported across managed and unmanaged windows, and a production-quality system needs to pay careful attention to threading issues.

We've already seen that when a solution combines both managed and unmanaged code, interesting issues related to the mismatch of object lifetime and memory management models can arise. They arise in the context of managed COM add-ins just as in general Automation, and we explored some of the more tactical problems and how to resolve them. In Chapter 8, we'll consider how this affects the design of your managed COM add-ins, as well as managed smart tags and managed RealTime Data components.

Finally, we worked through two approaches for using the methods exposed by a managed COM add-in as cell functions within an Excel worksheet. The first approach used an essentially vanilla managed COM add-in and a VBA wrapper. The second approach converted a vanilla managed COM add-in into an Automation add-in by virtue of a couple of minor tweaks.

Chapter 6

Smart Tags

Smart tags were introduced with Microsoft Office XP. A smart tag is an element of text (a string) in an Office document that is recognized as having custom actions associated with it. The list of elements recognized is determined by the business requirements and is completely open. For example, it might be a list of customer names, medical terms, product names or IDs, towns and cities, engineering acronyms, or financial instruments.

Smart tags enhance the power of Office with the ability to recognize the significance of a particular string and to respond with a list of possible actions. From that list, the user can select the most appropriate action based on the context. The exact nature of the actions offered is completely arbitrary—it's up to the application developer to determine the appropriate actions for each smart tag solution.

For example, if a string is recognized as a customer name, the list of actions might include querying a database or a Customer Relationship Management (CRM) system for further details, creating an e-mail to send to the customer, sending a message to a queue, or triggering a Microsoft BizTalk orchestration.

You can extend the capabilities of Office XP and Office 2003 by developing your own smart tag recognizer/action DLLs for use in Office documents. Microsoft Excel XP and Microsoft Word XP are the only Office XP applications that support smart tags. In Office 2003, smart tags are also supported in Microsoft Access and Microsoft Power-Point. Microsoft Outlook 2003 also supports smart tags when you use Word 2003 as the e-mail editor. Smart tags can also be used in the following scenarios:

- Office 2003 task panes, Microsoft Windows SharePoint Services, and Microsoft SharePoint Portal Server 2003

- Research task pane

- Microsoft Internet Explorer

One technology for building smart tag actions, the Information Bridge Framework (IBF), is a new solution model for Office 2003 that provides a declarative model for exposing information and actions from business systems that relate to phrases recognized by smart tags.

COM add-ins allow developers to extend Office by building solutions against a standard interface. Smart tags also allow developers to extend Office by building against a standard interface. In the case of COM add-ins, the interface is *IDTExtensibility2*. In the case of smart tags, the two primary interfaces are:

- **ISmartTagRecognizer**   For recognizing text that is typed into a document as a smart tag
- **ISmartTagAction**   For building a menu of possible actions and executing these actions on a particular smart tag string at the user's request

You don't have to implement both interfaces in the same DLL. If you like, you can have a recognizer DLL and then one or more action DLLs that extend a single smart tag type for different actions. Office 2003 also introduces the *ISmartTagRecognizer2* and *ISmartTagAction2* interfaces, which can be used in addition to the original pair. We'll see what extra functionality you get with these newer interfaces later in this chapter.

To build custom smart tag solutions, you must implement *ISmartTagRecognizer* and *ISmartTagAction*. As with COM add-ins, you can develop the solution using either managed or unmanaged code.

You can also build very simple smart tag solutions by writing a suitable XML file. This can be used by the Microsoft Office Smart Tag List (MOSTL) component, which implements *ISmartTagRecognizer* and *ISmartTagAction* internally. The MOSTL component reads the list of terms to be recognized in your XML file and invokes simple HTTP-based actions specified in your XML file. Clearly, this doesn't offer the sophistication of DLL-based smart tags, but it is a valid alternative for simple requirements.

A number of standard smart tags ship "out of the box" with Office. (This list varies with the Office versions, and not all are available for all languages.)

- Date actions (fdate.dll)
- Name recognizer (fname.dll) and Name actions (fperson.dll)
- Stock actions (fstock.dll)
- Place actions (fplace.dll)
- Microsoft Office Smart Tag List component (mofl.dll)

A number of "out of the box" Smart Tag Lists (that is, XML files) also ship with Office versions:

- Date recognizer (dates.xml)

- Phone recognizer (phone.xml)

- Stock recognizer (stocks.xml)

- Time recognizer (time.xml)

Notice the interesting separation of functionality between recognizer and action for both Dates and Stocks. The Date and Stock recognizers ship as Smart Tag Lists, while the Date and Stock actions ship as DLLs. This allows you to customize the lists of terms to be recognized while leveraging the same action functionality. Clearly, this is a good design feature for contexts in which the list of terms is subject to frequent change or where the terms need to support internationalization.

From a user's perspective, access to custom smart tags is managed through the Auto-Correct dialog box (Tools | AutoCorrect Options | Smart Tags tab). The exact format of the dialog box varies with the Office application.

The *ISmartTagRecognizer* interface derives from *IDispatch* and defines six read-only properties and one method, as described in Table 6-1.

Table 6-1 *ISmartTagRecognizer* Interface Members

Member	Description
ProgId	The programmatic identifier of the recognizer component
Name	A short title indicating what the recognizer does
Desc	A brief description of what the recognizer does
SmartTagCount	The number of smart tag types that the recognizer supports
SmartTagDownloadURL	The URL that is embedded in documents to let users download new or updated actions
SmartTagName	The unique identifiers of each smart tag type that the DLL supports
Recognize	Performs the recognition functionality and caches information about the recognition, which can later be used by the action component

The *ISmartTagAction* interface derives from *IDispatch* and defines 10 read-only properties and one method, as described in Table 6-2.

Table 6-2 *ISmartTagAction* Interface Members

Member	Description
ProgId	The programmatic identifier of the action component
Name	A short title indicating what the action does
Desc	A brief description of what the action does
SmartTagCount	The number of smart tag types that the DLL supports

Table 6-2   *ISmartTagAction* **Interface Members**

Member	Description
SmartTagName	The unique identifiers of each smart tag type that the DLL supports
SmartTagCaption	A caption for a smart tag type for use in the Smart Tag Actions menu
VerbCount	The total number of verbs supported by a DLL for a given smart tag type
VerbID	A unique integer identifier for a verb
VerbCaptionFromID	A caption for a smart tag type action for use in the Smart Tag Actions menu
VerbNameFromID	An identifier string for a verb not specific to any language
InvokeVerb	Performs some arbitrary functionality that corresponds to the VerbID passed in

6.1 Managed Smart Tags

Office 97	✖
Office 2000	✖
Office XP	✔
Office 2003	✔

In this section, we'll walk through the steps necessary to implement a managed custom smart tag DLL. In the sample folder is a set of JPG files—our smart tag will scan text entered in Word and Excel documents for strings that correspond to the file names of these JPGs. If we recognize a string, we'll offer the user two possible actions: to display a textual description of the item or to display the image. The images correspond to some of the items in the Northwind database Products table:

Marmalade.jpg	Schokolade.jpg	Tarte.jpg	Sauerkraut.jpg	Coffee.jpg

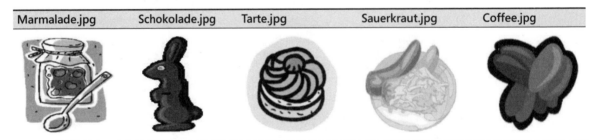

As with COM add-ins, while you're developing the custom smart tag, you should not have any Office applications running until you're ready to test the smart tag. This is because the set of smart tags available will be loaded by Office for the first Office application to run, so subsequent changes might not be picked up even if you run a different Office application.

Before you start, you should install the Smart Tag SDK (downloadable from *msdn.microsoft.com*). The Smart Tag DLLs and typelib are actually installed when you install Office. However, as a developer, it's useful to have the Smart Tag SDK installed, for the documentation, sample code, and tools. If you're targeting Office XP, you might also want to install the Advanced Smart Tag Tools, the Smart Tag Enterprise Resource Kit, and the Managed Smart Tag Shim. None of these is strictly necessary for this exercise, but all are useful to have.

The Smart Tag primary interop assemblies (PIAs) for Office XP are included in the Office XP PIAs, downloadable from *msdn.microsoft.com*. Office 2003 ships with a PIA for SmartTags, which is installed in the global assembly cache (GAC) along with all the other Office 2003 PIAs (assuming you choose to install .NET programmability support when you install or modify Office 2003).

 Note The sample solution for this topic can be found in the sample code at <install location>\Code\Office<n>\SmartTagDemo.

The Initial Project

1. To start the solution, create a new class library project called SmartTagDemo. Add a reference to the appropriate Smart Tag PIA for your version of Office.

2. When you create the new project, the Visual Studio Wizard generates a file named Class1.cs. You can safely delete this because we'll write our own classes from scratch.

3. Just as our managed smart tag code needs to be developed against an interop assembly (IA) to access the unmanaged smart tag DLL, Office will make use of our managed smart tag code only if we register it in the registry using the RegAsm.exe tool. This can be set up in Visual Studio to run as part of the build: go to Project | Properties | Configuration Properties, and set Register for COM Interop to True.

   Note that while this strategy still works in Office 2003, Office 2003 offers an alternative strategy that doesn't involve COM interop. (See Section 6.2, "Smart Tags and the VSTO Loader.")

4. Attach a *Guid* attribute at the assembly level (preferably in assemblyinfo.cs, where all the wizard-generated assembly-level attributes have been placed), set the version number to something known, and apply a strong-name keyfile:

   ```
   [assembly: Guid("64035657-17FE-4649-A02C-A377CCBE9111")]
   [assembly: AssemblyVersion("1.0.0.0")]
   [assembly: AssemblyKeyFile(@"..\..\SmartTagDemo.snk")]
   ```

Custom Action Behavior

Recall that for this exercise, we'll offer the user two possible actions: to display some text or to display a picture. To display text, we can use the standard *MessageBox* class. To display a picture, we'll create a custom dialog box. This functionality is not specific to smart tags, so we'll get this done and out of the way first.

1. Add a new Windows Form to the project, calling the file PictureDialog.cs. This will add a reference to the System.Windows.Forms.dll for you. When the user opts to show the image for a recognized string, we'll display this form. In Design view, put a *Label* control and a *PictureBox* control onto the form:

2. We won't embed our images as resources. To keep things simple, we'll just use external JPG files. (In this example, these are JPGs downloaded from the Office ClipArt library.) This approach makes it easier to move to the same design pattern as the Stock and Date smart tags use. That is, if we wanted to, we could separate out the recognizer and action behavior and put the recognizer behavior into a Smart Tag List. Having the JPGs used by the action behavior as external files allows us to keep an open-ended mapping between recognizer and action. We won't go to these lengths for this simple exercise, but you get the idea.

   When the user chooses to display a picture, we need to feed in the recognized string to work out which JPG to use. To enable this, we'll add a new public method to take in the currently recognized string. Set up a private string field to cache this:

```
private string filePath = String.Empty;

public void SetPicture(string fileName, string pathName)
{
    itemLabel.Text = fileName;
    filePath = Path.Combine(pathName, fileName +".jpg");
}
```

3. Get an event handler for the *Paint* event for the *PictureBox* control. Implement this to wrap the corresponding JPG file into a *Bitmap* object, and set this as the *Image* property of the *PictureBox* control:

```
private void itemPicture_Paint(
    object sender, System.Windows.Forms.PaintEventArgs e)
{
    if (filePath != String.Empty)
```

```
        {
            Bitmap b = new Bitmap(filePath);
            itemPicture.Image = b;
        }
    }
```

Implementing *ISmartTagRecognizer*

Now we'll turn our attention to the core smart tag functionality: implementing *ISmart-TagRecognizer* and *ISmartTagAction*.

1. Add another new class, calling the file Recognizer.cs. At the top, add a *using* statement for the *Microsoft.Office.Interop.SmartTag* namespace. For Office XP, this class needs to be COM-registered (so we need a GUID) and will implement *ISmartTagRecognizer*.

    ```
    [Guid("4EFA1F3F-A4D6-4c5b-8748-D7BAFD4CD7F6")]
    public class Recognizer : ISmartTagRecognizer
    {
    ```

2. For simplicity, we'll hardcode a string array for the names of our JPG files, so set this up as a field in the class:

    ```
    private string[] fileNames =
        {"Marmalade", "Schokolade", "Tarte", "Sauerkraut", "Coffee"};
    ```

3. We must now implement the five properties of the *ISmartTagRecognizer* interface, as indicated in the following code. First is the *ProgId*, which serves the same programmatic identification purpose as any COM *ProgId*—in this case, for our implementation of the *ISmartTagRecognizer* interface:

    ```
    public string ProgId
    {
        get
        {
            return "SmartTagDemo.Recognizer";
        }
    }
    ```

4. *SmartTagCount* is the count of the number of smart tags supported in this DLL. Based on this number, the host application will call into our *SmartTagName* property once for each smart tag supported. This is not the number of strings we recognize. Rather, it is the number of separate custom smart tag components in this DLL. It is normal to implement only one per DLL:

    ```
    public int SmartTagCount
    {
        get
        {
            return 1;
        }
    }
    ```

5. The *Desc* property is any suitable concise description of the smart tag:

```
public string get_Desc (int LocaleID)
{
    return "SmartTagDemo recognizes Northwind Groceries ";
}
```

6. The recognizer *Name* property should be friendly and can be up to 30 characters long. This string is displayed as a check box caption in the AutoCorrect dialog box in Office applications. If you don't supply a name, the recognizer is disabled.

```
public string get_Name(int LocaleID)
{
    return "SmartTagDemo Groceries Recognizer";
}
```

7. *SmartTagDownloadURL* is a URL that gets embedded in documents to allow users to download actions if they do not already have them installed for that particular smart tag. In our simple example, we won't support this, so set the return URL to a null string.

```
public string get_SmartTagDownloadURL(int SmartTagID)
{
    return null;
}
```

8. Upon initialization, if a recognizer returns, say, 3 from *SmartTagCount*, it will subsequently receive three calls to *SmartTagName*, with *SmartTagID* values ranging from 1 to 3. So, within this method, you would map the unique identifier to a corresponding string for the supported smart tag. The strings that are returned by this method must conform to the "namespaceURI#tagname" key style that defines a smart tag:

```
public string get_SmartTagName(int SmartTagID)
{
    return "Contoso/SmartTagDemo#Groceries";
}
```

9. In addition to the five properties we've just implemented, the *ISmartTagRecognizer* interface also defines one method, and this is where we do most of the work. The *Recognize* method is called and passed a text value (the string that the user has entered). We must search for recognized substrings within this text and set up the set of possible actions to offer the user. To do this, we create a property bag (an object that implements *ISmartTagProperties*) specifically for this *ISmartTagRecognizerSite* object so we can retrieve these properties later in our *ISmartTagAction* class:

```
public void Recognize(
    string Text,  IF_TYPE DataType,
    int LocaleID,  ISmartTagRecognizerSite RecognizerSite)
{
    int i;
```

```
        int startpos;
        int strlen;
        ISmartTagProperties propbag;

        int count = fileNames.Length;
        for (i = 0; i < count; i++)
        {
            startpos = Text.IndexOf(fileNames[i]) +1;
            strlen = fileNames[i].Length;
            while (startpos > 0)
            {
                // Commit the smart tag to the property bag.
                propbag = RecognizerSite.GetNewPropertyBag();
                RecognizerSite.CommitSmartTag(
                    "Contoso/SmartTagDemo#Groceries",
                    startpos, strlen, propbag);

                // Continue looking for matches.
                startpos = Text.IndexOf(
                    fileNames[i], startpos +strlen) +1;
            }
        }
    }
```

Note   Because we're keeping things simple, our string comparison is case-sensitive.

Implementing *ISmartTagAction*

The last piece of code is the action class. We'll call this class *Action*, although this name is arbitrary.

1. Add another new class, and call the file Action.cs. At the top, add a *using* statement for the *Microsoft.Office.Interop.SmartTag* namespace. As with the recognizer, for Office XP this class needs to be COM-registered, and it implements *ISmartTagAction*. We'll duplicate the hardcoded string array and set up another hardcoded string for the folder, where the JPG files reside. (Change the path according to where they are on your machine.)

    ```
    [Guid("992F12C7-9A7C-4a32-9244-332CEF8E4922")]
    public class Action:  ISmartTagAction
    {
        private string[] fileNames =
            {"Marmalade", "Schokolade", "Tarte", "Sauerkraut", "Coffee"};
        private string pathName = @"C:\ Interop\SmartTagDemo\";
    ```

2. The *ISmartTagAction* interface defines 10 properties, most of which we can implement very simply to return arbitrary strings. The *ProgId*, *SmartTagCount*, *SmartTagName*, *Desc*, and *Name* members have the same meanings as in the *ISmartTagRecognizer* interface:

```
public string ProgId
{
    get
    {
        return "SmartTagDemo.Action";
    }
}

public int SmartTagCount
{
    get
    {
        return 1;
    }
}

public string get_Desc(int LocaleID)
{
    return "Provides actions for the Groceries Smart Tag";
}

public string get_Name(int LocaleID)
{
    return " Groceries Smart Tag";
}

public string get_SmartTagName(int SmartTagID)
{
    return "Contoso/SmartTagDemo#Groceries";
}
```

3. The *SmartTagCaption* property allows you to supply a caption to be displayed on the menu for the smart tag:

```
public string get_SmartTagCaption(int SmartTagID , int LocaleID)
{
    return " Groceries Smart Tag";
}
```

4. The *VerbCaptionFromID* property allows you to supply a caption for each verb. This caption is displayed on the smart tag menu and should be a friendly string. You can opt to return null or an empty string, in which case the verb is not shown. In our example, we'll offer the user two possible actions, so we'll have two corresponding verbs:

```
public string get_VerbCaptionFromID(
    int VerbID, string ApplicationName, int LocaleID)
{
    switch(VerbID)
    {
        case 1:
            return "Show a description of this item";
        case 2:
            return "Show a picture of this item";
        default:
```

```
                return null;
        }
}
```

5. *VerbCount* should return the total number of verbs that the action handler sup-
    plies for a smart tag type:

    ```
    public int get_VerbCount(string SmartTagName)
    {
        if (SmartTagName.Equals("Contoso/SmartTagDemo#Groceries"))
        {
            return 2;
        }
        return 0;
    }
    ```

6. The *VerbID* property is a unique integer identifier for a verb. You can mix and
    match verbs for the various smart tag types they support. For example, a smart
    tag action DLL might support one verb for four smart tag types, or it might sup-
    port four variants of one smart tag verb for a smart tag type:

    ```
    public int get_VerbID(
        string SmartTagName, int VerbIndex)
    {
        return VerbIndex;
    }
    ```

7. The *VerbNameFromID* property is a language-agnostic identifier string for a verb:

    ```
    public string get_VerbNameFromID(int VerbID)
    {
        switch(VerbID)
        {
            case 1:
                return "ShowDescription";
            case 2:
                return "ShowPicture";
            default:
                return null;
        }
    }
    ```

8. The *ISmartTagAction* interface also defines one method, *InvokeVerb*, where most
    of the work is done. The method is called when a user chooses an option from
    the smart tag menu. If the user asks for a description, we'll just show a simple
    message box. If the user asks for a picture, we'll run up our custom dialog box:

    ```
    public void InvokeVerb(int VerbID,
        string ApplicationName, object Target,
        ISmartTagProperties Properties,
        string Text, string Xml)
    {
        foreach (string fileName in fileNames)
        {
            if (String.Compare(fileName, Text, true) == 0)
    ```

```
        {
            switch(VerbID)
            {
                case 1:
                    MessageBox.Show(
                        "Description: " +fileName);
                    break;
                case 2:
                    PictureDialog dlg = new PictureDialog();
                    dlg.SetPicture(fileName, pathName);
                    dlg.ShowDialog();
                    break;
            }
        }
    }
}
```

Building and Deploying

1. Finally, we'll build the project. For Office XP (which relies on you registering your DLL in the registry), our smart tag assembly must be somewhere where the COM runtime will find it. If you've left the project properties to Register For COM Interop, the RegAsm tool will have been invoked during the build of the project. This will register the assembly in the registry, including its path. Alternatively, you can put the assembly into the GAC (either from the command line with *gacutl /i* or by dragging and dropping into ...\windows\assembly). Because the smart tag solution might be used by multiple Office applications, it is reasonable to put the smart tag assembly in the GAC.

> **Note**   The alternative strategy available from Office 2003 is discussed in Section 6.2, "Smart Tags and the VSTO Loader."

2. The last step is to add two additional registry entries. You can do this interactively using RegEdit or by merging a .reg file. Sample .reg files are supplied with the sample code for this solution, for both registering and unregistering.

> **Warning**   Editing the registry incorrectly can cause serious problems that might require you to reinstall Windows. There is no guarantee that problems resulting from the incorrect use of RegEdit (including the use of .reg files) can be solved. Use RegEdit at your own risk.

3. To work with the registry interactively, run RegEdit and navigate to this key:

```
HKEY_CURRENT_USER\Software\Microsoft\Office\Common\Smart Tag\Actions
```

Add a new subkey, using the CLSID of our custom *SmartTagDemo.Action* class as the name:

```
HKEY_CURRENT_USER\Software\Microsoft\Office\Common\Smart Tag\Actions\
{992F12C7-9A7C-4a32-9244-332CEF8E4922}
```

Then navigate to this key:

```
HKEY_CURRENT_USER\Software\Microsoft\Office\Common\Smart Tag\Recognizers
```

Add a new subkey, using the CLSID of our custom *SmartTagDemo.Recognize* class as the name:

```
HKEY_CURRENT_USER\Software\Microsoft\Office\Common\Smart Tag\Recognizers\
{4EFA1F3F-A4D6-4c5b-8748-D7BAFD4CD7F6}
```

Note that while Office XP smart tags support the use of either a ProgId or a CLSID, there was a bug with that, and Office 2003 doesn't support it. So just use the CLSID throughout.

Instead of manually editing the registry, it is more sensible from a build-process and deployment perspective to script the registry changes. You can use a .reg file such as this to register the smart tag solution:

```
Windows Registry Editor Version 5.00

[HKEY_CURRENT_USER\Software\Microsoft\Office\Common\Smart Tag\Actions\
{992F12C7-9A7C-4a32-9244-332CEF8E4922}]

[HKEY_CURRENT_USER\Software\Microsoft\Office\Common\Smart Tag\Recognizers\
{4EFA1F3F-A4D6-4c5b-8748-D7BAFD4CD7F6}]
```

The corresponding .reg file to unregister the solution is shown below. The only difference between registering and unregistering is the minus sign (-) before the hive key used to unregister:

```
Windows Registry Editor Version 5.00

[-HKEY_CURRENT_USER\Software\Microsoft\Office\Common\Smart Tag\Actions\
{992F12C7-9A7C-4a32-9244-332CEF8E4922}]

[-HKEY_CURRENT_USER\Software\Microsoft\Office\Common\Smart Tag\Recognizers\
{4EFA1F3F-A4D6-4c5b-8748-D7BAFD4CD7F6}]
```

To test the solution, run Word or Excel. When the user types in one of our recognized strings, a faint underscore is displayed, along with a smart tag bullet, which drops down the Smart Tag menu. If the user chooses one of the options from our custom menu, we run up the corresponding message box or picture dialog box:

It's worth mentioning here that Excel accepts only recognitions that are the length of cell contents, whereas Word supports recognitions that are substrings. Therefore, using our smart tag demo, Excel and Word can recognize different strings, as shown in Table 6-3.

Table 6-3   String Recognition Differences Between Excel and Word

Input	Recognized?	
	Excel	Word
Tarte	✓	✓
TarteQ	✗	✓
Foo Tarte Q	✗	✓
Tarte foo Tarte bar	✓	✓

If the custom smart tag doesn't work, you can check two immediate environment settings. First, in an Office application, go to Tools | Macro | Security and relax the security level. You should do this only temporarily on the development machine, and you should reset the security level to whatever your organization mandates as soon as you can. Security issues with smart tag solutions are discussed further in Chapter 8, "Isolating Managed Extensions."

The second environment check you can make is to ensure that the custom smart tag solution is correctly registered. In an Office application, go to Tools | AutoCorrect Options | Smart Tags to make sure the custom smart tag is registered:

If this is not correct, you might need to check the registry manually using RegEdit (as described previously). If it still doesn't work, there's probably a bug in your code. In Office interop scenarios, managed exceptions often get absorbed by the interop layer or by Office itself. For further information, see Section 2.7, "Debugging Interop Solutions."

6.2 Smart Tags and the VSTO Loader

Office 97	⊗
Office 2000	⊗
Office XP	⊗
Office 2003	✓

Office 2003 extended the use of smart tags to cover not only Excel and Word, but also Access, PowerPoint, and Outlook. Several other enhancements were also made:

■ No need to register for COM Interop. Instead, the managed SmartTag assembly can be loaded using the VSTO CodeBehind loader (OTkLoadr.dll).

■ Office macro security can be set to High. A managed smart tag that leverages the VSTO loader is not subject to Office macro security checking at all.

■ Relies instead on .NET Code Access Security. Therefore, you must set up CAS policy security (in the same way as for Office 2003 VSTO CodeBehind assemblies).

■ No longer relies on direct COM interop. Your smart tag therefore doesn't need any GUIDs—in the assembly, the recognizer, or action classes. You should register the recognizer and action classes by fully qualified class name, not CLSID.

■ Optionally, you can implement *ISmartTagRecognizer2* in the recognizer class as well as *ISmartTagRecognizer*, and put the bulk of the processing in the new interface methods.

■ Optionally, you can implement *ISmartTagAction2* in the action class as well as *ISmartTagAction* and put the bulk of the processing in the new interface methods.

■ In Office XP, smart tag recognizers and actions are loaded only when an Office application is initially started. From Office 2003, you can reload smart tags without having to close and reopen the Office application. This clearly benefits users, and also developers who are iteratively developing or testing managed Smart Tag solutions.

The VSTO loader is part of Office 2003. Note that this is independent of the Visual Studio Tools for Office package, which is an extension to Visual Studio .NET 2003. However, you do need the .NET Framework version 1.1 to make use of this. It's also worth mentioning that a managed smart tag assembly loaded with the VSTO loader is loaded into a new AppDomain—not the default AppDomain, as with earlier managed smart tags. The implications of this are discussed fully in Chapter 8.

In the following exercise, we'll enhance our previous SmartTagDemo project to take advantage of the VSTO loader. The differences are as follows:

■ Don't register the assembly for COM interop, and remove any GUID attributes.

■ Add additional registry entries for the assembly path and the *Managed* value.

■ Set up Code Access Security policy to allow the assembly to execute with *Full-Trust* permissions.

> **Note**   The sample solution for this topic can be found in the sample code at
> <install location>\Code\VSTO\SmartTagDemo_otkloadr.

The Initial Project

1. Office 2003 ships with a PIA for SmartTags, which is installed in the GAC along with all the other Office 2003 PIAs (assuming you choose to install .NET programmability support when you install/modify Office 2003). To upgrade the earlier COM interop version of this exercise, remove the reference to Office XP Smart Tag PIA and replace it with a reference to the Office 2003 Smart Tag PIA. Add an appropriate namespace *using* statement at the top of the recognizer and action files.

   ```
   using SmartTagLib = Microsoft.Office.Interop.SmartTag;
   ```

2. Because we'll be using the VSTO loader, there is no need to register for COM Interop, so set the *Register for COM Interop* property to *False* in the project properties. There's also no need to have any GUIDs or ProgIDs for either the assembly itself, or for the recognizer and action classes, so comment out or delete all these attributes.

Implementing *ISmartTagRecognizer* and *ISmartTagAction*

1. For Office XP, the recognizer class needs to be COM-registered, but this is unnecessary for Office 2003 because we'll be using the VSTO loader. The class must implement *ISmartTagRecognizer* and can optionally implement *ISmartTag-Recognizer2*. We'll implement *ISmartTagRecognizer2* in a later exercise—for now, we'll just stick to our implementation of the primary *ISmartTagRecognizer* interface. The only change is to remove the *Guid* and *ProgId* attributes on the class:

   ```
   //[Guid("4EFA1F3F-A4D6-4c5b-8748-D7BAFD4CD7F6")]
   //[ProgId("SmartTagDemo.Recognizer")]
   public class Recognizer : SmartTagLib.ISmartTagRecognizer
   {
   ```

2. As with the recognizer, for Office XP the action class needs to have a GUID, but for Office 2003 this is unnecessary. The class must implement *ISmartTagAction* and can optionally implement *ISmartTagAction2*. Again, the only change is to remove the *Guid* and *ProgId* attributes:

   ```
   //[Guid("992F12C7-9A7C-4a32-9244-332CEF8E4922")]
   //[ProgId("SmartTagDemo.Action")]
   public class Action: SmartTagLib.ISmartTagAction
   {
   ```

Building and Deploying

1. Finally, we'll build the project. For Office XP, we put our smart tag assembly into the GAC, but this is unnecessary because now we're using the VSTO loader.

2. We do need to add two registry entries. Office will look for registered smart tags in a particular location. You can either run RegEdit and make the changes interactively or use a .reg file such as the one listed below (changing the path to wherever the DLL actually is on your machine).

> **Warning**   Editing the registry incorrectly can cause serious problems that might require you to reinstall Windows. There is no guarantee that problems resulting from the incorrect use of RegEdit (including the use of .reg files) can be solved. Use RegEdit at your own risk.

```
Windows Registry Editor Version 5.00

[HKEY_CURRENT_USER\Software\Microsoft\Office\Common\Smart Tag\Actions\
SmartTagDemo.Action]
"Filename"="C:\\SmartTagDemo_otkloadr\\bin\\SmartTagDemo_bin\\SmartTagDemo.dll"
"Managed"=dword:00000001
```

```
[HKEY_CURRENT_USER\Software\Microsoft\Office\Common\Smart Tag\Recognizers\Smart
TagDemo.Recognizer]
"Filename"="C:\\SmartTagDemo_otkloadr\\bin\\SmartTagDemo_bin\\SmartTagDemo.dll"
"Managed"=dword:00000001
```

This registers both the recognizer and action classes. The additional entries
required for the VSTO loader are the absolute path to the assembly and the
DWORD key *Managed*, set to 1.

For completeness, a corresponding .reg file to unregister this solution is shown
below:

```
Windows Registry Editor Version 5.00

[-HKEY_CURRENT_USER\Software\Microsoft\Office\Common\Smart Tag\Actions\
SmartTagDemo.Action]
"Filename"="C:\\SmartTagDemo_otkloadr\\bin\\SmartTagDemo_bin\\SmartTagDemo.dll"
"Managed"=dword:00000001

[-HKEY_CURRENT_USER\Software\Microsoft\Office\Common\Smart Tag\Recognizers\
SmartTagDemo.Recognizer]
"Filename"="C:\\SmartTagDemo_otkloadr\\bin\\SmartTagDemo_bin\\SmartTagDemo.dll"
"Managed"=dword:00000001
```

3. Finally, we need to set up CAS security policy. This can be done either interac-
    tively using the MsCorCfg.msc GUI utility or using the command-line (script-
    able) tool CASpol.exe. The following .cmd file will run three CASpol commands
    to set up security to allow our custom, managed smart tag to run (and pause at
    the end). Note that the first command turns off the standard policy change
    prompt, and the third one turns it on again. The first command adds a new code
    group for the folder that contains your DLL. It adds it to the *Office_Projects*
    group (and will fail if this group is not present). The second command adds a
    new code group for the DLL itself. We could achieve the desired security with
    just one code group for the DLL, but this pattern of an extra code group for the
    folder is consistent with the way VSTO projects are set up by default.

    You'll need to change the path according to where the DLL actually is on your
    machine. Also, each of the three CASpol commands should be on one line:

```
caspol -polchgprompt off -user -addgroup Office_Projects
-url C:\SmartTagDemo_otkloadr\bin\SmartTagDemo_bin\* Execution -name
"SmartTagDemo_bin"

caspol -user -addgroup "SmartTagDemo_bin" -
url C:\SmartTagDemo_otkloadr\bin\SmartTagDemo_bin\SmartTagDemo.dll FullTrust
-name "SmartTagDemo.dll"

caspol -polchgprompt on
pause
```

For completeness, a corresponding CASpol script to remove this CAS policy is listed below:

```
caspol -polchgprompt off -user -remgroup "SmartTagDemo_bin"
caspol -polchgprompt on
pause
```

4. Run Word or Excel to test. When the user types in one of our recognized strings, a faint underscore is displayed, along with a smart tag bullet—this drops down the Smart Tag menu. If the user chooses one of the options from our custom menu, we run up the corresponding message box. At runtime, the solution should look and behave the same as the previous non-VSTO-loaded version.

6.3 *ISmartTagRecognizer2* and *ISmartTagAction2*

Office 97	⊗
Office 2000	⊗
Office XP	⊗
Office 2003	✓

Office 2003 introduced a pair of additional smart tag interfaces, *ISmartTagRecognizer2* and *ISmartTagAction2*.

ISmartTagRecognizer2 is not an extension of *ISmartTagRecognizer*—rather, it is independently based on *IDispatch*. *ISmartTagRecognizer2* defines one read-only property and three methods, as shown in Table 6-4.

Table 6-4   *ISmartTagRecognizer2* Interface Members

Member	Description
PropertyPage	Provides a way to customize a smart tag recognizer to enable or disable particular features through the user interface.
SmartTagInitialize	Intended for whatever initialization you want to perform for your custom recognizer.
DisplayPropertyPage	Displays the property dialog box for the recognizer.
Recognize2	Performs the recognition functionality and caches information about the recognition, which can later be used by the action component. This can be implemented in a way that replaces the *ISmartTagRecognizer.Recognize* method.

The *ISmartTagAction2* interface derives from *IDispatch* and defines three read-only properties and two methods, as shown in Table 6-5.

Table 6-5   *ISmartTagAction2* Interface Members

Member	Description
ShowSmartTag-Indicator	Indicates whether the smart tag indicator should be shown.
IsCaptionDynamic	Determines whether a particular caption is dynamic or static.
VerbCaptionFromID2	A caption for a smart tag action for use in the Smart Tag Actions menu. This can be implemented in a way that replaces the *ISmartTagAction.VerbCaptionFromID* method.

Table 6-5   *ISmartTagAction2* Interface Members

Member	Description
SmartTagInitialize	Intended for whatever initialization you want to perform for your custom action component.
InvokeVerb2	Performs some arbitrary functionality that corresponds to the VerbID passed in. This can be implemented in a way that replaces the *ISmartTagAction.InvokeVerb* method.

A custom smart tag recognizer DLL must implement *ISmartTagRecognizer*, and it can also implement *ISmartTagRecognizer2*. Similarly, a custom smart tag action DLL must implement *ISmartTagAction* and can also implement *ISmartTagAction2*. Finally, a custom smart tag DLL that incorporates both a recognizer and action component must implement the earlier *ISmartTagRecognizer/ISmartTagAction* interfaces and can also implement the later *ISmartTagRecognizer2/ISmartTagAction2* interfaces.

A common pattern for a recognizer is to implement all the simple *ISmartTagRecognizer* properties (*ProgId*, *SmartTagCount*, *Name*, *Desc*, *SmartTagDownloadURL*, and *SmartTagName*) as before. Then implement the *Recognize* method as an empty no-op method, and instead put all the recognizer behavior into the new *Recognize2* method.

In the same way, a common pattern for an action component is to implement all the simple *ISmartTagAction* properties (*ProgId*, *SmartTagCount*, *Desc*, *Name*, *SmartTagCaption*, *SmartTagName*, *VerbCount*, *VerbID*, and *VerbNameFromID*) as before. Then implement the *VerbCaptionFromID* property to return an empty string, and the *InvokeVerb* method as a no-op method. You then put the custom behavior into the *VerbCaptionFromID2* property and the *InvokeVerb2* method.

At their simplest, the newer interfaces can have exactly the same functionality as you previously implemented for *ISmartTagRecognizer* and *ISmartTagAction* (allowing for naming differences). However, if you choose to implement these interfaces in your smart tag assemblies, you'll probably want to take advantage of their extended features. These include:

- **Dynamic captions**   In Office 2003, smart tag action menu captions can be altered at runtime. For example, the name of an action can depend on the string that has been smart-tagged.

- **Cascading menus**   In Office XP, smart tag menus support only one level of menu items—you cannot cascade or logically group menu items. In Office 2003, you have the ability to create cascading menus.

- **Tokenizer**   The tokenizer feature built into the smart tag infrastructure in Office 2003 breaks down strings, punctuation, and white space into actual words for use by the recognizer. This simplifies the development of recognizers for all languages—and especially those that do not have spaces between words, such as some East Asian languages.

In the following walk-through, we'll explore these new features. We could start from scratch, but to save time we'll copy and modify the SmartTagDemo solution from the previous example (available in the sample code).

> **Note** The sample solution for this topic can be found in the sample code at <install location>\Code\Office<n>\SmartTagDemo_otkloadr2.

Dynamic Captions

1. Take a copy of the previous SmartTagDemo_otkloadr solution (the version that uses the VSTO loader). Unregister the previous version from the registry, and remove the CAS security policy for the previous version. Clear any copies of the previous version out of the download cache, using *gacutil /cdl*.

2. For the first change, implement *ISmartTagRecognizer2* in the recognizer class:

```
public class Recognizer : SmartTagLib.ISmartTagRecognizer
    , SmartTagLib.ISmartTagRecognizer2
```

The *ISmartTagRecognizer2* interface has three methods and a property: *DisplayPropertyPage*, *get_PropertyPage*, *Recognize2*, and *SmartTagInitialize*. The first three can be implemented very simply: only the *PropertyPage* property needs any real work. (Set the return to *true*.)

```
public void DisplayPropertyPage (int SmartTagID, int LocaleID)
{
}

public bool get_PropertyPage (int SmartTagID, int LocaleID)
{
    return true;
}

public void SmartTagInitialize (string ApplicationName)
{
}
```

The fourth method, *Recognize2,* can be used to replace the older *ISmartTagRecognizer.Recognize* method. For now, simply cut and paste the code from the old method into the new method. You'll also have to make a couple of minor naming changes (from *RecognizerSite* to *RecognizerSite2*):

```
public void Recognize2 (
    string Text, SmartTagLib.IF_TYPE DataType, int LocaleID,
    SmartTagLib.ISmartTagRecognizerSite2 RecognizerSite2,
    string ApplicationName, SmartTagLib.ISmartTagTokenList TokenList)
{
    int i;
    int startpos;
    int strlen;
    SmartTagLib.ISmartTagProperties propbag;
    int count = fileNames.Length;
    for (i = 0; i < count; i++)
```

```
            {
                startpos = Text.IndexOf(fileNames[i]) +1;
                strlen = fileNames[i].Length;
                while (startpos > 0)
                {
                    propbag = RecognizerSite2.GetNewPropertyBag();
                    RecognizerSite2.CommitSmartTag2(
                        "Contoso/SmartTagDemo#Groceries",
                        startpos, strlen, propbag);
                    startpos = Text.IndexOf(fileNames[i], startpos +strlen) +1;
                }
            }
        }
    }
```

3. Change the action class to implement *ISmartTagAction2*:

   ```
   public class Action: SmartTagLib.ISmartTagAction,
       SmartTagLib.ISmartTagAction2
   ```

   ISmartTagAction2 has two methods and three properties: *SmartTagInitialize*, *InvokeVerb2*, *get_IsCaptionDynamic*, *get_ShowSmartTagIndicator*, and *get_VerbCaptionFromID2*. The first method and the first two properties are simple. (The *IsCaptionDynamic* property is what allows us to specify runtime captions for the Smart Tag menu.)

   ```
   public void SmartTagInitialize (string ApplicationName)
   {
   }

   public bool get_IsCaptionDynamic (
       int VerbID, string ApplicationName, int LocaleID)
   {
       return true;
   }

   public bool get_ShowSmartTagIndicator (
       int VerbID, string ApplicationName, int LocaleID)
   {
       return true;
   }
   ```

4. The *VerbCaptionFromID2* property can be used to replace the *ISmartTagAction.VerbCaptionFromID* property and is where we can specify runtime menu captions. The older *VerbCaptionFromID* property was passed only three parameters: *VerbID*, *ApplicationName*, and *LocaleID*. The new property is passed these three plus four more:

   ❑ The smart tag property bag. An action DLL can read, write, and modify these properties so that future action invocations can take advantage of the information.

   ❑ The text that has been recognized in the document.

   ❑ A read-only string that is an XML representation of the smart tag.

❑   A reference to the application-specific object that is responsible for calling the smart tag. In Excel, it is an Excel range object that points to the cell that the smart tag is attached to. In Word and PowerPoint, it is a range object that wraps around the block of text that the smart tag refers to. In Access, it is a control.

First cut and paste the code from the old method to the new one. Then modify it slightly to make the caption dynamic, based on the *Text* parameter supplied to us (that is, the text that was recognized in the document):

```csharp
public string get_VerbCaptionFromID2 (
    int VerbID, string ApplicationName, int LocaleID,
    SmartTagLib.ISmartTagProperties Properties,
    string Text, string Xml, object Target)
{
    switch(VerbID)
    {
        case 1:
            return String.Format("Show a description of {0}", Text);
        case 2:
            return String.Format("Show a picture of {0}", Text);
        default:
            return null;
    }
}
```

Of course, in our cutdown implementation of the old version of the property, we'll have to return some kind of string to satisfy the compiler, so just return an empty string.

5. *InvokeVerb2* is the newer equivalent of *ISmartTagAction.InvokeVerb*, so again just cut and paste the code from one to the other:

```csharp
public void InvokeVerb2 ( int VerbID, string ApplicationName,
    object Target, SmartTagLib.ISmartTagProperties Properties,
    string Text, string Xml, int LocaleID)
{
    foreach (string fileName in fileNames)
    {
        if (String.Compare(fileName, Text, true) == 0)
        {
            switch(VerbID)
            {
                case 1:
                    MessageBox.Show("Description: " +fileName);
                    break;
                case 2:
                    PictureDialog dlg = new PictureDialog();
                    dlg.SetPicture(fileName, pathName);
                    dlg.ShowDialog();
                    break;
            }
        }
    }
}
```

6. Build and test. Note that the menu captions are now dynamic:

Cascading Menus

1. Implementing cascading menus is simple. All you have to do is put three slash characters into the caption string as submenu separators. For example, you can change the code in *get_VerbCaptionFromID2* to offer an Options submenu, as shown below (including keyboard shortcut combinations):

```
switch(VerbID)
{
    case 1:
//      return String.Format("Show a description of {0}", Text);
        return String.Format(
            "&Options///Show a &description of {0} (otkloadr)", Text);
    case 2:
//      return String.Format("Show a picture of {0}", Text);
        return String.Format(
            "&Options///Show a &picture of {0} (otkloadr)", Text);
    default:
        return null;
}
```

2. Build and test.

The Tokenizer

1. The tokenizer can be used to replace tedious string parsing. To use this feature in the simplest possible manner, first find the *Recognize2* method, and comment out or delete all the code specific to string parsing. Inside the *for* loop, replace all the string-parsing code with token-processing code:

```
for (i = 0; i < namesCount; i++)
{
    SmartTagLib.ISmartTagToken token;
    int tokenCount = TokenList.Count;
    int j;
    for (j = 1; j <= tokenCount; j++)
    {
        token = TokenList.get_Item(j);
        if (fileNames[i] == token.Text)
        {
            propbag = RecognizerSite2.GetNewPropertyBag();
            RecognizerSite2.CommitSmartTag2(
                "Contoso/SmartTagDemo#Groceries",
                token.Start, token.Length, propbag);
        }
    }
}
```

2. Build and test. This should work exactly as before.

It's probably worth doing a "belt-and-braces" job and conditionally reinstating the earlier code that doesn't use a *TokenList*. If you use the *TokenList* object, it is recommended that you also trap for the case where the *TokenList* object is null or empty. This can happen if, for example, no word breaker for a particular language is installed:

```
for (i = 0; i < namesCount; i++)
{
    if (TokenList == null || TokenList.Count == 0)
    {
        int startpos = Text.IndexOf(fileNames[i]) +1;
        int strlen = fileNames[i].Length;
        while (startpos > 0)
        {
            propbag = RecognizerSite2.GetNewPropertyBag();
            RecognizerSite2.CommitSmartTag2(
                "Contoso/SmartTagDemo#Groceries",
                startpos, strlen, propbag);
            startpos = Text.IndexOf(
                fileNames[i], startpos +strlen) +1;
        }
    }
    else
    {
        SmartTagLib.ISmartTagToken token;
        int tokenCount = TokenList.Count;
        int j;
        for (j = 1; j <= tokenCount; j++)
```

```
            {
                token = TokenList.get_Item(j);
                if (fileNames[i] == token.Text)
                {
                    propbag =
                        RecognizerSite2.GetNewPropertyBag();
                    RecognizerSite2.CommitSmartTag2(
                        "Contoso/SmartTagDemo#Groceries",
                        token.Start, token.Length, propbag);
                }
            }
        }
```

Note that it's a known issue that the *TokenList* object (passed into the *Recognize2* method) and *Target* object (passed into the *InvokeVerb2* method) cause some applications (especially PowerPoint, Excel, and Access) to stay in memory. They must be aggressively released with an enforced garbage collection at the end of the method:

```
public void InvokeVerb2 ( int VerbID, string ApplicationName,
    object Target, SmartTagLib.ISmartTagProperties Properties,
    string Text, string Xml, int LocaleID)
{
// <code omitted for brevity>
    Target = null;
    GC.Collect();
    GC.WaitForPendingFinalizers();
    GC.Collect();
    GC.WaitForPendingFinalizers();
}

public void Recognize2 (
    string Text, SmartTagLib.IF_TYPE DataType, int LocaleID,
    SmartTagLib.ISmartTagRecognizerSite2 RecognizerSite2,
    string ApplicationName, SmartTagLib.ISmartTagTokenList TokenList)
{
// <code omitted for brevity>
    TokenList = null;
    GC.Collect();
    GC.WaitForPendingFinalizers();
    GC.Collect();
    GC.WaitForPendingFinalizers();
}
```

6.4 MOSTL Smart Tags

Office 97	✖
Office 2000	✖
Office XP	✔
Office 2003	✔

Instead of creating a custom smart tag DLL, you can write very simple custom smart tags by simply writing an XML file. If you then deploy this file to a well-known location, it will be picked up by Office via the Microsoft Office Smart Tag List (MOSTL) component. The MOSTL component is a generic smart tag recognizer and action handler. It implements the *ISmartTagRecognizer* and *ISmartTagAction* interfaces in a generic manner. You can use this instead of (or in addition to) writing custom smart tag DLLs. The MOSTL tool offers two main services:

- Acts as a recognizer that works with a list of terms that is maintained separately in an XML file

- Invokes HTTP-based actions associated with the recognized terms

To use this approach, you create an XML file containing the list of terms to be recognized, together with values that correspond to the properties of the *ISmartTagRecognizer* and *ISmartTagAction* interfaces. In addition, the file must correspond to the Smart Tag List schema. This schema changed between Office XP and Office 2003, although Office 2003 supports both for backward compatibility. Full details of this schema and the MOSTL tool are provided in the Smart Tag SDK, which is downloadable from the Microsoft Web site.

For some reason, there isn't a consensus on what to call XML-based smart tag solutions—you'll see them called XML smart tags, MOSTL smart tags, Smart Tag Lists, Smart Tag XML definitions, Smart Tag XML specifications, and other variations on the theme. I've decided to call them MOSTL smart tags.

MOSTL smart tags don't need to be registered in the same way that smart tag DLLs are. Instead, they are picked up by Office if they are deployed to one of the following locations:

- <drive>:\Program Files\Common Files\Microsoft Shared\Smart Tag\Lists

- <drive>:\Documents and Settings\<username>\Application Data\Microsoft\Smart Tag Lists

- The registered smart tag ListDirectory

If you deploy to the Documents and Settings folder, your smart tag will be able to roam with the user. The same is essentially true if you use a registered ListDirectory because the intention here is that the registered location for MOSTL smart tags is on some commonly accessible network server. This seems like a good idea but is not generally recommended. Office applications are not designed to be permanently connected, and although they can take advantage of network resources, it's not a good idea to tie them down in this way unless you have no alternative.

As you've seen from earlier sections in this chapter, the locations in the registry where smart tag information is kept are:

`HKEY_CURRENT_USER\Software\Microsoft\Office\Common\Smart Tag\Actions`

and:

`HKEY_CURRENT_USER\Software\Microsoft\Office\Common\Smart Tag\Recognizers`

The MOSTL component is registered in the following location, using a subkey that corresponds to its GUID:

```
{64AB6C69-B40E-40AF-9B7F-F5687B48E2B5}
```

If you wanted to register a server ListDirectory, you could create a new string value in this MOSTL GUID key, called *ListDirectory*. You would set the value of this to your server share URL:

```
Windows Registry Editor Version 5.00

[HKEY_CURRENT_USER\Software\Microsoft\Office\Common\Smart Tag\Actions\{64AB6C69-
B40E-40AF-9B7F-F5687B48E2B5}]
@=""
"ListDirectory"="\\\\Banana001\\SomeShare"

[HKEY_CURRENT_USER\Software\Microsoft\Office\Common\Smart Tag\Recognizers\{64AB6C69-
B40E-40AF-9B7F-F5687B48E2B5}]
@=""
"ListDirectory"="\\\\Banana001\\SomeShare"
```

Although this is not a recommended approach, one good reason for pointing out this registry key is so you know where the MOSTL component is registered. This information might be useful if your registry becomes corrupt and needs repairing. The key is vulnerable to corruption on a development machine simply because of the amount of registering and unregistering that you tend to perform on the *Smart Tag\Actions* and *Smart Tag\Recognizers* keys.

In the following exercise, we'll create another custom smart tag, but this time it will be a MOSTL smart tag that uses an XML file.

> **Note**   The sample solution for this topic can be found in the sample code at <install location>\Code\Office<n>\FruitBar.

1. First create a new XML file—you can do this with Notepad, or if you want color highlighting, you can use Visual Studio .NET:

```xml
<FL:smarttaglist xmlns:FL="urn:schemas-microsoft-com:smarttags:list">
    <FL:name>Fruit Terms</FL:name>
    <FL:description>A list of fruit for recognition, as well as a set
        of actions that work with them.</FL:description>
    <FL:smarttag type="urn:schemas-fruitbar-com:fruit#names">
        <FL:caption>FruitBar Inc</FL:caption>
        <FL:terms>
            <FL:termlist>Apple, Banana, Cherry, Peach, Plum</FL:termlist>
        </FL:terms>
        <FL:actions>
            <FL:action id="ItemInfo">
            <FL:caption>&amp;Item Information</FL:caption>
```

```
                <FL:url>http://localhost/fruitbar/fruitbar.aspx?name={TEXT}</FL:url>
                </FL:action>
                <FL:action id="FruitBarHome">
                <FL:caption>&amp;FruitBar Website</FL:caption>
                <FL:url>http://localhost/fruitbar/default.htm</FL:url>
                </FL:action>
            </FL:actions>
        </FL:smarttag>
</FL:smarttaglist>
```

Some of the entries in this XML file are more obvious than others. The friendly name and description will be familiar from the previous exercise. The smart tag type is defined by a unique namespace, specified as *namespaceURI#tagname*. The caption will be the caption at the top of the smart tag recognizer shortcut menu, and the list of terms is also self-evident.

We've defined two actions. The shortcut menu entries are Item Information and FruitBar Website, with automatic shortcuts indicated by the ampersand (*&*).

For the *Item Information* action, we specify a Web application URL, passing the recognized text ({TEXT}) as the parameter to the fruitbar.aspx page. For the *FruitBar Website* action, we simply specify the default.htm on the Web site. Of course, neither of these exists yet, so we must create them next.

2. In Visual Studio .NET, create a new Web application called FruitBar. The default (virtual) location will be *http://localhost/FruitBar*. When the wizard has generated the initial code, switch from the designer to the code view.

3. All we'll do is to load up a bitmap file that corresponds to the fruit name passed into the application and send this back to the client in the response stream. For simplicity, we can put all this code in the *Page_Load* method. Of course, you should change the path to where the files actually are on your machine:

```
string fruitName = Request.Params["name"];
if (fruitName != String.Empty)
{
    string imageFile =
        @"C:\Temp\OfficeInterop\Code\FruitBar\"
        + fruitName + ".jpg";
    try
    {
        Bitmap fruitImage = new Bitmap(imageFile);
        fruitImage.Save(Response.OutputStream, ImageFormat.Jpeg);
        fruitImage.Dispose();
    }
    catch (Exception ex)
    {
        Response.Write(ex.Message);
    }
    Response.End();
```

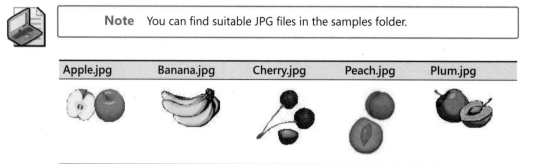

Note You can find suitable JPG files in the samples folder.

Apple.jpg	Banana.jpg	Cherry.jpg	Peach.jpg	Plum.jpg

4. Build the Web application. To test it, you can enter this URL in Internet Explorer:

   //localhost/FruitBar.aspx?name=Cherry

5. Also create a new HTML file and put some very simple text in the body. Save the file as default.htm in the FruitBar virtual directory:

```
<!DOCTYPE HTML PUBLIC "-//W3C//DTD HTML 4.0 Transitional//EN">
<html>
    <head>
        <title></title>
        <meta name="GENERATOR"
content="Microsoft Visual Studio.NET 7.0">
        <meta name="vs_targetSchema"
content="http://schemas.microsoft.com/intellisense/ie5">
    </head>
    <body>
    FruitBar Home Page
    </body>
</html>
```

6. Finally, copy or move the FruitBar.xml file into the default MOSTL XML list location: <drive>:\Program Files\Common Files\Microsoft Shared\Smart Tag\Lists. You might find a localized subfolder in this location (such as 1033). This is intended for MOSTL smart tags that are locale-specific. If your solution is not locale-specific, you should place it in the Lists parent folder itself.

   Run Word or Excel and test the new smart tags:

If you are doing a lot of MOSTL development, you might want to take advantage of the Smart Tag Enterprise Resource Kit (STERK). This is a set of tools downloadable from the Microsoft download site. It includes a MOSTL explorer tool and a tool for testing recognizers.

6.5 A MOSTL Generator

Office 97	❌
Office 2000	❌
Office XP	✅
Office 2003	✅

While custom smart tag DLLs offer open-ended flexibility, using XML lists with the MOSTL tool is more convenient. The only difficulty is in creating and maintaining the XML files. To mitigate this issue, you can create a managed COM add-in that generates a MOSTL XML file based on user input. This walkthrough describes a very simple starting point for such an add-in.

We will create an Office add-in with one custom command bar and one custom command bar button. When the user clicks the button, we'll display a managed Windows Forms dialog box to allow the user to input details of the smart tag list. We'll then write these details to an XML file in the correct format and put the file in the default location for XML lists. The initial project is a straightforward managed COM add-in, and you can refer back to Chapter 5, "Add-Ins," for a more detailed explanation of the add-in project plumbing.

 Note The sample solution for this topic can be found in the sample code at <install location>\Tools\MostlGenerator.

1. First create a new Shared Add-in Extensibility project called MostlGenerator. From the wizard choices, we'll select the C# language, both Excel and Word as host applications, some arbitrary *FriendlyName* and *Description*, and register the add-in for load on host application startup.

As usual with add-ins, we code the *OnConnection* method to call *OnStartupComplete*, and the *OnDisconnection* method to call *OnBeginShutdown*.

2. Declare a private field for the *CommandBar* that we'll add to the application's collection of bars. In *OnStartupComplete*, we'll set up our custom *CommandBar* and one button.

3. In the *Click* event handler for our button, we'll create and display our custom dialog box. (We'll write the code for this dialog box shortly.)

```
private void mostlGenerator_Click(
    Office.CommandBarButton cmdBarbutton, ref bool cancelButton)
{
    SmartTagDetailsForm form = new SmartTagDetailsForm();
    form.ShowDialog();
}
```

4. To create the dialog box, right-click the project in Solution Explorer, and select Add | Add Windows Form. Call the form SmartTagDetailsForm. In Design view, put six *Label* controls, five *TextBox* controls, a *DataGrid* control, and a *Button* control onto the form, as indicated below. For testing purposes, also put some test data into all the text boxes. Set the *Multiline* property of the Terms *TextBox* to *true*. For the *DataGrid*, set its *CaptionVisible* property to *false*:

5. In the new *SmartTagDetailsForm* class, declare a private field for a *DataTable*—this is for the smart tag Actions table, which we'll need across multiple methods:

```
private DataTable table;
```

6. In the form constructor, after the call to *InitializeComponent*, set up the *DataTable* with three columns and attach the table to the *DataGrid*:

```
table = new DataTable();
DataColumn col = new DataColumn("ID");
table.Columns.Add(col);
col = new DataColumn("Caption");
table.Columns.Add(col);
col = new DataColumn("URL");
table.Columns.Add(col);
stActions.DataSource = table;
```

7. Also, attach *DataGridTableStyle* and *GridColumnStylesCollection* support classes to the *DataGrid* so we can control the column widths:

```
DataGridTableStyle gts = new DataGridTableStyle();
stActions.TableStyles.Add(gts);
GridColumnStylesCollection gcs;
gcs = stActions.TableStyles[0].GridColumnStyles;
gcs[0].Width = 80;
gcs[1].Width = 80;
gcs[2].Width = 232;
```

8. Get a *Click* event handler for the Generate button, implement it to harvest all the user input from the *TextBox* and *DataGrid* controls, and use it to write out the XML file. You should, of course, put this in a *try...catch* block.

   Note also that, for brevity, we're omitting any validation. Realistically, we would enhance this with *Validating* event handlers on each input control, and an *Error-Provider*. We also assume the target location is fixed, although actually this is configurable. Finally, we ask only for the mandatory fields, and we could enhance this by asking for other elements such as locale ID and update information.

9. First set up an *XmlTextWriter* and write out the root starting element:

```
XmlTextWriter writer = new XmlTextWriter(
    @"C:\Program Files\Common Files\Microsoft Shared\Smart Tag\Lists\"
        +stName.Text +".xml", System.Text.Encoding.UTF8);
writer.Formatting = Formatting.Indented;

writer.WriteStartElement("FL", "smarttaglist",
    "urn:schemas-microsoft-com:smarttags:list");
```

10. Start a child element for the smart tag name, write out the value from the Name *TextBox*, and write the ending element tag:

```
writer.WriteStartElement("FL", "name", null);
writer.WriteString(stName.Text);
writer.WriteEndElement();
```

11. Similar code applies for the smart tag description:

```
writer.WriteStartElement("FL", "description", null);
writer.WriteString(stDescription.Text);
writer.WriteEndElement();
```

12. For the smart tag type, we need to write the user-supplied type as an attribute:

```
writer.WriteStartElement("FL", "smarttag", null);
writer.WriteAttributeString("type", stType.Text);
```

13. The caption is a simple element. The terms element contains a child *termlist* element:

```
writer.WriteStartElement("FL", "caption", null);
writer.WriteString(stCaption.Text);
writer.WriteEndElement();

writer.WriteStartElement("FL", "terms", null);
writer.WriteStartElement("FL", "termlist", null);
writer.WriteString(stTerms.Text);
writer.WriteEndElement();
writer.WriteEndElement();
```

14. There can be one or more actions, and we gather the details from the rows and columns in the *DataGrid*:

```
writer.WriteStartElement("FL", "actions", null);
int rowCount = table.Rows.Count;
for (int i = 0; i < rowCount; i++)
{
    writer.WriteStartElement("FL", "action", null);
    writer.WriteAttributeString("id", table.Rows[i][0].ToString());
    writer.WriteStartElement("FL", "caption", null);
    writer.WriteString(table.Rows[i][1].ToString());
    writer.WriteEndElement();
    writer.WriteStartElement("FL", "url", null);
    writer.WriteString(table.Rows[i][2].ToString());
    writer.WriteEndElement();
    writer.WriteEndElement();
}
```

15. Finally, close the *actions*, *smarttag*, and *smarttaglist* elements. Then close the *Xml-TextWriter* (and the underlying stream). (We'll leave the dialog box open in case the user wants to generate multiple list files.)

```
writer.WriteEndElement();       // actions
writer.WriteEndElement();       // smarttag
writer.WriteEndElement();       // smarttaglist
writer.Close();
```

16. Build and test. The resulting XML file should look something like the example below. Note that—for testing purposes—you can hook up the actions to existing Web pages:

```
<FL:smarttaglist xmlns:FL="urn:schemas-microsoft-com:smarttags:list">
    <FL:name>FooBar</FL:name>
    <FL:description>Some description of the smart tag</FL:description>
    <FL:smarttag type="urn:schemas-foobar-com:foo#names">
        <FL:caption>Foo Bar Inc</FL:caption>
        <FL:terms>
            <FL:termlist>Ant, Bee, Kind Dog, Elvis</FL:termlist>
```

```
        </FL:terms>
        <FL:actions>
            <FL:action id="itemInfo">
                <FL:caption>Foo Details</FL:caption>
            <FL:url>http://localhost/foobar/foobar.aspx?name={TEXT}</FL:url>
            </FL:action>
            <FL:action id="webSite">
                <FL:caption>Foo Web</FL:caption>
                <FL:url>http://localhost/foobar/default.htm</FL:url>
            </FL:action>
        </FL:actions>
    </FL:smarttag>
</FL:smarttaglist>
```

6.6 Troubleshooting Smart Tags

Office 97	✖
Office 2000	✖
Office XP	✔
Office 2003	✔

The general debugging techniques and tools discussed in Chapter 2, "Basics of Office Interoperability," are also applicable to smart tags. In addition, there are a few issues specific to managed smart tag solutions that we'll consider here.

If your managed smart tag solution fails, you can take a number of simple steps to check the health of the system. The first step is to make sure that your solution is being loaded by Word or Excel. In your target host, go to Tools | AutoCorrect Options, and then click the Smart Tags tab of the AutoCorrect Options dialog box. Check to see if the name of your solution appears in the list. If it is not, here are the possible reasons, listed in the order of likelihood:

■ **Your Office security settings are set to high or very high.**   If your organization's approved security configuration is to set Office security to high or very high, to clear the Trust All Installed Add-Ins And Templates check box, and to not sign your solution with a trusted publisher certificate, you have no alternative but to sign your solution according to your organization's standards. For testing purposes on the development machine, it might be appropriate to relax Office security to allow your unsigned smart tag solution to run, but this is a temporary measure and suitable only for developer testing. Note that this applies only to smart tag solutions that do not use the VSTO loader.

■ **The host application was not closed and reopened after compiling your solution.**   In Office XP, smart tag solutions are loaded only when an Office application is initially started. From Office 2003, smart tags can be reloaded without having to close and reopen the Office application. Reloading of smart tags while an application that supports smart tags is open isn't automatic. You can force a reload while an application is opened in two ways:

❑ **Run SmartTagInstall.exe.**   This tool is included in Office 2003. You can find it in the following directory location: <Drive>:\Program Files\Common Files\Microsoft Shared\Smart Tag. You can run this post-smart tag installation on the client machine. It will force the new smart tag (and also all other installed smart tags on the machine) to load/reload even if the applications that support smart tags are open. (Note: This tool doesn't work for PowerPoint.)

❑   **Run the following VBA code.**   When you run it, the reload happens only in the application where you run this command. For example, if you run the code in Word, reload will happen only for Word.

```
Application.SmartTagRecognizers.ReloadRecognizers
```

If you force a reload of smart tags while you're developing, it will cause your currently opened smart documents solution to be detached. This means you will need to reattach your solution for your currently opened smart documents to work again. You will also run into this issue if you install a new smart document solution or delete an existing one (because in these cases, too, all the smart tags/smart documents will be reloaded).

■   **One of your smart tag DLLs was disabled.**   A smart tag DLL that crashes at a critical point (typically, during initialization, when the host application itself was loading) will be disabled. To an extent, the behavior here is the same as for COM add-ins; details about disabled items are given in Section 5.5, "Tactical Add-In Issues."

■   **You have registry issues.**   You changed the CLSID or ProgId of the assembly itself or changed the recognizer or action classes, or the registry entries have become corrupted. Rebuilding your solution should fix this because RegAsm.exe is set to run as part of the build. Alternatively, you can run RegAsm directly on your assembly. Note that this applies to managed smart tags that don't use the VSTO loader.

For managed smart tags that use the VSTO loader, you should check that registration includes the absolute path to the assembly and that the DWORD key *Managed* is set to 1, as described previously.

■   **Your CAS policy is set incorrectly.**   For managed smart tags that use the VSTO loader, you should check that CAS security policy is correctly set up to grant FullTrust to the smart tag assembly and all its dependent assemblies.

■   **You have post-initialization failure.**   Your smart tag might load and successfully initialize but then fail silently at some point after initialization. In this case, the failure won't be entered into the Office Disabled List. Use a tool such as Process Explorer (*www.sysinternals.com*) to check that your smart tag assembly is being loaded. If it is, check for bugs in your code that don't cause crashes but do cause silent failure. For example, check that you are returning the correct value (usually 1) from your *SmartTagCount* property. You can use standard debugging techniques to track this kind of error—for instance, you can put *Debug.WriteLine* statements at interesting points in every method:

```
public string ProgId
{
    get
    {
        Debug.WriteLine("Recognizer.ProgID");
        return "SmartTagDemo.Recognizer";
    }
}
```

■ **You have conflicting recognizers.** The same text might be recognized by more than one smart tag solution. In this case, the user is presented with a cascading menu where action options from each of the different smart tags are combined. This isn't a bug. But if multiple recognizers try to recognize different parts of a string but not the same whole string, only one of the recognitions will be completed. Which one will win is undefined—that is, there are no set rules as to which recognizer will take precedence. Note that this is an issue only with Word because Excel works on the basis of complete cell contents—the partially overlapping substring issue is not possible with Excel.

Apart from the issue of partially overlapping substrings, the order of execution of recognizers is arbitrary. You should bear this in mind so you don't rely on your chosen strings always being recognized by any one specific smart tag. Also, you must not develop a smart tag that has any kind of sequence dependency on another smart tag.

■ **You have a performance problem.** Office runs smart tag recognizers on a background thread so as not to slow down the UI. You should not develop smart tags that put up any windows themselves because displaying windows causes the thread to be given a higher priority. This might then have a detrimental effect on the user experience.

As with all Office extensions—that is, add-ins, smart documents, RealTime Data components, and VSTO solutions, you should not build smart tags that rely on permanent database connections or network/Internet access because of the risk of diminishing the host application's responsiveness. You can by all means build solutions that rely on such resources, but you should build them to accommodate intermittent access.

Summary

Smart tags enable you to connect islands of information. You can build a solution where elements of text in a document can be linked to any amount of data held elsewhere. For example, something as seemingly trivial as the name of a company can be recognized by a smart tag and linked up to data held in a back-end CRM system or to a series of external Web services that feed financial information back to the document.

The list of terms you want to have your smart tag recognize is governed by the business requirements. Similarly, the actions you choose to attach to recognized terms is open-ended and determined by business requirements. The recognizer behavior and the action behavior can be built into a single DLL or can be in separate DLLs. You can even build a DLL for one set of functionality (typically the action component) while putting the other functionality (typically the recognizer) in a MOSTL XML file.

The MOSTL XML approach is useful for building recognizers that need to be kept up-to-date frequently. It's less useful for building action components because you're essentially limited to HTTP-based behavior. If you need a more powerful smart tag, you need to build DLLs that implement *ISmartTagRecognizer* and *ISmartTagAction*. If you're targeting Office 2003, you can optionally implement *ISmartTagRecognizer2* and *ISmartTagAction2*, which offer additional methods and properties to make the solution more sophisticated. These include dynamic captions in the Smart Tag menu, cascading menus, and a tokenizer that simplifies the development of recognizers for all languages.

Further information on smart tag development is available in the Microsoft Smart Tag SDK, downloadable from the Microsoft download site, along with sample code and tools. We'll look at the relationship between smart tags and smart documents in Chapter 11, "Smart Documents."

Chapter 7

Office Documents and Data

Getting data into and out of Microsoft Office documents is a common business requirement. This data might come from some back-end process, one or more Web services, or a database. In some solutions, the data is generated from within the Office document– particularly when the application is Microsoft Excel–and then fed back to server-side processes or databases.

Alongside the requirement to get data into and out of Office documents is the requirement to keep that data up-to-date, preferably in real or near-real time. In the past, this has often been accomplished through the use of Dynamic Data Exchange (DDE), but DDE is a technology that is not supported in Microsoft .NET, having been more or less superseded by other techniques such as remoting, Web services, and even COM interop itself in some circumstances.

This chapter explores three basic techniques for interchanging data between Office applications and managed code, and three techniques for keeping that data up-to-date.

The three basic data exchange techniques are:

- Using the .NET Framework class library classes to transfer directly between managed *DataSet* objects, *DataTable* objects, and elements within an Office document.

- Using the enhanced support for XML in later versions of Office, especially Excel.

- Using the *OleDbDataAdapter, OleDbDataReader*, and *OleDbCommand* classes, treating an Excel workbook file as just another OLE DB data source.

Using managed code, four techniques are available for keeping Office document data updated:

- Building a managed component, registering it for COM interop, and supplying it with some hook into the Office document (say, a *Document* or *Worksheet* object or a *Range*). You then have the component pump data into the document (and/ or copy data out of the document) repeatedly. The frequency of updates can be determined by the component or by some external configuration.

- If you're targeting Excel specifically (Excel XP and later), you can build a managed component that takes part in Excel's RealTime Data mechanism.

- Hooking up managed delegates (event handlers) to events exposed on the Office object model—for example, the *Worksheet Change* event that Excel fires when a change is made to a worksheet. This provides ongoing updates of changes to the document; you can then pick these up, perform some processing, and feed updated data back into the document.

- Connecting a managed COM add-in to an external component through remoting, and thereby supporting bidirectional updates in real time.

In this chapter, we'll examine the first three data update techniques, and we'll discuss some of the peculiarities in how events are exposed through Office interop assemblies (IAs). We'll consider the fourth technique in Chapter 9, "Web Services and Remoting."

Office 2003 offers greatly enhanced data capabilities, especially for Excel and Microsoft Word. Chapter 10, "Visual Studio Tools for Office," examines additional techniques for working with XML. These techniques are not specific to Visual Studio Tools for Office (VSTO), but rather to Office 2003; VSTO is often the most appropriate model to use for document-centric solutions.

7.1 Excel and SQL Data

Office 97	✓
Office 2000	✓
Office XP	✓
Office 2003	✓

The .NET Framework class library offers considerable support for data access in a set of ADO.NET classes that are reusable across a wide variety of application contexts. This is a major benefit for creating agile solutions: you can build a strongly typed dataset class that you can then consume in a Windows Forms application, an ASP.NET application, and a managed Office solution.

Data access with .NET is designed around a disconnected architecture. Applications are connected to the database only long enough to fetch or update the data. In a disconnected data model, it is impractical to go back to the database each time the application needs to process the next record. The solution, therefore, is to temporarily store the records retrieved from the database and work with this temporary set.

Traditional OLE DB includes the concept of the data provider, a piece of software that works at a slightly higher level than the raw database driver. In Microsoft ADO.NET, the OLE DB provider is called a *managed provider*. ADO.NET ships with two standard managed providers: one for Microsoft SQL Server and one for OLE DB data sources (including, of course, SQL Server). If you want to work with SQL Server databases, the SQL Server managed provider is much faster and more efficient than the generic OLE DB managed provider.

The class library offers a number of data access classes in the *System.Data* namespace. The most important of these classes are listed in Table 7-1.

Table 7-1 *System.Data* **Classes**

System.Data Class	Description
DataSet	Represents an in-memory cache of the record data you want to work on, including one or more tables
DataTableCollection	Represents the collection of tables in a *DataSet*
DataTable	Your coding representation of an individual data table, which includes one or more columns and one or more rows
DataRow	A row of data in a table
DataColumn	A column in a table

Two of the child namespaces, *System.Data.OleDb* and *System.Data.SqlClient*, offer the classes for the OLE DB managed provider and the SQL Server–specific managed provider, respectively, and they have many parallels. The most important classes in these two namespaces are listed in Table 7-2.

Table 7-2 *OleDb* **and** *SqlClient* **Classes**

System.Data.OleDb Class	Description	*System.Data.SqlClient* Class
OleDbCommand	Represents a SQL statement or stored procedure to execute at a data source	*SqlCommand*
OleDbCommandBuilder	Used to automatically generate single-table commands (such as *Insert*, *Delete*, and *Update*) that are used to reconcile changes made to a *DataSet* with the associated database	*SqlCommandBuilder*
OleDbConnection	Represents a connection to a data source	*SqlConnection*
OleDbDataAdapter	A set of data commands and a database connection that are used to fill the *DataSet* and update the data source	*SqlDataAdapter*
OleDbDataReader	Provides forward-only, read-only access to a stream of data rows from a data source	*SqlDataReader*

In the following example, we'll get some data from a SQL Server database and transfer it directly into cells in an Excel worksheet.

> **Note**   The sample solution for this topic can be found in the sample code at <install location>\Code\Office<n>\ExcelSQLDemo. Several of the examples in this chapter make use of the Northwind database. Access and SQL Server versions of this database ship with Office and with SQL Server. A copy of the version used in this chapter is also provided with the rest of the sample code.

1. Create a new Windows application called ExcelSQLDemo. Put a *Button* control on the form, label it *Transfer*, and get a *Click* handler. Add a reference to the Excel IAs. (In Solution Explorer, right-click and select Add Reference, click the COM tab, and select the appropriate Microsoft Excel Object Library from the list.)

2. Add a *using* statement for the Excel namespace (with an alias to cut down on typing effort) and for the *System.Data.SqlClient* namespace. (We'll be working with the *SqlConnection* and *SqlDataAdapter* classes.)

    ```
    using System.Data.SqlClient;
    using Excel = Microsoft.Office.Interop.Excel;    // not Office 97/2000
    ```

3. In the button *Click* handler, first set up a connection to the database and an arbitrary SELECT query. We'll use the simplest possible connection string. For our query, we'll request all products priced at more than $40, and we want the ProductID, ProductName, and UnitPrice columns returned. Pay careful attention to the use of semicolon delimiters within the query string. We should do this in a *try* block because making a connection to a database is one of the more vulnerable operations you can perform.

    ```
    try
    {
        SqlConnection connection = new SqlConnection (
            "data source=(local);"
            +"initial catalog=Northwind;"
            +"integrated security=SSPI");
        SqlDataAdapter adapter= new SqlDataAdapter(
            "SELECT ProductID, ProductName, UnitPrice FROM Products"
            +" WHERE UnitPrice > 40", connection);
    ```

4. Get the data from the database by filling a *DataSet* using the *SqlDataAdapter*. This gives us our disconnected data set, which we can work on locally. We know there is only one table in this data set, so we can cache a reference to the only *DataTable* in the collection:

    ```
    DataSet ds = new DataSet();
    adapter.Fill(ds," Products ");
    DataTable table = ds.Tables[0];
    ```

5. Launch Excel, and make sure there is an open workbook:

    ```
    Excel.Application xl= new Excel.Application();
    xl.Application.Workbooks.Add(true);
    ```

6. Put column headings into the active worksheet, using the column names from the *DataSet*. We'll get these from *DataColumn* objects, which are held in a collection in the *DataTable* that is associated with the *DataSet*. As a nod to usability, we'll make the headings bold:

```
int rowIndex = 1;
int colIndex = 0;
foreach(DataColumn col in table.Columns)
{
        colIndex++;
        Excel.Range cell = (Excel.Range)xl.Cells[1,colIndex];
        cell.Value2 = col.ColumnName;
        cell.Font.Bold = true;
}
```

7. Walk through every row returned in the data set, and for each of the three columns, copy the column data into a worksheet cell:

```
foreach(DataRow row in table.Rows)
{
    rowIndex++;
    colIndex = 0;
    foreach(DataColumn col in table.Columns)
    {
        colIndex++;
        xl.Cells[rowIndex,colIndex] =
            row[col.ColumnName].ToString();
    }
}
```

8. Make Excel visible, and finish off the *try/catch* block:

```
    xl.Visible = true;
}
catch (System.Exception ex)
{
    MessageBox.Show(ex.Message);
}
```

9. Build and test. The runtime behavior should look like this:

7.2 Excel and XML

Office 97	⊗
Office 2000	?
Office XP	✓
Office 2003	✓

Excel 2000 can read and write HTML files. It can read XML files but not write them, and it loses all information about the structure of the XML when it does read them.

Excel XP introduced functionality for both reading and writing files in XML format. An XML file that is well-formed can be opened directly in Excel XP both programmatically and through the UI.

Excel 2003 improves on that XML support and supports the use of customer-defined schemas. Developers are no longer limited to using the native Excel XML file format (XMLSS), as was the case with Excel XP. They can now create applications that are based on business-relevant XML definitions. So, instead of writing cumbersome XSLT files to transform XML data to and from XMLSS, developers can now attach their own schema and interchange data with Excel easily.

In the following example, we'll pull out some data from a SQL database and use it to create an XML file. We'll then load that XML into Excel (2000 or later).

> **Note**   The sample solution for this topic can be found in the sample code at this location: <install location>\Code\Office<n>\ExcelXMLDemo.

Generating an XML File

1. Create a new Windows application called ExcelXMLDemo. Put a *Button* control on the form, label it *Create XML*, and get a *Click* handler. Add *using* statements for all the namespaces we'll need:

    ```
    using System.Data.SqlClient;
    using System.Xml;
    using System.IO;
    using System.Xml.Xsl;
    using Excel = Microsoft.Office.Interop.Excel;
    ```

2. At class scope, add a string field for the database connection string and another string to hold the current path (so we know which folder we're reading/writing the file in), as in this example:

    ```
    private string connectionString ="data source=(local);"
        +"initial catalog= Northwind;integrated security=SSPI";
    private string currentPath;
    ```

3. In the form constructor (after the call to *InitializeComponent*), fill in the current path string. You can get this very easily from the *System.Environment* class:

    ```
    string currentLocation = System.Environment.CurrentDirectory;
    ```

4. At runtime, the current path for the application will depend on how you run the application. If you run it from within Visual Studio, the current path will be the .\bin\Debug subfolder of the solution folder. Because this is the target folder for the solution, the contents will be deleted during builds. To avoid confusion, we'll write our XML file to the solution folder, where it won't get deleted by a build. To do this, extract the solution folder path from the current path by using the *Substring* method:

```
currentPath = currentLocation.Substring(
    0, currentLocation.IndexOf(@"bin\Debug"));
```

5. Now we'll code the *Click* handler. First set up a *SqlConnection* using the connection string, and connect to the data source:

```
SqlConnection connection = new SqlConnection (connectionString);
try
{
    connection.Open();
```

6. Fill a *DataSet* with records from the Products table in the Northwind database:

```
SqlCommand command = new SqlCommand(
    "SELECT ProductID, ProductName, UnitPrice FROM Products"
    +" WHERE UnitPrice > 40", connection);
SqlDataAdapter adapter = new SqlDataAdapter();
adapter.SelectCommand = command;
DataSet dataset = new DataSet();
adapter.Fill(dataset);
```

7. Set up a *FileStream* and an *XMLTextWriter*:

```
string fileName = " Products.xml";
string filePath = Path.Combine(currentPath, fileName);
FileStream stream =
    new FileStream(filePath, FileMode.Create);
XmlTextWriter writer = new XmlTextWriter(
    stream, System.Text.Encoding.Unicode);
```

8. Write the XML from the dataset to the file, and close the XML writer (and therefore the file stream) and the database connection:

```
dataset.WriteXml(writer);
writer.Close();
connection.Close();
```

9. Code the *catch* block to clean up appropriately:

```
}
catch (System.Exception ex)
{
    MessageBox.Show(ex.Message);
    if (connection != null)
    {
        connection.Close(); // Multiple calls to Close is OK.
    }
}
```

10. Build and test. This should produce the output XML file (although you won't see anything on the screen to confirm this). The file should be in the current project folder, and you can open it in Microsoft Internet Explorer:

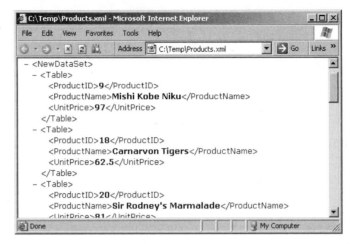

Applying an XSL File

As an additional step, we can write processing instructions into the XML file to make the parser (Internet Explorer or Excel in this case) use an XSL transform file.

1. Create a new XSL file, and add code to transform the data into tabular format, with the column headers rendered in some arbitrary background color. Save this as Products.xsl in the current project directory.

```
<xsl:stylesheet xmlns:xsl="http://www.w3.org/1999/XSL/Transform" version="1.0">
    <xsl:template match="/">
        <HTML>
            <HEAD>
                <STYLE>
                .HDR { background-color:bisque;font-weight:bold }
                </STYLE>
            </HEAD>
        <BODY>
            <TABLE>
                <COLGROUP WIDTH="100" ALIGN="CENTER"></COLGROUP>
                <COLGROUP WIDTH="200" ALIGN="LEFT"></COLGROUP>
                <COLGROUP WIDTH="100" ALIGN="LEFT"></COLGROUP>
                <TD CLASS="HDR">ProductID</TD>
                <TD CLASS="HDR">ProductName</TD>
                <TD CLASS="HDR">UnitPrice</TD>
                <xsl:for-each select="NewDataSet/Table">
                <TR>
                    <TD>
                        <xsl:value-of select="ProductID"/>
                    </TD>
                    <TD>
                        <xsl:value-of select="ProductName"/>
                    </TD>
```

```
            <TD>
                <xsl:value-of select="UnitPrice"/>
            </TD>
        </TR>
        </xsl:for-each>
    </TABLE>
</BODY>
</HTML>
    </xsl:template>
</xsl:stylesheet>
```

2. Add a check box to the form, with the name useXSL. In the *Click* handler for the original push button, before writing out the XML, we'll write out instructions to use the XSL:

```
if (useXSL.Checked)
{
    writer.WriteProcessingInstruction(
        "xml", "version='1.0'");
    writer.WriteProcessingInstruction(
        "xml-stylesheet",
        "type='text/xsl' href='Products.xsl'");
}
```

3. Build and test. When the user clicks the Create XML button, if he has checked the check box, the XSL instruction will be added. Now when you open the XML file in Internet Explorer, it should look like this:

When you open the XML file with Excel 2003 or Excel XP, you'll be prompted with a dialog box to open the file either with an XSL or without. The Products.xsl file will be listed as one of the options in the dialog box. If you choose to use the XSL, the data will be rendered almost identically to the way Internet Explorer renders it. If you choose to open the XML file without the XSL, it will look like this in Excel 2003 or Excel XP:

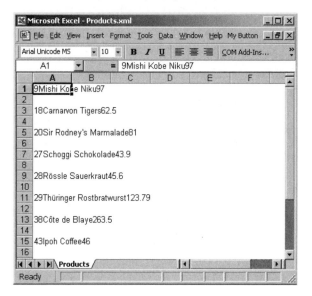

Remember that Excel 2000 can open XML files but that it loses all information about the structure. So, if you open the XML file in Excel 2000, it will look like this:

Automating Excel

It's a simple enhancement to automate Excel to load the generated XML file programmatically.

1. Add a second *Button* control to the form, and get a *Click* handler. Right-click on the project in Solution Explorer, and add a reference. In the dialog box, go to the COM tab and navigate to the appropriate Microsoft Excel type library to add references to the corresponding IAs.

2. In the *Click* handler, as before, we'll get a *SqlConnection* and fill a *DataSet*. (You can copy and paste most of this code):

```
SqlConnection connection = new SqlConnection (connectionString);
try
{
    connection.Open();
    SqlCommand command = new SqlCommand(
        "SELECT ProductID, ProductName, UnitPrice FROM Products"
        +" WHERE UnitPrice > 40", connection);
    SqlDataAdapter adapter = new SqlDataAdapter();
    adapter.SelectCommand = command;
    DataSet dataset = new DataSet();
    adapter.Fill(dataset);
```

3. This time–just for a change–we'll use the *XMLTextWriter* to generate an HTML file:

```
string htmlFile = " Products.html";
string htmlPath = Path.Combine(currentPath, htmlFile);
FileStream stream =
    new FileStream(htmlPath, FileMode.Create);
XmlTextWriter writer = new XmlTextWriter(
    stream, System.Text.Encoding.Unicode);

string xslFile = " Products.xsl";
string xslPath = Path.Combine(currentPath, xslFile);
XmlDataDocument xmlDoc = new XmlDataDocument(dataset);
XslTransform xslt = new XslTransform();
xslt.Load(xslPath);
xslt.Transform(xmlDoc, null, writer);

writer.Close();
connection.Close();
```

4. Automate Excel, make it visible (and set it under user control), and open the HTML file:

```
Excel.Application xl = new Excel.Application();
xl.Visible = true;
xl.UserControl = true;
Excel.Workbooks books = xl.Workbooks;
object missing = Type.Missing;
books.Open(htmlPath, missing, missing, missing,
    missing, missing, missing, missing, missing, missing,
    missing, missing, missing, missing, missing);
```

> **Version Notes**   The Workbooks.Open method in Excel 2000 takes fewer arguments than in Excel XP or Excel 2003. The Excel 2000 equivalent is as follows:
>
> ```
> books.Open(htmlPath, missing, missing, missing,
>     missing, missing, missing, missing, missing, missing,
>     missing, missing, missing);
> ```

5. Build and test. Open the HTML file in Excel (XP or later) or in Internet Explorer. This will again look like the previous version of the XML file that we transformed with XSL:

Using the Web Browser Control

As an aside, for testing the XML-generating section of the code, it would be handy to be able to view the generated data in the application itself. To achieve this, we can use the Microsoft Web Browser ActiveX control. (There's no equivalent in the .NET library.)

With the form open in the Forms Designer, open the toolbox (to any tab, but the Components tab is probably the most appropriate), right-click, and select Customize Toolbox (in Visual Studio .NET 2002), or Add/Remove Items (in Visual Studio .NET 2003). On the COM tab, find and check the entry for the Web Browser control. This will add a reference to the IA for shdocvw.dll.

1. Drop an instance of the Web Browser control onto the form.

2. In the code for the first button *Click* handler (the one that doesn't automate Excel), add this code at the end to load the XML file into the browser control:

```
object missing = Type.Missing;
axWebBrowser1.Navigate(filePath,
    ref missing, ref missing, ref missing, ref missing);
```

3. Build and test. The runtime behavior should look like this:

ProductID	ProductName	UnitPrice
9	Mishi Kobe Niku	97
18	Carnarvon Tigers	62.5
20	Sir Rodney's Marmalade	81
27	Schoggi Schokolade	43.9
28	Rössle Sauerkraut	45.6
29	Thüringer Rostbratwurst	123.79
38	Côte de Blaye	263.5
43	Ipoh Coffee	46
51	Manjimup Dried Apples	53
59	Raclette Courdavault	55

7.3 Excel and OLE DB

Office 97	✓
Office 2000	✓
Office XP	✓
Office 2003	✓

While you can use the Office IAs to interop with Excel through COM Automation, it is equally possible to work with Excel spreadsheets without using COM interop at all. You can do this by using the *OleDbDataAdapter*, *OleDbDataReader*, and *OleDbCommand* classes, treating an XLS file as just another OLE DB data source.

There are some limitations with this approach, of course—you don't have the rich set of Excel functionality available to you for building formulas, running macros, formatting, and so forth. However, if all you want is the data, using OLE DB is faster and simpler to develop. This technique also allows you to work with Excel workbook files without having Excel running or even installed on the machine.

In the following example, we'll explore the possibilities for reading and writing Excel spreadsheet data without using Excel.

> **Note** The sample solution for this topic can be found in the sample code at <install location>\Code\Office<n>\ExcelData.

1. Create a new Excel worksheet file (or use the one in the sample folder) called Contoso.xls. We want two sheets, as shown below. Note that the count of employees on the Summary sheet is a formula: *=COUNT(Employees!2:7)*. The Total Payroll is also: *=SUM(Employees!D2:D7)*.

Reading Excel Cell Data

1. Create a new console application called ExcelData. For simplicity, copy the Contoso.xls file into the bin\debug directory of the console application. You can do this manually or set it up as a post-build step in the project. The first thing we'll do is read the Site value from the Summary sheet. To do this, get the current directory and concatenate it with the name of the worksheet file:

   ```
   string filePath = Path.Combine(
       Directory.GetCurrentDirectory(), " Contoso.xls");
   ```

2. Build an OLE DB connection string for Excel. Note that the quotes (") in the *Extended Properties* string are important:

   ```
   string connectionString =
       "Provider=Microsoft.Jet.OLE DB.4.0;Data Source="
       + filePath +";Extended Properties=\"Excel 8.0;HDR=NO\"";
   ```

3. Set up an *OleDbConnection* based on this connection string, and open it:

```
OleDbConnection connection = null;
connection = new OleDbConnection(connectionString);
connection.Open();
```

4. Create an *OleDbCommand* for the SQL *SELECT* statement we want (the value of cell range B4 to B4), using the connection we just opened, as shown below. Note the $ character at the end of the worksheet name:

```
OleDbCommand command = null;
command = new OleDbCommand(
    "SELECT * FROM [Summary$B4:B4]", connection);
```

5. We can then get an *OleDbDataReader* initialized as a result of executing this command. Read the data via the reader, and extract the value (suitably cast):

```
OleDbDataReader reader = null;
reader = command.ExecuteReader();
reader.Read();

object oValue = reader.GetValue(0);
if (oValue != System.DBNull.Value)
{
    Console.WriteLine((string)oValue);
}
```

6. If you're running a console application in the debugger (with F5), it will close the console window at the end without pausing. If you run without the debugger (Ctrl+F5), you'll get a final prompt before the window closes. If you want a pause at the end in the debugger, you can simply put this extra line of code at the end of *Main*:

```
Console.ReadLine();
```

7. Close the reader and the connection, and then build and test:

```
reader.Close();
connection.Close();
```

8. At runtime, the console output so far should look like this:

```
London
```

WHERE Clause

1. Instead of specifying an absolute cell reference, we can use a conditional *SELECT* clause. For instance, to read the value corresponding to the Region entry in the Summary sheet, we can issue this command:

```
command = new OleDbCommand(
    "SELECT F2 FROM [Summary$] WHERE F1 = 'Region'",
    connection);
```

Note that F1 refers to field1, F2 to field2, and so on. Also note that the reader will only read values in F2 that have the same type as the first value in F2—in this case, strings. Bear in mind that we're treating an Excel spreadsheet as an OLE DB relational data source, where the data type of a column is fixed for all rows. The *OleDbDataReader* for Excel will figure out the data type based on the values it finds in the first *n* rows.

So in the example of our Contoso.xls, we can't read the numeric cells on the Summary sheet using a *WHERE* clause. Instead, we have to use absolute cell references.

2. With the sample Contoso.xls, the revised SELECT query above would produce this output:

```
South-East
```

Headers and Multiple Rows

1. Recall that our initial connection string specified *HDR=NO*. If we have column headings—as we do in the Employees worksheet—we should set the connection string to *HDR=YES* so that we can use the column heading values instead of F1, F2, and so on. With this change, the following code will read the first three columns for all rows in the Employees worksheet:

```
command = new OleDbCommand(
    "SELECT ID, LastName, FirstNames FROM [Employees$]",
    connection);
reader = command.ExecuteReader();

while (reader.Read())
{
    StringBuilder sb = new StringBuilder();
    object[] oValues = new object[3];
    reader.GetValues(oValues);
    int i;
    for (i = 0; i < 3; i++)
    {
        if (oValues[i] != System.DBNull.Value)
        {
            sb.Append((string)oValues[i]);
            if (i < 2) sb.Append(", ");
        }
    }
    Console.WriteLine(sb.ToString());
}
```

2. At runtime, the next set of console output should look like this:

```
A-123, Davolio, Nancy
A-456, Fuller, Andrew
B-789, Leverling, Janet
C-123, Peacock, Margaret
D-456, Buchanan, Steven
D-789, Suyama, Michael
```

UPDATE

1. We can update specific fields using a *WHERE* clause. For example, to update Janet Leverling's salary (employee ID B-789):

```
connection = new OleDbConnection(connectionString);
connection.Open();
OleDbCommand command = new OleDbCommand();
command.Connection = connection;

command.CommandText = string.Format(
    "UPDATE [Employees$] SET F4='{0}' WHERE F1='B-789'",
    99000);
command.ExecuteNonQuery();
```

Inserting a New Row

1. When you insert a complete row into the worksheet, this is done immediately after the last row. The following code uses the same connection and command as the previous one:

```
object[] employeeDetails = new object[]
    {"E-222", "Callahan", "Laura", 55000};
command.CommandText = string.Format(
    "INSERT INTO [Employees$] VALUES('{0}', '{1}', '{2}', {3})",
    employeeDetails);
command.ExecuteNonQuery();
```

Mixed Types

1. By default, the OLE DB provider reads the first eight rows to determine the data type of a column. The number of rows to read is determined by a DWORD registry value:

```
HKEY_LOCAL_MACHINE\SOFTWARE\Microsoft\Jet\4.0\Engines\Excel\TypeGuessRows
```

2. Suppose you need to deal with a column where some of the rows contain text and others contain numeric values. One solution is to force all values to be text on input, by prepending or appending a character. For example, the value 1234 becomes X1234, and later you strip off this character when you read the data back. The same character would be prepended to all values, whether text or numeric, so that all values get it stripped off later (to allow for the possibility that the prefix character is a legitimate part of an arbitrary text value).

An alternative approach is to read the data as text by switching to Import Mode. This is done by setting the *IMEX* value to 1 in the *Extended Properties*. For example, suppose we have an extra sheet with mixed data types in a column:

3. We can read this data as text using this connection string:

```
string connectionString =
    "Provider=Microsoft.Jet.OLE DB.4.0;Data Source="
    + filePath +";Extended Properties=\"Excel 8.0;IMEX=1;HDR=YES\"";
OleDbConnection connection = new OleDbConnection(connectionString);
connection.Open();
OleDbCommand command = new OleDbCommand(
    "SELECT Notes FROM [MixedTypes$]", connection);
```

4. The runtime output from this statement should look like this:

```
A123
456
B789
901
C234
567
```

7.4 Managed Data Feed

Office 97	✓
Office 2000	✓
Office XP	✓
Office 2003	✓

Suppose we want to build a managed component that feeds real-time data into an Excel worksheet. In the following exercise, we'll walk through one possible solution.

The basic model is to build a managed component, register it for COM interop, and supply it with a hook into the Office document—in this case, both a *Worksheet* reference and a cell *Range* reference. Then we'll have the component pump data into the document repeatedly. In a real system, the data itself would come from some back-end database or line-of-business system, a Web service, or some calculation engine. For our simple exercise, we'll use random numbers and pulse the updates on a simple timer.

Caution This example involves the use of VBA macro code. It is normally recommended that you set Office macro security to the highest possible level, not automatically trust installed add-ins and templates, and not trust access to the Visual Basic Project. To check your settings, go to Tools | Macro | Security. If you run the following sample application with the highest security settings, it will fail because of its use of VBA macro code unless you sign it. For the purposes of this exercise, you could relax your security settings while you're testing the application (or, alternatively, you could sign the solution as per your organization's standards). However, you should be sure to restore security to the settings approved by your organization immediately after testing.

Note The sample solution for this topic can be found in the sample code at <install location>\Code\Office<n>\LiveFeed.

A Managed "Live Data Feed" Component

1. Create a new class library project called LiveFeed. Set the project properties to register the assembly for COM interop. Recall that this will invoke the RegAsm.exe tool as part of the build to put entries for this assembly into the registry, including a /codebase path. It will also build a COM typelib for the assembly.

2. When you build managed components that are intended to be used from COM clients, it's generally useful to be as precise as possible (for deployment and maintenance issues, if nothing else). So, it's generally a good idea to strong-name your assembly and also to set a specific version number. For a production system, a strong-named keypair is generated and kept secure by some responsible party in your organization. For the purposes of these tutorial exercises, you can generate an ad hoc keypair.

   To generate a strong-named keypair, use the SN.exe utility that ships with the .NET Framework SDK. At the Visual Studio .NET command prompt, navigate to the current solution folder, and execute SN.exe on the command line. In this example, we'll create a keypair file called LiveFeed.snk:

   ```
   sn -k LiveFeed.snk
   ```

3. Apply the keypair to the assembly by using the *AssemblyKeyFile* attribute—a stub for this is usually generated by the project wizard in the assemblyinfo.cs file:

   ```
   [assembly: AssemblyKeyFile(@"..\..\LiveFeed.snk")]
   ```

4. At the same time, you can specify a known version number:

   ```
   [assembly: AssemblyVersion("1.0.0.0")]
   ```

   Note that while the Office XP and Office 2003 PIAs are strong-named and GAC-deployed, if you autogenerate IAs using TlbImp (as you must for Office 97 and Office 2000), these will not be strong-named and so cannot be GAC-deployed.

For the scenario described here, this is not a problem. If you're not using the Office XP or Office 2003 PIAs, you should not strong-name your *LiveFeed* assembly because when you build a strong-named assembly, the compiler insists that all its dependent assemblies are also strong-named.

5. Generate a GUID and attribute the assembly with this GUID. To do this, go to the Tools menu and select Create GUID. From the list of formats, choose the simple Registry Format. When you click Copy, this copies a new GUID to the clipboard. You can then paste it into an assembly-level *Guid* attribute. For code hygiene, this should be put in the assemblyinfo.cs along with all the other assembly-level attributes. The *Guid* attribute is defined in the *System.Runtime.InteropServices* namespace, so you'll need to put a *using* statement for that namespace at the top of the file.

    ```
    [assembly: Guid("C430AC92-76C0-4c5c-B191-E858D000F77A")]
    ```

    This assembly GUID is used for the registered typelib.

6. Back in the main class file, we'll need to use Excel *Worksheet* and *Range* types, so add a reference to the Excel IA. Also add a *using* statement for the Excel namespace:

    ```
    using Excel = Microsoft.Office.Interop.Excel;   // not Office 97/2000
    ```

7. While we're up at the top of the file, you should also add namespace *using* statements to allow us to use the threading and regular expression classes:

    ```
    using System.Threading;
    using System.Text.RegularExpressions;
    ```

8. COM development relies heavily on the use of interfaces. You could even say that COM development is interface-based. That is, clients and servers communicate by commonly recognized interfaces—they do not rely on any knowledge of the internal implementation of those interfaces.

    For this reason, we must define an interface to be used by the client, with a new GUID and a *Guid* attribute. We should also mark the interface as visible to COM. This interface needs only two methods, one to connect the Excel *Worksheet* to the managed assembly and start the live feed, and the second to stop the live feed. When we connect, we will specify the *Worksheet* object to connect to and the cell reference (in the conventional alphanumeric form, as in *A1*).

    ```
    [ComVisible(true)]
    [Guid("0345EDC8-EECC-4052-8BDC-155E259AE917")]
    public interface ILiveFeed
    {
        void BindToSheet(Excel.Worksheet sheet, string cellRef);
        void StopFeed();
    }
    ```

    As with the assembly/typelib GUID, this interface is registered in the registry. Note that this interface must be defined within the namespace in the project but not inside any class.

9. Define a class to implement this interface. The project wizard will have generated a skeleton class called *Class1*. You can either delete this and start from scratch or just rename *Class1* to *LiveFeedClass*. Again, use a new GUID and *Guid* attribute, and mark the class *ComVisible*. Another definite requirement for COM interop is that the class you expose to COM must have a default constructor:

```
[ComVisible(true)]
[Guid("9891CEB8-EA3A-4b2b-8759-9DD2A3F1F3C4")]
public class LiveFeedClass : ILiveFeed
{
    public LiveFeedClass() {}
```

10. Declare private fields for the Excel cell *Range* we're going to feed the data into and a *Timer* to pulse the live data values:

```
private Excel.Range range = null;
private Timer timer;
```

11. In the first interface method, we'll get a reference to the *Range* that corresponds to the chosen cell reference and cache it for later use. Then we'll create a *Random* number generator (by default, *Random* uses a seed based on system time), set up a *TimerCallback* delegate, and start a one-second *Timer*:

```
public void BindToSheet(Excel.Worksheet sheet, string cellRef)
{
    range = ((Excel.Range)sheet.get_Range(cellRef, Type.Missing));
    Random rand = new Random();
    TimerCallback timerDelegate = new TimerCallback(LiveData);
    timer = new Timer(timerDelegate, rand, 0, 1000);
}
```

12. You can take the code for the method that converts from alphanumeric cell references to row, column coordinates from the following:

```
private void CellToRowCol(string cell, out int row, out int col)
{
    const int maxRows = 65536;
    row = 0;
    col = 0;

    Regex nonAlpha = new Regex (@"(\d+)");
    string[] values = nonAlpha.Split(cell);
    if (values.Length < 2)
    {
        throw new Exception("invalid cell reference");
    }

    row = Convert.ToInt32(values[1]);
    if (row < 0 || row > maxRows)
    {
        row = 0;
        string errorMessage = String.Format(
            "Row number outside valid range: {0}..{1}",
            0, maxRows);
        throw new Exception(errorMessage);
```

```
    }

    char[] alphaChars = values[0].ToUpper().ToCharArray();

    // Convert each character in the string to numeric equivalent.
    int[] numerics = new int[alphaChars.Length];
    for (int i = 0; i < alphaChars.Length; i++)
    {
        // Subtract 64 ('A' -1 because column A == 1 not 0)
        numerics[i] = Convert.ToInt32(alphaChars[i]) - 64;
    }
    col = numerics[0];
    if (numerics.Length == 2)
    {
        col = col * 26 +numerics[1];
    }
}
```

13. In the *TimerCallback* delegate method, we'll set the next random number into the chosen cell *Range*:

```
public void LiveData(object o)
{
        range.Value2 = ((Random)o).Next(0, 451);
}
```

14. Finally, in the second interface method, we'll kill off the *Timer*:

```
public void StopFeed()
{
    timer.Dispose();
    timer = null;
}
```

15. Build the project and check that the correct registry settings have been made and that the type library has been generated. The typelib should be registered against the GUID we used for the assembly, under HKCR\TypeLib:

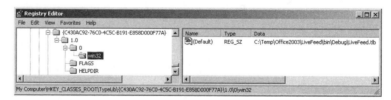

The managed component itself (*LiveFeed.LiveFeedClass*) should be registered by both a ProgId and a CLSID, under HKCR:

Finally, the *ILiveFeed* interface should be registered, under HKCR:

Excel VBA Client

1. Run Excel, and open a new worksheet. Switch to Design Mode, and put the following controls onto the sheet: a *Label* ("Cell to Feed"), a *TextBox* in the adjacent cell, and two *Button* controls:

2. Double-click one of the *Button* controls to get to the VBA code. Go to Tools | References, and add a reference to the type library for the managed Live Feed component.

3. At the top of the code sheet, declare a variable for the COM callable wrapper (CCW) to the managed LiveFeed component. Then code the two button *Click* handlers: the first one to start the live feed, and the second to stop it:

```
Public ccw As LiveFeed.ILiveFeed

Public Sub cmdStartFeed_Click()
    Set ccw = New LiveFeed.LiveFeedClass
    ccw.BindToSheet Sheet1, cellToFeed.Value
End Sub

Public Sub cmdStopFeed_Click()
    ccw.StopFeed
    Set ccw = Nothing
End Sub
```

4. In the VBA code above, I've used *Call* statements. You can omit these if you like, but then you have to also omit the parentheses:

```
ccw.BindToSheet Sheet1, cellToFeed.Value
```

5. Save the workbook (and add it to the solution if you like). Then test it by entering a suitable cell reference in the text box and clicking the Start Feed button. The managed component should start pumping updated values into the chosen cell.

7.5 Real-Time Data in Excel

Office 97	✗
Office 2000	✗
Office XP	✓
Office 2003	✓

Excel XP introduced a new worksheet function named *RTD* that supports the retrieval of real-time data. A perfect example of its use is for accessing real-time stock market data from market data vendors such as Reuters and Bloomberg. In previous versions of Excel, this was accomplished by using DDE or through custom developed worksheet functions such as *BLP* (Bloomberg) or *RTGet* (Reuters).

To bring data into a spreadsheet using the *RTD* function, you must have a RealTime Data (RTD) server to supply the data. An RTD server is an automation server (DLL or EXE) that receives requests for data from Excel, passes the request on to some real-time data source, retrieves data from the source, and passes the data back to Excel. The server must implement the *IRtdServer* interface, which is summarized in Table 7-3.

Table 7-3   The *IRtdServer* Interface

IRtdServer Method	Description
ServerStart	Called by Excel the first time a topic is requested.
ServerTerminate	Called by Excel when no more topics are required—when all *RTD* functions are deleted or Excel is closed.
Heartbeat	Called by Excel to find out if the RTD server is still running. If Excel does not receive the proper response, it displays a message box asking if it should attempt to reconnect to the server.
ConnectData	Called by Excel to request a new topic from the server when an *RTD* function is placed in a worksheet.
DisconnectData	Called when Excel no longer needs a topic—when an *RTD* function is deleted or Excel closes. Also (and perhaps more commonly) used when a topic has been changed. For example, if I have only one *RTD* stock function using ticker "ORCL" and I change the ticker to "MSFT", the "ORCL" topic will no longer be needed and will therefore be disconnected, and the "MSFT" topic will be created.
RefreshData	Called by Excel to get new values for *RTD* functions from the server after an update notify message is received from the server.

RTD uses a hybrid push and pull mechanism:

- **Push**   When the RTD server wants to give Excel an update, it notifies Excel by calling the *UpdateNotify* method on the Excel *IRTDUpdateEvent* interface. The RTD server can do this whenever and as frequently as it wants. Excel just notes that the RTD server wants to give it an update.

- **Pull**   When Excel is ready for the update, it grabs the update from the RTD server by calling the *RefreshData* method of the *IRtdServer* interface, which is implemented by the RTD server.

> **Note**   The sample solution for this topic can be found in the sample code at <install location>\Code\Office<n>\MarketData.

A Managed RTD Component

1. Create a new class library project called MarketData. Set the project properties to register the assembly for COM interop. We don't need to deploy this assembly to the GAC; we can rely instead on the (default) */codebase* switch to RegAsm. However, if you do want to GAC-deploy this assembly, use SN.exe to generate a strong-named keyfile and apply this keyfile in the assemblyinfo.cs. Also set a specific version number.

2. Add references to the Office XP and Office 2003 PIAs for Excel. Add a *using* statement for the Excel namespace. Also add *using* statements for the *System.Timers*, *System.Collections*, and *System.Runtime.InteropServices* namespaces.

3. The project wizard will have generated code that includes a *MarketData* namespace, which contains a class named *Class1*. Change the name of *Class1* to something meaningful, such as *Stock*, and declare the *Stock* class to implement the *Excel.IRtdServer* interface. Attribute the *Stock* class to make it visible to COM and to associate a *ProgId*:

```
[ComVisible(true)]
[ProgId("MarketData.Stock")]
public class Stock : Excel.IRtdServer
{
```

4. When you type in the interface implementation, you should get a ToolTip inviting you to press Tab to generate skeleton implementations for all the interface methods. If you miss the ToolTip, you can get skeleton implementations another way. In Solution Explorer, select ClassView, and then expand the *IRtd-Server* interface. Right-click on each method in turn, and select Add | Override to generate a skeleton implementation for the method in the *Stock* class.

5. Declare an *ArrayList* field in the class. This will hold our collection of stock items. Initialize this in the constructor to a new *ArrayList*. Also declare a *Timer*— we'll use this to trigger repeated updates to the data:

```
private Timer timer;
private ArrayList dataCollection;

public Stock()
{
    dataCollection = new ArrayList();
}
```

A Stock Data Class

1. Add a new class to the project called *StockData*. This will be a simple class to encapsulate the stock data (name and price). Set up private fields and public properties for the name (such as "MSFT"), the price, and the TopicID (a unique value that Excel will assign):

```
private string name;
public string Name { get { return name; } }

private double price;
public double Price { get { return price; } }

private int topicID = -1;
public int TopicID
{
    get { return topicID; }
    set { topicID = value; }
}
```

2. In the constructor, we'll generate a random value to use for the initial price:

```
public StockData(string name)
{
    this.name = name;
    Random random = new Random();
    price = random.NextDouble() * 100;
}
```

3. Write an update method to simulate market movements in stock price, using randomly generated values. Use a second random value to determine whether the simulated price change should be an increase or decrease:

```
public void Update(Random random)
{
    double priceChange = random.NextDouble();
    if (random.Next(1, 10) < 5)
    {
        price -= priceChange;
    }
    else
    {
        price += priceChange;
    }
}
```

4. Override *Equals* and *GetHashCode* so we can put instances of this type into a collection and perform operations such as *Contains*:

```
public override bool Equals(object obj)
{
    StockData tmp = (StockData)obj;
    if (tmp != null)
    {
        if (tmp.name == this.name)
        {
            return true;
        }
    }
    return false;
}

public override int GetHashCode()
{
    return this.name.GetHashCode();
}
```

IRtdServer Methods

1. Back to our main RTD *Stock* class. We must now implement the *IRtdServer* methods. When we used the wizard to autogenerate the skeleton methods, code was generated for the *IRtdServer.Heartbeat* method to return 1. This tells Excel that the real-time server is still alive. If for some reason this wasn't done (or if you chose to code the methods manually instead of autogenerating them), you can do this now:

```
public int Heartbeat() { return 1; }
```

2. As a new field in the class, declare a reference to the *IRTDUpdateEvent* interface. Excel exposes the *IRTDUpdateEvent* interface so we can call into its *UpdateNotify* method to tell Excel that we have new data ready:

```
private Excel.IRTDUpdateEvent xlUpdateEvent;
```

3. Implement the *IRtdServer.ServerStart* method. This will be called just after the constructor. Recall that we autogenerated a skeleton for this—so we just need to flesh it out now. We need to cache the *IRTDUpdateEvent* reference that Excel passes us. We'll also set up a timer (with a 1000-millisecond interval) to trigger the simulated data updates. Add a handler for this event (we'll write our custom *TimerEventHandler* method later). Finally, return 1 if all is OK:

```
public int ServerStart(
    Microsoft.Office.Interop.Excel.IRTDUpdateEvent CallbackObject)
{
    xlUpdateEvent = CallbackObject;
    timer = new Timer(1000);
    timer.AutoReset = true;
    timer.Elapsed += new ElapsedEventHandler(TimerEventHandler);
    return 1;
}
```

4. Implement *ServerTerminate* (that is, flesh out the autogenerated skeleton) to clean up, by setting the cached *IRTDUpdateEvent* reference to null, stopping the timer, and setting the reference to null:

```
public void ServerTerminate()
{
    xlUpdateEvent = null;
    if (timer.Enabled)
    {
        timer.Stop();
    }
    timer = null;
}
```

5. Implement the *IRtdServer.ConnectData* method. This is called when a file is opened that contains real-time data functions or when a user types in a new formula that contains the *RTD* function. First make sure the timer has been started, and set the *GetNewValues ref* parameter to *true* to indicate that new values will be acquired.

```
public object ConnectData(
    int TopicID, ref System.Array Strings, ref bool GetNewValues)
{
    if (!timer.Enabled)
    {
        timer.Start();
    }

    GetNewValues = true;
```

When a workbook with *RTD* functions is saved as an Excel spreadsheet, the values of these functions are saved with the workbook. When such a workbook is opened, the *ConnectData* method is called for each new *RTD* function. If the *GetNewValues* parameter is set to *true*, the saved value is discarded and the return value from the *ConnectData* method is used. If the *GetNewValues* parameter is set to *false*, the saved value is used until that topic has been updated, and the return value from the *ConnectData* method is ignored.

6. The array of strings passed in will be the parameters to the *RTD* function in the worksheet. In our example, we're only expecting one string—the stock name. Extract this string from the array and cache it. Then check to see if the requested stock item is already in our collection. If not, create a new data item to represent it, set its *TopicID* from the value passed in by Excel, and add the item to our collection. Finally, return the current price:

```
string stockName = (string)Strings.GetValue(0);
StockData dataItem = null;
if (!dataCollection.Contains(stockName))
{
    dataItem = new StockData(stockName);
    dataItem.TopicID = TopicID;
    dataCollection.Add(dataItem);
```

```
    }
    else
    {
        foreach (StockData sd in dataCollection)
        {
            if (sd.Name == stockName)
            {
                dataItem = sd;
                break;
            }
        }
    }

    return dataItem.Price;
}
```

It has to be said that this is heavily simplified: we don't care what string is passed—we just assume that the string corresponds to a stock name. An empty string could even be passed, and we'd still return a new *StockData* item.

7. Implement *IRtdServer.DisconnectData*. This is called from Excel for each previously connected use of the *RTD* function in the worksheet (that is, when the user deletes a previous use of *RTD*). We'll implement this to walk the collection of data items, and if we find one that matches the specified *TopicID*, we'll remove it from the collection:

```
public void DisconnectData(int TopicID)
{
    foreach (StockData dataItem in dataCollection)
    {
        if (dataItem.TopicID == TopicID)
        {
            dataCollection.Remove(dataItem.Name);
        }
    }

    // If we've emptied the collection, stop the timer.
    if (dataCollection.Count == 0 && timer.Enabled)
    {
        timer.Stop();
    }
}
```

8. The last *IRtdServer* method to implement is *RefreshData*. Excel will call this method when it is ready to receive our data. We must change the value of the *TopicCount* to the number of elements in the array that we return. The data returned to Excel will be a *Variant* containing a two-dimensional array. The first dimension represents the list of topic IDs. The second dimension represents the values associated with the topic IDs:

```
public System.Array RefreshData(ref int TopicCount)
{
    object[,] variants = new object[2, dataCollection.Count];
    int itemCount = 0;
    for ( ; itemCount < dataCollection.Count; itemCount++)
```

```
    {
        StockData dataItem =
            (StockData)dataCollection[itemCount];
        variants[0, itemCount] = dataItem.TopicID;
        variants[1, itemCount] = dataItem.Price;
    }

    TopicCount = itemCount+1;
    return variants;
}
```

9. Implement our custom handler for the timer events. We'll use this to update the price of all the stock data items in our collection and to notify Excel that the updated data is available:

```
private void TimerEventHandler(
    object sender, ElapsedEventArgs e)
{
    Random random = new Random();
    foreach (StockData dataItem in dataCollection)
    {
        dataItem.Update(random);
    }
    xlUpdateEvent.UpdateNotify();
}
```

10. Build the project.

The Excel Client

1. Run Excel, and open a new worksheet. In a cell of your choice, type the *RTD* worksheet function, using the *ProgId* of our managed RTD server, and any arbitrary stock name:

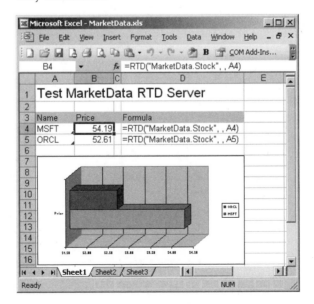

7.6 Sinking Office Events

Office 97
Office 2000
Office XP
Office 2003

Once you've connected to an Office application (or any other COM object), it's a relatively simple matter to hook up a client-side sink to the COM application's events. Recall from Section 2.4, "Interface/Class Ambiguity," that IAs for Office applications expose events through separate interfaces. For example, the Excel *Worksheet* class derives from both the *_Worksheet* interface and the *DocEvents_Event* interface. You can't see the *Worksheet* class in the Object Browser, but you can see the *Worksheet* interface that maps directly to the class. The *DocEvents_Event* interface defines events (that is, managed delegate types) named *DocEvents_XXXEventHandler*—for example, the *DocEvents_ChangeEventHandler*:

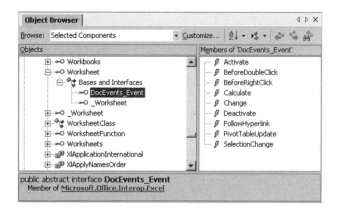

As you peruse the Object Browser, you might notice another set of classes with names such as *DocEvents_SinkHelper*. The *XXX_SinkHelper* classes implement their corresponding *XXX* interfaces (e.g., *DocEvents_SinkHelper* implements *DocEvents*) and have both a method and a delegate field that correspond to each event on the interface.

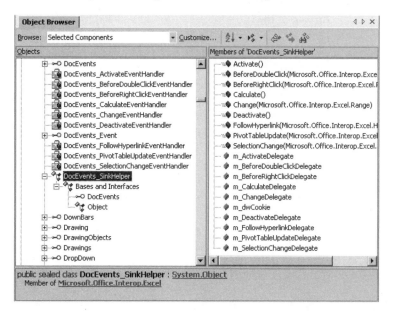

If you can't see any *XXX_SinkHelper* classes in the Object Browser, it's probably because your project is a default project built against the IAs for Office 97, Office 2000, or Office XP. Unless you do something about it, you'll see these classes only in a project that uses the Office 2003 PIAs.

This needs a little explanation. These *XXX_SinkHelper* classes are used internally by the IA and should not be used directly in your code. They had to be made public for reasons having to do with the way the IAs are implemented, but for all intents and purposes you should treat them as private (that is, invisible). So, the fact that we can't see them in a default project using Office 97, Office 2000, or Office XP is a good thing, right? And the fact that we can see them in a project using the Office 2003 PIAs is bad, right? Wrong and wrong. Unfortunately, even though we shouldn't use them directly, we do need them to be publicly accessible, which makes them visible in the Object Browser.

In the following exercise, we'll write a simple client application to sink Excel's *Change* event, which fires when the user (or an external link) changes the contents of a cell. For Office 2003, hooking up Excel events is simple because the *XXX_SinkHelper* classes are declared public. For Office 97, Office 2000, and Office XP, it's a little more interesting—we have to modify the IA to make these classes public.

 Note   The sample solution for this topic can be found in the sample code at <install location>\Code\Office<n>\ExcelEvents.

The Core Solution

1. Create a new Windows application called ExcelEvents. Add a reference to the Excel IA. (In Solution Explorer, right-click and select Add Reference, click the COM tab, and select the appropriate Microsoft Excel Object Library from the list.) Add a *using* statement for the Excel namespace and the *System.Runtime.InteropServices*.

2. Put two *Button* controls, a *Label*, and a *TextBox* on the form. When the user clicks the Run Excel button, we'll run Excel. When the user clicks the Hook button, we'll hook up our event handler. When the user changes the contents of a cell in the worksheet, we'll get the event and put the value into our *TextBox*. Set the Enabled property of the Hook button to *false*—we don't want the user to try to hook an event until she has started Excel. Set the *ReadOnly* property of the *TextBox* to *true*.

3. Declare a *Worksheet* reference as a new field in the class. We'll assign this a value in the Run Excel button handler, but we need the reference to persist across method calls because we'll use it later in the Hook button handler. Also declare a *bool* variable, which we'll toggle on and off based on whether we've hooked Excel events:

```
private Excel.Worksheet sheet = null;
private bool hooked = false;
```

4. Enhance the wizard-supplied *Dispose* method. If we have a live reference to a *Worksheet*, we should be careful to release it before the application dies. To do this, set the reference to *null* and force a double garbage collection in the usual way:

```
protected override void Dispose(bool disposing)
{
    if (sheet != null)
    {
        sheet = null;
        GC.Collect();
        GC.WaitForPendingFinalizers();
        GC.Collect();
        GC.WaitForPendingFinalizers();
    }

    if (disposing)
    {
        if (components != null)
        {
            components.Dispose();
        }
    }
    base.Dispose(disposing);
}
```

5. In the Run Excel button handler, launch Excel through automation, make it visible, add a new *Workbook* to the collection, and cache the active *Worksheet*. (This assumes that Excel is set to open at least one worksheet when a new *Workbook* is created). Disable the Run Excel button, and enable the Hook button:

```
private void runExcel_Click(object sender, System.EventArgs e)
{
    Excel.Application xl = new Excel.Application();
    xl.Visible = true;
    Excel.Workbook book =
        xl.Workbooks.Add(Excel.XlSheetType.xlWorksheet);
    sheet = (Excel.Worksheet)book.ActiveSheet;
    runExcel.Enabled = false;
    hookEvent.Enabled = true;
}
```

Recall that the *Application* class is not listed in the Object Browser, even though the *Application* interface is listed. Of course, you can't declare an instance of an interface, but there's a little syntactic sugar provided by the compiler that instantiates an *Application* class, not an *Application* interface. As discussed in Section 2.4, "Interface/Class Ambiguity," you should not be tempted to use the *ApplicationClass* class type at all.

6. Now we'll set up a delegate method to be called when Excel fires a *Change* event for the sheet. This method should take a *Range* parameter and return void. We'll simply extract the value from the current range (that is, the cell that has changed), convert it to a string, and put it into our *TextBox*:

```
public void OnCellChanged(Excel.Range range)
{
    cellValue.Text = range.Value2.ToString();
}
```

7. In the Hook button handler, test to see if we've already hooked the sheet—if so, remove the delegate, toggle the flag off, and change the button text to *Hook*. Otherwise, add the delegate, toggle the flag on, and change the button text to *Unhook*:

```
private void hookEvent_Click(object sender, System.EventArgs e)
{
    if (hooked)
    {
        sheet.Change -=
            new Excel.DocEvents_ChangeEventHandler(OnCellChanged);
        hooked = false;
        hookEvent.Text = "Hook";
    }
    else
    {
        sheet.Change +=
            new Excel.DocEvents_ChangeEventHandler(OnCellChanged);
        hooked = true;
        hookEvent.Text = "Unhook";
    }
}
```

8. Build and test. When you change any cell in the hooked sheet, the corresponding value is put in the *TextBox*. This stops when you unhook the event.

> **Caution**   There is an inherent danger in this simple code: because we hook only the *Change* event, we don't know when the worksheet is deleted or the workbook (or Excel) is closed. Realistically, we would also hook these events so we don't attempt to unhook our *Change* event handler from a sheet that's no longer live.

Private Sink Helpers (Pre–Office 2003)

If you're using autogenerated IAs (such as for Office 97 or Office 2000) or the Office XP PIAs, you'll find that everything works up to the point where you try to add the event handler.

The *XXX_SinkHelper* event wrapper classes in the IAs for Excel 97, Office 2000, and Office XP have access privileges that are too strict. Because these wrapper classes are marked as private, the *QueryInterface* call is disallowed by the CLR and returns *E_NOINTERFACE*. This generally translates to a *System.InvalidCastException*.

To work around this problem, you can manually modify the IA generated for Excel to relax the access privileges for the event wrapper classes. The next few instructions show you how to do this. The sample code also includes a set of generated IAs for Office 97, Office 2000, and Office XP that you could use instead. You'll find these in the following folders:

<install location>\Code\Office97\Office97InteropAssemblies

<install location>\Code\Office2000\Office2000InteropAssemblies

<install location>\Code\OfficeXP\Interop.Excel_publicSinkHelpers

In those folders, you'll find two versions of the Excel IA: one named Interop.Excel.dll, and the other named Interop.Excel_public SinkHelpers.dll. The first is a standard generation of the Excel IA. The second is a version of the Excel IA that has been modified to make the event handlers public. Internally, the metadata for the assembly is identified as *Interop.Excel*. Therefore, before you can use this file, you should take a copy of it and rename it to Interop.Excel.dll. Put the copy somewhere appropriate, and then add a reference in your project to this copy. You can't reference the assembly until you rename it because otherwise its internal name would conflict with its external name and the runtime would fail to find it.

Whenever you add a reference to the Excel IA, this cross-references the Office and Visual Basic Editor (VBE) IAs. When your solution uses the PIAs, and when you get Visual Studio to dynamically generate new IAs from COM typelibs, these additional dependencies are pulled in. If, instead, you use pregenerated IAs, these additional dependencies are not pulled in. In most situations, when you use an Office application IA (such as Interop.Excel.dll), you also need the core Office and VBE IAs.

For Office 97 and Office 2000, the folder locations listed above include not only the standard and modified Excel IAs, but also pregenerated IAs for Word, Office, and the VBE. If you add references to pregenerated IAs in those folder locations, Visual Studio will add the folder to your dependency search list for the solution. Unfortunately, this means Visual Studio will see the standard Interop.Excel.dll in that folder and will use that version instead of the modified version. If you add the references to the pregenerated IAs for Office and VBE after the reference to the modified version of the Excel IA, Visual Studio will overwrite the modified Excel assembly with the standard one it found in the same location. Therefore, you should add references to Interop.Office.dll and Interop.VBIDE.dll first, and add a reference to the (renamed) modified Excel IA last.

For Office XP, the sample code includes only the standard and modified Excel IAs. It doesn't include pregenerated IAs for Office and the VBE—the latter assemblies do not need to be modified or generated ad hoc because Microsoft supplies all the PIAs for Office XP.

If you want to build your own modified version of the Excel IA, here are the steps:

1. Save and close your Visual Studio .NET project.

2. Open a Visual Studio .NET command prompt and change the directory to the output directory of your project (for example, the <project>\bin\debug directory).

3. Use Ildasm.exe to extract the intermediate language from the autogenerated Excel IA:

    ```
    ildasm.exe /source Interop.Excel.dll /output=Interop.Excel.il
    ```

    Note that ildasm.exe is likely to be at C:\Program Files\Microsoft Visual Studio .NET\FrameworkSDK\Bin.

4. Open Interop.Excel.il in a text editor such as WordPad, and search for declarations of classes that end in _SinkHelper. Change the access privileges of the _SinkHelper classes from private to public, and then save and close Interop.Excel.il. (Note: you must change only the class declarations—not comments, definitions of class methods, and so on.) You're looking to change entries like this one, for example:

    ```
    .class private auto ansi sealed DocEvents_SinkHelper
    ```

    Change it to this:

    ```
    .class public auto ansi sealed DocEvents_SinkHelper
    ```

5. At the Visual Studio .NET command prompt, use Ilasm.exe with the /dll switch to recompile the intermediate language file into an IA, as follows:

    ```
    ilasm.exe /dll Interop.Excel.il /output=Interop.Excel.dll
    ```

Note that ilasm.exe is typically not in the same place as ildasm.exe–it's likely to be somewhere like C:\WINDOWS\Microsoft.NET\Framework\<framework version>. For example:

C:\WINDOWS\Microsoft.NET\Framework\v1.0.3705

6. Open your project in Visual Studio .NET. Remove the reference to the autogenerated IA, and add a reference to the Interop.Excel.dll that you created above using ilasm. If you have used the same name for this assembly as for the original autogenerated version, you might find that when you rebuild, the modified assembly is overwritten with a new autogenerated one. To prevent this, you should set the Local Copy property of this assembly to *false*.

Tracking Cell References

As an interesting aside, suppose we want to track the cell reference as well as the cell value. For example, we might hook *Change* events for the sheet, but we might only be interested in certain cells changing–not necessarily all the cells in the sheet. For this, we need the cell reference. The *Change* event fired does provide us with a *Range* object, which has properties for both value and row/column. The only work we need to do is to convert row/column references into the more familiar alphanumeric references.

1. Put another *Label* on the form (labeled Cell Ref) and a corresponding read-only *Textbox*. Then use the *get_Address* accessor method exposed by the *Range* object and specify A1 reference style (as opposed to R1C1 style):

```
public void OnCellChanged(Excel.Range range)
{
    cellValue.Text = range.Value2.ToString();
    object missing = Type.Missing;
    cellRef.Text = range.get_Address(missing, missing,
        Excel.XlReferenceStyle.xlA1, missing, missing);
}
```

2. Build and test:

> **Note**   The sample code also includes a more sophisticated version of this project that synchronizes a selected range of cells in an Excel worksheet with a *DataGrid* on a Windows Forms application.

Summary

In this chapter, we looked at three ways to meet the business requirement of getting data into and out of Office documents, and three ways to keep that data up-to-date.

We saw that the .NET Framework class library supports data access in at least two distinct ways: through the use of ADO.NET classes such as *DataSet* and *XXXDataAdapter*, and through classes that support XML, such as *XmlTextWriter*. Word and Excel increasingly support XML themselves, and we explored this trend by using multiple versions of Excel to generate and manipulate XML, XSL, and HTML files.

XML actually permeates the whole class library, and even within ADO.NET classes such as the *DataSet*, there is built-in support for XML. We considered a little-known and somewhat limited (but potentially very useful) technique for treating Excel workbooks as OLE DB data sources. In Chapter 10, we will examine the enhanced XML capabilities of Office 2003.

To meet the requirement of keeping Office document data up-to-date, we considered three baseline techniques:

- Registering a managed component for COM interop and supplying it with a hook into the Office document. The component can then pump data into the document (and/or copy data out of the document) repeatedly, at whatever frequency makes sense for the context.

- Building a managed component that takes part in Excel's RealTime Data mechanism—a very elegant mechanism supported by Excel XP and later.

- Hooking up managed delegates to events exposed on the Office object model. This is a simple technique that can be built into a more complex system where changes to document data are made to trigger other processing, which might feed back into the document data.

During our exploration of Office events, we encountered an interesting anomaly in the way published events were exposed in IAs prior to Office 2003. The fix for this involves dropping down to the level of intermediate language code, but fortunately this problem has been eliminated in later versions of Office.

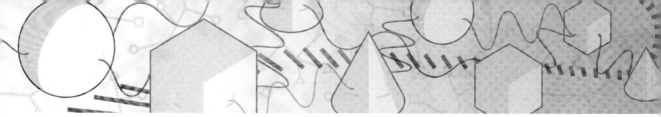

Chapter 8

Isolating Managed Extensions

In addition to using techniques such as automation, Web services, and remoting, Microsoft Office developers can also use a number of more formalized protocols. Office interop protocols include managed COM add-ins, RealTime Data components, smart tags, smart documents, and Visual Studio Tools for Office (VSTO). This list is in chronological order, from oldest to most recent. In this chapter, we'll focus on issues that arise with three of these protocols: COM add-ins, RealTime Data components, and some managed smart tags. It is no coincidence that these are all the older protocols. Also, only some smart tags—the older ones—pose a problem.

> **Note**   The discussion in this chapter applies to managed extensions only—it does not apply to unmanaged extensions.

These three protocols are designed for different purposes, but they share two common features: by default, they all use the default AppDomain in the Office host application, and they are all subject to Office macro security. A brief summary of these three protocols is in order here:

- **COM add-ins**   Office 2000 and later can be extended using a COM add-in, which is a component that implements the *IDTExtensibility2* interface. You can create COM add-ins in unmanaged code or in managed code. Any managed assembly can implement COM interfaces and then be registered for use by COM-aware clients. Unmanaged COM DLLs are typically registered with the RegSvr32.exe tool. Managed COM DLLs are registered with the RegAsm.exe tool.

- **RealTime Data components**   Microsoft Excel XP introduced a new worksheet function called *RTD* that supports the retrieval of real-time data. To bring data into a spreadsheet using the *RTD* function, you build a component that implements the *IRtdServer* interface. As with COM add-ins, you can develop RealTime Data components in either unmanaged or managed code.

- **Smart tags**   Office XP and later can be extended using a smart tag solution, which is a component that recognizes text within a document or workbook, and performs custom actions based on that recognition. A smart tag DLL implements the *ISmartTagRecognizer* and/or *ISmartTagAction* interface. You don't have to implement both interfaces in the same DLL—if you like, you can have a recognizer DLL and then one or more action DLLs that extend a single smart tag type for different actions. You can develop smart tags in either unmanaged or managed code.

AppDomain Isolation

With managed code, you can run several AppDomains in a single process with a similar level of isolation to what you would get between separate processes, but without incurring the overhead of cross-process calls or process switching. You can create multiple AppDomains in a process and load one or more DLLs or EXEs into each AppDomain. The CLR gives every managed application a default AppDomain when it starts. Every unmanaged application (such as an Office application) that uses the runtime also gets a default AppDomain when it loads managed assemblies.

If you build VSTO solutions, they will use the COM shim provided by the VSTO loader. A *shim* is a small component that sits between the Office host application and your managed extension. With Office 2003, you can optionally load managed smart tag solutions with the same VSTO loader and therefore leverage the same in-built COM shim. In the same way, managed Smart Document solutions also use the VSTO loader. If you're building a managed extension and you don't use the VSTO loader, by default your assembly will be put into the default AppDomain along with all other unshimmed add-ins, RealTime Data components, and smart tags.

There are two reasons for using a COM shim (either the in-built COM shim provided by the VSTO loader or a custom COM shim):

- **Security**   If you set the Office macro security level to High (or Very High in Office 2003), as is recommended, Office will examine the DLLs it loads for digital signatures. When you deploy a managed extension, the DLL that Office examines for signatures is always MSCoree.dll. This is the .NET CLR engine, which in turn loads your custom managed extension DLL. The problem is that you cannot digitally sign MSCoree.dll. Therefore, you must interpose a COM shim DLL (which you can sign) as the first DLL that Office examines for signatures.

- **Isolation**   If you don't use a standard COM shim (such as the VSTO loader) or provide your own custom COM shim, your extension DLL is loaded into the default AppDomain along with all other unshimmed extensions. Therefore, if any one of those extensions misbehaves, you run the risk that they will damage your solution. Your solution might run perfectly well for years until the user installs a new managed extension that causes problems. By the same token, if your code misbehaves, you risk damaging every other add-in, RealTime Data component, and smart tag in the default AppDomain. Also, if an add-in crashes, its filename will be registered in the load blacklist (on a per-application basis). In the case of a managed add-in, the only filename that Office knows about is MsCoree.dll. So if one managed add-in dies and gets blacklisted, on next bootup *every* managed add-in is blacklisted, and none of them will be loaded.

The message should be clear: both for enhanced security and for isolation between solutions, you are strongly encouraged to shim your managed extension.

8.1 The COM Shim Wizard

Office 97	⊗
Office 2000	?
Office XP	✓
Office 2003	✓

You can write a COM shim yourself, or you can use the COM Shim Wizard, which is actually a set of five Microsoft Visual Studio wizards that generate COM shims for managed extensions. The wizards are freely downloadable from the Microsoft Download Center and are also supplied with the sample code for this book. The general sequence for developing a shimmed extension assembly is summarized here:

1. Build your managed extension. By default, this registers the unshimmed extension.

2. Run the COM Shim Wizard from Visual Studio, specifying the managed extension you want to provide a shim for.

3. Build the wizard-generated shim. This registers the unmanaged shim DLL and effectively unregisters the managed extension.

4. Optionally (but highly recommended), you can digitally sign the shim so you can keep Office macro security at its highest level.

When you create a managed extension project, the project typically includes a step that runs RegAsm.exe on the target assembly. This puts entries in the registry so that Office will load the .NET runtime engine MSCoree.dll and then your custom extension assembly.

The COM Shim Wizard generates a Visual C++ project, either as a new solution or added to your managed extension solution as a new project. The wizard also includes a post-build step to run RegSvr32.exe on the shim. This replaces any registry entries for your original unshimmed assembly (or creates new entries if there were none before for this extension assembly). These entries ensure that Office loads the shim instead of your original extension. The shim then loads your original extension assembly into a new AppDomain. Therefore, your original managed extension assembly no longer needs to be registered for COM interop itself.

Although it is an optional step, you are encouraged to digitally sign the shim with Authenticode. If you do so, you can then set the Office macro security level to High or Very High. This approach gives you both the benefits of using a shim. Just using the shim gives you AppDomain isolation and gives you the opportunity to sign your code. However, to get the additional benefits of heightened security, you do need to sign the shim.

> **Note**   If you don't want to use the COM Shim Wizard, you can write appropriate
> shim code yourself, if you want, using the code generated by the wizard as a guideline.
> The concept of using a COM shim for managed extensions is widely recognized and
> recommended. However, the implementation details can be varied to suit differing
> requirements. Also, the current shim documented here uses CLR hosting, and this is
> not always a suitable technique. A valid alternative to CLR hosting would be to intro-
> duce an additional managed helper DLL, registered for COM interop. The unmanaged
> shim would load this additional helper DLL, which would in turn create a new AppDo-
> main and load the actual managed extension into the newly created AppDomain. In
> such an implementation, the new managed add-in helper DLL would be identical for
> all shims but would add to the complexity of the shim model.

The current implementation of the shim is a Visual C++ ATL COM DLL. It exposes a COM-creatable class that acts as a proxy to the real managed extension class. The COM Shim Wizard registers the CLSID and ProgId for this class in the registry. In the case of COM add-ins and smart tags, the wizard also registers this class against all the target Office applications you choose. So, when the host Office application starts, it will load the COM shim DLL, not the managed extension.

When the COM shim is loaded, it creates an instance of a second class—the CLR *Loader* class. The CLR *Loader* object loads the .NET runtime, creates a new AppDo-main, and loads the managed extension assembly into that new AppDomain. It cre-ates an instance of the managed extension class that implements the target interface (that is, *IDTExtensibility2*, or *ISmartTagRecognizer* and/or *ISmartTagAction*, or *IRtd-Server*) and caches the interface pointer. Subsequently, any calls from Office into this interface are handled first by the proxy class. The proxy class merely passes those calls on through the cached pointer to the "real" extension class in the managed extension assembly. Figure 8-1 summarizes the load-time behavior.

COM add-ins can be set to load when the targeted Office application(s) starts up and can also be loaded and unloaded through the UI, using the Com Add-ins toolbar option. In Office XP, smart tag recognizers and actions are loaded only when an Office application is initially started. In Office 2003, you can reload smart tags without hav-ing to close and reopen the Office application.

A RealTime Data component is loaded only when the user enters or modifies a cell for-mula that refers to that component. In the cell formula, the Excel *RTD* function must be passed the ProgId of the component. It is this ProgId that the COM Shim Wizard registers for the COM shim. Therefore, when such a formula is entered in a cell in Excel, the shim is loaded at that point. The subsequent behavior is the same as for add-ins and smart tags. So the only variation from the flowchart in Figure 8-1 is that the RealTime Data component is triggered not when Excel starts but at a later point.

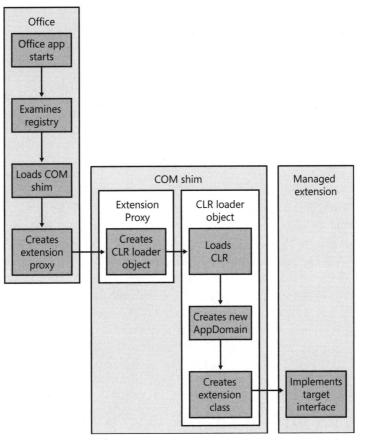

Figure 8-1   Load behavior of the COM shim.

How the Wizard Works

The COM Shim Wizard is designed to be as streamlined as possible. The whole idea is to encourage developers to use COM shims for their managed extensions. To support this, the wizard has a simple UI that asks a few simple questions and does all the hard work in the background. The aim is to allow developers to produce Visual C++ ATL COM shims without ever touching C++ code. The COM Shim Wizard is actually a set of five wizards, one for each type of managed extension assembly that you can shim:

- A managed COM add-in assembly

- A managed RealTime Data component assembly

- A managed assembly that implements both *ISmartTagRecognizer* and *ISmart-TagAction*

- A managed assembly that implements only *ISmartTagRecognizer*
- A managed assembly that implements only *ISmartTagAction*

The COM Shim Wizard follows the same pattern as most of the standard Visual Studio .NET wizards. When you install the wizard, it deploys a number of text files to the installed location for Visual Studio .NET. These text files list the five additional wizards and their properties, including icons to be used in the Visual Studio project dialog boxes. The installation also copies five sets of template files that form the basis of the code generated when the wizard runs. Five JScript files are deployed, in the standard manner; these are the controlling scripts that run when the user starts the wizard.

Two of the wizard components, the AppDomainHarvester.dll and ComShimHarvester.dll, will be installed in the global assembly cache (GAC), so you need to have admin rights on your machine in order to install the wizard. The ComShimHarvester is also registered as a COM server in the registry. This component is used by the scripts to ask a few simple questions and to reflect over the target managed extension assembly that the developer is intending to shim. This reflection process harvests metadata from the assembly such as the fully qualified name of the class that implements the target interface (*IDTExtensibility2, ISmartTagRecognizer*, etc.), the public key token that forms part of the assembly's strong name (if present), any relevant GUIDs and ProgIds, and so on. These details are then used to complete the template source files that are generated for the shim and the registry information. The following exercises assume that you have installed the COM Shim Wizards.

8.2 Creating an Add-In Shim

Office 97	✖
Office 2000	✔
Office XP	✔
Office 2003	✔

In this first exercise, we'll create an example shim for a managed COM add-in. This is the most commonly used type of managed Office extension. It is also the type of extension that requires the most input from the developer to establish the precise registry requirements.

> **Note** The sample solution for this topic can be found in the sample code at <install location>\Code\Office<n>\MyOfficeAddin_Shimmed.

1. Start Visual Studio .NET. From the File menu, select New and then Project. In the New Project dialog box, expand the Visual C++ Projects node, and select the child node COM Shims:

2. Choose the Addin Shim Wizard, give it a suitable name, and specify a suitable location. Then click OK.

3. The wizard runs the COMShimHarvester component, which offers the main COM Shim Wizard page. If you know the full path to the managed extension assembly you want to shim, you can type it into the first text box. Alternatively, you can click the Browse button to open a File dialog box within which you can navigate to the assembly. When you installed the wizards, several sample extensions were also copied. For experimenting with the wizard, you can choose one of these to shim—for example, TestAddin.dll.

4. When you've selected the assembly you want to shim, the COMShimHarvester opens it, harvests the name and public key token of the assembly and the name of the class that implements *IDTExtensibility2*, and populates the text boxes in the dialog box. By default, it also generates a new GUID and ProgId. This is useful if your original assembly omitted either the GUID or ProgId. However, you will more likely want to reuse the GUID and ProgId of the original. Therefore, you have the option to use the original values, by selecting the check box in the dialog box:

If you are not sure whether you should reuse the original GUID and ProgId or use the wizard-generated ones, it is recommended that you reuse the original values.

5. When you click Next, you'll be given the opportunity to specify additional information that will be entered in the registry. This information is the same as in the original Visual Studio Add-in Wizard —that is, choices to specify a suitable description and friendly name, the load behavior of the add-in, and the list of target host applications.

6. By default, the wizard uses the fully qualified type name of the class that implements the target interface for both *Description* and *Friendly Name*. You probably want to change these to something more meaningful, and you'll certainly want to specify the host applications you want to use this add-in for:

7. When you click Next, the wizard offers a final page, summarizing the choices you made. Click Finish to generate the new shim project and code. In Solution Explorer, the list of source files in the shim project should look something like this:

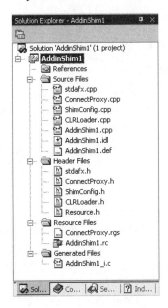

8. You can now build the shim project. The wizard-generated project includes a final build step that runs RegSvr32.exe on the target DLL to register the shim, so you don't need to register it manually. You can then test your add-in. For example, the test add-in we used in this exercise offers a custom button at the end of the Tools menu in Excel and Microsoft Word.

9. The wizard cannot make any assumptions about the location to which you will end up deploying the add-in solution. However, it is a requirement that the shim and the extension assembly be in the same folder (unless the extension assembly is deployed to the GAC). Therefore, before you can test the solution, you should copy or move the extension assembly to the same folder as the shim. If you do it the other way round and copy/move the shim to the folder where the managed extension assembly is, you'll have to reregister the shim because when you build the shim, registry entries are added that include its current path.

10. If you need to reregister the shim at any time, simply run RegSvr32.exe on it. For example, open a command window and type this command:

regsvr32 /s AddinShim1.dll

11. When you reach the stage in development when you no longer need to register the unshimmed assembly, you can turn off registration in the project. To do this, right-click the project in Solution Explorer, and select Properties. In the Properties dialog box, navigate to Configuration Properties and select the Build child node. Set the Register For COM Interop setting to False.

12. When you deploy your solution (including both the shim and the managed extension), you'll probably use an MSI, set up to register the shim appropriately. Therefore, uninstalling simply involves running the MSI again (or going to Control Panel | Add/Remove Programs). During the development phase, if you ever need to unregister the shim, you can use RegSvr32.exe. For example, you can open a Visual Studio .NET command window and type this command:

regsvr32 /u AddinShim1.dll

13. If the shim was registered after the managed extension assembly and you have unregistered the shim, there is no need to unregister the managed extension assembly. However, if you want to unregister the managed extension assembly, you can do so with RegAsm.exe. To do this, open a command window and type this command:

regasm /unregister TestAddin.dll

Note that you might unregister the shim and/or the managed extension assembly multiple times—this will not do any harm.

8.3 Creating a Smart Tag Shim

Office 97	✗
Office 2000	✗
Office XP	✓
Office 2003	✓

We'll now use the wizard to create a shim for a managed smart tag assembly that implements both *ISmartTagRecognizer* and *ISmartTagAction*. Although there are two interfaces involved, the wizard actually requires less input from the developer—mainly because smart tag solutions need fewer registry entries.

 Note The sample solution for this topic can be found in the sample code at <install location>\Code\Office<n>\SmartTagDemo_Shimmed.

1. After you've installed the COM Shim Wizard, start Visual Studio. From the File menu, select New and then Project, and expand the Visual C++ Projects node. Select the ST Recognizer + Action Shim project type, and use suitable name and location values. Then click OK. The second page in the dialog box is where you specify the managed assembly you want to shim. This is somewhat longer than the page used for add-ins because two interfaces are involved.

As with the add-in, type the path to your smart tag assembly or click the Browse button to navigate to it. Select your smart tag assembly, and the wizard will populate the fields in the dialog box with details harvested from the assembly. At this point, you have the option to reuse the GUID and ProgId from the original assembly for both the *Recognizer* and *Action* classes. In most situations, you should reuse these values. If you're not sure whether you need to, the recommendation is to reuse the original values:

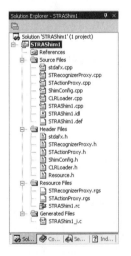

2. For smart tags and RealTime Data components, there are no further details to be registered, so this is the only input page in the dialog box. Click Next to get to the final Summary page.

3. When you click Finish, the wizard will generate the project and code for the shim. In Solution Explorer, you should see a project file listing like this:

4. You can then build the shim—which registers it—and then test your solution.

5. The COM Shim Wizard behavior described in Section 8.2, "Creating an Add-In Shim," and Section 8.3, "Creating a Smart Tag Shim," is representative of all five of the extension types.

8.4 Shim Wizard Internals

Office 97	✖
Office 2000	❓
Office XP	✔
Office 2003	✔

The main reason for this COM Shim Wizard is to protect developers from the chore of working with C++ code directly. Normally, you wouldn't want to generate the shim until you'd finished developing the managed extension assembly. Realistically, however, development is an iterative process, and you might find that you need to make changes to the assembly after you've generated the shim. You might want to test the solution both with and without the shim, and testing with the shim might highlight issues that require you to change the assembly. Whatever path you end up following, the generated shim code will likely continue to work regardless of any changes you make to the assembly.

Because there are minimal dependencies in the shim code on the managed extension code, you can generally continue to develop your managed extension project even after you have generated the shim. Even if you do change any of those dependencies, you can always simply run the wizard again to regenerate the shim project. You need to change or regenerate the shim only if you change any of the following:

- The namespace and/or type name of the class that implements the target interface (*IDTExtensibility2*, *ISmartTagRecognizer*, *ISmartTagAction*, or *IRtdServer*)
- The CLSID or ProgId of the class that implements the target interface
- For COM add-ins only, the list of target host applications
- For COM add-ins only, the load behavior of the add-in
- For COM add-ins only, the per-user or per-machine registration

If you do make any of the listed changes, and if you choose to manually edit the shim code, there are only three source files in the shim project that you would ever need to change, listed in Table 8-1.

Table 8-1   Shim Source Files Subject to Change

File	Description
ShimConfig.cpp	This file contains the name and public key token of the class that implements the target interface.
xxxProxy.rgs	This is the registry script that gets built into the shim DLL. The exact name will vary according to the type of extension, but it will always have an .rgs extension. In the case of the combined SmartTag Recognizer and Action shim, there will be two .rgs files—one for the *Action* class and one for the *Recognizer* class. The values in the registry scripts correspond to the choices made in the COMShimHarvester for load behavior, target host applications, etc.
xxxShim.idl	This is the MIDL source file that gets built into the type library for the shim. You will need to change this file only if you change the CLSID of the class(es) that implements the target interface(s).

The following steps detail the changes you might need to make to the shim code. The values that you might need to change are highlighted in bold in the code listings.

First look at the ShimConfig.cpp file. The code snippet shown is an example Shim-Config.cpp used for a managed COM add-in:

```
static LPCWSTR szAddInAssemblyName =
    L"TestAddin, PublicKeyToken=ddf2e0af5633d44c";
static LPCWSTR szConnectClassName =
    L"TestAddin.Connect";
```

This is another ShimConfig.cpp file—this time for a combined SmartTag Recognizer and Action assembly:

```
static LPCWSTR szSmartTagsAssemblyName =
    L"TestSmartTagRecognizerAction, PublicKeyToken=921d58dbc288bb6b";
static LPCWSTR szRecognizerClassName =
    L"TestSmartTagRecognizerAction.Recognizer";
static LPCWSTR szActionClassName =
    L"TestSmartTagRecognizerAction.Action";
```

The variables that are dependent on the managed assembly are listed in Table 8-2.

Table 8-2   ShimConfig.cpp Variables

Variable	Description
szXXXAssemblyName	The name of the managed assembly, listing the name of the DLL file itself (without the .dll extension) and the public key token.
szXXXClassName	The fully qualified name of the class that implements the target interface, in the form *namespace.classname*.

Here is an example of an IDL file. You would only ever need to change the CLSID of the coclass. In this example, the CLSID is *7f20788f-7f95-43b4-8224-b1db54cd7fb7*.

```
import "oaidl.idl";
import "ocidl.idl";

[
    uuid(7B7FEE35-BE47-4ABC-87AA-347BAE716DB7),
    version(1.0),
    helpstring("AddinShim1 1.0 Type Library")
]
library AddinShim1Lib
{
    importlib("stdole2.tlb");

    [
        uuid(7f20788f-7f95-43b4-8224-b1db54cd7fb7),
        helpstring("ConnectProxy Class")
    ]
    coclass ConnectProxy
    {
        [default] interface IUnknown;
    };

};
```

The third file that contains dependencies is the registry script.

> **Warning**   Changing this file and rebuilding the corresponding project is equivalent to editing the registry. Editing the registry incorrectly can cause serious problems that might require you to reinstall Windows. There is no guarantee that problems resulting from the incorrect use of .rgs files can be solved. You should back up your registry before building a project in which you have manually edited the .rgs file.

The next example (ConnectProxy.rgs) is for a managed COM add-in that is intended to be hosted in Excel and Word:

```
HKCR
{
    TestAddin.SomeProgId = s 'Connect Class'
    {
        CLSID = s '{7f20788f-7f95-43b4-8224-b1db54cd7fb7}'
    }
    NoRemove CLSID
    {
        ForceRemove '{7f20788f-7f95-43b4-8224-b1db54cd7fb7}' = s 'Connect Class'
        {
            ProgID = s 'TestAddin.SomeProgId'
            InprocServer32 = s '%MODULE%'
            {
                val ThreadingModel = s 'Apartment'
            }
        }
    }
}
 HKCU {
    NoRemove Software
    {
        NoRemove Microsoft
        {
            NoRemove Office
            {
                NoRemove Excel
                {
                    NoRemove Addins
                    {
                        ForceRemove TestAddin.SomeProgId
                        {
                            val 'Description' = s 'Adds a button to the Tools menu.'
                            val 'FriendlyName' = s 'TestAddin.Connect'
                            val 'LoadBehavior' = d 3
                        }
                    }
                }
                NoRemove Word
                {
                    NoRemove Addins
                    {
                        ForceRemove TestAddin.SomeProgId
                        {
                            val 'Description' = s 'Adds a button to the Tools menu.'
                            val 'FriendlyName' = s 'TestAddin.Connect'
```

```
                    val 'LoadBehavior' = d 3
                 }
              }
           }
        }
     }
  }
}
```

Table 8-3 lists the values that are dependent on the managed assembly.

Table 8-3   Add-In Registry Script Variables

Variable Value	Description
TestAddin.SomeProgId	Occurs four times. This is the registered ProgId of the class that implements the target interface.
7f20788f-7f95-43b4-8224-b1db54cd7fb7	Occurs two times. This is the CLSID of the class that implements the target interface and is the same as the CLSID of the coclass in the IDL file.
'Adds a button to the Tools menu.'	Any arbitrary description.
'TestAddin.Connect'	Any meaningful name for the extension.
3	The value of the *LoadBehavior* key. A value of *3* indicates that this add-in will be loaded when the host application starts. The only useful alternative value to put in this script is *0* (zero), which indicates that the add-in will be loaded only when the user asks for it via the COM Add-ins dialog box.
HKCU	Standard abbreviation for the registry hive HKEY_CURRENT_USER. If you want to register this add-in for all users on the machine, use *HKLM* instead (short for HKEY_LOCAL_MACHINE).

In addition to the variables listed in Table 8-2, the registry script for an add-in lists the host applications that will load the add-in. In the foregoing example, the script has entries for Excel and Word. To remove one of these entries—say, the Excel entry—you remove the entire node from *NoRemove Excel* down to the closing brace for that node. If you need to add a node, you can model it on the examples given above. You should not remove any other nodes. If you need to unregister the add-in, use RegSvr32.exe to unregister the shim.

If you want to see what the registry script entries should look like for add-ins that target other host applications, the simplest thing to do is to use the wizard to generate a shim, selecting all the host applications. Then model your manual script on that. Note that the nodes for the Office applications are slightly different from those for Visual Studio and other applications, and that 'MS Project' will be in quotes because of the space between the words.

Another example of a registry script is provided below—this time for a combined SmartTag Recognizer and Action assembly. The script for the Action registry entries is shown, and there will be a second .rgs file for the Recognizer entries that follows the same general pattern.

```
HKCR
{
    TestSmartTagRecognizerAction.SomeActionProgId = s 'STRecognizerProxy Class'
    {
        CLSID = s '{d47d6baa-3989-46e8-adca-250dde710df2}'
    }
    NoRemove CLSID
    {
        ForceRemove {d47d6baa-3989-46e8-adca-250dde710df2} = s 'STActionProxy Class'
        {
            ProgID = s 'TestSmartTagRecognizerAction.SomeActionProgId'
            InprocServer32 = s '%MODULE%'
            {
                val ThreadingModel = s 'Apartment'
            }
        }
    }
}
HKCU
{
    NoRemove Software
    {
        NoRemove Microsoft
        {
            NoRemove Office
            {
                NoRemove Common
                {
                    NoRemove 'Smart Tag'
                    {
                        NoRemove Actions
                        {
                            ForceRemove {d47d6baa-3989-46e8-adca-250dde710df2}
                        }
                    }
                }
            }
        }
    }
}
```

Table 8-4 lists the values that are dependent on the managed assembly.

Table 8-4   Smart Tag Registry Script Variables

Variable Value	Description
TestSmartTagRecognizer-Action.SomeActionProgId	Occurs two times. This is the registered ProgId for the class that implements *ISmartTagAction*.
d47d6baa-3989-46e8-adca-250dde710df2	Occurs three times. This is the CLSID for the class that implements *ISmartTagAction*.

Note that for smart tag shims and RealTime Data component shims, you should not remove any of the nodes. If you need to unregister the smart tag or RealTime Data shim, use RegSvr32.exe to unregister the shim, as in this example:

regsvr32 /u STRAShim1.dll

Additional Shim Wizard Features

Here is a summary of the features of the COM Shim Wizard that were not described earlier.

- The wizard allows you to shim strong-named and delay-signed assemblies. Re-signing a delay-signed assembly does not require any changes to the shim.

- The wizard allows you to shim simple- or weak-named assemblies. As a matter of general .NET security, you are encouraged to strong-name your assemblies. If you attempt to shim an assembly that is not strong-named, the wizard will warn you of this, but it will allow you to shim the assembly if you choose to go ahead anyway.

- If the managed assembly is missing GUIDs and/or ProgIds, a fresh GUID is generated and the fully qualified class name of the class that implements the target interface is used for the ProgId.

- The wizard supports managed assemblies that use the Office 2003 PIAs, the Office XP PIAs, or custom-generated IAs for Office. The name of the PIA or IA is not significant. When you generate custom IAs for Office—which you should normally do only for versions of Office that don't ship with PIAs (Office 97 and Office 2000)—the IAs might have arbitrary names and arbitrary namespaces. For this reason, the wizard allows for arbitrary names and namespaces.

- In addition to using the wizard to create a new solution, you can also use the wizard to add a new shim project to an existing solution. In this way, you can add your shim to your existing managed extension solution. If you do this, you might also want to set the managed project as a dependency of the shim project. Whenever you build the shim, the managed assembly will be built first if it has been changed.

- From Office 2003, you can optionally implement *ISmartTagRecognizer2* as well as *ISmartTagRecognizer*. You can also implement *ISmartTagAction2* as well as *ISmartTagAction*. Because you can use the VSTO loader for Office 2003 smart tags, it is unlikely that you will want to shim an assembly that implements the newer *ISmartTagRecognizer2* and *ISmartTagAction2* interfaces. Therefore, the COM Shim Wizard does not support shimming these interfaces. However, if your component implements both *ISmartTagRecognizer* and *ISmartTagRecognizer2*, you can still shim the component for the older *ISmartTagRecognizer* interface. The same goes for *ISmartTagAction/ISmartTagAction2*.

The MSI for the COM Shim Wizard also installs a set of sample managed extension assemblies for testing purposes. The installer does not register these—it merely unzips them and copies them to the file system at your chosen location. These samples are summarized in Table 8-5.

Table 8-5   Managed Extension Samples Provided with the COM Shim Wizard

Sample	Description
TestAddin	Puts a custom button at the end of the Tools menu (in Excel or Word). When the user clicks the button, the add-in displays a message.
TestRealTimeData	A simple RTD feed that produces dummy stock data. An example of its use is in TestRealTimeData.xls.
TestSmartTagAction	A smart tag assembly that contains only action functionality. An example of its use is in TestSmartTagData.xls.
TestSmartTagRecognizer	A smart tag assembly that contains only recognizer functionality. An example of its use is in TestSmartTag-Data.xls.
TestSmartTagRecognizerAction	A smart tag assembly that contains both recognizer and action functionality. An example of its use is in TestSmartTagData.xls.

Known Issues

The RealTime Data component shim works successfully for Excel 2003. For Excel XP, you can successfully generate a RealTime Data shim and both the shim and the managed RealTime Data assembly will be loaded, but the *RTD* cell function will fail. This is a known limitation in the current release of the COM Shim Wizard.

8.5 Config Files

Office 97	?
Office 2000	✓
Office XP	✓
Office 2003	✓

Most applications have some information that should be abstracted out from the code to an external file that can be configured separately as requirements change, without you having to rebuild the code. Back in the old days, we used INI files for persisting application configuration (user preferences, dependent file locations, etc.). Then we started using the registry. With .NET, you can use the registry if you like. You can also use XML config files. An application config file is an XML file saved with a .config extension. Visual Studio .NET supports this as a predefined project item and through its XML editor.

The runtime supports loading config files for EXE assemblies as long as you adhere to the naming and deployment standard. For example, if your application is called Contoso.exe, its config file would be Contoso.exe.config, and it would be saved in the same folder as the EXE itself. The runtime will search for and load such a config file for a managed EXE. It won't do this for DLLs. However, you can create any arbitrary

XML file (or any other file, for that matter) and explicitly load it in your own code, regardless of whether your code is in an EXE or a DLL.

This all holds true in the context of Office interop as well. That is, if you build a managed EXE to interop with Office, you can take advantage of the CLR's automatic loading of the application's config file. If you build a managed DLL to interop with Office, you can load such a file explicitly in your code.

In the following exercise, we'll build a managed COM add-in to make use of an XML config file. The add-in will put one custom button onto the Tools menu. When the user clicks the button, we'll display a message. Config files can be used in any Office interop scenario, and the technique is not restricted to add-ins, although we're using add-ins here to illustrate the technique. We'll write a config file for our assembly and deploy it to the same location as the assembly itself. In the config, we'll set up two values: an integer and a string. We'll use the integer for the FaceId of our custom button, and we'll use the string for the message displayed when the user clicks the button.

> **Note**   The sample solution for this topic can be found in the sample code at <install location>\Code\Office<n>\ExtensionConfig. There are three versions of the solution in this folder, corresponding to the three major steps described next.

Custom XML Parsing

Create a new Shared Add-in project called ExtensionConfig. To simplify testing, deselect all application hosts except one (say, Excel). Specify that the add-in should load when the host application loads but should not be available to all users on the machine.

When the wizard has generated the initial project, add a reference to System.Windows.Forms.dll and *using* statements for the *System.Windows.Forms*, *System.Reflection* and *System.Xml* namespaces. We'll be using a *MessageBox*, getting *Assembly* information, and doing some XML parsing.

We need to make some generic enhancements to two of the wizard-generated methods. You can refer back to Section 5.1, "Managed COM Add-Ins," for further information on the reasons behind these changes. In *OnConnection*, we invoke our *OnStartupComplete* method, and in *OnDisconnection*, we invoke our *OnBeginShutdown* method:

```
public void OnConnection(object application,
    Extensibility.ext_ConnectMode connectMode,
    object addInInst, ref System.Array custom)
{
    applicationObject = application;
    addInInstance = addInInst;
    if (connectMode !=
        Extensibility.ext_ConnectMode.ext_cm_Startup)
```

```
        {
            OnStartupComplete(ref custom);
        }
    }

    public void OnDisconnection(
        Extensibility.ext_DisconnectMode disconnectMode,
        ref System.Array custom)
    {
        if (disconnectMode !=
            Extensibility.ext_DisconnectMode.ext_dm_HostShutdown)
        {
            OnBeginShutdown(ref custom);
        }
        applicationObject = null;
    }
```

Declare class fields for the custom command bar button and for the two values that will be configured:

```
private CommandBarButton button;
private int buttonFaceId;
private string messageText;
```

OnStartupComplete is where we do all the work of setting up the custom button and the event handler. Most of this code should be familiar from many earlier examples of building custom command bars, so it doesn't need any explanation here (beyond a few comments inline). The only new features are the call to the *GetConfiguration* method—this is a custom method we will write to get the configured values from the config file—and the use of the configured *buttonFaceId* value:

```
public void OnStartupComplete(ref System.Array custom)
{
    string buttonName = "ConfiguredButton";

    try
    {
        GetConfiguration();

        // Find the Tools command bar.
        Type applicationType = applicationObject.GetType();
        CommandBars bars = (CommandBars)
            applicationType.InvokeMember(
                "CommandBars",
                BindingFlags.GetProperty,
                null, applicationObject, null);
        CommandBar bar = bars["Tools"];

        // Add our custom button to the bar, if it's not already there.
        object missing = Type.Missing;
        CommandBarButton tmp = (CommandBarButton)
            bar.FindControl(MsoControlType.msoControlButton,
            missing, buttonName, true, true);
        if (tmp == null)
        {
```

```
            // It's not there, so add our button to the commandbar.
            button = (CommandBarButton) bar.Controls.Add(
                MsoControlType.msoControlButton, 1, missing,
                missing, true);
            button.FaceId = buttonFaceId;
            button.Caption = buttonName;
        }
        else
        {
            // The button is already there, so just get a reference.
            button = tmp;
            button.FaceId = buttonFaceId;
        }

        button.Click +=
            new _CommandBarButtonEvents_ClickEventHandler(
                button_Click);
    }
    catch (Exception ex)
    {
        MessageBox.Show(ex.Message);
    }
}
```

Write the *Click* event handler for the button to display a message using the configured string value:

```
private void button_Click(
    CommandBarButton cmdBarbutton, ref bool cancelButton)
{
    MessageBox.Show(messageText);
}
```

Let's step aside now and create the config file. Add a new item to the project: an application config file. This will add a skeleton XML file called app.config. For EXE projects, this would be copied to the target location as <applicationName>.exe.config as part of the build. However, for DLL projects (including add-in solutions), this is not done. So, add a post-build step to do this directly:

```
copy "$(SolutionDir)app.config" "$(TargetDir)$(TargetFileName).config"
```

If you're building the sample solutions instead of working through from scratch, you will of course be building and installing the setup project as well. If you do this, and you run the solution from Visual Studio, the current directory will be the directory where Visual Studio put the assembly when it built it, and all will be fine. If you run the host application independently (as you would on the end-user's machine), the assembly will run from its registered location—the solution directory, not the target directory. To accommodate this, you can either copy the config file manually to the solution directory or add this post-build step and build the solution again:

```
copy "$(SolutionDir)app.config" "$(SolutionDir)$(TargetFileName).config"
```

We're using the same naming convention as standard .NET managed EXEs use, but this is by no means essential unless you want to use the standard *ConfigurationSettings* class to read it. In fact, we could use any file, and are not even restricted to XML—but we'll keep to the standard here for the sake of consistency.

Edit app.config to add entries for two custom properties: *buttonFaceId* and *messageText*:

```
<?xml version="1.0" encoding="utf-8" ?>
<configuration>
    <appSettings>
        <add key="buttonFaceId" value="1809" />
        <add key="messageText" value="Hello World" />
    </appSettings>
</configuration>
```

Our custom *GetConfiguration* method will load this XML file, read it into an *XmlDocument*, and extract the attribute values. First we'll work out the path to the current assembly, load the config file from that path, and then navigate to the inner *appSettings* node using *SelectSingleNode*. Then we'll walk the children of this node to find all the attributes. Of course, everything in the XML file is text, which is fine for the string value, but we do need to convert the *ColorIndex* and *FontSize* values to integers:

```
private void GetConfiguration()
{
    string codeBase =
        Assembly.GetExecutingAssembly().CodeBase + ".config";

    XmlDocument configData = new XmlDocument();
    configData.Load(codeBase);
    XmlNode node = configData.SelectSingleNode(
        "/configuration/appSettings");
    foreach (XmlNode childNode in node.ChildNodes)
    {
        XmlAttributeCollection attribs = childNode.Attributes;
        switch (attribs[0].Value)
        {
            case "buttonFaceId":
                buttonFaceId =
                    Convert.ToInt16(attribs[1].Value);
                break;
            case "messageText":
                messageText = attribs[1].Value;
                break;
        }
    }
}
```

Build and test. At the bottom of the host application's Tools menu, there should be a new button, ConfiguredButton, with an associated icon.

Shimmed AppDomain Configs

Alternatively, you can leverage the standard .NET EXE configuration loading if you name your config according to the EXE name—that is, the name of the Office application with *config* on the end. Try it: rename the config from *TestConfig.dll.config* to *Excel.exe.config*. You can even set this up as an additional post-build step:

```
copy "$(SolutionDir)app.config" "$(SolutionDir)$(TargetName)_bin\Excel.exe.config"
```

You can then greatly simplify the code required for accessing the configuration data. Specifically, you can add a *using* statement for the *System.Configuration* namespace and then replace all the custom XmlDocument code with just two lines—using the *ConfigurationSettings.AppSettings* collection:

```
private void GetConfiguration()
{
    buttonFaceId = Convert.ToInt16(
        ConfigurationSettings.AppSettings["buttonFaceId"]);
    messageText =
        ConfigurationSettings.AppSettings["messageText"];
}
```

> **Warning** You should not use config files with managed COM add-ins or smart tags unless you are using a shim or unless you use the DLL name as the base name, not the host EXE name. The danger here is that if you don't use a shim, the add-in or smart tag will be loaded into the default AppDomain along with all other unshimmed managed add-ins and smart tags. Because configs are loaded on a per-AppDomain basis, if you use the host EXE as the base name, you will clearly risk overwriting some other component's config.

The runtime resolves config files on a per-AppDomain basis, so it looks for this renamed config file in the same place it found the extension assembly if a new App-Domain has been created for the extension assembly. Placing such a config file in the same directory as the assembly works for the case where the COM shim is used because each COM shim instance creates a separate AppDomain for its managed assembly.

We must therefore shim our add-in. The simplest way is to run the COM Shim Wizard, as described earlier. After you've built your shim, don't forget to copy your original managed add-in assembly to the same folder as the shim, plus your config file.

Multiple Configured Add-Ins

In the sample solutions, you will find a second managed COM add-in, called Another-Extension. This has almost identical behavior to the current add-in but uses a different name for its button, so both buttons should appear on the Tools menu. Both add-ins use a config file, which they parse with the *ConfigurationSettings* class, and therefore both name their configs according to the host application (in this example, Excel.exe.config).

If both add-ins were loaded into the default AppDomain, there would be a conflict and only one of the configs would ever be used. However, we're using the COM shim, which creates a separate AppDomain for each add-in and supports separate config files, so all is well. Both config files are named Excel.exe.config, but they're in different locations in the file system. This location is the registered location for each of the shim components, and the shim creates a separate AppDomain for each one, so it loads each one's config independently.

> **Caution**   You could use the host EXE as the base name for your config file and then deploy the config file to the location where the host application is—typically, C:\Program Files\Microsoft Office\Office11\. This is definitely discouraged—again, you run the risk of multiple solutions overwriting each other's config files. The recommendation is to deploy the config to the location where your solution is. You might then use either the DLL or the host EXE as the base name, depending on whether you want to use the standard *ConfigurationSettings* class or custom parsing code based on *XmlDocument*.

On a positive note, the VSTO loader also creates a separate AppDomain for each VSTO solution that is loaded into an Office application. In this case also, you can use an independent config file for each solution, all named after the host application (such as Excel.exe.config), all in different locations. See Chapter 10, "Visual Studio Tools for Office," for more details.

Summary

As with any other managed applications, managed Office extensions are given a default AppDomain, and by default all managed DLLs are loaded into this same AppDomain. The VSTO loader creates a fresh AppDomain for each managed smart tag or smart document solution that it loads. The VSTO loader is a COM shim that sits between the Office host application and your managed code.

Over the years, many Office extensions—predominantly add-ins—have been built that do not use a shim and are loaded into the default AppDomain. As more and more managed extensions are deployed, it has become more obvious that this situation is fragile. The recommendation is that you should ensure that your managed extensions use an unmanaged (COM) shim. There are two reasons to use a COM shim—either the built-in COM shim provided by the VSTO loader or a custom COM shim:

- **Security**   With Office security set to High/Very High, when you deploy an unshimmed managed extension, the DLL that Office examines for signatures is always MSCoree.dll. You cannot digitally sign MSCoree.dll. Therefore, you need to interpose a COM shim DLL (which you can sign) as the first DLL that Office examines for signatures.

- **Isolation**   If you don't use a COM shim, your extension is loaded into the default AppDomain along with all other unshimmed extensions. Every assembly in the same AppDomain is vulnerable to damage that might be caused by every other assembly in the AppDomain. Configuration is another reason why isolation is a good thing—if an extension DLL lives in its own AppDomain, it can use its own config file without risking any interference with any other config files.

From a wider perspective, it is clear that all the newer protocols—such as VSTO, VSTO-loaded smart tags, and smart documents—do not suffer the same problems as the older protocols, which is good news for Office developers going forward.

Chapter 9
Web Services and Remoting

The Microsoft Office applications were originally designed to be client-side UI-intensive end-user applications, and they fulfill this role extremely well. They also expose extensive programmability features, and many solutions based around Office are also client-side UI-intensive. On the other hand, it is increasingly common to build Office-based solutions that are distributed and that leverage existing systems that might even reside on non-Windows platforms.

The .NET Framework offers two broad technologies for building enterprise-strength distributed systems: ASP.NET Web services and .NET Remoting. To be sure, you can build solutions using older interprocess communication protocols such as named pipes, sockets, and mailslots. However, the support for these in .NET is considerably less than for Web services and remoting.

In some cases, the same application requirements can be met by either Web services or remoting. Both can enable cross-process communication, but they are designed to benefit different target audiences. Web services provide a simple programming model and a wide reach. Remoting provides a more complex programming model and has a much narrower reach.

The ASP.NET Web services infrastructure provides a simple API for Web services based on mapping SOAP messages to method calls. The clients of ASP.NET Web services do not have to know anything about the platform or the object model used to build them. The services themselves don't have to know anything about the clients. The only requirement is that both parties agree on the format of the SOAP messages being sent. This format is defined by the Web service's contract, expressed using Web Services Description Language (WSDL) and XML Schema (XSD).

.NET Remoting provides a functionally rich infrastructure for distributed objects. It exposes the full-object semantics of .NET to remote processes using plumbing that is both flexible and extensible. Where Web services provide a simple programming model based on message passing, remoting offers much more complex functionality based on passing objects or object references.

One major difference is that Web services are platform-agnostic—the client might be a .NET client on Windows and the server might be a console application on a UNIX platform, or vice-versa. To use remoting, however, both ends of the conversation need to be built using .NET.

In this chapter, we'll consider the options for building solutions that integrate Office applications with Web services and with remoting. Office can consume Web services in two basic ways: using the SOAP toolkit with VBA; and using managed Web service proxies. Once we've examined these basic tools, we'll consider the latest Web Services Enhancements (WSE) library, which allows you to enhance Web services in a variety of ways, including improving security.

As more and more systems are built using Web services, the need for Office to support their use has increased. Office 2003 includes a new Research task pane that uses Web services to bring search results into Office. It is relatively simple to build a Web service that conforms to the Research pane requirements, and this is becoming a common strategy for bringing data from server-side resources (both internal and external) into Office.

Another example of this trend is the Information Bridge Framework (IBF), which was released in June 2004. It offers a number of server-side components, a significant library, and a tool set for building solutions that bring line-of-business data into Office. IBF is considerably more complex than the Research Services SDK and is well worth a close look. Unfortunately, a detailed discussion of IBF is beyond the scope of this book.

Finally, we'll spend some time working through a complex solution that uses remoting with Office. This solution also makes use of remoted delegates—events fired across processes. We'll use these remoted delegates to allow Office to sink events fired from a managed component.

The sample solutions presented in this chapter make use of ASP.NET Web services. For these to work, you must have Microsoft Internet Information Services (IIS) installed on the local machine or on another machine that is accessible on the intranet or Internet. However, the techniques explored in these solutions are not specific to ASP.NET, so if you have access to Web services on some other platform, they'll do just as well.

9.1 The SOAP Toolkit

Office 97	✓
Office 2000	✓
Office XP	✓
Office 2003	✓

Two Microsoft toolkits are available to support development of solutions that integrate Office and Web services:

- The Microsoft SOAP Toolkit
- The Microsoft Office XP Web Services Toolkit and Office 2003 Web Services Toolkit

The Office Web Services Toolkit is essentially an extension of the SOAP Toolkit. The SOAP Toolkit includes the following components:

- The *SoapClient* client-side component, which acts as a proxy to the target Web service described by a WSDL file. This WSDL file describes the service(s) and operations of the service offered by the server.

- A server-side component that maps invoked XML Web service operations to COM object method calls, as described by the WSDL and Web Services Meta Language (WSML) files. The WSML file is necessary for the implementation of the Microsoft SOAP Toolkit.

- The components needed to construct, transmit, read, and process SOAP messages. These processes are collectively referred to as marshaling and unmarshaling.

- A WSDL/WSML Generator tool, which generates the WSDL and WSML files, relieving you of the tedious process of manually creating such files.

All the real work is done by the SOAP Toolkit. The Office XP Web Services Toolkit uses the same core components and adds developer support in terms of the Web Service References Tool. This tool integrates with the Visual Basic Editor in Office applications and allows you to autogenerate VBA code to use the SOAP toolkit components. The Office 2003 Web Services Toolkit offers essentially the same functionality as the Office XP Web Services Toolkit, but for Office 2003. The Office 2003 Web Services Toolkit uses Office SOAP 3.0.

The Web Service References Tool provides an interface for discovering Web services, selecting the services you want, and creating classes that act as Web service proxies for your VBA projects.

When you add a reference to a Web service using the tool, a *SoapClient* proxy class is added to your VBA project. The proxy class is added to your project as a class module with the name of the Web service prefixed with *clsws*. This proxy class wraps calls to the Web service. You can use this proxy class to easily access the functionality that the Web service provides and incorporate that functionality into your Office solution. When you implement a Web service in your Office solution, your Office solution is considered a Web service client.

The proxy class uses SOAP and MSXML to interact with a Web service. Because the proxy class wraps calls to the Web service, you do not need to write the code yourself to interact with SOAP and MSXML.

In the following exercise, we'll use the Office XP or Office 2003 Web Services Toolkit to integrate a Microsoft Excel worksheet with a Web service. Note that if you're developing with earlier versions of Office, you can either use the Office Web Services Toolkit on a development machine and copy the generated VBA code (or the document/ worksheet where the code resides) to the production pre–Office XP machines, or you can simply write the VBA code manually. Regardless of the Office version, your code will use the SOAP Toolkit underneath.

Caution This example involves the use of VBA macro code. It is normally recommended that you set Office macro security to the highest possible level, not automatically trust installed add-ins and templates, and not trust access to the Visual Basic project. To check your settings, go to Tools | Macro | Security. With the security settings at their highest, the following sample application will fail because of its use of VBA macro code unless you sign it. For the purposes of this exercise, you can relax your security settings while you're testing the application. However, you should be sure to restore security to the settings approved by your organization immediately after testing.

Note The sample solution for this topic can be found in the sample code at <install location>\Code\Office<n>\OfficeWeb. This contains a "blank" solution that contains only OfficeWeb.xls—we're only using Visual Studio for consistency with the rest of the sample solutions. The exercise also uses a simple Web service; the files for this are in <install location>\Tools\WebServices\WebTempConv.

A Sample Web Service

This chapter uses a simple Web service. If you want to focus on the consumption of Web services in your Office solution, you can simply use the sample code for the Web service itself while working through the Office interop portions. However, the instructions for creating the Web service from scratch are also given here.

In this exercise, we'll create a simple Web service that exposes temperature conversion functions.

1. Create a new C# ASP.NET Web Service project (not a Web application) called WebTempConv. Note that Visual Studio puts this in the default Web directory, probably c:\inetpub\wwwroot, which is published as http://<servername>. The wizard generates several files.

2. The first file to consider is Service1.asmx—this is what the client will be requesting, and the code in this file will trigger the C# code-behind. If you just double-click this file, it opens in the designer. For this exercise, this is not useful—we want to see the code instead. To see the code, right-click the .asmx file in Solution Explorer, and choose Open with either Source Code Text Editor or HTML/XML Editor:

```
<%@ WebService Language="c#" Codebehind="Service1.asmx.cs"
Class="WebTempConv.Service1" %>
```

3. As you can see, the code behind the Service1.asmx file is in the file Service1.asmx.cs. This is a C# file that is not normally listed in Solution Explorer. However, you can find it if you click the Show All Files button. You

must then right-click it and select View Code.

If you examine the code in this file, you'll see that it consists of a single class called *Service1*, derived from *System.Web.Services.WebService*. Apart from the familiar *InitializeComponent* method that the designer uses, the only other code of note is a commented-out sample *HelloWorld* method. The wizard provides that to indicate how to write a simple Web service method.

4. Next we add our custom methods to perform temperature conversion and decorate them with the *WebMethod* attribute:

```
[WebMethod]
public double F2C(double val)
{
    return ((5.0/9.0) * (val - 32.0));
}

[WebMethod]
public double C2F(double val)
{
    return ((val * (9.0/5.0)) + 32.0);
}
```

5. Build the project, and test it by running Microsoft Internet Explorer and requesting the TempConv page—that is, <servername>/WebTempConv/Service1.asmx. By default, the Web service is built on the local machine, so you can use *localhost* as the *servername*.

Instead of explicitly running Internet Explorer, you can also just execute the project within Visual Studio to run it in situ. Alternatively, you can right-click the .asmx file in Solution Explorer, and select View In Browser. You'll see links that you can use to invoke the *F2C* and *C2F* Web methods, as well as some explanatory information on the syntax:

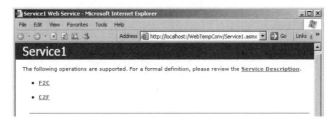

Click on either the *F2C* or *C2F* link, and you'll be offered a text box for typing in the parameter. You'll also see the SOAP and HTTP messages that will be built (both outgoing and incoming). If you type a value (say, 212) into the *F2C* parameter value box and click Invoke, your input will be passed to the Web service and you'll get the appropriate response, as XML in the browser.

A Web Service Proxy

If you are using the sample code for the WebTempConv Web service, instead of working through the exercise above, you'll need to build the service from the sample solution. You also need to set it up in IIS.

1. To set up the service, go to the IIS MMC snap-in, select and right-click the *Default Web Site* node, and select New | Virtual Directory. Create a new vdir with the name *WebTempConv*, and point it to the location where the WebTempConv project files are. Accept all other defaults. When you've done this, the WebTemp-Conv virtual directory should appear in the IIS tree.

2. With the Web service set up, we can start on the Office development: run Excel and open a new workbook with at least one worksheet. Go to the Visual Basic Editor, and then choose Tools | Web References to run the Web References Tool. In the first dialog box, select the Web Service URL option and type in the URL for the WebTempConv service on your local machine, as shown here. (Note: If you're not using the Office XP or Office 2003 Web Services Toolkit, see the next section, "SOAP Toolkit Code," for instructions.) Clicking the Search button finds the service and populates the Search Results treelist. Select the box next to Service1, and click the Add button.

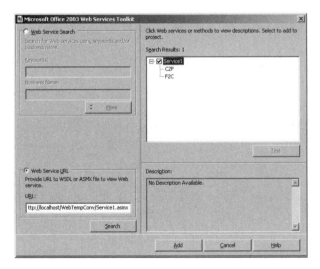

This generates a new class module in your VBA project, named something like *clsws_Service1*. This class is a proxy based on the WSDL from Service1. If you examine the code, you'll see a *Class_Initialize* subroutine that is called each time the class is instantiated. It instantiates a *SoapClient* (actually, for version 3.0, a *SoapClient30*) proxy object and initializes it with the WSDL from Service1.

```
Private sc_Service1 As SoapClient30
Private Const c_WSDL_URL As String =
```

```
"http://localhost/WebTempConv/Service1.asmx?wsdl"
Private Const C_SERVICE As String = "Service1"
Private Const C_PORT As String = "Service1Soap"
Private Const C_SERVICE_NAMESPACE As String = "http://tempuri.org/"

Private Sub Class_Initialize()
    Dim str_WSML As String
    str_WSML = ""
    sc_Service1 = New SoapClient30

    sc_Service1.MSSoapInit2(C_WSDL_URL, str_WSML, C_SERVICE, C_PORT,
        C_SERVICE_NAMESPACE)
End Sub
```

The tool also generates proxy functions for the Web methods in the Web service. For example, the proxy to the *F2C* method converts from Fahrenheit to Celsius:

```
Public Function wsm_F2C(ByVal dbl_val As Double) As Double
    On Error GoTo wsm_F2CTrap
    wsm_F2C = sc_Service1.F2C(dbl_val)
    Exit Function
    wsm_F2CTrap:
    Service1ErrorHandler("wsm_F2C")
End Function
```

3. In the Project Explorer pane, right-click on the project and insert a new module. Add code to the module to define VBA functions that wrap calls to the proxy—we need these additional wrappers in a module so we can call the functions directly from worksheet cells. In each wrapper, instantiate the *clsws_Service1* proxy and call either the *wsm_F2C* or *wsm_C2F* proxied method:

```
Option Explicit

Public Function F2CWrapper(val As Double) As Double
    Dim service As clsws_Service1
    Set service = New clsws_Service1
    F2CWrapper = service.wsm_F2C(val)
End Function

Private Function C2FWrapper(val As Double) As Double
    Dim service As clsws_Service1
    Set service = New clsws_Service1
    C2FWrapper = service.wsm_C2F(val)
End Function
```

4. In the worksheet, put some arbitrary values in two of the cells (the pale shaded ones in the following screenshots). We'll convert one of these from Fahrenheit to Celsius, and the other from Celsius to Fahrenheit. In the adjacent cells (the dark shaded ones), put cell formulas to call the two VBA wrapper functions. Here is how the cell should look as you're typing in the formula (in cell C2 in this example):

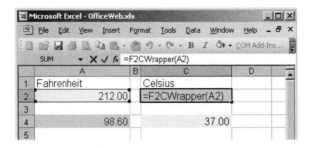

This is how it should look after you press Enter and the formula has called into the Web service to return the value:

SOAP Toolkit Code

If you're not using the Office XP or Office 2003 Web Services Toolkit, you can enter the VBA code manually. To mirror what is produced by the toolkit, you must create a class module in your workbook for the *SoapClient30* proxy and a regular module for the Web method wrappers.

1. To do this, open the workbook in Excel and go to the Visual Basic Editor. Create a new class module, calling it *clsws_Service1*. This class will be a VBA proxy to the target Web service. At the top, set up some private class variables:

```
Private sc_Service1 As SoapClient30
Private Const c_WSDL_URL As String =
"http://localhost/WebTempConv/Service1.asmx?wsdl"
Private Const c_SERVICE As String = "Service1"
Private Const c_PORT As String = "Service1Soap"
Private Const c_SERVICE_NAMESPACE As String = "http://tempuri.org/"
```

2. Define a *Class_Initialize* subroutine—this will be called each time the class is instantiated (like a constructor):

```
Private Sub Class_Initialize()
      Dim str_WSML As String
      str_WSML = ""

      'Create a new SoapClient object, and initialize it to the target WSDL.
      sc_Service1 = New SoapClient30()
      sc_Service1.MSSoapInit2(c_WSDL_URL, str_WSML, c_SERVICE,
C_PORT, C_SERVICE_NAMESPACE)
```

```
'Use the proxy server defined in IE's LAN settings.
sc_Service1.ConnectorProperty("ProxyServer") = "<CURRENT_USER>"

'Autodetect proxy settings if IE is set to autodetect.
sc_Service1.ConnectorProperty("EnableAutoProxy") = True
End Sub
```

The *Class_Terminate* subroutine works like a destructor:

```
Private Sub Class_Terminate()
        On Error GoTo Class_TerminateTrap
        sc_Service1 = Nothing
        Exit Sub
Class_TerminateTrap:
        Service1ErrorHandler("Class_Terminate")
End Sub
```

The *Service1ErrorHandler* sub is a common error-handling routine that is callable from anywhere in the class:

```
Private Sub Service1ErrorHandler(ByVal str_Function As String)
        If sc_Service1.FaultCode <> "" Then
            Err.Raise(vbObjectError, str_Function, sc_Service1.FaultString)
        Else
            Err.Raise(Err.Number, str_Function, Err.Description)
        End If
End Sub
```

3. Finally, add a regular module, and code the wrappers to the two Web service methods:

```
Public Function wsm_F2C(ByVal dbl_val As Double) As Double
        On Error GoTo wsm_F2CTrap
        wsm_F2C = sc_Service1.F2C(dbl_val)
        Exit Function
wsm_F2CTrap:
        Service1ErrorHandler("wsm_F2C")
End Function

Public Function wsm_C2F(ByVal dbl_val As Double) As Double
        On Error GoTo wsm_C2FTrap
        wsm_C2F = sc_Service1.C2F(dbl_val)
        Exit Function
wsm_C2FTrap:
        Service1ErrorHandler("wsm_C2F")
End Function
```

4. Save everything, and test the solution.

UDDI

For a further example of using the Web Service References Tool, we'll use the Universal Discovery, Description, and Integration (UDDI) feature. UDDI is a specification used by businesses to register information such as the Web services they expose. This information can be consumed by business partners so they can interact with the exposed Web services.

Open the worksheet and go to the Visual Basic Editor again. Go to Tools | Web References. In the Web References Tool dialog box, select the Web Service Search option, type in the keyword *airport*, and click Search. UDDI is used to find published Web services that match this keyword.

From the search results, select the box next to the AirportWeather service—a useful little service that reports weather conditions at airports. Click Add to generate the SoapClient proxy code.

Add a *Button* control to the worksheet, set its *Name* property to *cmdWeather* and its *Caption* to "Get Weather", and double-click it to get a *Click* handler. Code this to instantiate the *clsws_AirportWeather* proxy, and call the *wsm_getTemperature* proxy method. Pass it the code string for your favorite airport (say, "KSEA"):

```
Private Sub cmdWeather_Click()
    Dim service As New clsws_AirportWeather
    MsgBox service.wsm_getTemperature("KSEA")
End Sub
```

Build and test. When the user clicks the button, the application calls out to the Web service to get the current temperature at the chosen airport:

> **Microsoft Excel**
>
> The Temperature at Seattle, Seattle-Tacoma International Airport, WA, United States is 60.1 F (15.6 C)
>
> [OK]

> **Note**   The AirportWeather service used here is like all publicly available services in that it might not be offered indefinitely. If you can't find the service when you try this exercise, try a different service instead. A good place to start looking is *http://test.uddi.microsoft.com/*.

9.2 Managed Web Service Proxies

Office 97	?
Office 2000	?
Office XP	✓
Office 2003	✓

The SOAP Toolkit and the Office Web Services Toolkit require you to use VBA-based client-side Web service proxy code. This is all well and good, but you might want to move away from VBA. If that is your aim, you can build client-side Web service proxy code using .NET instead. The version block at the beginning of this section needs clarifying: the core technique explained in this section (a managed Web service proxy) can be built with all four versions of Office. The only question is how to hook the Web service proxy into Office. You have several choices—and you'll often be faced with these same choices when you design Office solutions with managed code:

- Build a separate Windows Forms application that makes the Web service calls and automates Office from the outside.

- Build a managed component that makes the Web service calls, and register it for COM interop—you then need VBA code in the Office document to instantiate and control your managed component.

- Build a managed COM add-in that makes the Web service calls. (This restricts you to Office 2000 and later.)

- Build a managed automation add-in that makes the Web service calls. (This restricts you to Excel XP and later.)

- Build a Visual Studio Tools for Office solution that makes the Web service calls. (This restricts you to Microsoft Word 2003 and Excel 2003.)

Which option you choose will depend on whether you are constrained to use a particular version of Office and whether the solution requirement is more application-centric or more document-centric. In this section, we'll work through an example using a managed automation add-in—arguably the most elegant of the solution models, although the most restrictive as to host application.

> **Note** The sample solution for this topic can be found in the sample code at <install location>\Code\Office<n>\WebAddin. The Web service itself can be found at <install location>\Tools\WebServices\WebTempConv.

We'll build functionality that's similar to the Automation add-in in Section 5.7, "Excel Automation Add-Ins." To avoid any conflict, if you built that add-in sample and installed it, you should remove it before proceeding with this example. You can simply deselect the box next to its name in the Add-ins dialog box in Excel (Tools | Add-ins). If you prefer, you can uninstall it altogether—although this is not strictly necessary. You can also refer to Section 5.7 for more detailed information about building an Automation add-in.

1. To start, create a Shared Add-in project called WebAddin. Select only Excel as the application host, and supply a suitable name and description. Don't select either of the final check boxes—we don't want this add-in to load when the host application loads because that would load it as a COM add-in, not as an Automation add-in.

2. Automation add-ins need a couple of extra registry entries over and above the normal entries for COM add-ins. So, once the wizard has generated the add-in project, select the setup project, and click the Registry Editor button. In the registry editor, create an additional subkey of HKEY_CLASSES_ROOT named *CLSID* and leave all properties at their defaults. Create another new key that is a child of CLSID, with the GUID of the *Connect* class, delimited with braces, such as: {EE337219-ADD7-4FF9-86AE-C31111B281E4}. Set the *AlwaysCreate* property to *True*. Create a final key that is a child of this GUID key, named *Programmable*. This key needs no value. Set the *AlwaysCreate* property to *True* for this key also.

3. The *Connect* class is already attributed with a *Guid* and a *ProgId*. Add a third attribute for *ClassInterface*, specifying *AutoDual* as the type. Recall that using *AutoDual* class interfaces is normally discouraged because such interfaces allow clients to bind to a specific interface layout that might change as the class evolves, thereby breaking the client. However, using an *AutoDual* class interface gives us a registered type library, which is essential for an Automation add-in.

```
[GuidAttribute("EE337219-ADD7-4FF9-86AE-C31111B281E4"),
ProgId("WebAddin.Connect"),
ClassInterface(ClassInterfaceType.AutoDual)]
public class Connect : Object, Extensibility.IDTExtensibility2
{
```

4. Add stubs for two public methods that we'll expose to Excel and that will act as wrappers for the Web service methods. Bearing in mind the problem we had in Chapter 5, "Add-Ins," with the very short *C2F* and *F2C* method names, we'll avoid that here by using unambiguous names for the methods that will be used from Excel cells:

```
public double FtoC(double val)
{
}

public double CtoF(double val)
{
}
```

5. Now we're ready to add a reference to our chosen Web service. Right-click the project in Solution Explorer, and select Add Web Reference. In the Add Web Reference dialog box, type the URL for the Web service (*http://localhost/WebTempConv/Service1.asmx*) and click Go. When the wizard returns with the Service1 information, change the Web reference name from localhost to WebTempConv:

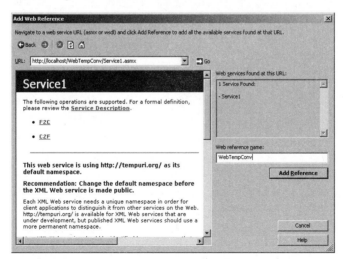

6. Then click Add Reference. This generates a C# source file based on the Web service WSDL. By default, you cannot see this file, but if you click the Show All Files button and expand the *WebTempConv* node in the tree, you'll see it listed as Reference.cs.

The generated class is a client-side proxy to the Web service and is derived from *SoapHttpClientProtocol*. The significant features of this class are listed below (with comments and attributes removed for brevity). It's worth noting that the constructor sets up the URL for the Web service and that there are wrapper methods for the Web service methods. You'll see that there are in fact both synchronous and asynchronous wrappers for each method.

```csharp
namespace WebAddin.WebTempConv
{

    public class Service1 : SoapHttpClientProtocol
    {

        public Service1() {
            this.Url = "http://localhost/WebTempConv/Service1.asmx";
        }

        public System.Double F2C(System.Double val) {
            object[] results = this.Invoke("F2C", new object[] {
                    val});
            return ((System.Double)(results[0]));
        }

        public System.IAsyncResult BeginF2C(System.Double val,
            System.AsyncCallback callback, object asyncState) {
            return this.BeginInvoke("F2C", new object[] {
                    val}, callback_u32 ?asyncState);
        }

        public System.Double EndF2C(System.IAsyncResult asyncResult) {
            object[] results = this.EndInvoke(asyncResult);
            return ((System.Double)(results[0]));
        }

        public System.Double C2F(System.Double val) {
            object[] results = this.Invoke("C2F", new object[] {
                    val});
            return ((System.Double)(results[0]));
        }

        public System.IAsyncResult BeginC2F(System.Double val,
            System.AsyncCallback callback, object asyncState) {
            return this.BeginInvoke("C2F", new object[] {
                    val}, callback, asyncState);
        }

        public System.Double EndC2F(System.IAsyncResult asyncResult) {
            object[] results = this.EndInvoke(asyncResult);
            return ((System.Double)(results[0]));
        }
    }
}
```

7. Note the namespace given in the generated code. Back in the *Connect* class, add a *using* statement for this namespace. Then flesh out the stubs we created earlier: instantiate the service proxy, and call the appropriate Web method proxy:

```
public double FtoC(double val)
{
    Service1 s = new Service1();
    return s.F2C(val);
}

public double CtoF(double val)
{
    Service1 s = new Service1();
    return s.C2F(val);
}
```

8. Change the add-in project properties—go to Configuration Properties | Debugging, and set the *Start Application* value to launch Excel instead of Visual Studio. Then build the add-in project.

9. As with our previous Automation add-in project, we need to build and run the setup project so the additional registry entries are made. After you build the add-in, build the setup, and install it, you can test it. In Excel, go to Tools | Add-ins to get the list of Automation add-ins. Click the Automation button to get a list of all programmable automation servers registered on the machine. Select your add-in component from the list, and click OK. If you get the message "Cannot find add-in 'mscoree.dll'. Delete from list?" click No.

10. Back in the Add-ins dialog box, the new WebAddin add-in should be listed. Close the dialog box. In Excel, in any cell, make a call to the *FtoC* method or the *CtoF* method exposed by our Automation add-in to convert from Fahrenheit to Celsius:

9.3 WSE Security

Office 97	②
Office 2000	✓
Office XP	✓
Office 2003	✓

Web Services Enhancements (WSE) 2.0 for Microsoft .NET, which you can download for free from the Microsoft Download Center, is a .NET class library for building Web services. It implements the latest Web services protocols, including WS-Security, WS-SecureConversation, WS-Trust, WS-Policy, WS-SecurityPolicy, WS-Addressing, and WS-Attachments. WSE allows you to add these capabilities at design time using code or at deployment time through the use of an XML policy file.

You can apply the WSE features to an existing Web service or to a new one, and to client-side code that consumes the Web service. The basic mechanism is a series of filters that build additional SOAP header information for an outgoing message or that parse and process additional SOAP headers for an incoming message. Filters can be applied at both the Web server and at the client end.

WSE uses the mechanisms defined in the WS-Security specification to place security credentials in the SOAP headers. This is done by having a client obtain security credentials (known as *tokens*) from a source that is trusted by both the sender and receiver. When the Web server receives the SOAP request, it does not need to make another network request to the client's computer or to a trusted third party to verify the integrity of the security tokens. Instead, WSE cryptographically verifies that the credentials are authentic before passing execution to the Web service. Using the new WSE features, you can also digitally sign the message and/or encrypt it.

In the following exercise, we'll build a managed COM add-in that uses the same WebTempConv Web service introduced in the previous section, "Managed Web Service Proxies." The add-in will offer a custom toolbar with two text boxes and a button. The idea is that the user will enter a value in the first text box, and we'll hand that value off to the Web service method and put the return value into the second text box. The button acts as a toggle to switch the direction of the temperature conversion between Celsius and Fahrenheit. The significant change from the previous version of this solution is that we'll secure the Web service calls using WSE security.

In this case, the mechanism used to connect to the Office application is a managed COM add-in, which therefore restricts this particular implementation of the solution to Office 2000 and later. However, as with the previous solution, the core techniques of using a managed Web service proxy and using WSE security are usable with all four versions of Office.

 Note   The client-side (managed add-in) part of the sample solution for this topic can be found in the sample code at <install location>\Code\Office<n>\WseAddin. The WSE-enabled Web service itself can be found at <install location>\Tools\WebServices\WebTempConv_WSE.

The Core Add-In

1. Create a Shared Add-in project called WseAddin. Select your preferred Office application(s) as the host, and supply a suitable name and description. Select the box that sets up the registry to have Office load this add-in when the host application loads.

   When the wizard has generated the initial code, add a reference to System.Windows.Forms.dll and a corresponding *using* statement for the namespace—we'll be using the *MessageBox* class for convenience during testing, and we'll also add a custom dialog box in the last phase.

2. We need to make some generic enhancements to two of the wizard-generated methods. You can refer back to Section 5.1, "Managed COM Add-Ins," for further information on the reasons behind these changes. Briefly, we'll create our custom toolbar in *OnStartupComplete* and delete it in *OnBeginShutdown*. We will ensure that these methods are invoked not only when the host application starts up and shuts down (the normal route), but also when the add-in is connected or disconnected through the UI.

Declare some class fields for the custom toolbar, the three controls on the bar, and a *bool* flag to hold the current state of the conversion direction:

```
private CommandBar wseBar;
private CommandBarComboBox btnInput;
private CommandBarComboBox btnOutput;
private CommandBarButton btnDirection;
private bool isFtoC = true;
```

OnStartupComplete is where we do all the work of setting up the toolbar, the buttons, and the event handlers. First start a *try* block and get the collection of command bars in the host application (using late binding, as usual):

```
public void OnStartupComplete(ref System.Array custom)
{
    string barName = "WseTempConv";
    object missing = Type.Missing;

    try
    {
        CommandBars bars = null;
        Type applicationType = applicationObject.GetType();
        bars = (CommandBars)applicationType.InvokeMember(
            "CommandBars", BindingFlags.GetProperty,
            null, applicationObject, null);
```

3. Add a new toolbar—you specify a toolbar by specifying a *CommandBar* that is not a menu. We want this bar to be temporary—it will be created each time the host application starts or the user connects the add-in and will be deleted each time the host application stops or the user disconnects the add-in:

```
bool isMenuBar = false;
bool isTemporary = true;
wseBar = bars.Add(barName,
    MsoBarPosition.msoBarTop,
    isMenuBar, isTemporary);
```

4. Next we'll add the three controls. We need a text box for the incoming temperature value, a button to toggle the direction of conversion between Fahrenheit and Celsius, and a second text box for the conversion result. The order you add the buttons in is significant—that's the order in which they'll be presented in at runtime. For the button, we'll set the *FaceId* to *85*—this has an image of the character

F. This indicates to the user that we start off with the conversion direction from Fahrenheit to Celsius.

```
// Add an text box for the incoming temperature value.
btnInput = (CommandBarComboBox)wseBar.Controls.Add(
    MsoControlType.msoControlEdit, 1,
    missing, missing, true);
btnInput.Width = 50;
btnInput.Tag = "Input";
btnInput.Enabled = true;

// Add a button to toggle the direction of conversion F<->C.
string tagName = "Toggle Convert Direction";
btnDirection = (CommandBarButton)wseBar.Controls.Add(
    MsoControlType.msoControlButton, 1,
    missing, missing, false);
btnDirection.FaceId = 85;
btnDirection.Tag = tagName;
btnDirection.TooltipText = tagName;
btnDirection.Enabled = true;

// Add an text box for the conversion result.
btnOutput = (CommandBarComboBox)wseBar.Controls.Add(
    MsoControlType.msoControlEdit, 1,
    missing, missing, false);
btnOutput.Width = 50;
btnOutput.Tag = "Output";
btnOutput.Enabled = true;
```

5. Finally, we'll hook up event handlers for the input and direction controls. We're interested in the *Change* event on the input text box and the *Click* event on the direction button. Then make sure the new bar is visible and close off the *catch* block.

```
btnInput.Change +=
    new _CommandBarComboBoxEvents_ChangeEventHandler(
    btnInput_Change);
btnDirection.Click +=
    new _CommandBarButtonEvents_ClickEventHandler(
    btnDirection_Click);

        wseBar.Visible = true;
    }
    catch(Exception ex)
    {
        MessageBox.Show(ex.StackTrace, ex.Message);
    }
}
```

OnBeginShutdown just needs to delete the toolbar:

```
public void OnBeginShutdown(ref System.Array custom)
{
    if (wseBar != null)
    {
        wseBar.Delete();
    }
}
```

6. Having set up the command UI, we need to handle the events fired when the user works with these commands. Write a new method for the *Change* event on the input text box to correspond with the event hookup we've just done. This method will be invoked when the user enters something into the input text box and presses Return.

   The idea is that eventually we'll take the input string, convert it to a double, hand it off to the Web service method, convert the return value to a string, and put it into the output text box. For ease of testing, we'll do this in stages. For now we can do all these things except the Web method call. For this phase, just echo the input value into the output text box:

   ```
   private void btnInput_Change(
       CommandBarComboBox cmdBarComboBox)
   {
       try
       {
           string inputString = cmdBarComboBox.Text;
           double inputNumber = double.Parse(inputString);
           btnOutput.Text = inputNumber.ToString();
       }
       catch (Exception ex)
       {
           MessageBox.Show("Invalid Input");
       }
   }
   ```

7. Write a second custom method to handle the *Click* event on the direction button. We use this to toggle the conversion direction between Fahrenheit and Celsius. All we have to do is toggle the state of our *bool* field and reset the *FaceId* between *F* and *C*:

   ```
   private void btnDirection_Click(
       CommandBarButton Ctrl, ref bool CancelDefault)
   {
       try
       {
           if (isFtoC)
           {
               btnDirection.FaceId = 82;   // 'C'.
               isFtoC = false;
           }
           else
           {
               btnDirection.FaceId = 85;   // 'F'.
               isFtoC = true;
           }
       }
       catch (Exception ex)
       {
           MessageBox.Show(ex.StackTrace, ex.Message);
       }
   }
   ```

8. At this point, you should build and test the basic add-in before we go ahead and add the Web service proxy. This is how it should look at runtime, with the input value mirrored in the output text box:

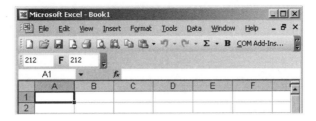

The Web Service Proxy

1. The procedure for adding the client-side Web service proxy is the same as in the previous solution. Right-click the project in Solution Explorer, and select Add Web Reference. In the Add Web Reference dialog box, type the URL for the Web service (*http://localhost/WebTempConv/Service1.asmx*), and click Go.

2. When the wizard returns with the Service1 information, change the Web reference name from *localhost* to *WebTempConv*. Then click Add Reference. This generates a C# source file based on the Web service WSDL. By default, you cannot see this file, but if you click the Show All Files button and expand the *WebTempConv* node in the tree, you'll see it listed as Reference.cs.

3. Before we layer on the WSE security features, it's worth checking that the basic functionality of the Web service is working correctly. In the Connect.cs, add a *using* statement for the freshly minted *WseAddin.WebTempConv* namespace. Then go back to the *Change* event handler for the input text box and make a call to the Web service, putting the result in the output text box:

```csharp
private void btnInput_Change(
    CommandBarComboBox cmdBarComboBox)
{
    try
    {
        string inputString = cmdBarComboBox.Text;
        double inputNumber = double.Parse(inputString);
        //btnOutput.Text = inputNumber.ToString();
        Service1 s = new Service1();
        if (isFtoC)
        {
            btnOutput.Text = s.F2C(inputNumber).ToString();
        }
        else
        {
            btnOutput.Text = s.C2F(inputNumber).ToString();
        }
    }
    catch (Exception)
```

```
    {
        MessageBox.Show("Invalid Input");
    }
}
```

Now when you test the solution, with the default conversion direction of Fahrenheit to Celsius, an input of 212 should result in an output of 100. If you toggle the conversion direction, the same 212 input should result in an output of 413.6.

The WSE Client Proxy

WSE offers many security features that we could use in our solution, including encrypting and signing SOAP messages and adding security headers. In our example, we'll add a username/password security token to each Web method call.

For simplicity, we'll use the user's logon username and password—that is, a Windows domain account. When the application makes a Web service call, we'll prompt the user to supply a valid username and password. This information can be used to construct a suitable token, which is then added to the SOAP headers that go along with the Web service call. The WSE library includes default handling for this scenario, as long as we send the username and password in cleartext. Of course, for a production system, this is not acceptable, and we'd have to use other classes in the WSE library to increase the security of the call. Most commonly, in fact, we'd use a Kerberos token rather than a Username token, and we'd probably encrypt the message as well—but we'll keep things simple here.

1. Add a new Windows Form to the application called LogonDialog, and populate it with appropriate controls:

Also set the form's *AcceptButton* property to the name of the OK button, and set the *DialogResult* property of the OK button to *OK*. This means users only have to type in the information and press Return—they don't actually have to click the button. Also set *BackColor* to *ControlLightLight*, *FormBorderStyle* to *FixedDialog*, and turn off both *MaximizeBox* and *MinimizeBox*. Set the *PasswordChar* property of the *Password* text box to an asterisk (*).

2. In the following code snippets, the assumption is that the Password text box is named *password*, and the Username text box is named *username*. We will need to get the strings supplied by the user for these values from code outside the dialog class. However, by default, such controls in a form are declared private. Instead of changing this standard behavior, it is better to expose a public property for each one and to make that property effectively read-only:

```
public string Username
{
    get { return username.Text; }
}

public string Password
{
    get { return password.Text; }
}
```

3. To use WSE, we need to add a reference to the WSE assembly; this will be listed on the .NET tab of the Add Reference dialog box as Microsoft.Web.Services2.dll.

    When you added a reference to the Web service, the wizard generated a Web service proxy derived from *SoapHttpClientProtocol*. We need to change this if we want to hook up WSE. To do this, go to the Reference.cs wizard-generated proxy file and add a *using* statement for the *Microsoft.Web.Services2* namespace. Then you can change the inheritance of the *Service1* proxy class to the WSE *WebServicesClientProtocol*:

```
public class Service1 :
    //System.Web.Services.Protocols.SoapHttpClientProtocol
    Microsoft.Web.Services2.WebServicesClientProtocol
{
```

    We're developing this solution incrementally, and we started off with a regular (non-WSE-enabled) Web service and proxy. If we'd started off with a WSE-enabled Web service, the wizard-generated proxy would already provide a *WebServicesClientProtocol*-based class and we wouldn't have to make this manual change.

4. Back in the *Connect* class, add *using* statements at the top for the WSE *Security* and *Security.Tokens* namespaces:

```
using Microsoft.Web.Services2.Security;
using Microsoft.Web.Services2.Security.Tokens;
```

5. Update the *Change* event handler: display our new *LogonDialog* to harvest a suitable username and password from the user, use these to build a new *UsernameToken* object, and attach this token to the Web service *RequestSoapContext*. Also sign the message with the token:

```
try
{
    string inputString = cmdBarComboBox.Text;
```

```
                        double inputNumber = double.Parse(inputString);
                        Service1 s = new Service1();

                        UsernameToken token = null;
                        LogonDialog dlg = new LogonDialog();
                        if (dlg.ShowDialog() == DialogResult.OK)
                        {
                            token = new UsernameToken(
                                dlg.Username, dlg.Password,
                                PasswordOption.SendPlainText);
                        }

                        s.RequestSoapContext.Security.Tokens.Add(token);
                        s.RequestSoapContext.Security.Elements.Add(
                            new MessageSignature(token));

                        if (isFtoC)
                        {
                            btnOutput.Text = s.F2C(inputNumber).ToString();
                        }
                        else
                        {
                            btnOutput.Text = s.C2F(inputNumber).ToString();
                        }
                    }
```

6. Although we haven't finished the solution, you should build and test at this point to make sure all the client-side processing is correct. When the user enters a value in the input box and presses Return, the solution displays the *LogonDialog* to prompt for username and password. At this stage, you can enter whatever you like in these boxes:

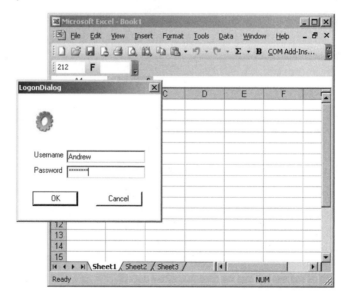

The result of testing at this stage should be an error. Although all the client code is correct, the Web service itself currently doesn't understand the additional security information we've supplied.

The WSE Web Service

The final piece of the puzzle is to enhance the Web service so it can deal with the additional security information. There are two main tasks to perform:

- Update the web.config for the Web service so it uses the additional WSE features.

- Enhance the existing Web methods to test for valid security information.

When you install WSE, you get a wizard added to the Visual Studio Solution Explorer shortcut menu. This wizard essentially runs the WSE Configuration Editor tool, which modifies the web.config XML file for WSE features. This tool is not a one-off wizard—you can continue to use it to maintain your web.config if you need to. You can also run the tool independently of Visual Studio—by default, there is a shortcut at Start | Programs | Microsoft WSE 2.0. You don't have to use the tool at all if you don't want to—if you prefer, you can make the WSE configuration changes by directly editing the web.config. We'll look next at how to use the tool and what changes you have to make if you edit the configuration manually.

1. The first task is to update the web.config. Open the WebTempConv Web service solution. Right-click on the project in Solution Explorer, and select WSE Settings 2.0. This runs the Configuration Editor. On the General tab, select both boxes—we want to enable this project for WSE and we want to enable WSE Soap Extensions.

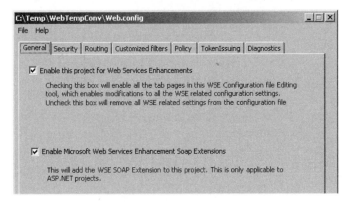

Selecting these options adds some new nodes to the web.config and also adds a reference in the project to the WSE assembly.

2. On the Diagnostics tab, select the Enable Message Trace check box. This is a debugging convenience—if we turn this on, WSE will write XML trace output for both the incoming and outgoing messages into files that we specify here.

Choose appropriate file names for the trace logs, such as InputTrace.xml and OutputTrace.xml.

Close the tool to persist the changes to the web.config. If you want to make the changes manually instead of using the Configuration Editor, here are the new entries that correspond to the choices we made in the tool. Note that some of the strings (in quotes) in this listing have been split over multiple lines, but in the web.config file they must each be on one line:

```xml
<configSections>
    <section name="microsoft.web.services2"
    type="Microsoft.Web.Services2.Configuration.WebServicesConfiguration,
    Microsoft.Web.Services2, Version=2.0.0.0, Culture=neutral,
    PublicKeyToken=31bf3856ad364e35" />
</configSections>

<microsoft.web.services2>
    <security>
        <x509 allowTestRoot="false" allowRevocationUrlRetrieval="true"
        verifyTrust="true" allowUrlRetrieval="false"
        storeLocation="LocalMachine" />
<defaultTtlInSeconds>300</defaultTtlInSeconds>
<timeToleranceInSeconds>300</timeToleranceInSeconds>
    </security>
    <diagnostics>
        <trace enabled="true" input="InputTrace.xml"
output="OutputTrace.xml" />
<detailedErrors enabled="false" />
<policyTrace enabled="false" />
    </diagnostics>
</microsoft.web.services2>

<system.web>
    <webServices>
        <soapExtensionTypes>
            <add type="Microsoft.Web.Services2.WebServicesExtension,
            Microsoft.Web.Services2, Version=2.0.0.0, Culture=neutral,
            PublicKeyToken=31bf3856ad364e35" priority="1" group="0" />
        </soapExtensionTypes>
    </webServices>

    <!-- standard entries here... -->
</system.web>
```

3. The second task is to update the Web methods. At the top of the Service1.asmx.cs file, add *using* statements for the main *WSE Security* namespace and the namespace where the security token classes are defined:

```csharp
using Microsoft.Web.Services2;
using Microsoft.Web.Services2.Security.Tokens;
```

4. Write a new method to walk the collection of *SecurityToken* objects in the SOAP headers sent in from the client with each message. Examine each one to see if it is a *UsernameToken*. At this point, you can perform whatever additional checks you want to authorize the method call. The following example checks the

incoming username and the user's role membership. Obviously, hardcoding these tests is not realistic, but you get the idea. If we authorize this call, we'll return an appropriate *bool* value to indicate this:

```
private bool IsMessageSigned()
{
    SoapContext requestContext = RequestSoapContext.Current;
    if (requestContext == null)
    {
        throw new ApplicationException(
            "Either a non-SOAP request was received or " +
            "WSE is not properly installed.");
    }

    foreach (SecurityToken token in requestContext.Security.Tokens)
    {
        if (token is UsernameToken)
        {
            UsernameToken user = (UsernameToken)token;
            if (user.Username == "Andrew")
            {
                if (user.Principal.IsInRole(
                    "BUILTIN\\Administrators"))
                {
                    return true;
                }
            }
        }
    }
    return false;
}
```

5. We can then update both of our Web methods with a call to this new method. Only if the call is correctly signed do we return the conversion value—otherwise, we throw an exception. This exception is propagated back to the client.

```
[WebMethod]
public double F2C(double val)
{
    if (!IsMessageSigned())
    {
        throw new ApplicationException(
            "The request is not correctly signed.");
    }

    return ((5.0/9.0) * (val - 32.0));
}
```

6. Test the client add-in again. Now the username and password information should be correctly handled on the server, and the add-in should display expected results in the toolbar.

As an aside, you might want to check the trace logs. For example, in InputTrace.xml you should be able to identify the additional security information, including the (cleartext) username and password, and the message body.

9.4 Research Services

Office 97	⊗
Office 2000	⊗
Office XP	⊗
Office 2003	✓

Excel 2003, Word 2003, and Microsoft PowerPoint 2003 include a new Research task pane. This task pane allows users to search local and remote data sources from within Office. Out of the box, the Research task pane includes resources such as the Encarta World Dictionary, the Encarta Encyclopedia, MSN Money Stock Quotes, and others. These resources are made available as Web services.

As a developer, you can provide additional research resources by simply providing Web services that conform to the Research Services protocol. Office clients contact the service in two scenarios: when the user registers the service for the first time (or updates it later), and when the user queries the service. You must therefore provide a Web service (or two Web services) that implement the *Registration* and *Query* methods that respond to these two events. Office passes your Web methods an XML payload that conforms to the published request schema for registration or query. You then parse this XML and compose a response that conforms to the published response schema for registration or query.

The Research Services SDK is a free download available from the Microsoft Download Center—it contains a schema and API reference, simple tools, sample code, and documentation. Also, the OfficeZealot team—who works very closely with Microsoft to produce a number of tools for Office development—has put together a freely downloadable class library and a set of wizards that greatly simplify the development of research services. See *www.officezealot.com*.

In the following exercise, we'll build two research services: the first using the Research Services SDK, and the second using the Research Services Class Library (RSCL).

> **Note**   The sample solution for the raw SDK research service can be found in the sample code here: <install location>\Tools\WebServices\SimpleResearchService. The RSCL-based sample code can be found here: <install location>\Tools\WebServices\ SimpleRascal.

Raw SDK Research Service

Create an ASP.NET Web Service project called SimpleResearchService. When the wizard has generated the skeleton code, go to the code for Service1.asmx and add *using* statements at the top for *System.IO* and *System.Xml*—we'll be manipulating XML files in our solution. Then attribute the Web service class with the Research Services namespace, and declare the required two Web methods. We could put each of these methods in a separate Web service, but for our simple sample there's no need:

```
[WebService(Namespace="urn:Microsoft.Search")]
public class SimpleResearchService: System.Web.Services.WebService
{
```

```
    [WebMethod]
    public string Registration(string registrationRequest)
    {
        return String.Empty;
    }

    [WebMethod]
    public string Query(string queryXml)
    {
        return String.Empty;
    }
}
```

When we get a registration or query request from Office, we must compose a schema-conformant XML response packet. In both cases, we can compose this XML either programmatically or by loading predefined XML, or some combination of the two. For registration, it makes sense to allow the information to be configurable and therefore abstracted to a separate XML file. For queries, the information is more likely to be dynamic, so it is more useful to compose the XML programmatically.

We'll start with the registration method. We'll create a new XML file that we can load at runtime and submit back as our response packet. Add a new XML file to the project called Registration.xml, and remove the wizard-generated starter code. We want to end up with a simple XML file that looks like this:

```xml
<ProviderUpdate xmlns="urn:Microsoft.Search.Registration.Response">
   <Status>SUCCESS</Status>
   <Providers>
      <Provider>
         <Message>Introductory service setup message.</Message>
         <Id>{9F834983-4B66-4d47-A61F-FB2A50BA9B2E}</Id>
         <Name>Simple Research Provider</Name>
         <QueryPath>
            http://localhost/SimpleResearchService/Service1.asmx
         </QueryPath>
         <RegistrationPath>
            http://localhost/SimpleResearchService/Service1.asmx
         </RegistrationPath>
         <Type>SOAP</Type>
         <Services>
            <Service>
               <Id>{DF73D049-5FCE-44c5-B87F-6AF84472FBE8}</Id>
               <Name>Simple Research Service</Name>
               <Description>My first Research service.</Description>
               <Copyright>(c) Andrew Whitechapel 2003.</Copyright>
               <Display>On</Display>
               <Category>INTRANET_GENERAL</Category>
               <Parental>Unsupported</Parental>
            </Service>
         </Services>
      </Provider>
   </Providers>
</ProviderUpdate>
```

Clearly, some of this information depends on the specifics of your solution, so let's walk through it from the top. We'll consider the overall structure first. The whole registration response packet is termed a *ProviderUpdate* because it will be used on first registration and for subsequent updates for this service provider. There must be one (and only one) *Provider*, and there can be one or more *Service* nodes.

The *ProviderUpdate* must include the research services target namespace and must indicate a *SUCCESS* status code. The *Message* is optional: if you provide a message string here, it will be displayed in the initial dialog box when the user first registers or updates the Research task pane with your service. The *Id* element must be a unique GUID—you can get this from the GUIDGen tool in Visual Studio | Tools. The *Name* element is an arbitrary string name for your provider, which is also displayed in the various dialog boxes offered by the Research task pane.

```
<ProviderUpdate xmlns="urn:Microsoft.Search.Registration.Response">
   <Status>SUCCESS</Status>
   <Providers>
      <Provider>
         <Message>Introductory service setup message.</Message>
         <Id>{9F834983-4B66-4d47-A61F-FB2A50BA9B2E}</Id>
         <Name>Simple Research Provider</Name>
```

You must provide the URLs to the services that implement the *Query* and *Registration* methods. In our example, these methods are implemented by the same service. The provider *Type* must be *SOAP*.

```
         <QueryPath>
            http://localhost/SimpleResearchService/Service1.asmx
         </QueryPath>
         <RegistrationPath>
            http://localhost/SimpleResearchService/Service1.asmx
         </RegistrationPath>
         <Type>SOAP</Type>
```

There can be one or more *Services* for each *Provider*, although in our example there's only one. Each *Service* must have a unique GUID identifier and a suitable *Name*. The *Description* and *Copyright* information (if supplied) will be displayed in various Research task pane dialog boxes—clearly, you should supply whatever strings are appropriate for your solution. The *Display* element indicates whether this service is visible. The *Category* element defines the category under which the service shows in the UI—the possible values include INTRANET_GENERAL, BUSINESS_FINANCE, SCIENCE_BIOLOGY, and MEDICAL_GENERAL (defined in the published schema). The *Parental* element indicates whether the service supports filtering of potentially offensive content:

```
         <Services>
            <Service>
               <Id>{DF73D049-5FCE-44c5-B87F-6AF84472FBE8}</Id>
               <Name>Simple Research Service</Name>
               <Description>My first Research service.</Description>
```

```
            <Copyright>(c) Andrew Whitechapel 2003.</Copyright>
            <Display>On</Display>
            <Category>INTRANET_GENERAL</Category>
            <Parental>Unsupported</Parental>
        </Service>
    </Services>
```

When you've completed this file to your satisfaction, save it. Then go back to the
Service1.asmx.cs code and implement the *Registration* method. Because we've
abstracted all the registration information to a configurable file, implementing the
Registration method is simple. All we do is find the file, load it up, and read it into a
string. Bear in mind that we're running in a Web service, so the current path is the
path to the CLR (almost certainly %WINDIR%\system32)—hence the use of *MapPath*
in the code snippet:

```
[WebMethod]
public string Registration(string registrationRequest)
{
    string xmlFile = Path.Combine(
        HttpContext.Current.Server.MapPath("."), "registration.xml");
    StreamReader reader = new StreamReader(xmlFile);
    string registrationXml = reader.ReadToEnd();
    reader.Close();
    return registrationXml;
}
```

At this point, you can build and test your service. We haven't implemented the *Query*
method yet, so users cannot use our service for any searches—but they can register it.
Open Word, Excel or PowerPoint, go to the View menu, and make sure the task pane
is visible. In the task pane, select Research from the Other Task Panes drop-down list.
In the Research task pane, click the Research Options link at the bottom to open the
Research Options dialog box:

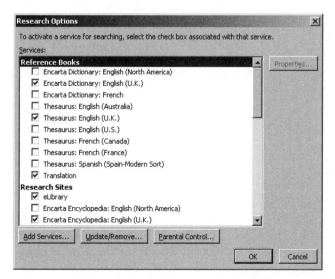

In the dialog box, click Add Services, enter the URL (including the *http://* prefix) to your new service, and click Add. If your service is built correctly, this will display your introductory service setup message, followed by a final confirmation page that includes a list of the services that will be installed for this provider. Click Install to complete the registration of this provider and its services:

Once registration is complete, you can start using the service. In the Office Research task pane, type in a term to search for, and select your new service in the drop-down list. At this point, we haven't implemented the *Query* method, so you should get an empty result packet:

If registration was successful, we can now turn to the *Query* method. We'll return a response packet that illustrates some of the typical contents, including a title, a hyperlink, an image, some formatting, and some text. The text will be conditional upon the specific query we receive (in a very simple way). We could again implement this by loading an external XML file, and we want to end up with XML that looks like this:

```
<ResponsePacket xmlns="urn:Microsoft.Search.Response">
    <Response domain="{DF73D049-5FCE-44C5-B87F-6AF84472FBE8}">
        <QueryID>{3CB6A657-9446-432C-A82A-191881ACBF3C}</QueryID>
        <Range>
            <Results>
                <Document xmlns="urn:Microsoft.Search.Response.Document">
                    <Title>Electrons</Title>
                    <Action>
                        <LinkUrl>http://www.microsoft.com</LinkUrl>
                    </Action>
                    <Media type="IMAGE">
                        <SrcUrl>
                            C:\Temp\SimpleResearchService\Electrons.wmf
                        </SrcUrl>
                        <AltText>Electrons</AltText>
                    </Media>
                </Document>
                <Content xmlns="urn:Microsoft.Search.Response.Content">
                    <HorizontalRule />
                    <P>Hello world</P>
                    <HorizontalRule />
                </Content>
            </Results>
        </Range>
        <Status>SUCCESS</Status>
    </Response>
</ResponsePacket>
```

However, queries tend to require dynamic information, so it's more realistic to build the XML query response packet entirely programmatically.

In the *Query* method, we first need to parse the incoming query request XML: load this into an *XmlDocument* and select the *Query* node. From that node, we can extract the domain (which is supplied with the request to identify the service that is being requested). We extract it because we need to feed the same information back when we send our response. Similarly, we extract the query ID—a dynamically generated GUID that the task pane attaches to each query—and send it back with our response. Finally, we need to extract the query term itself so we can use it to compose a conditional response:

```
[WebMethod]
public string Query(string queryXml)
{
    XmlDocument xmlQuery = new XmlDocument();
    xmlQuery.LoadXml(queryXml);
```

```
XmlNamespaceManager nm =
    new XmlNamespaceManager(xmlQuery.NameTable);
nm.AddNamespace("msq", "urn:Microsoft.Search.Query");
XmlNode queryNode =
    xmlQuery.SelectSingleNode(
        "/msq:QueryPacket/msq:Query", nm);
string domain =
    queryNode.Attributes.GetNamedItem("domain").Value;
string queryId = xmlQuery.SelectSingleNode(
    "/msq:QueryPacket/msq:Query/msq:QueryId", nm).InnerText;
string queryTerm = xmlQuery.SelectSingleNode(
    "//msq:QueryText", nm).InnerText;
xmlQuery = null;
```

We'll build the XML string in memory, using a *MemoryStream* object and an *XmlText-Writer*. Set these up, and set the formatting to *Indented*—this is simply for easy viewing. Then write out the start of the XML document:

```
MemoryStream stream = new MemoryStream();
XmlTextWriter writer = new XmlTextWriter(stream, null);
writer.Formatting = Formatting.Indented;
writer.WriteStartDocument();
```

Write out the start elements for the entire *ResponsePacket*, the *Response*, and the *Results*, including the service domain and query ID information extracted from the incoming request packet:

```
writer.WriteStartElement("ResponsePacket",
    "urn:Microsoft.Search.Response");
writer.WriteStartElement("Response");
writer.WriteAttributeString("domain", domain);
writer.WriteElementString("QueryID", queryId);
writer.WriteStartElement("Range");
writer.WriteStartElement("Results");
```

Begin the *Document* element. Now for our first discretionary piece of data: we'll write out a title:

```
writer.WriteStartElement("Document",
    "urn:Microsoft.Search.Response.Document");
writer.WriteElementString("Title", "Electrons");
```

Add a link to some Web site (or other URL) of your choice:

```
writer.WriteStartElement("Action");
writer.WriteStartElement("LinkUrl");
writer.WriteString("http://www.microsoft.com");
writer.WriteEndElement(); // LinkUrl
writer.WriteEndElement(); // Action
```

Include an image–the sample solution includes a small Windows metafile, but you can use any image you like:

```
writer.WriteStartElement("Media");
writer.WriteAttributeString("type", "IMAGE");
writer.WriteElementString("SrcUrl",
HttpContext.Current.Server.MapPath(".") +"\\Electrons.wmf");
writer.WriteElementString("AltText", "Electrons");
writer.WriteEndElement(); // Media
```

Close the *Document* element, and begin the *Content* element. We'll put out a simple string that is partially composed from the incoming query term, topped and tailed with horizontal lines:

```
writer.WriteEndElement(); // Document

writer.WriteStartElement("Content",
    "urn:Microsoft.Search.Response.Content");
writer.WriteStartElement("HorizontalRule");
writer.WriteEndElement(); //Horizontal rule
writer.WriteElementString("P", "Hello " +queryTerm);
writer.WriteStartElement("HorizontalRule");
writer.WriteEndElement(); //Horizontal rule

writer.WriteEndElement(); // Content
```

Close off all the end elements, and make sure the *XmlTextWriter* flushes all data out to the stream. Finally, move the stream into a string by using a *StreamReader*, and return this XML string:

```
writer.WriteEndElement(); // Results
writer.WriteEndElement(); // Range
writer.WriteElementString("Status", "SUCCESS");
writer.WriteEndElement(); // Response
writer.WriteEndElement(); // ResponsePacket

writer.WriteEndDocument();
writer.Flush();
stream.Position = 0;
StreamReader reader = new StreamReader(stream);
return reader.ReadToEnd();
```

Build and test again. This time, when the user searches our research service, he'll get back our populated response packet with dynamic text:

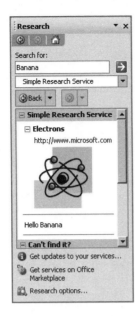

Research Services Class Library

When you install the Research Services Class Library (RSCL) Toolkit, you get a class library, a set of Visual Studio wizards, sample solutions, and documentation. The RSCL simplifies the creation of research services by abstracting often-used features of the Research task pane into a simple object model wrapper. The wrapper produces the XML defined by the research service's XML schemas. Using the RSCL, a developer can focus mostly on the business logic of the solution rather than the XML plumbing code of research services.

1. After you install the RSCL Toolkit, run the wizard. You'll be prompted to supply all the mandatory and optional information required for registration of your service. The wizard then generates a project, including an enhanced web.config, a reference to the RSCL assembly, and skeleton code. The Web service derives from the RSCL ResearchWebService, which derives in turn from the familiar System.Web.Services.WebService.

2. Look first at the web.config file. This has a new config section, with all the information you provided to the wizard:

```
<configSections>
    <section name="RSCL.ResearchService"
type="Microsoft.Samples.Office.ResearchService.Config.RSCLConfigLoader,RSCL,1.1
.4322.573,Culture=neutral, PublicKeyToken=null" />
</configSections>

<!-- RSCL web.config section -->
<RSCL.ResearchService>
    <Provider>
        <Name>Contoso Research Services</Name>
```

```
        <Message>Welcome to Contoso</Message>
        <AboutPath></AboutPath>
        <ID>{406790cc-2446-4bef-8209-9dff22990817}</ID>
    </Provider>
    <Service>
        <Name>Simple Rascal Service</Name>
        <Description>A simple service demonstrating the OfficeZealot RSCL toolk
it</Description>
        <Category>RESEARCH_GENERAL</Category>
        <ID>{575440db-b8b0-4db5-8ca9-d579abcd648c}</ID>
    </Service>
</RSCL.ResearchService>
```

This config information is used by the *Registration* method in the Web service class:

```
public override RegistrationResponse Registration(RegistrationRequest request)
{
    RegistrationResponse response = new RegistrationResponse();
    return response;
}
```

The wizard also generates a stub *Query* method, with a dummy code block indicating the sort of code you need to add to return query responses:

```
public override QueryResponse Query(QueryRequest request)
{
    QueryResponse response = new QueryResponse();
    DocumentResponseWriter doc = new DocumentResponseWriter();
    doc.WriteItem(
        "Sample Response Title","Sample Response Description");
    response.WriteResponse(doc);
    return response;
}
```

At this point, the research service compiles and runs. However, because no business logic has been provided in the *Query* method, the research service can only be registered, and no search results are returned.

3. Add some code to the *Query* method to experiment with some of the features of the *DocumentResponseWriter* and the *ContentResponseWriter* classes. For example, add a hyperlink and an image, and write out the incoming query text. Also, insert a button to insert the incoming query text into the current document, and add a line separator:

```
public override QueryResponse Query(QueryRequest request)
{
    QueryResponse response = new QueryResponse();
    DocumentResponseWriter doc = new DocumentResponseWriter();
    doc.WriteItem(
        "Sample Response Title","Sample Response Description");
    response.WriteResponse(doc);

    ContentResponseWriter content = new ContentResponseWriter();
    content.WriteHyperlink(
        "http://www.fourthcoffee.com/", "Fourth Coffee");
```

```
content.WriteImage(
    HttpContext.Current.Server.MapPath(".")
    +"\\Coffee.wmf", "Coffee");
content.WriteParagraph(request.QueryText);
content.WriteInsertTextIntoDocumentButton(
    request.QueryText);
content.WriteHorizontalLineSeparator();
```

4. Another nice feature is the ease with which you can run further queries on the same service from the query response. To test this, switch on the incoming query text, and offer the user an alternative query. In our example, if the user queries for "Espresso," we'll offer the option to run a new query for "Latte," and vice versa:

```
content.WriteParagraph(
    @"<Char bold=""true"">New query:</Char>",
    false);
switch (request.QueryText.ToLower().Trim())
{
    case "espresso":
        content.WriteNewQuery(
            "Latte", "Latte", "Query for 'Latte'");
        break;
    case "latte":
        content.WriteNewQuery(
            "Espresso", "Espresso", "Query for 'Espresso'");
        break;
}

response.WriteResponse(content);
return response;
}
```

5. Build and test. This is how it should look at runtime, once you've registered the service:

9.5 Remoting with Office

Office 97	?
Office 2000	✓
Office XP	✓
Office 2003	✓

.NET Remoting is a set of classes and a framework that allows objects to interact with one another across application domains. In many ways, this can be seen as an evolved alternative to DCOM. You can use remoting to build distributed systems where objects communicate across application domains, across processes on the same machine, or across machines in a LAN or WAN. In practice, when you build distributed systems across machines, you are often better served by using Web services. That said, in some scenarios remoting is useful, particularly if performance is a major factor.

When you develop an object and you want to make it remotable, you have a choice as to how the object is remoted:

- **Marshal by value (MBV) objects**   A complete copy of the object is made when the object is passed from one application to another. You could argue that this means the object isn't really remoted at all because the client will have a complete copy and there's no assumption that the client and server objects are connected or synchronized in any way. The standard way to implement an MBV object is to make it serializable.

- **Marshal by reference (MBR) objects**   A reference to the object—*ObjRef*—is made when the object is passed from one application to another. When the object reference arrives in the remote application, it is used to dynamically create a proxy to the original object. The client's method calls are executed on the proxy. This is the more usual definition of a remotable object.

The Remoting framework provides a number of services, including object activation and lifetime management, and communication channels for transporting messages to and from remote applications. An object used in remoting falls into one of two general categories, depending on how it is created or activated:

- **Client-activated object (CAO)**   This is a server-side object that is activated upon request from the client. When a client uses the new operator to create a remote CAO, an activation request message is sent to the remote application that is acting as the host for the CAO, and an *ObjRef* is returned. Note that clients can use the new operator or the *Activator.CreateInstance* method.

   A CAO can store state information between method calls for its specific client, but not across different clients because each client will use a different instance of the CAO. Also, a client can pass constructor parameters to a CAO, which is not possible with a server-activated object (SAO). The lifetime of a CAO is determined by a lease-based system. The object is available for garbage collection when the lease expires or when there are no longer any client references.

- **Server-activated object (SAO)**   This is an object created by a hosting server application. When a client uses the new operator to "create" a remote SAO, an activation request message is sent to the server. The server either creates a fresh instance of the requested object or uses an existing instance—either way, an *ObjRef* is returned and the client ends up with a client-side proxy. However, there is no activation until the first method call is made from the client on the proxy. Note that clients can use the new operator or the *Activator.GetObject* method. SAOs can be further divided into:

  - **Single Call objects**   The objects service one and only one incoming request. Single Call objects are useful in scenarios where the objects are required to do a finite amount of work. These objects cannot hold state information between method calls. However, Single Call objects can be configured in a load-balanced fashion.

  - **Singleton objects**   These objects are intended to service multiple clients and therefore share data by storing state information between client invocations. They are useful in cases in which data needs to be shared explicitly between clients and also in which the overhead of creating and maintaining the object is substantial.

To support customization, Remoting offers a number of hooks that provide access to the messages and the serialized stream before the stream is transported over the channel. Formatters are used for encoding and decoding the messages before they are transported by the channel. Applications can use binary encoding where performance is critical, or XML encoding where interoperability with other remoting frameworks is essential.

You must host your remotable object in some way, and you have three options:

- **Managed executable**   Remoting objects can be hosted in any regular .NET EXE or a managed Windows service.

- **IIS**   By default, remoting objects hosted in IIS receive messages through the HTTP channel. This is most appropriate when you want to build a remoting solution that spans multiple machines. Hosting in IIS gives you built-in scalability, failover robustness, and security.

- **.NET Component Services**   Remoting objects can be hosted in the .NET Component Services infrastructure to take advantage of the various COM+ services, such as Transactions, JIT Activation, and Object Pooling.

You can specify the configuration for a remoting application using either code or XML config files. The main advantage of using config files is that they abstract the configuration information from the code so that you can make changes later by just changing the config file, as opposed to editing and recompiling the source file. Abstracting the specifics of the system in this way also supports location transparency—the code doesn't need to have any knowledge of how the system is actually deployed at any given time.

Config files are used by both client and server and typically include:

- Host application information
- Object names
- Object URIs
- Channels to be used
- Lease expiry information

Remoting can be used by any .NET component that you choose to use with Office, regardless of how you integrate that component with Office. Unlike protocols such as Add-ins, Smart Tags, Smart Documents, Remoting is not specific to Office and has no Office-specific features. That said, in one Office development scenario it can be very useful. Recall that it is a relatively simple matter to hook up your managed code to events fired by an Office application. For this to work, you obviously need information about the Office application (from its type library, via the interop assembly) so you can correctly hook up your event sink.

Suppose, however, that you want to fire events in your managed code, and you want Office to sink them. Clearly, this would imply that the Office application must have information about your managed code. Certainly, you can expose your managed code through a registered type library and a runtime COM callable wrapper (CCW), but the Office application can't hook up your events because it wasn't written to know anything about them. On the other hand, you can write an add-in that knows about your events.

One additional issue is that both Office applications and Windows Forms controls can execute only on the thread on which they are created. An event fired from a remote object will come in on a different thread. If you want to update an Office or Windows Forms UI control from another thread, you must marshal the call to the thread that created the control. Five methods on a control are safe to call from any thread: *InvokeRequired*, *Invoke*, *BeginInvoke*, *EndInvoke*, and *CreateGraphics*. For all other method calls on a control, you should pass a delegate to that method as a parameter to the control's *Invoke* or *BeginInvoke* method. These methods ensure that the delegate method is executed on the thread that owns this control's underlying window handle.

Remoting fully supports event-driven programming and callback functions using synchronous and asynchronous delegates. Delegates are serializable MBV objects, but the objects to which they refer can be MBV or MBR. Therefore, we can set up a system that uses remotable delegates to implement events fired across application domains (and across processes, and even across machines).

In the following example, we'll build a solution that allows Office (using our add-in) to respond to events fired from our managed code, using a remoted SAO. The vehicle we'll use to illustrate this model is a simple broadcast chat system. This will involve multiple projects, and we'll build the solution in two main phases, starting with the remotable object and a simple Windows Forms client application, and only later implementing an Office add-in client. The first-phase projects will be built in the following order:

- **ChatCoordinator** An SAO that fires events
- **ChatServer** A server-side console application that hosts the *ChatCoordinator* SAO
- **WinChat** A Windows Forms client that both initiates and responds to remote chat messages
- **ChatDelegate** A remotable delegate that sinks events fired by the ChatCoordinator and asynchronously updates the WinChat UI

Phase 1 is summarized in Figure 9-1.

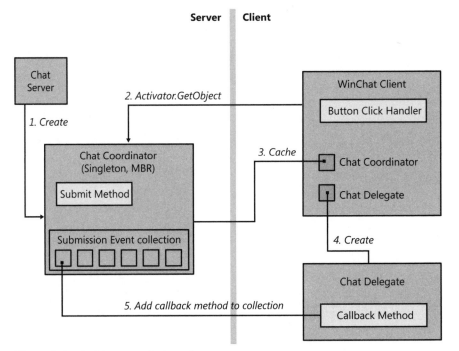

Figure 9-1 Architecture of phase 1.

In the second phase, we'll add an additional project, OfficeChat, a managed COM add-in client that both initiates and responds to remote chat messages.

Phase 2 is summarized in Figure 9-2.

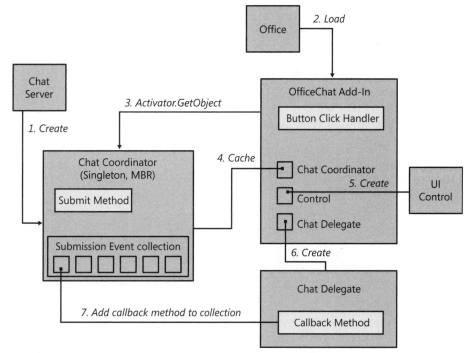

Figure 9-2   Architecture of phase 2.

In this example, the mechanism used to connect to the Office application is a managed COM add-in, which therefore restricts this particular implementation of the solution to Office 2000 and later. However, the core remoting techniques are isolated in the managed code and are therefore usable with all four versions of Office.

> **Note**   The sample solution for this topic can be found in the sample code at <install location>\Code\Office<n>\Chat. The solution includes multiple projects. This is a lengthy example, with a lot of moving parts—in fact, it's probably the most complex example in the book.

ChatCoordinator SAO

1. Create a class library project called ChatCoordinator. You can delete the wizard-generated *Class1* class, but keep the file. At the top of the file, add *using* statements for the main remoting namespaces:

```
using System.Runtime.Remoting;
using System.Runtime.Remoting.Services;
```

2. Before creating the SAO class, create a custom *EventArgs* class for encapsulating the chat message that clients will send and the alias name each client will use to identify itself. When we send a chat message, we'll send it as one of these custom *EventArgs* objects. Therefore, the class needs to be remotable, and in this case MBV remotable is fine:

```
[Serializable]
public class SubmitEventArgs : EventArgs
{
    public string payload;
    public string alias;

    public SubmitEventArgs(string payload, string alias)
    {
        this.payload = payload;
        this.alias = alias;
    }
}
```

3. We can also declare the delegate type that will be used to handle the events that will be fired in this solution:

```
public delegate void SubmissionEventHandler(
    object sender, SubmitEventArgs submitArgs);
```

4. The *ChatCoordinator* class itself is the primary remoted object, an MBR SAO. In the (default) constructor, just print out a message to the console—we'll be hosting this SAO in a console application. You can print any message you like (or none), although printing the hash code for the object provides some identity information.

We must override the *InitializeLifetimeService* method to return *null*—to ensure that when created as a *Singleton*, the first instance never dies, regardless of the time between chat users.

The real work is done in the custom *Submit* method. The client calls this method to submit a message to the chat system. When we get the call in our SAO, we'll print out the message to the server console and then broadcast it by invoking the remote client's (or clients') *Submission* methods. To do this, we need to have an event field of the delegate type we devised earlier. The idea is that clients will implement a method of the form of the delegate so we can invoke it without having any other knowledge about the clients.

```
public class ChatCoordinator : MarshalByRefObject
{
    public ChatCoordinator()
    {
        Console.WriteLine("ChatCoordinator created. Instance="
            + this.GetHashCode().ToString());
    }

    public override object InitializeLifetimeService()
```

```
    {
        return null;
    }

    public event SubmissionEventHandler Submission;

    public void Submit(string payload, string alias)
    {
        Console.WriteLine("{0}-> {1}.", alias, payload);

        SubmitEventArgs e = new SubmitEventArgs(payload, alias);
        if (Submission != null)
        {
            Submission(this, e);
        }
    }
}
```

5. All parties involved in the chat system need to have minimal type information about the ChatCoordinator, so for simplicity we'll deploy it to the global assembly cache (GAC). To do this, go to the Properties for the project and navigate to Common Properties | Build Events. Set the Post-build Event command line to run the GAC installer utility, specifying its full path (the default path is shown below) and the name of the *ChatCoordinator* assembly, using the *$(TargetPath)* macro:

   "C:\program files\Microsoft Visual Studio .NET 2003\SDK\v1.1\Bin\gacutil" /i "$(TargetPath)"

6. To deploy to the GAC, the assembly must be strong-named. So, generate or acquire a strong-named keypair file and apply it with the *AssemblyKeyFile* attribute in the assemblyinfo.cs file. Build the project, and check that ChatCoordinator.dll is correctly installed in the GAC.

Chat Server Host

This application is about as simple as it gets. All it needs to do is host the *ChatCoordinator* SAO and stay alive until it's no longer needed. We'll set up the remoting information using a config file.

1. Create a new console application called ChatServer—for convenience, you can add this project to the existing solution, although this is not essential. Add a *using* statement for the main remoting namespace, and add a reference to the *ChatCoordinator* assembly.

2. We need only one class, with one method—the skeleton class supplied by the wizard will do fine (although you might want to rename it). Set up the SAO hosting operation by specifying the config file. Stay alive by the simple expedient of issuing a *Console.ReadLine* statement:

```
public class ServerProcess
{
    public static void Main(string[] Args)
    {
        RemotingConfiguration.Configure("ChatServer.exe.config");
        Console.WriteLine(
            "Host appdomain started - press Enter to stop it.");
        Console.ReadLine();
    }
}
```

3. Add an application configuration file to the project—this is one of the predefined project item types, so you'll find it in the Add New Item dialog box. In this way, the file will be copied to ChatServer.exe.config as part of the build. In the config, we need to specify the class name and assembly name for the *ChatCoordinator* SAO, an arbitrary name (objectUri) for the service, and the fact that we want a *Singleton* object.

4. We also need to specify the attributes of the channel we want to use—in this case, the TCP communication protocol—using some port that won't conflict with anything else (8081), and we must specify that we support SOAP and binary formatting:

```
<configuration>
    <system.runtime.remoting>
        <application>
            <service>
                <wellknown
                type="Chat.ChatCoordinator, ChatCoordinator"
                objectUri="Chat" mode="Singleton" />
            </service>
            <channels>
                <channel ref="tcp" port="8081">
                    <serverProviders>
                        <provider ref="wsdl" />
                        <formatter
                            ref="soap" typeFilterLevel="Full" />
                        <formatter
                            ref="binary" typeFilterLevel="Full" />
                    </serverProviders>
                    <clientProviders>
                        <formatter ref="binary" />
                    </clientProviders>
                </channel>
            </channels>
        </application>
    </system.runtime.remoting>
</configuration>
```

5. Build the server. You should test the server, of course, but it won't instantiate the ChatCoordinator until we have at least one client request.

Chat Delegate

This is basically a wrapper for a remotable delegate. We need this extra piece because not only are we using remoting to talk across applications, but also we need to update the UI of a Windows or Office client from a remote object (on a thread that is not the same as the client's UI thread).

1. Add another new project to the solution: a class library called *ChatDelegate*. Add a reference to the *ChatCoordinator* assembly, and add a *using* statement for the *ChatCoordinator* assembly's main namespace.

2. Declare a custom interface. To make our solution as loosely coupled (and therefore agile) as possible, we don't want to have to have any detailed information about our clients. That is, we don't want to care whether our clients are Windows Forms, console, Office or ASP.NET applications, or indeed user controls or other class libraries. The only requirement we stipulate is that they implement this custom interface.

3. The interface needs one method—the callback method that clients will implement to update their own UI. It also needs a property that is a reference to a UI artifact (a control or form of some kind that lives on the same thread as the client's main UI). We need this property to be only readable, not writable:

```
public interface IConnect
{
    void AddIncomingMessage(string message);

    Control UI
    {
        get;
    }
}
```

4. Declare a custom delegate type. Clients will implement a method that takes this form to update their own UI:

```
public delegate void AddMessageDelegate(string message);
```

The remotable delegate class itself is a wrapper to this delegate. It needs to be MBR and to have fields where it can cache the reference to the client's implementation of the *IConnect* interface. As with the *ChatCoordinator*, this remotable object must override the *InitializeLifetimeService* method.

5. The class needs just one custom method that conforms to the *Submission-EventHandler* delegate type that we defined in the *ChatCoordinator* assembly. The *ChatCoordinator* SAO will call back into this method to send a chat message. When we get the call, we wrap the client method that we ultimately want to call in a delegate of our own, so we can invoke it asynchronously. This ensures that the call is marshaled onto the same UI thread as the control that we use to make the *BeginInvoke* call.

```
public class CallbackWrapper : MarshalByRefObject
{
    private IConnect connect;
    private Control ui;

    public CallbackWrapper () {}
    public CallbackWrapper (IConnect connect)
    {
        this.connect = connect;
        ui = connect.UI;
    }

    public override object InitializeLifetimeService()
    {
        return null;
    }

    public void SubmissionCallback (
        object sender, SubmitEventArgs submitArgs)
    {
        if (submitArgs.payload.Length > 0)
        {
            string message = submitArgs.alias +"-> "
                +submitArgs.payload;
            AddMessageDelegate md =
                new AddMessageDelegate(
                    connect.AddIncomingMessage);

            try
            {
                if (!ui.IsDisposed)
                {
                    ui.BeginInvoke(md, new object[]{message});
                }
            }
            catch (Exception ex)
            {
                MessageBox.Show(ex.Message);
            }
        }
    }
}
```

6. We want our *ChatDelegate* to be usable by multiple clients, so for convenience, strong-name it and GAC-deploy it. You can set up a post-build event in the same way we did for the *ChatCoordinator*. Then build the project and check that it is correctly installed in the GAC.

A WinChat Client

Our first client will be a simple Windows Forms application, with a *TextBox* for the user to type in a message, a *Button* to send the message, and a *ListBox* to list the ongoing chat conversation.

1. Add a new Windows Forms project to the solution, called WinChat. Put suitable controls on the form. In the following code listings, the *TextBox* is named *txtOutgoing*, and the *ListBox* is named *lstConversation*. Set the *DialogResult* property of the Send button to OK, and set the *AcceptButton* property of the form to the *btnOK* button. This way, the user doesn't have to click the button to send a message—he can just press Return at the end of the message. Pressing Return defaults to the same behavior as clicking the button.

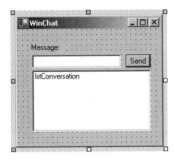

2. Add references to the *ChatCoordinator* and *ChatDelegate* assemblies, and add *using* statements for all the remoting namespaces we'll need, plus the *ChatCoordinator* and *ChatDelegate* namespaces.

```
using System.Runtime.Remoting;
using System.Runtime.Remoting.Channels;
using System.Runtime.Remoting.Services;
using System.Runtime.Remoting.Channels.Tcp;

using ChatCoordinator;
using ChatDelegate;
```

3. Set the class to implement the *ChatDelegate.IConnect* interface. If you click Tab after typing in this interface name in the inheritance list for the class, the wizard generates skeleton implementations for the interface members. If you forget to do that, you can always type them in manually. (Recall that there are only two members.)

4. We'll implement the *AddIncomingMessage* method to add the incoming message to our list box. We'll implement the *UI* property to return the form itself:

```
public void AddIncomingMessage(string message)
{
    lstConversation.Items.Add(message);
    lstConversation.SelectedIndex = lstConversation.Items.Count -1;
}

public Control UI
{
    get { return this; }
}
```

5. We need fields for the *ChatCoordinator* SAO and the *ChatDelegate.CallbackWrapper* class, plus strings for the server URL and our chosen chat alias. This alias will be used outside the class, so expose it with a property:

```
private ChatCoordinator coordinator;
private CallbackWrapper callback;
private string serverUrl = String.Empty;
private string alias;

public string Alias
{
    get { return alias; }
    set { alias = value; }
}
```

6. We'll be using an XML config file for the remoting information on the client also. The same config file can also double up for nonremoting information. Each deployed instance of the application will have its own config file and can therefore configure a different alias. In the form's constructor, get the configured alias name. We'll use it initially just to set the caption in the form—later, we'll send the alias with all messages we send. At the same time, get the configured URL for the server. Finally, make a call to a custom *StartChat* method (which we haven't written yet), and enable the Send button:

```
public WinChatForm()
{
    InitializeComponent();

    alias = (string)ConfigurationSettings.AppSettings["userAlias"];
    this.Text = this.Text +" - " +alias;
    serverUrl =
        (string)ConfigurationSettings.AppSettings["serverUrl"];

    StartChat();
    btnSend.Enabled = true;
}
```

7. In the form's *Dispose* method, be sure to clean up. This should ideally include unhooking the event sink from the *ChatCoordinator*:

```
protected override void Dispose(bool disposing)
{
    if (coordinator != null && callback != null)
    {
        coordinator.Submission -=
            new SubmissionEventHandler(
                callback.SubmissionCallback);
    }

    if (disposing)
    {
        if (components != null)
        {
            components.Dispose();
        }
    }
    base.Dispose(disposing);
}
```

8. The most critical work is done in the custom *StartChat* method. This is where we set up and register the remoting channel we want to use. Because the attributes of the channel might need to change over time, we abstract all the details to an external config file. Therefore, all we have to do in code is to point the remoting infrastructure at that config file. This configures and registers the channel for us, based on the information we specify in the config file. We can then get a reference to the remote *ChatCoordinator* object and hook up the event handler.

```
public void StartChat()
{
    try
    {
        RemotingConfiguration.Configure("WinChat.exe.config");
        coordinator = (ChatCoordinator)
            Activator.GetObject(typeof(ChatCoordinator),
            serverUrl);
        callback = new CallbackWrapper(this);
        coordinator.Submission +=
            new SubmissionEventHandler(
                callback.SubmissionCallback);
    }
    catch (Exception ex)
    {
        MessageBox.Show(ex.Message);
    }
}
```

9. The last method to implement is a *Click* handler for the *Button*. Generate the skeleton by double-clicking on the button in the Forms Designer. When the user clicks the Send button, we gather the text from the *TextBox* and submit it to the *ChatCoordinator*, along with our alias:

```
private void btnSend_Click(
    object sender, System.EventArgs e)
{
    string outgoingMessage = txtOutgoing.Text;
    if (outgoingMessage.Length > 0)
    {
        coordinator.Submit(outgoingMessage, this.alias);
        txtOutgoing.Text = String.Empty;
    }
}
```

10. Add an application config file to the project, in the usual way. This needs to have almost the same basic remoting configuration as the server—the *ChatCoordinator* class and assembly, the URL to the registered well-known service provider (including the port we expect the server to use), and channel information.

11. We also specify two custom application settings, for our alias and for the server URL. (This last part is just a convenience—we could parse the config file and extract the same information from the *<wellknown>* element instead.) The point is that we can retrieve our custom *<appSettings>* entries using the standard *ConfigurationSettings* class without having to do any XML parsing manually.

```
<configuration>
    <system.runtime.remoting>
        <application>
            <client>
                <wellknown
                type="Chat.ChatCoordinator, ChatCoordinator"
                url="tcp://localhost:8081/Chat" />
            </client>
            <channels>
                <channel ref="tcp" port="0">
                    <clientProviders>
                        <formatter ref="binary" />
                    </clientProviders>
                    <serverProviders>
                        <formatter ref="binary" typeFilterLevel="Full" />
                    </serverProviders>

                </channel>
            </channels>
        </application>
    </system.runtime.remoting>

    <appSettings>
        <add key="userAlias" value="Andrew" />
        <add key="serverUrl" value="tcp://localhost:8081/Chat" />
    </appSettings>

</configuration>
```

12. Build the client project. Then test the entire remoted chat system. Run Chat-Server first so it is waiting for potential clients to ask for the *ChatCoordinator* SAO. Then run two or more instances of the WinChat client. If you set these up in different locations and with different aliases in their configs, you can follow what's happening more easily:

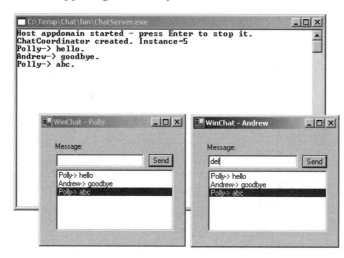

As you can see, when you type a message in one client and click Send, the message is sent to the ChatCoordinator, which prints it to the ChatServer console and then broadcasts it to all clients (including the original sender). Each client can do whatever it likes with the incoming message—in this example, we add the alias and the message payload to our conversation list.

The runtime process is summarized in Figure 9-3.

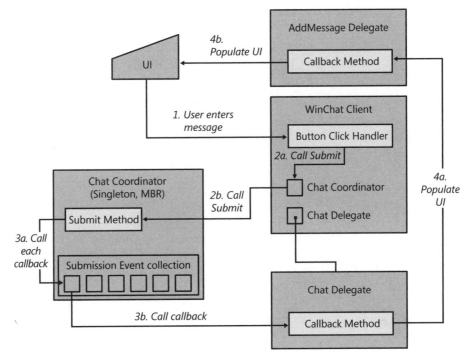

Figure 9-3   Runtime process of phase 1.

OfficeChat Add-In Client

To get an Office application to act as a client in this remoted chat system, we'll build an add-in. This will offer a custom command bar with four controls: a button to start the chat conversation, a text box for the user to type in a message, a combo box for the ongoing conversation, and a second button to stop chatting.

1. Create a Shared Add-in project called OfficeChat. Select your preferred Office application as the host—you might want to register this add-in against more than one host (say, Word and Excel), although this is not essential. Supply a suitable name and description. Select the box that sets up the registry to have Office load this add-in when the host application loads. When the wizard has generated the initial code, add references (and namespace *using* statements) to System.Windows.Forms.dll and the *ChatCoordinator* and *ChatDelegate* assemblies.

2. We need to make some generic enhancements to two of the wizard-generated methods. You can refer back to Section 5.1, "Managed COM Add-Ins," for further information on the reasons behind these changes. Briefly, we'll create our custom toolbar in *OnStartupComplete* and delete it in *OnBeginShutdown*. In *OnConnection*, we'll invoke our *OnStartupComplete* method, and in *OnDisconnection*, we'll invoke our *OnBeginShutdown* method. Additionally (as with the WinChat client), we must clean up at the end—so we'll add code to *OnDisconnection* to unhook the *ChatCoordinator* event sink.

3. We'll keep the *OnStartupComplete* method clean and put all the work in custom methods (which we haven't written yet). The first method will find and load the config file, and the second will set up our custom command bar:

```
public void OnStartupComplete(ref System.Array custom)
{
    GetConfiguration();
    SetupCommandBars();
}
```

4. Now declare some class fields for the custom toolbar and the four controls on the bar. We also need the same fields as the WinChat client—that is, references to the *ChatCoordinator* and a *ChatDelegate.CallbackWrapper*, and strings for our alias and the server URL. Declare a third string field for the path to our configuration file. With our WinChat client, we didn't need this because we could make the standard assumption that the config file was deployed to the same location as the EXE. With this OfficeChat add-in, we can still assume that the config is in the same place as the DLL, but because the DLL is running in the process of the host Office application, we need to do some extra work to find the location of the DLL.

The most important additional field we need is a *Control*. Recall that we need to ensure that remoted event callbacks update our UI on the same thread as our UI. With the WinChat client, we could simply use the main form for this, relying on the fact that *System.Windows.Forms.Form* derives from *System.Windows.Forms.Control*, which has thread-safe asynchronous methods such as *BeginInvoke*. For an Office add-in, we could get hold of the window handle for the host application and dynamically construct a *Control* around that, but it's just simpler to have a *Control* field.

```
private CommandBar chatBar;
private CommandBarButton btnStartChat;
private CommandBarComboBox btnMessage;
private CommandBarComboBox btnConversation;
private CommandBarButton btnStopChat;

private ChatCoordinator coordinator;
private CallbackWrapper callback;
private string configPath;
private string serverUrl;
private string userAlias;
```

```
public string Alias
{
    get { return userAlias; }
    set { userAlias = value; }
}

public Control control;
```

5. Set the class to implement the *ChatDelegate.IConnect* interface. Implement the *AddIncomingMessage* method to add the incoming message to our command bar combo box. Implement the *UI* property to return our *Control* field:

```
public void AddIncomingMessage(string message)
{
    btnConversation.AddItem(message,
        btnConversation.ListCount+1);
    btnConversation.ListIndex = btnConversation.ListCount;
}

public Control UI
{
    get { return control; }
}
```

6. Remoting information will be abstracted to a config file, and we'll use the same config file for other configuration details that are separate from the remoting information. Write the custom *GetConfiguration* method we called in *OnStartup-Complete* to find the config file, and cache it for use later when we want to set up the remoting channel.

    With the WinChat client, we could use the standard *ConfigurationSettings* class to work with the config. However, this relies on the fact that EXEs can have application configs. There is no support for DLLs that have configs, and of course our add-in is a DLL, so we have to parse the config ourselves with the *XmlDocument, XmlNode,* and *XmlAttributeCollection* classes. From the config, apart from the remoting information, we need to extract the server URL and the alias to use for this client:

```
private void GetConfiguration()
{
    string assemblyLocation =
        Assembly.GetExecutingAssembly().Location;
    configPath = assemblyLocation + ".config";

    try
    {
        XmlDocument configData = new XmlDocument();
        configData.Load(configPath);
        XmlNode node = configData.SelectSingleNode(
            "/configuration/appSettings");

        foreach (XmlNode childNode in node.ChildNodes)
        {
            XmlAttributeCollection attribs = childNode.Attributes;
            switch (attribs[0].Value)
```

```
                    {
                        case "userAlias":
                            userAlias = attribs[1].Value;
                            break;
                        case "serverUrl":
                            serverUrl = attribs[1].Value;
                            break;
                    }
                }
            }
            catch (Exception ex)
            {
                MessageBox.Show(ex.Message);
            }
        }
```

7. *SetupCommandBars* is the second custom method called in *OnStartupComplete*.
    It sets up our custom command bar and its controls and hooks up event han-
    dlers for them. There's nothing especially unusual about any of this—it follows
    the same pattern we've seen many times since we first looked at add-ins in Chap-
    ter 5. Briefly, we're adding a new command bar to the host application's collec-
    tion and adding four cont

    rols—two buttons, a text box, and a combo box.

8. The event handlers for the buttons are also fairly straightforward. We need a
    Click event handler for the first button, to start the chat conversation. We'll do
    all the work in a *StartChat* custom method, leaving the *Click* handler to fix up
    the UI for us:

```
private void btnStartChat_Click(
    CommandBarButton cmdBarbutton, ref bool cancelButton)
{
    if (serverUrl.Length > 0)
    {
        StartChat();
        btnStartChat.Enabled = false;
        btnMessage.Enabled = true;
        btnConversation.Enabled = true;
        btnStopChat.Enabled = true;
    }
}
```

9. We also need a *Change* event handler for the first combo box. This is where the
    user types in messages to be sent. We'll get the *Change* event when the user
    presses Return, so we don't need another button for the send behavior. When
    we get this *Change* event, we get the text out of the combo box and submit it to
    the *ChatCoordinator*:

```
private void btnMessage_Change(
    CommandBarComboBox cmdBarComboBox)
{
    string outgoingMessage = cmdBarComboBox.Text;
```

```
        if (outgoingMessage.Length > 0)
        {
            coordinator.Submit(outgoingMessage, this.userAlias);
            cmdBarComboBox.Text = String.Empty;
        }
    }
```

10. We don't need any event handlers for the second combo box because this is where we list the ongoing conversation, and the user won't be typing into it. The second button is to allow the user to stop a conversation—she can, of course, stop sending messages simply by doing nothing, but she might want to stop receiving messages. We'll clean up the *Control* (we'll re-create it each time the user starts a conversation) and fix up the UI:

```
private void btnStopChat_Click(
    CommandBarButton Ctrl, ref bool CancelDefault)
{
    try
    {
        control.Dispose();
        control = null;

        btnStartChat.Enabled = true;
        btnMessage.Enabled = false;
        btnConversation.Enabled = false;
        btnStopChat.Enabled = false;

        btnMessage.Clear();
        btnConversation.Clear();
    }
    catch (Exception ex)
    {
        MessageBox.Show(ex.Message);
    }
}
```

11. The last method to implement is our custom *StartChat* method. This is almost identical to the *StartChat* method in the *WinChat* class. The only differences are that in this version, we use our previously cached path to the config file and we create a new *Control* each time the user starts a conversation:

```
public void StartChat()
{
    control = new Control();
    control.CreateControl();

    try
    {
        RemotingConfiguration.Configure(configPath);

        coordinator = (ChatCoordinator)
            Activator.GetObject(
                typeof(ChatCoordinator), serverUrl);
```

```
            callback = new CallbackWrapper(this);
            coordinator.Submission +=
                new SubmissionEventHandler(
                callback.SubmissionCallback);
        }
        catch (Exception ex)
        {
            MessageBox.Show(ex.Message);
        }
    }
```

12. Add a new XML file to the project called OfficeChat.config. This will be almost identical to the WinChat config. The only difference will be the alias name. Set this to something different from the WinChat alias–you can use any appropriate string:

```
<add key="userAlias" value="Excel" />
```

13. Before building, set up a post-build step to copy this config to the target location, using the target basename. This copies the file to a file called OfficeChat.dll.config in the same place as the add-in DLL itself.

copy "$(ProjectDir)\OfficeChat.config" "$(TargetPath).config"

14. Build and test. Run ChatServer first. Then run your host Office application and one or more instances of WinChat. You can now chat between Office and external applications:

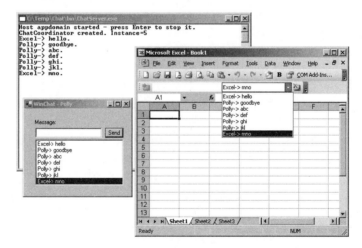

If you registered the add-in for more than one host, you can also chat across multiple Office applications. Once that's working to your satisfaction, you can deploy the solution to another machine, change the config files (replace localhost with the deployed server URL), and chat across machines.

Of course, the ability to chat between Office applications and other applications might actually be useful, but the important point is that you can use the combination of remoting and COM add-ins to extend the event capabilities of Office according to your business requirements.

Summary

The two main technologies that the .NET Framework offers for supporting distributed systems are ASP.NET Web services and .NET Remoting. Web services provide a simple API based on mapping SOAP messages to method calls. Each end of a Web service call doesn't need to know anything about the platform, the operating system, or the development infrastructure used to build the other end. This allows you to build loosely coupled systems that are adaptable to change. Remoting, on the other hand, relies on both ends being built with .NET because the infrastructure exposes .NET objects and object references.

We examined the two basic ways that Office can consume Web services: using the SOAP Toolkit with VBA and using managed Web service proxies. Using managed proxies is clearly more powerful and flexible and gives you access to the full richness of the .NET class library. The only continuing issue is how to connect your managed code to Office. If you're targeting Office 97, you won't be able to avoid using some VBA to hook things up. For Office 2000 and later, you can eliminate VBA altogether if you wish, and the range of options for integrating managed code continues to grow.

The industry is generally focused on the use of Web services, and the WSE library is a good example of implementing widely agreed-upon standards to allow you to build distributed systems across platforms and technologies. The basic WSE mechanism is a series of filters that build additional SOAP header information for outgoing and/or incoming messages, at the client and/or server end. You can invent your own custom filters to perform whatever processing you wish, and plug them seamlessly into the WSE-enabled Web service call. Or you can use any of the filters supplied with the WSE library—and we experimented in a very simple way with some of the WSE security features.

The Office 2003 Research task pane is another example of how Office itself is evolving to provide explicit support for Web services. It's easy to see how you can build custom applications that use both Office and Web services to bring both external and internal data together where an information worker can easily manipulate it. This approach has the benefits of reusing existing server-side applications, reusing the standard Web service infrastructure, and reusing Office applications that the user is already familiar with. You end up with a better system, at a lower initial cost and lower ongoing support cost.

If you worked through the sample remoting solution and came out the other end in one piece, you can pat yourself on the back. This was a very complex solution involving not only a managed Office add-in but also a console application, a Windows Forms application, two class libraries, and two levels of remoting—including remoted delegates and an asynchronously updated UI. It should be clear from this that while remoting gives you a lot of power to achieve sophisticated functionality, it is hard work to develop with. Also, remoting is a more tightly coupled technology and doesn't lend itself to agile, service-oriented systems.

Chapter 10
Visual Studio Tools for Office

One of the many enhancements to Microsoft Office introduced with Office 2003 is the Visual Studio Tools for Office (VSTO) toolkit. This toolkit seamlessly integrates with Microsoft Visual Studio .NET 2003 to allow you to build managed assemblies that are associated with particular Excel workbooks or Word documents. This is a modern alternative to the traditional approach of using VBA code embedded within a workbook or document.

This technology applies only to Office 2003 and later, so all references in this chapter to "Office" refer to those versions only. Office 2003 has been enhanced to support managed "code-behind" assemblies, so it's not possible to hook an Office 2003 code-behind assembly into an earlier version of Office. If you have some functionality that you want to make available to earlier versions as well as Office 2003, you can always implement it as a COM add-in instead of as a code-behind assembly. The two technologies serve different purposes, although some of the development processes involved are similar.

Some of the techniques discussed in this book are application-centric and some are document-centric. Application-centric techniques include COM add-ins, smart tags, and RealTime Data components—these extend the host application in a way that can be generically useful across multiple documents. Traditional VBA is very much a document-centric approach because the code is embedded in the workbook or document itself. Embedding code in a document has a number of disadvantages: it's difficult to impose any kind of source control, maintenance and versioning is difficult, and users are often tempted to relax their Office macro security settings. VSTO is also a document-centric development model, with the significant advantage that the code is not embedded in the document.

Just as modern ASP.NET separates code out to managed code-behind assemblies, so does the modern Office solution model. This feature can be seen as one of the pluggable technologies that can be used to build Office-based smart clients. The seamless integration with Visual Studio, the fact that the Office PIAs are referenced in the project, and the familiar use of the Office application object model make this toolkit look deceptively simple. Indeed, VSTO is simple to use, but behind the scenes there is a very significant change in architecture. The crucial difference is that Microsoft Word 2003 and Excel 2003 have been enhanced specifically to be able to use managed assemblies. Developing solutions with earlier versions of Office was entirely dependent on COM interop. Office 2003 is the first version of Office to have knowledge of the .NET runtime.

This can be seen as the first step in moving Office away from traditional VBA towards the .NET managed world. This book is entirely about developing solutions in managed code that interoperate with Office. VSTO is a strong indicator that Microsoft is keen to support this approach. Making Office .NET-aware makes many things much easier when you build managed solutions with Office.

10.1 VSTO Code-Behind Assemblies

Office 97	✗
Office 2000	✗
Office XP	✗
Office 2003	✓

Visual Studio Tools for Office allows you to create code-behind assemblies for Excel workbooks, Word documents, and Word templates. In this section, we'll explore the basic concepts and techniques for creating VSTO solutions.

This walkthrough assumes you have installed all the prerequisites (including the .NET Framework version 1.1, Visual Studio .NET 2003, all the Office 2003 PIAs, and the VSTO package).

Our first example will be a minimal Excel solution. We'll take some time to consider exactly what the wizard generates for us in terms of code, project files, document information, and security policy. The only custom functionality we'll build in will be to put a simple "Hello World" string into the solution workbook.

> **Note** The sample solution for this topic can be found in the sample code at <install location>\Code\VSTO\ExcelProject1.

First create a new project. Select Microsoft Office System Projects, Visual C# Projects, and then Excel Workbook. For simplicity, we'll leave the project name as the default ExcelProject1.

You have the choice of either selecting an existing workbook to associate with this new assembly or getting the wizard to create a new workbook for you. If you already have an existing workbook that you want to use, the wizard will take a copy of it. However, for our purposes, we want to start from scratch (and this is likely to be the sensible choice in most cases), so we'll select the Create New Document setting. We could give the document a different name from the assembly, and we could specify a different location, but these would both make life confusing for our first project, so we'll accept all the defaults.

If you examine the Security Settings tab, you'll see that you can either allow the wizard to modify the local user security policy specifically for this assembly or not. Most of the time, you'll accept the default (update the local security policy). This causes the wizard to generate a default security policy for the solution. If you don't allow it to do this, the solution won't run until you set up a suitable policy yourself. We will see later that the default policy is not always adequate, and you are likely to change it anyway. For now, however, it's better to have some policy than none.

In addition to generating source code files, the wizard makes Code Access Security policy changes, specifically to the User-level policy. If you run up the .NET Framework Configuration tool (MSCorCfg.msc), you can see these entries.

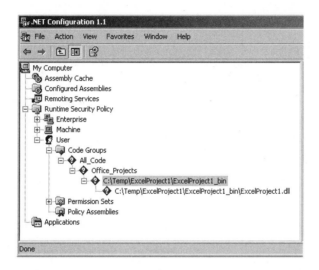

The folder that contains the assembly (and all subfolders) is granted Execution permission based on the URL evidence of a specific folder path (the path to the ExcelProject1_bin folder). The assembly itself is granted FullTrust permission, based on the URL evidence of a specific file path (the path to the ExcelProject1.dll assembly).

As you can see, security permissions are granted on the basis of URL—that is, location evidence. So if you move the assembly to another location, you have to change the security policy for it—otherwise, it won't run.

The generated project will contain references to the appropriate Office PIAs—in this case to *Excel*, the *Microsoft.Office.Core*, and *VBIDE*. A fresh Excel workbook is created and attached to the assembly. When you build the solution, a new folder is created, named in this case ExcelProject1_bin. When the project is built, the output files are put in the usual obj and bin folders, and a copy of the target assembly is put into the *_bin folder, together with its pdb (for possible debugging use). Click the Show All Files button in Solution Explorer to see all the files:

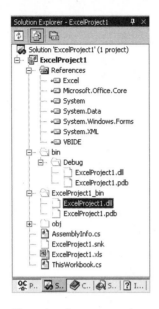

The wizard generates three main files: two C# source files and an Excel workbook. AssemblyInfo.cs is the standard assemblyinfo.cs generated for many other C# projects and contains nothing unusual. The other C# file, by default named ThisWorkbook.cs, is much more interesting. Let's examine all the code (with comments removed for clarity).

The ThisWorkbook.cs file contains a namespace, named as usual with the name of the solution, in this case ExcelProject1. In the namespace is one class, named by default *OfficeCodeBehind*, with a do-nothing default constructor. Note that these names have no significance, and you are at liberty to change them to anything you like. However, if you do so, you must ensure that the *DescriptionAttribute* is updated accordingly. The constructor is not required, although you can use it for all the usual constructor reasons if you wish. There is currently no way for a nondefault constructor to be invoked by the VSTO load mechanism.

The first item of note is the assembly-level *DescriptionAttribute*, which specifies the Office startup class. A code-behind assembly must specify that one of its classes is the startup class. The Office application looks for the startup class and invokes the *_Startup* and *_Shutdown* methods on that class when loading and unloading the assembly.

```
[assembly:System.ComponentModel.DescriptionAttribute("OfficeStartupClass, Version=
1.0, Class=ExcelProject1.OfficeCodeBehind")]
```

The *Class* value in this attribute—in this case, set to *ExcelProject1.OfficeCodeBehind*—looks like a COM ProgId but isn't: it's the fully qualified name of the class in its namespace. The component is not attributed *ComVisible*, nor is the project marked "Register for COM Interop." The Office application does not use COM interop, in the sense of a COM callable wrapper (CCW), when it uses the managed code-behind assembly. Effectively, the only calls that Office makes into the managed assembly are to _Startup and _Shutdown, which are methods known to Office. All other interop between the assembly and the Office application is driven by the assembly, which can choose to use COM interop via a runtime callable wrapper (RCW) in the usual way.

The startup class has two private fields, which represent the current running instance of the Office application (Excel) and the current workbook that loaded this assembly. There are also internal properties associated with these fields, and they should be familiar to you as standard Excel object model types:

```
internal Excel.Application ThisApplication
{
    get { return thisApplication; }
}

internal Excel.Workbook ThisWorkbook
{
    get { return thisWorkbook; }
}

private Excel.Application thisApplication = null;
private Excel.Workbook thisWorkbook = null;
```

The class also has two event fields, for the *Workbook.Open* and *Workbook.BeforeClose* events. These are hooked up to event handler methods in the special *_Startup* method. Recall that Excel calls the *_Startup* method when it loads the assembly. Indeed, all the *_Startup* method does is to assign values to the *Application* and *Workbook* fields and hook up the event handlers:

```
private Excel.WorkbookEvents_OpenEventHandler openEvent;
private Excel.WorkbookEvents_BeforeCloseEventHandler beforeCloseEvent;

public void _Startup(object application, object workbook)
{
    this.thisApplication = application as Excel.Application;
    this.thisWorkbook = workbook as Excel.Workbook;

    openEvent= new
    Excel.WorkbookEvents_OpenEventHandler (
    ThisWorkbook_Open);
    thisWorkbook.Open += openEvent;

    beforeCloseEvent = new
    Excel.WorkbookEvents_BeforeCloseEventHandler(
    ThisWorkbook_BeforeClose);
    thisWorkbook.BeforeClose += beforeCloseEvent;
}
```

To correspond with these events, the wizard has given us custom event handler methods, which are called when the workbook is opened and closed. Note the *Cancel* parameter in the *BeforeClose* handler: if you set this to *true*, the workbook will not close after this method returns. We can put whatever appropriate code we like in these methods, although the wizard-generated implementations are very minimal.

```
protected void ThisWorkbook_Open()
{
}

protected void ThisWorkbook_BeforeClose(ref bool Cancel)
{
    Cancel = false;
}
```

It won't be obvious until you've worked with VSTO solutions for a while, but the model is heavily event-based. That is, the host application fires events in the usual way, and your code-behind assembly will respond to these events. Your code can do whatever it likes, of course, and some of what it does is likely to trigger further events on the host application.

The special _Shutdown_ method is called when Excel unloads the assembly, and the wizard takes this opportunity to clean out application and workbook references (which lead to the release of the corresponding COM objects):

```
public void _Shutdown()
{
    thisApplication = null;
    thisWorkbook = null;
}
```

We're also given two custom (overloaded) *FindControl* methods. The purpose of these helpers is to find a specific control in either the active worksheet or any specified worksheet. If you supply only the name of the control you want, the assumption is that it's in the current worksheet—otherwise, you must also specify the worksheet. Excel holds its controls and embedded/linked objects in its *OLEObjects* collection. This supports indexing into the collection using the name of the control.

```
object FindControl(string name )
{
    return FindControl(name, (Excel.Worksheet)
    ThisWorkbook.ActiveSheet);
}

object FindControl(string name, Excel.Worksheet sheet )
{
    Excel.OLEObject theObject;
    try
    {
        theObject = (Excel.OLEObject) sheet.OLEObjects(name);
        return theObject.Object;
    }
    catch
    {
    }
    return null;
}
```

Let's now build and execute. When you execute this type of solution, you're actually executing the relevant Office application. If you look in the project properties and go to Configuration Properties | Debugging, you'll see that the *Debug Mode* property is set to Program, Start Application is set to Excel.exe, and Command Line Arguments is set to ExcelProject1.xls.

Another artifact of the way the wizard produces a VSTO project is in a special element that it places in the .csproj file. You should never need to change this, but it might be worth knowing about it in case the .csproj gets corrupted in some way. If you want to look at this, open the .csproj file in a text editor such as Notepad. Look for the custom *UserProperties* element:

```
<UserProperties
    OfficeDocumentPath = ".\EXCELPROJECT1.XLS"
    OfficeProjectType = "XLS"
    OfficeProject = "true"
    TrustedAssembly = "C:\Temp\ExcelProject1\ExcelProject1_bin\ExcelProject1.dll"
/>
```

There is no GUI way to change this using Visual Studio. You could change it by manually editing the .csproj file, but this is generally not recommended. One significance of this entry is that if the specified file is not found, you get an error when you try to build the solution. The assembly will be built but won't be copied to the target execution folder (*_bin).

Another point to note is that Visual Studio uses the *TrustedAssembly* attribute to grant *FullTrust* to the assembly when it is first built. If you don't want this default behavior, you can remove the *TrustedAssembly* attribute.

When the code-behind assembly is used, Word and Excel use a special unmanaged COM DLL to load the CLR and the code-behind assembly. This resides in the file OTkLoadr.dll and is known commonly as the VSTO Loader. The general sequence of operations for the loading of a VSTO solution is shown in Figure 10-1.

So far, the code-behind assembly we've built doesn't do anything special. It could, of course, perform any regular Office automation tasks because it has access to the object model of the hosting application. Let's make a simple enhancement: we'll add code to the generated *Workbook.Open* event handler to insert some text into cell A1, and then build and test:

```
protected void ThisWorkbook_Open()
{
    Excel.Worksheet sheet =
    (Excel.Worksheet)thisApplication.ActiveSheet;
    Excel.Range range = (Excel.Range)sheet.Cells[1,1];
    range.Value2 = "Hello World";
}
```

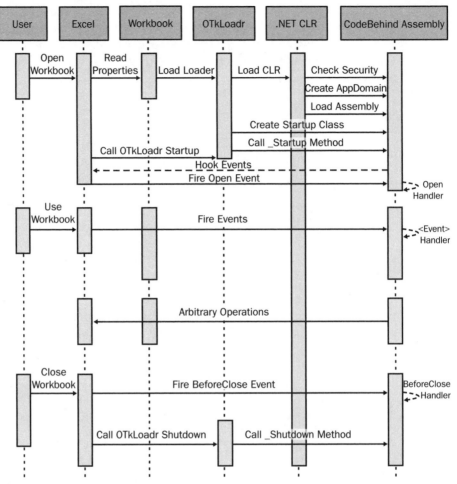

Figure 10-1 VSTO load sequence.

It's also worth running a tool such as Process Explorer (from *www.sysinternals.com*) to see where Office is running your solution from. Assemblies in VSTO solutions are loaded by the VSTO Loader and run from the download cache, which is a subdirectory of the user's profile.

While there are distinct project types for Word documents and Word templates, there is no option to create an Excel template project. If you want template behavior in an Excel code-behind project, you can take the following steps:

1. Create an Excel workbook project.

2. Make the workbook itself read-only.

3. In the handler for the *Workbook.Open* or *Workbook.BeforeSave* event, call the *Workbook.SaveAs* method to save a copy of the workbook to a new name and location.

4. To prevent this handler from saving again when the copy workbook is opened or saved, put a test in against some property of the original workbook (read-only, original date-timestamp, original name/location, etc.).

Finally, a common question is "Can I build a VSTO solution that exposes functions that can be called from Excel cells?" The only managed technique for doing this seamlessly is to use managed Automation add-ins. (See Section 5.8, "Excel Automation Add-Ins.") You can achieve part of the requirement with VSTO by exposing your VSTO assembly for COM interop, as detailed in Section 4.2, "Managed CCW in VBA." You can find an example of using this approach with a VSTO solution in the sample code at <install location>\Code\VSTO\ManagedCellFunctions.

10.2 Custom Document Properties

Office 97	✖
Office 2000	✖
Office XP	✖
Office 2003	✔

When you create a new VSTO code-behind project and create a new Word document or Excel workbook at the same time, the new workbook or document is given two additional custom properties. Similarly, if you choose to attach a new VSTO project to an existing workbook or document, a copy of the file is made, and this copy is edited to include these two custom properties.

In our simple Excel example, note the custom document properties in the .xls file. To see this, open the file in Excel, and go to File | Properties | Custom. The VSTO properties are _AssemblyLocation0_ (set to .*ExcelProject1_bin* in this example), and _AssemblyName0_ (set to *ExcelProject1*—that is, the name of the DLL without the extension). Note that _AssemblyLocation0_ can be a relative or absolute path and can be local, UNC, or HTTP.

Following from this, a reasonable question is, "Can you associate an unrelated workbook to an existing code-behind assembly?" The answer, of course, is Yes. Try it: create a new Excel workbook, independently of Visual Studio. Go to File | Properties | Custom, and add the new custom properties. Set _AssemblyLocation0_ to the location of the assembly (.*ExcelProject1_bin* in this example), and set _AssemblyName0_ to the name of the DLL (*ExcelProject1* in this example). If you deploy the workbook to a location where (a) the relative path to the assembly is valid and (b) the location has been granted security permissions, the solution will run.

A related question is, "Can you associate a single code-behind assembly with multiple workbooks?" The answer, again, is Yes, although of course these will be independent instances of the assembly and not shared in any way. It is standard practice to build reusable components in assemblies, so this is nothing new. However, if you want to reuse assemblies across VSTO solutions, it is probably more useful if you have a unique primary assembly for each solution and then have that primary assembly reuse other assemblies as dependencies in the normal way. It is unlikely that a reusable assembly will be useful as a primary VSTO assembly, simply because if it is, there's probably not enough difference between the solutions to justify them being different solutions. These are design choices and are not constrained in any way by VSTO itself.

The VSTO toolkit ships with an ActiveX control called the Persistence Control, which is intended for use by administrators to modify the custom assembly name and location properties of an Excel or Word file from a script. The *ProgID* of the Persistence Control is *OfficeToolkit.Persistence*, and it is housed in the file OTkPerst.dll. A JScript example of how to use this is given below.

> **Note** The scripts for this topic can be found in the sample code at <install location>\Code\VSTO\PersistenceControl.

```
// SetAssembly.js

if (WScript.Arguments.Length < 3)
{
    WScript.Echo("Usage: SetAssembly <document> <assembly> <location>\n" +
        " <document> is the name of a Word document or Excel spreadsheet\n" +
        " <assembly> is the name of the assembly, without the extension\n" +
        " <location> can be a relative path, and should end in a slash")
    WScript.Quit(1)
}

var doc = WScript.Arguments(0)
var asm = WScript.Arguments(1)
var loc = WScript.Arguments(2)

WScript.Echo("Updating '" + doc + "', setting _AssemblyName='" + asm
    + "' and _AssemblyLocation='" + loc + "'")

try
{
    var control = new ActiveXObject("OfficeToolkit.Persistence")
    control.SetAssemblyNameAndLocation(doc, asm, loc)
    WScript.Echo("Name and location successfully set")
}
catch(e)
{
    WScript.Echo("Error:" + e.number + ": " + e.description)
    WScript.Quit(2)
}
```

Here is an equivalent VBScript example:

```
' SetAssembly.vbs
If (WScript.Arguments.Length < 3) Then
    WScript.Echo "Usage: SetAssembly <document> <assembly> <location>" & VbCrLf _
        & " <document> is the name of a Word document or Excel spreadsheet" & VbCrLf _
        & " <assembly> is the name of the assembly, without the extension" & VbCrLf _
```

```
        & "  <location> can be a relative path, and should end in a slash"
        WScript.Quit 1
End If


Dim doc
Dim asm
Dim loc


doc = WScript.Arguments(0)
asm = WScript.Arguments(1)
loc = WScript.Arguments(2)


WScript.Echo "Updating '" & doc & "', setting _AssemblyName='" & asm _
        & "' and _AssemblyLocation='" & loc & "'"


On Error Resume Next


Dim control
Set control = CreateObject("OfficeToolkit.Persistence")
control.SetAssemblyNameAndLocation doc, asm, loc


If (Err.Number <> 0) Then
        WScript.Echo "Error:"  & VbCrLf & Err.Number & ": " & Err.Description
        WScript.Quit 2
Else
        WScript.Echo "Name and Location successfully set."
End If
```

Another situation where the Persistence Control comes in handy is when administrators need to change or update the assembly reference in multiple documents or workbooks at once—for example, if the administrator is moving some documents from *http://someserver1/example1* to *http://someserver008/example008*. In this situation, we could do something like this, where *GetDocNames* can be a custom method to retrieve file names from a spreadsheet, directory listings, and so forth.

```
...
var doc = GetDocNames()
...
for (var i in doc)
   control.SetAssemblyLocation(doc[i], asm, loc)
...
```

10.3 Debugging VSTO Solutions

Office 97	⊗
Office 2000	⊗
Office XP	⊗
Office 2003	⊘

VSTO solutions share many of the general COM interop techniques and debugging issues, as discussed in Chapter 2, "Basics of Office Interoperability." However, a couple of additional debugging issues are specific to VSTO solutions:

- Clearing the cached shadow copy
- Avoiding swallowed exceptions

Clearing the Cached Shadow Copy

The VSTO loader uses shadow copying to support the use of in-place updates of shared assemblies. This allows developers and administrators to update an assembly even if it is currently being used by an application. One side effect of shadow copying is that if your assembly is strong-named and you have disabled version increment, the CLR fusion (assembly loader) will decide to use the cached copy of your assembly and not the new copy.

At runtime, a VSTO code-behind assembly is loaded into an AppDomain with its *ShadowCopyFiles* property set to *true*—so the assembly will actually be copied into a shadow directory (a subdirectory in the user's profile, similar to the Internet Explorer assembly download cache) and executed from there. This will be in the user's profile: %userprofile%\Local Settings\Application Data\assembly\... (for example, C:\Documents and Settings\<username>\Local Settings\Application Data\assembly\...).

This will contain subdirectories with hash-like names. If you like, you can examine these subdirectories and their contents. However, the exact file system layout of the download cache is an implementation detail that might well change with future releases of the framework, so you shouldn't rely on it.

During development, it's a good idea to clear out this download cache from time to time, to make sure the latest version of your assembly is being loaded. To ensure that your most current copy of assembly is loaded instead of a cached copy, you can do any of the following:

- Manually increment the assembly version number. You can do this by modifying the *AssemblyVersion* number in the *AssemblyInfo* file.

- Don't strong-name your assembly until you are ready to release.

- Clear the download cache.

The recommended way to clear the download cache is to use the GacUtil.exe tool with the */cdl* (clear download) switch: *gacutil /cdl*. You can even set this as a post-build event in your project properties.

Clearing the download cache will succeed only if the shadow copy cache is not in use. To make sure it's not, you might need to close Excel and Word (and Outlook if you use Word as the e-mail editor), and sometimes Visual Studio as well (which means that setting it as a post-build step won't always work). One thing you shouldn't do is to manually delete files or folders in the download cache. The download cache is in a series of subdirectories in your user profile folder, but the folder names have been obfuscated to discourage you from interfering with them. You could navigate your way around and examine each assembly to see if it is one you want to delete, but this is not recommended. This would have the desired effect of removing the shadow copies, but it would also confuse the CLR loader which tracks cache quota values. So, don't do it—use gacutil instead.

Avoiding Swallowed Exceptions

By default, if your code-behind assembly throws an exception, it won't be exposed by Excel or Word—in essence, it gets caught and absorbed. You should do two things to mitigate this:

- Always include structured exception handling (SEH) code (that is, *try/catch* blocks) in your code.
- Change the default debugger options to break into the debugger when an exception is thrown. To do this, in Visual Studio, go to Debug | Exceptions. In the Exceptions dialog box, select Common Language Runtime Exceptions, and select the Break Into The Debugger option.

Note that if you use this setting, you'll likely get one or more messages indicating that a *FileIOException* was thrown during the attempt to load MSOSEC.DLL. You can safely ignore these, but if you want to do away with them altogether, you can put MSOSEC.DLL into the GAC. Further details are supplied in Section 12.7, "VSTO Deployment Options." You'll find MSOSEC.DLL in the installed location for Office 2003:

C:\Program Files\Microsoft Office 2003\OFFICE11\ADDINS\msosec.dll

To experiment with the VSTO debugging techniques, we'll create an Excel code-behind solution and introduce some deliberate errors. The solution will add a custom button to the first visible command bar it finds. When the user clicks the button, we'll put up a message box. The code is basically the same as the first Office add-in example used in Section 5.1, "Managed COM Add-Ins."

> **Note**   The sample solution for this topic can be found in the sample code at <install location>\Code\VSTO\BugBehind.

Create a new VSTO Excel project called BugBehind. Accept all defaults. Build (to set up the security policy) and test the generated workbook to ensure everything works as expected before making any changes.

In the *ThisWorkbook_Open* method, we'll get hold of the collection of *CommandBars* and then find the first visible one. Note that unlike Office COM add-ins, where the *applicationObject* is a simple object, in VSTO code *thisApplication* is a strongly typed *Excel.Application* or *Word.Application* object, so we can access the object model more directly:

```
Office.CommandBars oCommandBars;
Office.CommandBar oBar = null;

oCommandBars = thisApplication.CommandBars;
foreach (Office.CommandBar b in oCommandBars)
{
    if (b.Visible == true)
    {
        oBar = b;
        break;
    }
}
```

Next add a custom button to the end of the command bar and hook up a *Click* event handler to this button:

```
object omissing = Missing.Value;
myButton = (Office.CommandBarButton) oBar.Controls.Add(
    Office.MsoControlType.msoControlButton,
    omissing, omissing, omissing, omissing);
myButton.Caption = "My Button";
myButton.Style = Office.MsoButtonStyle.msoButtonCaption;

myButton.Click +=
    new Office._CommandBarButtonEvents_ClickEventHandler(
    this.myButton_Click);
```

Implement the *Click* handler initially to just show a message:

```
private void myButton_Click(
    Office.CommandBarButton cmdBarbutton, ref bool cancel)
{
    MessageBox.Show("You Clicked MyButton");
}
```

Finally, in the *ThisWorkbook_BeforeClose* method, clean up the custom button:

```
protected void ThisWorkbook_BeforeClose(ref bool Cancel)
{
    if (myButton != null)
    {
        object omissing = Missing.Value ;
        myButton.Delete(omissing);
        myButton = null;
    }
    Cancel = false;
}
```

Build and test—at this stage, everything should work. At least, we haven't introduced any deliberate errors yet.

Now introduce a deliberate error into the *Click* handler, and test again (using F5 to run in the debugger):

```
private void myButton_Click(
    Office.CommandBarButton cmdBarbutton, ref bool cancel)
{
    // Throw an arbitrary exception.
    throw new ApplicationException("Deliberate error");

    // We won't get here because the previous line will
    // have thrown us out of the scope of this method.
    MessageBox.Show("You Clicked MyButton");
}
```

You should find that although we're clearly throwing an exception, there is no report of this anywhere—it just gets swallowed up and lost. Change the debugger behavior by choosing Debug | Exceptions. Select Common Language Runtime Exceptions, and select the Break Into The Debugger option, as shown earlier in this section.

When you test again, the runtime will break into the debugger when the exception is thrown:

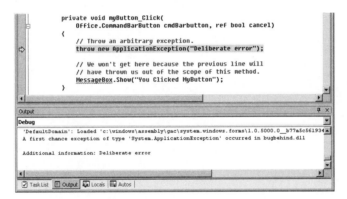

Of course, if you continue past the exception, you'll be back in Excel. The exception is still being thrown, and we can spot this happening and look at what's going on in memory at that time. This is a big improvement, and it should be all you need to identify and fix the bug. However, we're still not catching the exception ourselves, and that would be even better.

So, the next step is to put some SEH into our code. Wrap the code in the *Click* handler with *try/catch* blocks, and report on any exception caught:

```
try
{
    throw new ApplicationException("Deliberate error");
    MessageBox.Show("You Clicked MyButton");
}
catch (Exception ex)
{
    MessageBox.Show(ex.Message);
}
```

Now, even when you run without the debugger (that is, using Ctrl+F5), you'll be alerted to the exception. If you put a breakpoint on the line of code in the *catch* block and run in the debugger, you'll be able to examine the values of all objects in scope in memory at the point the exception is thrown, plus all the usual Visual Studio debugging reports (call stack, threads, memory, registers, etc.).

Finally, note that if you ever need to open the Office document without running the code in the code-behind assembly, you can do this by holding down the Shift key while opening the document. (Note that this works only if you run Excel or Word and then open the workbook or document, not if you double-click on the .doc or .xls file directly.)

10.4 Word Code-Behind

Office 97	✕
Office 2000	✕
Office XP	✕
Office 2003	✓

The procedure for creating a VSTO project for Word is almost identical to that for creating a VSTO project for Excel. The VSTO wizards for Office 2003 offer three project types: Excel workbook, Word document, and Word template. In this walkthrough exercise, we'll create two projects: one for a Word document and one for a Word template. First we'll create an assembly that hooks the *Open* event on a Word document and inserts "Hello World".

> **Note**   This section includes two solutions. They can be found in the sample code at <install location>\Code\VSTO\WordProject1 and <install location>\Code\VSTO\WordTemplateProject1.

Word Document Project

Create a new project. Select Microsoft Office System Projects, Visual C# Projects, and Word Document. For simplicity, we'll leave the project name as the default WordProject1. Accept the defaults for the remaining wizard choices: create a new document, and allow the security policy to be updated. The wizard will add new code group entries under the User security policy and create the project with two C# source code files and a Word document. As with Excel, assemblyinfo.cs contains nothing unusual. The code in ThisDocument.cs will be similar to ThisWorkbook.cs, which is generated for an Excel project. Let's focus here on the differences.

First, of course, the fields and properties that represent the hosting application and document are Word-specific instead of Excel-specific:

```
internal Word.Application ThisApplication
{
    get { return thisApplication; }
}

internal Word.Document ThisDocument
```

```
{
    get { return thisDocument; }
}

private Word.Application thisApplication = null;
private Word.Document thisDocument = null;
```

Similarly, the event fields and handlers are specific to Word events fired when the document is opened or closed:

```
private Word.DocumentEvents2_OpenEventHandler openEvent;
private Word.DocumentEvents2_CloseEventHandler closeEvent;
```

The special _Startup_ method caches the host application and document references and hooks up the event handlers, just as with our Excel project. The event handlers themselves are empty, as before.

There is one additional piece of code at the end of the _Startup_ method that we didn't see in the Excel solution. This code checks and conditionally toggles the _FormsDesign_ property of the document. The reason for this is that when Word is in forms design mode, event procedures don't run, which means our _Open_ event handler won't run. So, the extra code turns off forms design mode and invokes the _Open_ event handler directly:

```
public void _Startup(object application, object document)
{
    this.thisApplication = application as Word.Application;
    this.thisDocument = document as Word.Document;

    openEvent = new
        Word.DocumentEvents2_OpenEventHandler(
            ThisDocument_Open);
    thisDocument.Open += openEvent;

    closeEvent = new
        Word.DocumentEvents2_CloseEventHandler(
            ThisDocument_Close);
    ((Word.DocumentEvents2_Event)thisDocument).Close
        += closeEvent;

    if (ThisDocument.FormsDesign == true)
    {
        thisDocument.ToggleFormsDesign();
        ThisDocument_Open();
    }
}
```

The _Shutdown_ method clears the host object references, and the simple version of _Find-Control_ finds the specified control in this document—again, just like the Excel version.

The second overload of *FindControl* is more complex. Unlike Excel, Word doesn't hold its embedded controls in an *OLEObjects* collection. Instead, these are held in two collections: the *InlineShapes* collection of *InlineShape* objects, and the *Shapes* collection of *Shape* objects. Rather than simply indexing into the collection, we have to instantiate each control and invoke its *Name* property to find out whether this is the control we're looking for:

```
foreach (Word.InlineShape shape in document.InlineShapes)
{
    if (shape.Type ==
    Word.WdInlineShapeType.wdInlineShapeOLEControlObject)
    {
        object oleControl = shape.OLEFormat.Object;
        Type oleControlType = oleControl.GetType();
        string oleControlName =
            (string) oleControlType.InvokeMember("Name",
            System.Reflection.BindingFlags.GetProperty,
            null, oleControl, null);
        if (String.Compare(oleControlName, name, true,
            System.Globalization.CultureInfo.InvariantCulture)
            == 0)
        {
            return oleControl;
        }
    }
}

foreach (Word.Shape shape in document.Shapes)
{
    if (shape.Type ==
    Microsoft.Office.Core.MsoShapeType.msoOLEControlObject)
    {
        object oleControl = shape.OLEFormat.Object;
        Type oleControlType = oleControl.GetType();
        string oleControlName =
            (string) oleControlType.InvokeMember("Name",
            System.Reflection.BindingFlags.GetProperty,
            null, oleControl, null);
        if (String.Compare(oleControlName, name, true,
            System.Globalization.CultureInfo.InvariantCulture)
            == 0)
        {
            return oleControl;
        }
    }
}
```

Fortunately, all the tricky stuff is done for us by the wizard, so we don't have to worry about the idiosyncrasies of the Excel vs. Word object models and the requirements of their late-bound collections.

As before, we'll add some code to the *Open* event handler to put a simple "Hello World" string into the document:

```
protected void ThisDocument_Open()
{
    object start = 0;
    object end = 0;
    Word.Range range =
        (Word.Range)thisDocument.Range(ref start, ref end);
    range.InsertAfter("Hello World");
}
```

Build and test—this is how the solution should look at runtime:

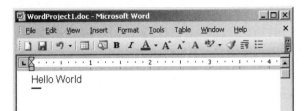

Word Template Project

In addition to creating a code-behind assembly for a Word document, you can create a code-behind assembly for a Word template. Let's do that now, just to see what the differences are.

First create a new project: Microsoft Office System Projects | Visual C# Projects | Word Document Template. Leave the project name as the default WordTemplate-Project1, and accept the defaults for the remaining wizard choices. The wizard will add new code group entries under the User security policy and create the project with two C# source code files and a Word template document (called, in this example, WordTemplateProject1.dot). The code in ThisDocument.cs will be similar to This-Document.cs, which is generated for a Word Document project.

The code has only two real differences. The first is that there are three event handlers—the additional handler is for the *New* event. The *New* event is fired when a new document is created from the template; it is not fired when the document is opened subsequently. The *Open* event is fired when documents that were created from the template are opened and when the template itself is opened for editing, but not when a new document is created from the template:

```
private Word.DocumentEvents2_NewEventHandler newEvent;
```

The second difference is that in the *_Startup* method, there is an additional test for an open document before invoking the *Open* event handler:

```
if (ThisDocument.FormsDesign == true)
{
    thisDocument.ToggleFormsDesign();
    if (ThisDocument.Path != "")
        ThisDocument_Open();
}
```

Build the solution and test it.

10.5 XML Lists

Office 97	⊗
Office 2000	⊗
Office XP	⊗
Office 2003	⊘

Excel 2003 has been enhanced with additions to the object model such as *ListColumn*, *ListDataObject*, *ListFormat*, and *ListRow*. These allow you to create, modify, and navigate data lists in a workbook.

In the following example, we'll pull out some data from the Northwind SQL database, write it out to an XML file, and load that XML file into a workbook list. Then we'll explore the features offered to create a list programmatically and to navigate and manipulate this list.

> **Note** The sample solution for this topic can be found in the sample code at <install location>\Code\VSTO\XmlList.

Importing a List from XML

Create a new Excel code-behind project called XmlList, with all defaults. Build and test the solution before making any changes, to make sure both the code and the security policy are set up correctly.

Next write a new method, called *GetSupplierData*, and put a call to this method in the *ThisWorkbook_Open* event handler. In this method, connect to the Northwind database, and build a dataset of all the suppliers. The following code listing uses the simplest possible SQL connection string and a straightforward SQL SELECT statement.

Once we get the data back from the database, we can use the *DataSet.WriteXml* method to write it out to an XML file. From there, we can use the Excel *OpenXML* method to load this file into a workbook, specifying the new *XlXmlLoadOption* enumeration to specify that we'll import the XML into a list object:

```
private void GetSuppliersData()
{
    SqlConnection connection = null;
    string connectionString =
        "Data Source=localhost;Integrated Security=SSPI;"
        +"Initial Catalog=Northwind;";
    string xmlFile = "Suppliers.xml";
```

```
try
{
    // Connect to the SQL database, and build a
    // dataset of all the Suppliers.
    connection = new SqlConnection(connectionString);
    connection.Open();
    SqlDataAdapter adapter = new SqlDataAdapter(
        "SELECT * FROM Suppliers", connection);
    DataSet suppliers = new DataSet();
    adapter.Fill(suppliers);

    // Write the data out to an XML file, then load
    // the XML file into a new workbook.
    suppliers.WriteXml(xmlFile);
    connection.Close();
    thisApplication.Workbooks.OpenXML(xmlFile, missing,
        Excel.XlXmlLoadOption.xlXmlLoadImportToList);
}
catch (Exception ex)
{
    MessageBox.Show(ex.Message);
}
finally
{
    if (connection != null)
    {
        connection.Close();
    }
}
}
```

Build and test. You might get a notification message indicating that Excel will infer a schema from the XML—if so, you can click OK. When you run the solution, it should look something like this:

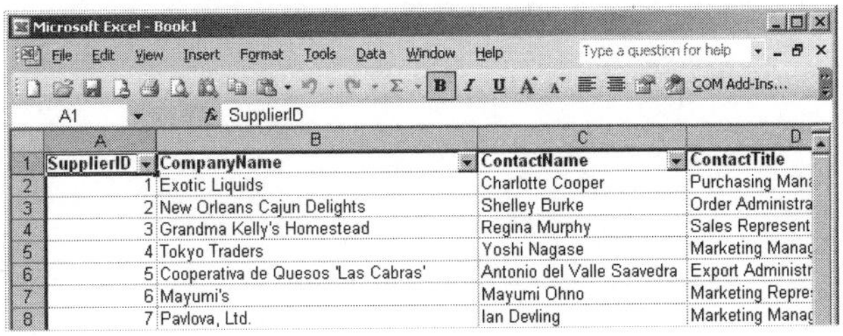

Notice the blue border that surrounds the data in the worksheet. This is an XML list, and it allows users to work with XML datasets as a whole instead of on a cell-by-cell basis.

A moment's reflection (in your head, not in the code) should tell you that the XML file (a fragment of which is shown below) has been flattened into a two-dimensional spreadsheet format. Each row represents a different supplier. This was all done automatically with no need to write an XSL Transform.

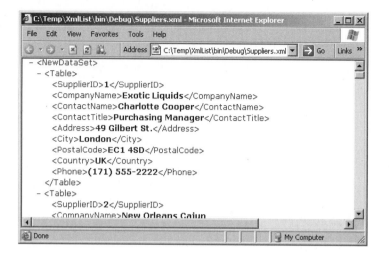

Let's experiment with the UI capabilities of lists. First click on the down-arrow next to the Country header, and select any country from the list—the supplier list will be filtered to the selected country:

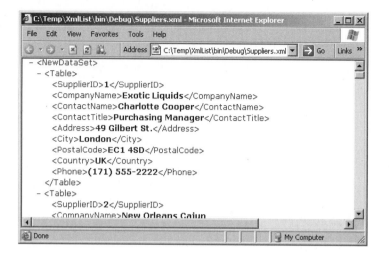

As another experiment, click the down-arrow next to CompanyName and select Sort Ascending.

In addition to analyzing the data, you can edit the data and export it back out again. One of the benefits of the XML list is that it acts like a database table: an insert row appears at the bottom of the list and allows you to add new rows to the data while maintaining the integrity of the XML dataset. To test this, remove any filters on the data, and then scroll down to the bottom and add a new row. Then go to Data | XML | Export, and type a new filename to export to. Examine the resulting XML file.

Creating a List Programmatically

Instead of importing XML data into a list, we can also create lists programmatically. Recall that when we imported the XML file in the previous example, this created a second workbook—our original workbook was untouched. In this section, we'll programmatically create a list in our original workbook:

Continue with the current solution, close Excel, and create a new method called *CreateList*. Put a call to this method in the *ThisWorkbook_Open* event handler. In the new method, create the skeleton list by adding a new *ListObject* to the worksheet's collection of *ListObject* objects.

Next build the column headings—we'll put arbitrary data into the list, and we'll have three columns. So, in row 1, columns 1, 2, and 3, put headings such as, ID, Name, and Email. Use the *Range* property exposed by the *ListObject*. Use this same property (with different index values) to insert some arbitrary data into the same three columns, for the next three rows.

When all the data is in, set appropriate column widths. Finally—just for fun—navigate to an arbitrary list element and display its data value:

```
private void CreateList()
{
    try
    {
        // Create the skeleton list.
        Excel.Worksheet sheet =
            (Excel.Worksheet)thisWorkbook.ActiveSheet;
        Excel.ListObject list =
            sheet.ListObjects.Add(
            Excel.XlListObjectSourceType.xlSrcRange,
            sheet.Cells[1,1], missing,
            Excel.XlYesNoGuess.xlYes, missing);

        // Build column headings.
        ((Excel.Range)list.Range[1,1]).Value2 = "ID";
        ((Excel.Range)list.Range[1,2]).Value2 = "Name";
        ((Excel.Range)list.Range[1,3]).Value2 = "Email";
```

```
                // Insert some arbitrary data.
                ((Excel.Range)list.Range[2,1]).Value2 = "123";
                ((Excel.Range)list.Range[2,2]).Value2 = "Kim Akers";
                ((Excel.Range)list.Range[2,3]).Value2 =
                    "kim.akers@contoso.com";

                ((Excel.Range)list.Range[3,1]).Value2 = "789";
                ((Excel.Range)list.Range[3,2]).Value2 = "Lori Penor";
                ((Excel.Range)list.Range[3,3]).Value2 =
                    "lorip@cohowinery.com";

                ((Excel.Range)list.Range[4,1]).Value2 = "456";
                ((Excel.Range)list.Range[4,2]).Value2 = "Julia Ilyina";
                ((Excel.Range)list.Range[4,3]).Value2 =
                    "jilyina@fourthcoffee.com";

                // Set appropriate column widths.
                ((Excel.Range)sheet.Cells[1,1]).ColumnWidth = 10;
                ((Excel.Range)sheet.Cells[1,2]).ColumnWidth = 15;
                ((Excel.Range)sheet.Cells[1,3]).ColumnWidth = 30;

                // Navigate to an arbitrary value.
                MessageBox.Show(
                    ((Excel.Range)
                    list.ListColumns[3].Range[3,1]).Value2.ToString());
            }
            catch (Exception ex)
            {
                MessageBox.Show(ex.Message);
            }
        }
```

Build and test.

10.6 XML Data Form

Office 97	✗
Office 2000	✗
Office XP	✗
Office 2003	✓

Excel 2003 extends the XML support built into Excel XP. Excel XP supports flattened XML data and XML spreadsheet formatted data; Excel 2003 allows you to display and access user-defined XML. You can also create a mapping between a user-defined XML schema and an Excel workbook, either interactively through the new XML Source Task Pane or programmatically via the enhanced object model.

Excel 2003 also supports XPath, an expression language used to access or refer to parts of an XML document. The Excel object model now includes classes such as *XmlMap* and *XPath*. For example, the *Workbook* now has a collection of *XmlMaps*, and the *Range* object has an *XPath* property. Of course, you can also use the *XmlDocument*, *XmlNode*, *XmlTextReader*, and related classes already in the .NET Framework class library.

In the following exercise, we'll create a code-behind project to use the new XML capabilities of Excel to view data from the Northwind database in a worksheet. The main tasks to cover are:

- Set up a custom *CommandBar* with a drop-down combo box to allow the user to choose a data record.

- Get a set of data from the Northwind database in XML format and use it to populate the combo box.

- Create and attach an XML schema (XSD) based on the SQL data.

- Build a form with XML tags from the schema.

- Query the SQL database to populate the form dynamically, based on the user's selection from the combo box.

The Northwind sample database is a commonly used sample that ships with Microsoft SQL Server and with later versions of Office. A version of it is also supplied with the sample code for this document. If you don't already have the Northwind database attached to your SQL Server, you'll need to attach it for this exercise to work.

> **Note**   The sample solution for this topic can be found in the sample code at <install location>\Code\VSTO\XmlDataViewer.

A Custom Command Bar

First create a new Excel code-behind project called XmlDataViewer. Accept all defaults. Build (to set up the security policy) and test the generated workbook to ensure that everything works as expected before making any changes.

Declare some variables at the class level for use in several methods—specifically, for the new *CommandBar*, the combo box, an event handler for the *Change* event on the combo box, the *Missing.Value* that we'll need for a number of Excel method calls, and a connection string for the Northwind database:

```
private CommandBar dataBar;
private CommandBarComboBox dataList;
private _CommandBarComboBoxEvents_ChangeEventHandler dataListChange;
private object missing = Type.Missing;
private string connectionString =
        "Data Source=localhost;Integrated Security=SSPI;"
        +"Initial Catalog=Northwind;";
```

Also set up a class variable for the names of the fields in the Suppliers table. We could (and probably should) extract these dynamically from the dataset or the schema, but for simplicity we'll just hardcode them here:

```
private string[] fields =
    new string[12]
        {
            "SupplierID", "CompanyName", "ContactName",
```

```
                    "ContactTitle", "Address", "City", "Region",
                    "PostalCode", "Country", "Phone", "Fax",
                    "HomePage"
            };
```

Write a new custom method called *SetupBar*—we'll call this from the *ThisWorkbook_Open* event handler to create our custom *CommandBar*. The code, listed below, uses familiar techniques to set up a new command bar with a combo box of a suitable size. Don't forget to wrap this (as always) in suitable *try/catch* exception handling blocks:

```csharp
private void SetupDataBar()
{
    try
    {
        // Add a new bar to the collection.
        dataBar = thisApplication.CommandBars.Add(
            "Northwind Data", MsoBarPosition.msoBarTop,
            missing, (object)true);

        // Add a combo box to the bar.
        dataList = (CommandBarComboBox)
            dataBar.Controls.Add(
            MsoControlType.msoControlDropdown,
            missing, missing, missing, (object)true);
        dataList.Caption = "Supplier:";
        dataList.Style = MsoComboStyle.msoComboLabel;
        dataList.ListIndex = 0;
        dataList.Width = 230;

        // Hook up a handler for the combo box Change event.
        dataListChange =
            new
                _CommandBarComboBoxEvents_ChangeEventHandler(
            DataListChangeHandler);
        dataList.Change += dataListChange;

        // Make the bar visible.
        dataBar.Visible = true;
    }
    catch (Exception ex)
    {
        MessageBox.Show(ex.Message);
    }
}
```

Write a stub for the combo box *Change* event handler. This will be fully implemented much later on, when we have something meaningful to do when the user selects a value from the combo box. For now, just put up a message box to indicate that something at least is happening:

```csharp
private void DataListChangeHandler(CommandBarComboBox cb)
{
    MessageBox.Show(dataList.Text);
}
```

If you build and run the solution at this point (and therefore run Excel and open the workbook), you should see the custom *CommandBar*:

Populating the List from SQL Data

Now we'll open the Northwind database, read all the company names from the Suppliers table, and add these to the combo box. Create another custom method, called *BuildSupplierList*. Again, we'll call this method at the end of the *ThisWorkbook_Open* event handler. Use structured exception handling as normal.

At the top of the method, clear any current contents of the combo box. Then connect to the SQL database and build a dataset of all the company names in the Suppliers table. Get the data in the *DataSet* as an XML string, using *StringWriter* and *String-Reader*. Parse the XML string with *XmlTextReader*, putting each *CompanyName* into the combo box. Finally, make sure the database connection is closed, even if an exception throws us out of the *try* block:

```
private void BuildSupplierList()
{
    SqlConnection connection = null;

    try
    {
        dataList.Clear();

        // Connect to the SQL database.
        // Build a dataset of all the Supplier names.
        connection =
            new SqlConnection(connectionString);
        connection.Open();
        SqlDataAdapter adapter = new SqlDataAdapter(
            "SELECT CompanyName FROM Suppliers",
            connection);
        DataSet suppliers = new DataSet();
        adapter.Fill(suppliers);

        // Get the dataset as an xml string.
        StringWriter writer = new StringWriter();
        suppliers.WriteXml(writer, XmlWriteMode.IgnoreSchema);
        StringReader reader = new StringReader(writer.ToString());
        XmlTextReader xmlReader = new XmlTextReader(reader);

        // Read the CompanyName nodes in the XML and
        // add each one to the combo box.
        while (xmlReader.Read())
        {
            if (xmlReader.NodeType == XmlNodeType.Element
                && xmlReader.Name == "CompanyName")
```

```
                    {
                        string supplierName = xmlReader.ReadString();
                        dataList.AddItem(supplierName, missing);
                    }
                }
            }
            catch (Exception ex)
            {
                MessageBox.Show(ex.Message);
            }
            finally
            {
                // Close the connection on the way out.
                if (connection != null)
                {
                    connection.Close();
                }
            }
        }
    }
```

Build and test again. The combo box should be populated as shown here, and when you change the selection, the *Change* event handler will pop up a message box.

Creating an XSD

We can use the Visual Studio .NET IDE to create an XSD for the Suppliers table (the whole table this time, not just the *CompanyName* field). To do this, right-click the project in Solution Explorer and choose Add Component. In the Add New Item dialog box, select XML Schema and type in a suitable name—we'll use the name Suppliers.xsd.

When you click Open, this creates a skeleton schema. To complete this, open Server Explorer (from the sliding tab or from the View menu). Navigate down to the Northwind database for your SQL Server, and open the *Tables* node. Drag and drop the Suppliers table onto the schema designer surface.

This schema is listed in XML format below. Note that the *elementFormDefault* attribute is set to "unqualified". You can change this property in the designer. If you don't set it to unqualified, every element will be qualified with a namespace. This can be cumbersome to work with, and in our example, we don't need namespaces to avoid name clashes because the data is so simple.

```xml
<?xml version="1.0" encoding="utf-8" ?>
<xs:schema id="Suppliers" targetNamespace="http://tempuri.org/Suppliers.xsd"
elementFormDefault="unqualified"
    xmlns="http://tempuri.org/Suppliers.xsd"
    xmlns:mstns="http://tempuri.org/Suppliers.xsd"
    xmlns:xs="http://www.w3.org/2001/XMLSchema"
    xmlns:msdata="urn:schemas-microsoft-com:xml-msdata">
    <xs:element name="Document" msdata:Locale="en-GB">
        <xs:complexType>
            <xs:choice maxOccurs="unbounded">
                <xs:element name="Suppliers">
                    <xs:complexType>
                        <xs:sequence>
                            <xs:element name="SupplierID" msdata:ReadOnly="true"
                                msdata:AutoIncrement="true" type="xs:int" />
                            <xs:element name="CompanyName" type="xs:string" />
                            <xs:element name="ContactName" type="xs:string"
                                minOccurs="0" />
                            <xs:element name="ContactTitle" type="xs:string"
                                minOccurs="0" />
                            <xs:element name="Address" type="xs:string"
                                minOccurs="0" />
                            <xs:element name="City" type="xs:string"
                                minOccurs="0" />
                            <xs:element name="Region" type="xs:string"
                                minOccurs="0" />
                            <xs:element name="PostalCode" type="xs:string"
                                minOccurs="0" />
```

```
                              <xs:element name="Country" type="xs:string"
                                    minOccurs="0" />
                              <xs:element name="Phone" type="xs:string"
                                    minOccurs="0" />
                              <xs:element name="Fax" type="xs:string"
                                    minOccurs="0" />
                              <xs:element name="HomePage" type="xs:string"
                                    minOccurs="0" />
                        </xs:sequence>
                     </xs:complexType>
                  </xs:element>
               </xs:choice>
            </xs:complexType>
            <xs:unique name="DocumentKey1" msdata:PrimaryKey="true">
               <xs:selector xpath=".//mstns:Suppliers" />
               <xs:field xpath="mstns:SupplierID" />
            </xs:unique>
         </xs:element>
      </xs:schema>
```

Next we'll attach the XSD to the Excel workbook. We can do this either interactively or programmatically. Just for the exercise, we'll try both options.

To attach a schema interactively, open the workbook in Excel and display the XML task pane (choose View | Task Pane, and select XML Source from the task pane drop-down list). On the XML task pane, click XML Maps, and then click Add. Browse to Suppliers.xsd and add it to the maps. Then click Rename and change the name to Suppliers:

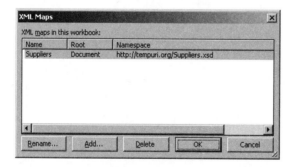

Once you've added the XSD to the workbook, the XML task pane will display a tree representation of the schema. Note that because we set the *elementFormDefault* attribute to unqualified, there are no namespace prefixes on the elements. However, there is a namespace on the root element ("ns1"). In the XSD designer properties, we could set the corresponding form property of the *Document* element, but this is not supported by the Excel schema. The net result is that we're stuck with the namespace on the root element.

If we want to continue working with the workbook interactively, we can drag and drop treenodes from the Suppliers schema onto the worksheet surface. Try this out, just for fun. However, don't save any changes you make because we'll achieve the same results programmatically in the next section, "Building a Form." At this point, click XML Maps again, and then delete this Suppliers mapping—we'll add it programmatically instead. Close Excel.

To attach a schema programmatically, we first need to put the schema file in some location that we can find. The simplest location for our current purposes is where the assembly will be loaded from. At present, the Suppliers.xsd schema file is in the solution folder. So, set up a post-build step to copy it to the special VSTO _bin folder:

copy "$(SolutionDir)Suppliers.xsd" "$(SolutionDir)$(TargetName)_bin"

Create a custom method called *CreateSchema*, and add a call to this method at the end of the *ThisWorkbook_Open* event handler. When we've attached the schema, we'll save the workbook, so if we're writing a method to add the schema programmatically, we must first check to see if it has already been added.

First declare an *XmlMap* reference as a class field variable—we'll be using this across multiple methods. In this method, try to get the "Suppliers" map from the *XmlMaps* collection, and assign it to this field. If this throws a *COMException*, it is almost certainly because the "Suppliers" index value is invalid.

If the *XmlMap* reference is still null after this operation, we don't already have a Suppliers map, so we can add it now. We can use the static *Assembly.GetExecutingAssembly* method to get the full path to the current assembly and split off the assembly name itself, leaving the folder path. This is where we copied the schema to.

While we're here, we might as well make the XML task pane visible and select the Suppliers map in the task pane.

```csharp
private void CreateSchema()
{
    try
    {
        try
        {
            // If we already have a Suppliers map, or if the
            // Maps collection is null, this will throw.
            supplierMap = thisWorkbook.XmlMaps["Suppliers"];
        }
        catch (System.Runtime.InteropServices.COMException) {}

        if (supplierMap == null)
        {
            // We don't yet have a Suppliers map, so add it now.
            string assemblyPath =
                Assembly.GetExecutingAssembly().CodeBase;
            string assemblyDir =
                assemblyPath.Substring(0,
                assemblyPath.LastIndexOf('/'));
            string xsdPath = Path.Combine(assemblyDir,
                "Suppliers.xsd");

            supplierMap =
                thisWorkbook.XmlMaps.Add(xsdPath, missing);
            supplierMap.Name = "Suppliers";
            thisWorkbook.Save();
        }

        // Make the XML task pane visible.
        thisApplication.DisplayXMLSourcePane(supplierMap);
    }
    catch (Exception ex)
    {
        MessageBox.Show(ex.Message);
    }
}
```

Build and test. Note that for a production system, you're more likely to attach the XSD interactively or have the location of the XSD set in a config file, but it is sometimes useful to do it programmatically.

Building a Form

In this section, we'll programmatically build a user form from the XML nodes in the attached schema. This is what we'll end up with:

Write another custom method, called *BuildXmlDocument*. In this method, we'll fill column 1 with labels, using the names of the fields in the Suppliers table in the Northwind database. Then we'll set up corresponding XML nodes alongside in column 2. Note that we have to specify the root element namespace prefix ("ns1"). After setting up the XML nodes, set the column widths to something reasonable for the expected data:

```
private void BuildXmlDocument()
{
    try
    {
        Excel.Worksheet sheet =
            (Excel.Worksheet)thisWorkbook.ActiveSheet;
        int row = 2;
        int col = 1;
        for (int i = 0; i < 12; i++)
        {
            // Fill in the field name in Column 1.
            Excel.Range label =
                (Excel.Range)sheet.Cells[row+i,col];
            label.Value2 = fields[i];

            // Setup an XML node alongside, in Column 2.
            Excel.Range data =
                (Excel.Range)sheet.Cells[row+i, col+1];
            string elementXPath =
                String.Format(
                "/ns1:Document/Suppliers/{0}", fields[i]);
            data.XPath.SetValue(
                supplierMap, elementXPath, missing, false);
        }

        // Set the column widths to something reasonable.
        ((Excel.Range)sheet.Cells[1,1]).ColumnWidth = 20;
        ((Excel.Range)sheet.Cells[1,2]).ColumnWidth = 40;
```

```
        }
        catch (Exception ex)
        {
            MessageBox.Show(ex.Message);
        }
    }
}
```

Build and test.

Dynamic Queries

The final piece of the puzzle is to dynamically update the contents of the XML nodes with Supplier data, according to the user's current selection from the combo box. To achieve this, first write a custom method to query the database given the *Company-Name* string. Call this method *GetSupplierRecord*, and set it to take in a string (the *CompanyName* selected by the user) and return a string (the XML representation of the Supplier data).

We'll be using the *CompanyName* as part of our select query, but we know that the values in this column might contain apostrophes or single quote marks. So, we need to massage the incoming supplier name to protect these. To do this, use the *Regex* class from the *System.Text.RegularExpressions* namespace to replace all instances of the apostrophe with two apostrophes.

Connect to the database, and get a *DataSet* that includes all rows for the specified supplier. Then return the record data as an XML string, making sure to close the database connection on the way out.

```
private string GetSupplierRecord(string supplierName)
{
    SqlConnection connection = null;

    try
    {
        // Protect any apostrophes in the supplier name.
        Regex rx = new Regex("[']");
        string safeSupplierName = rx.Replace(supplierName, "''");

        // Connect to the database, and get all rows for the
        // specified supplier.
        connection =
            new SqlConnection(connectionString);
        connection.Open();
        SqlDataAdapter adapter = new SqlDataAdapter(
            String.Format(
                "SELECT * FROM Suppliers "
                +"WHERE CompanyName='{0}'",
                safeSupplierName), connection);
        DataSet supplier = new DataSet("Document");
        adapter.Fill(supplier, "Suppliers");
```

```
            // Return the record data as an XML string.
            StringWriter supplierXml = new StringWriter();
            supplier.WriteXml(
                supplierXml, XmlWriteMode.IgnoreSchema);
            supplierXml.Close();
            return supplierXml.ToString();
        }
        catch (Exception ex)
        {
            MessageBox.Show(ex.Message);
            return String.Empty;
        }
        finally
        {
            if (connection != null)
            {
                connection.Close();
            }
        }
    }
}
```

Now update the combo box *Change* event handler to call this new method to populate the XML nodes on the sheet. Use the XML string returned by this method to build an *XmlDocument*.

Then use the supplier data to populate the XML nodes in the worksheet. Note that the XPath expression to specify the data for the current field does not include the namespace prefix on the root element. In the code where we set up the form, we had to specify the namespace because we were setting up an XML node in the worksheet. Now we're only traversing the XML document to find the data.

```
private void DataListChangeHandler(CommandBarComboBox cb)
{
    // Get the selected supplier data as an XML document.
    XmlDocument document = new XmlDocument();
    string supplierName = dataList.get_List(dataList.ListIndex);
    string supplierRecord = GetSupplierRecord(supplierName);
    document.LoadXml(supplierRecord);

    try
    {
        // Use the supplier data to populate the XML nodes.
        Excel.Worksheet sheet =
            (Excel.Worksheet)thisWorkbook.ActiveSheet;
        int row = 2;
        int col = 2;
        for (int i = 0; i < 12; i++)
        {
            Excel.Range data =
                (Excel.Range)sheet.Cells[row+i, col];
            string supplierXPath =
                String.Format(
                "/Document/Suppliers/{0}", fields[i]);
```

```
            XmlNode node =
                document.SelectSingleNode(supplierXPath);
            if (node == null)
            {
                data.Value2 = String.Empty;
            }
            else
            {
                data.Value2 = node.InnerText;
            }
        }
    }
    catch (Exception ex)
    {
        MessageBox.Show(ex.Message);
    }
}
```

Build and test. The runtime behavior should look like this:

As a means of further exploration, it would be relatively simple to extend this example to support editing the data and inserting/updating back to the database.

10.7 VSTO and Web Services

Office 97	✗
Office 2000	✗
Office XP	✗
Office 2003	✓

Chapter 9, "Web Services and Remoting," discussed the use of Web services with Office solutions and considered the SOAP Toolkit, managed Web service proxies, Web Services Enhancements, and Research Services. Now, we'll consider Web services in a VSTO solution. In essence, the Web service proxying behavior is the same–the difference is in how we hook all the pieces together.

In the following exercise, we'll build a VSTO solution to consume a dummy stock price Web service. We'll put traditional MSForms buttons on the worksheet and hook them up to event handlers in the *OfficeCodeBehind* class. One button starts a timer, and the other stops it. We'll have a handler for the timer events that calls the Web service each time to get the latest price. For simplicity, our solution is interested only in the price of one stock. So, from a technology perspective, we have:

- A VSTO solution

- Traditional worksheet controls

- A Web service with a managed client-side proxy.

> **Note** The sample solution for this topic can be found in the sample code at <install location>\Code\VSTO\VstoWeb. The dummy stock Web service can be found at <install location>\Tools\WebServices\StockService.

The dummy Web service has only one method, listed here, which generates dummy stock prices using the *Random* class to generate random numbers:

```
public class StockData : System.Web.Services.WebService
{
    // (standard initialization code omitted for brevity)

    [WebMethod]
    public double GetPrice()
    {
        Random randomPrice = new Random();
        return randomPrice.NextDouble() * 100;
    }
}
```

The following exercise focuses on the VSTO solution and assumes that you have already built or installed the stock Web service. To install the Web service on the local machine, go to the IIS MMC snap-in, expand the Web Sites node, and right-click on the Default Web Site node. Choose New | Virtual directory. In the dialog box, type the name *StockService* and the full path to where you put the Web service solution. You can leave all other settings at their defaults.

Create a new VSTO Excel project called VstoWeb. Accept all defaults. Build (to set up the security policy) and test the generated workbook, to ensure everything works as expected before making any changes.

Add two button controls to the form named *cmdStart* and *cmdStop,* captioned Start and Stop. Declare some class fields in the *OfficeCodeBehind* class. We need a timer, a cell range, and two *CommandButton* references. Use the fully qualified timer name instead of adding a *using* statement for the namespace (which would add ambiguity because the *Timer* class could be confused with the *Timer* class in the *System.Windows.Forms* namespace, which the wizard has already included).

```
private System.Timers.Timer stockTimer;
private Excel.Range a1;
private MSForms.CommandButton startButton;
private MSForms.CommandButton stopButton;
```

Implement the *ThisWorkbook_Open* method to set up a one-second autoreset timer, and hook up an event handler for it. Don't enable the timer, however, because that's what the Start button is for. In the same method, cache a reference to some arbitrary cell in the active worksheet (cell A1 in the example code).

Also use the *FindControl* method that the VSTO wizard always provides to find the two buttons, so we can hook up *Click* event handlers for them:

```
protected void ThisWorkbook_Open()
{
    stockTimer = new System.Timers.Timer(1000);
    stockTimer.AutoReset = true;
    stockTimer.Elapsed +=
        new System.Timers.ElapsedEventHandler(
        TimerEventHandler);

    Excel.Worksheet sheet =
        (Excel.Worksheet)ThisWorkbook.ActiveSheet;
    a1 = (Excel.Range)sheet.Cells[1,1];

    startButton = (MSForms.CommandButton)
        FindControl("cmdStart");
    startButton.Click +=
        new
        MSForms.CommandButtonEvents_ClickEventHandler(
        StartClickEventHandler);

    stopButton = (MSForms.CommandButton)
        FindControl("cmdStop");
    stopButton.Click +=
        new
        MSForms.CommandButtonEvents_ClickEventHandler(
        StopClickEventHandler);
}
```

Because we are creating a timer when the workbook is opened, we should be careful to clean it up when the workbook is closed. The VSTO wizard gave us a standard *ThisWorkbook_BeforeClose* event handler, along with a comment that this method might be called multiple times and the value assigned to the *Cancel* parameter might be ignored if other code or the user intervenes—for example, if the user chooses to close the workbook, gets a display alert that the contents have changed, and then chooses to cancel the close. In this simple example, we will ignore any complexity around this event and just kill off our timer.

```
protected void ThisWorkbook_BeforeClose(ref bool Cancel)
{
    if (stockTimer.Enabled)
```

```
    {
        stockTimer.Stop();
    }
    stockTimer = null;

    Cancel = false;
}
```

The event handlers for our Start and Stop buttons are completely trivial: we just enable or disable the timer so it starts or stops firing timer events:

```
private void StartClickEventHandler()
{
    stockTimer.Enabled = true;
}

private void StopClickEventHandler()
{
    stockTimer.Enabled = false;
}
```

Before we can code the timer event handler, we need to add a reference to the Web service. Right-click the project in Solution Explorer, and choose Add Web Reference. In the dialog box, type in the URL to the dummy stock service (*http://localhost/ StockService/StockData.asmx*) and click Go.

When the wizard comes back with the service information, type *StockService* as the Web reference name, and click Add Reference.

Finally, implement the timer event handler to instantiate the Web service proxy and call its *GetPrice* method. Put the returned value into the cell whose reference we cached earlier:

```
private void TimerEventHandler(
    object sender, System.Timers.ElapsedEventArgs e)
{
    StockData stock = new StockData();
    a1.Value2 = stock.GetPrice();
}
```

Build and test. This is how the solution should look at runtime:

10.8 VSTO Configs

Office 97	⊗
Office 2000	⊗
Office XP	⊗
Office 2003	✓

Chapter 8, "Isolating Managed Extensions," discussed the isolation of managed extensions used with Office, focusing on managed COM add-ins, managed smart tags, and managed RealTime Data components. The major point is that you should apply a shim to these extensions so they get the benefit of AppDomain isolation, individual security, and independent configurability. VSTO solutions also require these benefits. Fortunately, the VSTO loader creates a separate AppDomain for each VSTO solution it loads, as well as for VSTO-loaded smart tags and smart documents. Therefore, it is trivial to plug into this mechanism to provide for per-solution configuration.

In the following exercise, we'll build a VSTO solution to make use of an XML config file. Such config files can be used in any Office interop scenario, and the technique is not restricted to VSTO. We'll write a config file for our assembly and deploy it to the same location as the assembly itself. In the config, we'll set up two values: a string and an integer. We'll use the string to put into a cell in the associated workbook, and we'll use the integer for the font size of this string.

> **Note**   The sample solution for this topic can be found in the sample code at <install location>\Code\VSTO\TestConfigs.

Create a new VSTO Excel project called TestConfigs. Accept all defaults. Build (to set up the security policy) and test the generated workbook, to ensure that everything works as expected before making any changes.

Add a new item to the project: an application config file. This adds a skeleton XML file called app.config. For EXE projects, this is copied to the target location as <applicationName>.exe.config as part of the build. However, for DLL projects (including VSTO solutions), this is not done. So, add a post-build step to do this directly:

copy "$(SolutionDir)app.config" "$(SolutionDir)$(TargetName)_bin\$(TargetFileName).config"

Edit the app.config to add entries for two custom properties: *messageText* and *fontSize*:

```xml
<?xml version="1.0" encoding="utf-8" ?>
<configuration>
    <appSettings>
            <add key="messageText" value="Hello World" />
            <add key="fontSize" value="36" />
    </appSettings>
</configuration>
```

In the *OfficeCodeBehind* class, declare two class fields to hold these configured values:

```csharp
private string messageText;
private int fontSize;
```

In the *ThisWorkbook_Open* method, make a call to a custom method called *GetConfiguration* (which we haven't written yet). This gets the configured values from the config file so we can use them in the solution. We'll put the configured text into a cell in the active worksheet and set the size of the font according to the configured value:

```
protected void ThisWorkbook_Open()
{
    try
    {
        GetConfiguration();

        Excel.Worksheet sheet =
            (Excel.Worksheet)thisWorkbook.ActiveSheet;
        Excel.Range cell = (Excel.Range)sheet.Cells[1,1];
        cell.Value2 = messageText;
        cell.Font.Size = fontSize;
    }
    catch (Exception ex)
    {
        MessageBox.Show(ex.Message);
    }
}
```

Code the custom *GetConfiguration* method to load this XML file, read it into an *XmlDocument*, and extract the attribute values. First we'll work out the path to the current assembly, load the config file from that path, and then navigate to the inner *appSettings* node using *SelectSingleNode*. Then we'll walk the children of this node to find all the attributes. Of course, everything in the XML file is text, which is fine for the string value, but we do need to convert *fontSize* to an integer:

```
private void GetConfiguration()
{
    string codeBase =
        Assembly.GetExecutingAssembly().CodeBase + ".config";

    XmlDocument configData = new XmlDocument();
    configData.Load(codeBase);
    XmlNode node = configData.SelectSingleNode(
        "/configuration/appSettings");

    foreach (XmlNode childNode in node.ChildNodes)
    {
        XmlAttributeCollection attribs = childNode.Attributes;
        switch (attribs[0].Value)
        {
            case "messageText":
                messageText = attribs[1].Value;
                break;
            case "fontSize":
                fontSize = Convert.ToInt16(
                    attribs[1].Value);
                break;
        }
    }
}
```

Build and test. This is how your solution should look at runtime:

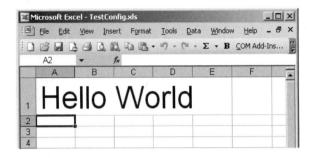

As an alternative, you can leverage the standard .NET EXE configuration loading if you name your config according to the EXE name—that is, the name of the Office application with *.config* on the end (in this example, *Excel.exe.config*). You can even set this up as an alternative post-build step:

copy "$(SolutionDir)app.config" "$(SolutionDir)$(TargetName)_bin\Excel.exe.config"

You can then greatly simplify the code required for accessing the configuration data. Specifically, you can replace all the custom *XmlDocument* code with just two lines—using the *ConfigurationSettings.AppSettings* collection:

```
private void GetConfiguration()
{
    messageText =
        ConfigurationSettings.AppSettings["messageText"];
    fontSize = Convert.ToInt16(
        ConfigurationSettings.AppSettings["FontSize"]);
}
```

The runtime resolves config files on a per-AppDomain basis, so it looks for this renamed config file in the same place it found the code-behind assembly if a new App-Domain has been created for the code-behind assembly. This is the case if the assembly was loaded by the VSTO loader, which does indeed create a new AppDomain for the assembly.

Summary

Just like traditional VBA, VSTO is a document-centric technology. The big difference is that VSTO separates out the code from the document and at the same time moves the code from an older procedural language to a modern managed language. Unlike with VBA, with VSTO you have complete access to the full richness of the .NET Framework and its library. You can build agile, reusable components, surround them with robust and repeatable development and testing processes, enforce coding standards guidelines, and apply sophisticated source control management. Moreover, security for

VSTO is more flexible, more finely-grained, and potentially more powerful than traditional macro-based Office security.

The significance of VSTO should not be underestimated. It represents the first step on a road that is moving Office away from traditional VBA toward the .NET managed world. Of course, VBA will continue to be supported for years to come. However, most people recognize the benefits of moving to .NET. That implies moving from a development process that has traditionally often been unstructured and error-prone to one in which any number of powerful support tools can be applied to improve the quality of the code produced and to improve the development experience. Office has been used as the basis of serious development for many years, but it hasn't had the tool support that other development platforms have enjoyed. VSTO can be seen as an indicator that Office is finally being recognized as a serious development platform. It also represents a wonderful opportunity to consolidate the many different approaches available for Office development.

Chapter 11

Smart Documents

Smart documents are documents in Microsoft Word 2003 or workbooks in Microsoft Excel 2003 that have some associated intelligence. You can build two kinds of smart document solutions: simple XML-based solutions and sophisticated DLL-based solutions:

- **XML-based solutions**   You can create very simple smart documents by writing an XML file that conforms to the Microsoft Office Smart Tag List (MOSTL) schema. Using this approach, you don't need a custom DLL. Instead, all the "intelligence" is listed in the XML file. You are restricted to displaying static text in the task pane, as well as minimal functionality.

- **DLL-based solutions**   Sophisticated smart documents require a custom DLL. In this DLL, you write a component that implements the *ISmartDocument* interface. For DLL-based smart documents, you have three technology choices for building the solution:

  - ❑   Using an unmanaged COM DLL, developed in any language that supports the creation of COM objects, and directly implementing the *ISmartDocument* interface.

  - ❑   Using a managed DLL assembly, developed in any managed language, and directly implementing the *ISmartDocument* interface.

  - ❑   Using a managed DLL assembly, developed in any managed language, and using the Vertigo Smart Document Wrapper (which implements *ISmartDocument* on your behalf).

Among the factors to consider when choosing between managed and unmanaged DLLs are the following:

- Word and Excel are themselves COM servers, and the COM runtime DLLs are part of Microsoft Windows, so if your users don't have the Microsoft .NET Framework deployed, they cannot use managed smart documents but they can use COM-based smart documents.

- Managed smart documents use the VSTO loader, which brings with it greater flexibility in loading/unloading assemblies, isolation of assemblies through separate AppDomains, and .NET security enforcement.

DLL-based smart document solutions comprise, at a minimum, a set of three artifacts. These are their simplest forms:

- An XML schema attached to the document/workbook
- A DLL (managed or unmanaged) that contains the custom code
- An XML manifest that lists the DLL and additional files

Here is a high-level overview of how DLL-based smart documents are implemented and how they appear to the user:

1. You map an XML schema to a document or workbook, mapping individual elements in the document or cells in the workbook to elements in the schema. The schema elements are entirely arbitrary—you decide what you want them to be.

2. You develop a custom DLL that puts one or more controls onto the Office task pane (specifically, the Document Actions task pane). These controls can be standard controls such as labels, text boxes, list boxes, and buttons, or they can be ActiveX controls. These controls can have any code behind them that you want.

3. When the user puts the cursor into a mapped document element or mapped worksheet cell, the task pane responds by dynamically displaying the set of controls that you have decided are appropriate to show the user when he's working on that element. If the user interacts with any of these controls, your custom DLL will take whatever action you programmed into it.

The document or workbook thus has elements or cells mapped to a custom schema, and your custom DLL knows what controls to put into the task pane for each element in the schema and how to respond when the user works with a control.

Your custom DLL can rely on dependent DLLs or on external files such as XML files, HTML files, XSLTs, bitmap files, Word documents, and Excel workbooks. The whole set of files required for a given smart document to work is called an XML Expansion Pack (XEP). The XEP includes the XEP manifest file. This is an XML file that lists all the files in the XEP, including their locations, namespaces, and so forth, and basically acts as an install/uninstall bootstrapper. Before a smart document will work, the XEP must be attached to the Microsoft Office application, and that is done through the manifest file.

Regardless of whether you choose managed or unmanaged code for your solution, you'll need to become familiar with the smart document API, and especially the *ISmartDocument* interface. This interface is not as obvious in its behavior as some interfaces, and it's worth taking time to understand it. A good starting point is to consider the sequence of operations that take place inside the smart document components in Word and Excel. At a high level, there are four stages in the initialization of a smart document, and they correspond to four sets of *ISmartDocument* functions that Office calls, in sequence. The *PopulateXXX* functions are called for each control that you define—so if you define only, say, a check box control, only the *PopulateCheckbox* function is called. The fifth stage also corresponds to a set of *ISmartDocument* functions, but these might or might not ever be called. These are essentially event handlers for user interaction on the controls, although they can be triggered by other runtime behavior. Figure 11-1 illustrates the high-level view.

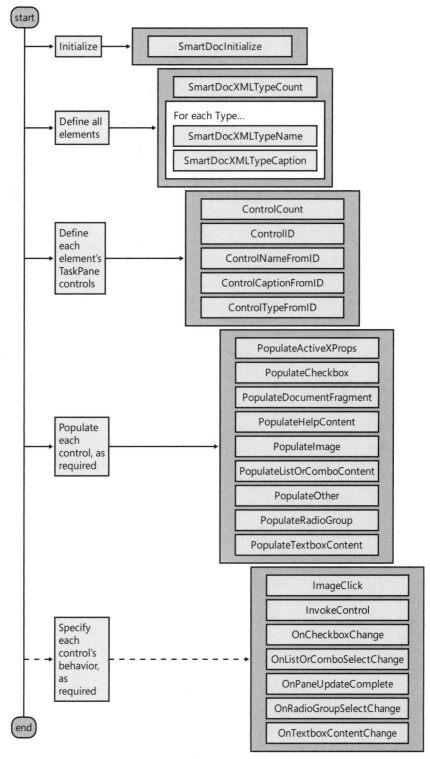

Figure 11-1 Smart document initialization.

11.1 Smart Documents Core

Office 97	✖
Office 2000	✖
Office XP	✖
Office 2003	✔

Smart documents can be as sophisticated as you like. However, all smart documents must implement the *ISmartDocument* interface, and certain core operations must be performed regardless of how simple or sophisticated your smart document solution is. In this section, we'll look at these core operations and the concepts that underlie them.

In the following exercise, we'll create a simple smart document. We'll use Excel for the host application. In our XML schema, we'll define two elements. We'll map two cells in a workbook, one to each of our custom elements. When the user puts the cursor in the first mapped cell, we'll display a text box on the task pane to provide some additional information on this element type. When the user puts the cursor in the second mapped cell, we'll display a text box and also a button. We'll develop a managed smart document DLL to implement this functionality. We'll implement the button handler code to perform some simple arbitrary operation such as showing a message box. Finally, we'll write an XEP manifest and a batch file to set up security policy for our solution.

> **Note**   The sample solution for this topic can be found in the sample code at <install location>\Code\Office2003\BasicXlSmartDoc.

The Initial Project

Logically, we should start with the XML schema. However, it's more convenient if we start with our DLL project. That way, we can add all related files–including the schema, the XEP manifest, a batch file for setting .NET security policy, and .reg files for registering and unregistering our component–into the same project, for ease of handling. This is only for convenience; none of these additional files is actually built into the assembly.

1. First create a new Class Library project called BasicXlSmartDoc. Add a reference to the Smart Tags PIA. This will be listed on the COM tab as Microsoft Smart Tags 2.0 Type Library. The smart document object model is closely related to the smart tag object model, so they're both in the same type library and the same PIA. Note that if you've added this reference correctly, in the Properties window it should show up with a path such as C:\WINDOWS\assembly\ GAC\Microsoft.Office.Interop.SmartTag\11.0.0.0__71e9bce111e9429c\ Microsoft.Office.Interop.SmartTag.dll–that is, the location of the PIA in the GAC. The *CopyLocal* property should be set to *False*.

2. When you create the class library project, the wizard generates a class called *Class1*. Rename this to something more meaningful, such as *ExcelExpansion*. The significant step is to specify that this class implements the *ISmartDocument* interface. To implement an interface, type the colon and the interface name, and then

press Tab to get stubs for all the methods. Your code should end up looking something like this:

```
public class ExcelExpansion : ISmartDocument
{
    public ExcelExpansion()
    {
    }

    #region ISmartDocument Members

    public void PopulateCheckbox(int ControlID, string ApplicationName,
        int LocaleID, string Text, string Xml, object Target,
        ISmartDocProperties Props, ref bool Checked)
    {
        // TODO:  Add PopulateCheckbox implementation
    }

    public int get_ControlID(string XMLTypeName, int ControlIndex)
    {
        // TODO:  Add  get_ControlID implementation
        return 0;
    }
    .
    .
    .
```

3. Before we get stuck into the code, we'll add an XML Schema file to the project. You can call this whatever you like, but for consistency we'll call it BasicXlSmart-Doc.xsd. We'll specify a custom namespace and two custom elements. When Excel invokes our *ISmartDocument* interface methods, these elements will be known as "types." The namespace we specify in the schema will also be specified in our custom DLL. Recall that the data elements in the workbook will eventually be mapped to this schema. Therefore, this schema acts as the link between the workbook and the code in our custom DLL. You can use any names you like for your schema namespace and elements; an example is given here:

```
<?xml version="1.0" encoding="UTF-8"?>
<xsd:schema xmlns:xsd="http://www.w3.org/2001/XMLSchema"
    xmlns="urn:schemas-microsoft-com.BasicXlSmartDoc"
    targetNamespace="urn:schemas-microsoft-com.BasicXlSmartDoc"
    elementFormDefault="qualified"
    attributeFormDefault="unqualified"
    id="SomeInfo">

<xsd:complexType name="exampleType">
    <xsd:all>
        <xsd:element name="SomeType" type="xsd:string"/>
        <xsd:element name="AnotherType" type="xsd:string"/>
    </xsd:all>
</xsd:complexType>

<xsd:element name="example" type="exampleType"/>

</xsd:schema>
```

4. Now we'll turn to the code. We'll follow the sequence of operations in the flow-chart above. First we need to specify some constants that we'll be using through-out the code. The namespace must be the same as the one we wrote into the XML schema. Similarly, the "type" names must correspond to our two schema elements (and they are case-sensitive). Finally, we have two "types":

```
const string NAMESPACE = "urn:schemas-microsoft-com.BasicXlSmartDoc";
const string SOMETYPE = NAMESPACE + "#SomeType";
const string ANOTHERTYPE = NAMESPACE + "#AnotherType";
const int TYPESCOUNT = 2;
```

5. The first method to be called is *SmartDocInitialize*. This runs when a user attaches an XEP to a document or workbook, or when a user first opens a smart document with this expansion pack attached. We don't actually have anything special to do here, so we can leave this blank:

```
public void SmartDocInitialize(string ApplicationName, object Document,
    string SolutionPath, string SolutionRegKeyRoot)
{
}
```

Defining All Elements

1. Next we'll code the three methods that are called to allow us to define all the elements we will use in our smart document: *SmartDocXmlTypeCount*, *SmartDocXmlTypeName*, and *SmartDocXmlTypeCaption*. These are actually parameterized properties rather than methods, but they are represented in C# as methods. (See Section 2.6, "Visual Basic .NET vs. C#," for an explanation of parameterized properties.) The first of these is *SmartDocXmlTypeCount*, which is called so that we can specify the number of elements from the schema that have assigned actions in the smart document. We have two elements, and both have assigned actions:

```
public int SmartDocXmlTypeCount
{
    get
    {
        return TYPESCOUNT;
    }
}
```

2. Next is SmartDocXmlTypeName: we implement this to specify the name of an element for which smart document actions are defined. The format for this name is <namespace>#<xmlelementname>. We've already defined constants for these strings. When this method is called, we are passed an integer index value to allow us to determine which element we need to supply the name for. These are arbitrary values starting at 1. The method is called the same number of times as there are elements. So, the first time, this method is called—with XMLTypeID

set to 1— for the first element in the schema. The second time—with *XMLTypeID* set to 2—is for the second element in the schema:

```
public string get_SmartDocXmlTypeName(int XMLTypeID)
{
    string typeName = "";

    switch (XMLTypeID)
    {
        case 1:
            typeName = SOMETYPE;
            break;
        case 2:
            typeName = ANOTHERTYPE;
            break;
    }
    return typeName;
}
```

3. The *SmartDocXmlTypeCaption* property is where we specify the caption that should be displayed in the Document Actions task pane for a specific element. Again, we're passed in the index number each time this method is called:

```
public string get_SmartDocXmlTypeCaption(int XMLTypeID, int LocaleID)
{
    string typeCaption = "";

    switch (XMLTypeID)
    {
        case 1:
            typeCaption = "Some Type";
            break;
        case 2:
            typeCaption = "Another Type";
            break;
    }
    return typeCaption;
}
```

Defining Each Element's Task Pane Controls

1. Now we must implement the methods that are called to allow us to define how many and which controls are to be displayed in the Document Actions task pane when the user is working with a particular mapped element in the workbook. Again, all five of these are actually parameterized properties: *ControlCount, ControlID, ControlNameFromID, ControlCaptionFromID,* and *ControlTypeFromID.*

2. The first one is *ControlCount,* where we specify how many controls should be displayed for each element. When the user is on the cell mapped to our first element, we'll display just one control (a text box). When the user is on the

cell mapped to our second element, we'll display two controls (a text box and a button):

```
public int get_ControlCount(string XMLTypeName)
{
    int numberOfControls = 0;

    switch (XMLTypeName)
    {
        case SOMETYPE:
            numberOfControls = 1;
            break;
        case ANOTHERTYPE:
            numberOfControls = 2;
            break;
    }

    return numberOfControls;
}
```

3. The second property is *ControlID*. We must specify a unique ID for each control. This can be confusing, particularly if we want to reuse the same control across multiple elements. By default, the smart document object model assigns a non-unique control index number to each control associated with a *namespace#element* name. While the control index number is unique for each control for each *namespace#element* name, it is not unique across all of the controls in the smart document. An example of this numbering schema is given in Table 11-1.

Table 11-1 Default, Nonunique Control IDs

Smart Document Type (*namespace#element*)	Control	Control Index
urn:schemas-microsoft-com.BasicXlSmartDoc#SomeType	Text box	1
urn:schemas-microsoft-com.BasicXlSmartDoc#AnotherType	Text box	1
urn:schemas-microsoft-com.BasicXlSmartDoc#AnotherType	Button	2

A standard approach to resolving this numbering is to specify a *ControlID* that is unique by using some arbitrary increment between elements. It's usual to use an increment of 100—this allows you to have up to 100 controls on display per element, which is far more than you would (or should) ever need. Following this pattern, our *ControlID* properties would be as indicated in Table 11-2.

Table 11-2 Numbering Scheme for Unique Control IDs

Smart Document Type (*namespace#element*)	Control	Unique *ControlID*
urn:schemas-microsoft-com.BasicXlSmartDoc#SomeType	Text box	1
urn:schemas-microsoft-com.BasicXlSmartDoc#AnotherType	Text box	101
urn:schemas-microsoft-com.BasicXlSmartDoc#AnotherType	Button	102

4. When this method is called, we're told the "type" and the index. We just have to map the permutations of "type" and index to a unique integer value:

```
public int get_ControlID(string XMLTypeName, int ControlIndex)
{
    int controlID = 0;

    switch (XMLTypeName)
    {
        case SOMETYPE:
            controlID = ControlIndex;
            break;
        case ANOTHERTYPE:
            controlID = ControlIndex + 100;
            break;
    }

        return controlID;
}
```

5. The *ControlNameFromID* property specifies a string that can be used to access each of the controls in the Document Actions task pane for a smart document by using the *SmartTagActions* collection within an application's VBA object model. This name can be any name you like. We'll assign each control a name composed of the element name plus *ControlID*.

For example, the button control will be named *urn:schemas-microsoft-com.BasicXlSmartDoc102*. Then, if you want to access that control from the VBA object model, you can access it by using *SmartTagActions("urn:schemas-microsoft-com.BasicXlSmartDoc102")*. This might seem a little cumbersome, but (a) there's a good chance we won't be using this control with VBA anyway and (b) it does reduce the chance of any name clashes.

```
public string get_ControlNameFromID(int ControlID)
{
    string controlName = "";
    controlName = NAMESPACE + ControlID.ToString();
    return controlName;
}
```

6. The *ControlCaptionFromID* property specifies the caption we want displayed in the task pane for each control:

```
public string get_ControlCaptionFromID(
    int ControlID, string ApplicationName, int LocaleID,
    string Text, string Xml, object Target)
{
    string controlCaption = "";

    switch (ControlID)
    {
        case 1:
            controlCaption = "Enter some value:";
            break;
```

```
        case 101:
            controlCaption = "Please enter your name:";
            break;
        case 102:
            controlCaption = "Test button";
            break;
    }
    return controlCaption;
}
```

7. The final property, *ControlTypeFromID*, specifies a *C_TYPE* constant, which represents the type of control (button, text box, list box, etc.):

```
public C_TYPE get_ControlTypeFromID(
    int ControlID, string ApplicationName, int LocaleID)
{
    C_TYPE type = new C_TYPE();

    switch (ControlID)
    {
        case 1:
            type = C_TYPE.C_TYPE_TEXTBOX;
            break;
        case 101:
            type = C_TYPE.C_TYPE_TEXTBOX;
            break;
        case 102:
            type = C_TYPE.C_TYPE_BUTTON;
            break;
    }
    return type;
}
```

Populating Each Control

If we want any initial values in any of our controls, we must implement the corresponding *PopulateXXX* method. For example, you would use *PopulateListOrCombo-Content* to put strings in a list box or a combo box. We have only text boxes and a button, and those don't need any initial values in our example. Therefore, you can leave all these *PopulateXXX* methods blank.

Specifying Control Behavior

The last set of code implementations specify what should happen when the user interacts with each of our controls. In this simple example, we'll just put up a message box in each case. We have two types of controls (text box and button), so we have two methods to implement. The first is the *OnTextboxContentChange* method. This is called when a text box loses the focus—the user has moved to another control on the task pane or to another cell in the workbook. We'll implement this to put up a message box with the text the user has typed in the text box:

```
public void OnTextboxContentChange(
    int ControlID, object Target, string Value)
{
    if (Value.Length > 0)
    {
        MessageBox.Show("Hello, " + Value);
    }
}
```

When the user clicks the button, the *InvokeControl* method is called. (This method is also called when the user clicks a hyperlink or document fragment control.) Again, we'll just display a simple message box:

```
public void InvokeControl(int ControlID, string ApplicationName,
    object Target, string Text, string Xml, int LocaleID)
{
    switch ( ControlID)
    {
        case 102:
            MessageBox.Show("This is an example of a button.");
            break;
    }
}
```

Deployment

All the code's done—the remaining *ISmartDocument* methods can be left blank for this exercise. You can now build the assembly. Before you can test the smart document solution, however, you have to create some deployment files. Specifically, we need an XEP manifest file, a batch file to set up .NET security, and (optionally) a .reg file to register our component.

1. First we need the XEP manifest. The idea is to support zero-touch deployment of smart documents. It is a single XML file that contains the deployment information needed to set up the smart document components when a document is loaded into the host application. The manifest acts as an installer: when the XEP is attached, the manifest writes the appropriate registry keys, runs a batch file or MSI file, and so on. It also performs the reverse uninstall behavior when the XEP is detached.

2. We'll take the manifest in sections. At the top of the file is the standard smart documents schema namespace and version number. The update frequency allows the smart document to download updated files at specified intervals (20160 minutes is 14 days)—we won't be using that in our solution.

```
<?xml version="1.0" encoding="UTF-8" standalone="no"?>
<manifest xmlns=
    "http://schemas.microsoft.com/office/xmlexpansionpacks/2003">
    <version>1.0</version>
    <updateFrequency>20160</updateFrequency>
```

3. The *uri* element defines the XML namespace of the project. The *<solution>* block has a GUID that identifies this solution (which must be unique), the predefined *smartDocument* type, a friendly (locale-attributed) alias for the solution, and the *ProgId* of the target host application (in this case, Excel):

```xml
<uri>urn:schemas-microsoft-com.BasicXlSmartDoc</uri>
<solution>
    <solutionID>
        {73DF8F6A-2413-414f-9DAD-5BCBD4F2C747}
    </solutionID>
    <type>smartDocument</type>
    <alias lcid="1033">BasicXlSmartDoc</alias>
    <documentSpecific>False</documentSpecific>
    <targetApplication>Excel.Application.11</targetApplication>
```

4. The *<file>* block identifies the managed assembly, with its full path and the fully qualified name of the class that implements *ISmartDocument*. If you change the .NET namespace of the class, you must change the *<CLSNAME>* element's value. The .NET namespace is different from the XML namespace discussed earlier. The *<CLSNAME>* element's value is the namespace and class name of the class that will be the *solutionActionHandler*—that is, the class that drives the smart document.

The *<runFromServer>* element specifies that the assembly will be used from its existing location. If the *<runFromServer>* tag is omitted, the file is downloaded to the smart document solution folder and is used from there. By default, this solution folder is in the user's profile, under C:\Documents and Settings\<user-Name>\Local Settings\Application Data\Microsoft\Schemas\<uri>\<solutionID>. Using *<runFromServer>* is extremely convenient for assemblies because you do not have to delete the expansion pack and then re-add it to the document after every recompile to allow debugging of the newly created assembly. However, *<runFromServer>* is generally only for development use—in a production environment, it can cause performance issues and unnecessary dependence on the network.

Only two of the elements in the manifest are specific to managed solutions: *<managed>* and *<CLSNAME>*. For an unmanaged solution, these two elements are replaced with the *<CLSID>* element.

```xml
<file>
    <type>solutionActionHandler</type>
    <version>1.0</version>
    <filePath>
        C:\Temp\BasicXlSmartDoc\bin\debug\BasicXlSmartDoc.dll
    </filePath>
    <CLSNAME>
        BasicXlSmartDoc.ExcelExpansion
    </CLSNAME>
    <managed/>
    <runFromServer>True</runFromServer>
</file>
</solution>
```

5. In addition to the assembly, the manifest also lists other solution resources—which minimally include the schema file.

```
    <solution>
        <solutionID>
            {73DF8F6A-2413-414f-9DAD-5BCBD4F2C747}
        </solutionID>
        <type>schema</type>
        <alias lcid="1033">BasicXlSmartDoc</alias>
        <file>
        <type>schema</type>
        <version>1.0</version>
        <filePath>BasicXlSmartDoc.xsd</filePath>
        </file>
    </solution>
</manifest>
```

6. Note that if you copy and paste this file into your solution, you should replace the GUID used to identify the solution in the *<solutionID>* elements—these IDs should be unique across all expansion packs deployed. You can use any identifier you like for this, but it is common practice to use GUIDs. Also, the path to the DLL will need changing, as will the name of the class that you've written to implement *ISmartDocument* if you've deviated from the suggested names in this exercise.

7. The *<managed>* element in the manifest causes a key for this solution to be written to the registry. This key should be present under the HKEY_CURRENT_USER\Software\Microsoft\Office\Common\Smart Tag\Actions\<Smart Document assembly ProgID> key. It should have a name of Managed, a type of REG_DWORD, and a value of 1. When the user attaches the XEP to the Office application, the appropriate registry key is written:

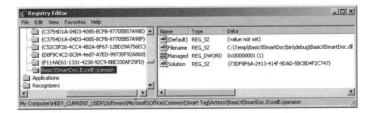

Likewise, when you detach an XEP, the registry entry is removed.

8. An alternative approach is to use a .reg file, which can be merged into the registry with RegEdit. This approach might be more familiar to administrators and might fit in with existing script-based admin procedures. An example is given below. The following .reg file adds a new key under HKCU for our custom *SmartDoc* class, including the path to the DLL (which you obviously have to change to match where the DLL actually is on your machine). Again, note that there are six lines in this example file (including the blank line) and that lines can be word-wrapped in this document.

> **Warning**   Editing the registry incorrectly can cause serious problems that require you to reinstall Windows. There is no guarantee that problems resulting from the incorrect use of RegEdit (including the use of .reg files) can be solved. Use RegEdit at your own risk.

```
Windows Registry Editor Version 5.00

[HKEY_CURRENT_USER\Software\Microsoft\Office\Common\Smart Tag\Actions\
BasicXlSmartDoc.ExcelExpansion]
"Solution"="BasicXlSmartDoc.ExcelExpansion"
"Managed"=dword:00000001
"Filename"="C:\\Temp\\BasicXlSmartDoc\\bin\\Debug\\BasicXlSmartDoc.dll"
```

9. Once you're sure the .reg file is correct, you can double-click it to merge it into the registry. It's probably also worthwhile to write a second .reg file to unregister the component. This is the same as the file for registering the component, but with a minus sign (-) in front of the HKEY_CURRENT_USER entry.

10. Regardless of how you register the solution, you must set up .NET security policy for it. You can do this by writing a simple batch file. Security should be set up according to your organization's specific requirements. However, the smart document DLL must be granted FullTrust permission. It is recommended that you use a strong form of evidence, such as strongname evidence (and preferably strongname evidence scoped to a particular zone or URL), but for simplicity we'll use URL evidence in this exercise. To set up security, recall that you can use either the CASPol.exe command-line utility (which you can therefore write scripts or batch files for) or the MSCorCfg.msc MMC snap-in. The following screenshot illustrates MSCorCfg with the code group we want to set up:

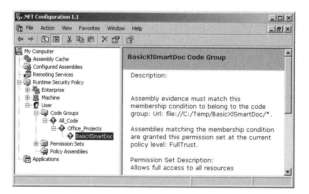

11. If you prefer to use CASPol, it's probably more convenient to write a batch file (and there's good reason for this, which you'll see in a moment). The following batch file gives FullTrust permission to everything in the specified path and below, at the User policy level, based on URL evidence. Note that it also assumes that you already have the *Office_Projects* code group (created when you build a

standard VSTO project). This code group has no special meaning; it is a convenience for grouping managed Office solutions. It is arbitrary, and you can use whatever code group names you like.

```
CD %windir%\microsoft.net\framework\v1.1.4322
caspol -polchgprompt off -user -addgroup Office_Projects -url
"C:\Temp\ BasicXlSmartDoc\*" FullTrust -name "BasicXlSmartDoc"
caspol - polchgprompt on
pause
```

Note that the lines have been wrapped: there are two CASPol commands, and each must be on one line. Instead of changing the current directory to the location of CASPol.exe, you can either extend the *PATH* in your environment to include this location or run the command from a Visual Studio .NET command prompt.

12. It's also useful, at least during development, to have a batch file that removes a code group:

```
CD %windir%\microsoft.net\framework\v1.1.4322
caspol.exe -polchgprompt off -user -remgroup  BasicXlSmartDoc
caspol -polchgprompt on
pause
```

When you're sure the CASPol commands are correct, you can run the batch file. Alternatively, you can include the batch file in the XEP manifest. Remember that the XEP manifest acts as an install/uninstall bootstrapper. To do this, simply add another *<file>* element within the *<solution>* element with a path to the batch file. The following listing shows the relevant part of the manifest that incorporates the batch file:

```
<solution>
    ... (standard elements omitted for brevity)
    <file>
        <type>installPackage</type>
        <version>1.0</version>
        <filePath>
            C:\Temp\BasicXlSmartDoc\SetupPolicy.bat
        </filePath>
    </file>

</solution>
```

The only downside to adding the policy setup batch file to the manifest is that the policy will be re-created each time the user updates the XEP or deletes it and adds it again. If you want to support this behavior properly, the batch file should include commands that at least test for the existence of the code group before attempting to add it.

13. Lastly, smart documents require XML expansion pack manifest files to be digitally signed. During development, you can disable this functionality if you wish: run the DisableManifestSecurityCheck.reg file. This changes the registry setting so Office 2003 will not require that your manifest files be signed during testing. This is the file:

```
Windows Registry Editor Version 5.00
[HKEY_LOCAL_MACHINE\Software\Microsoft\Office\Common\Smart Tag]
"DisableManifestSecurityCheck"=dword:00000001
```

> **Important** You are strongly discouraged from disabling XML expansion pack manifest security checking *except* within a testing environment and not on end users' machines. The option to disable XML expansion pack security checking is included to make it easier for developers to test their smart documents during the development phase. In Chapter 12, "Security," we'll see how to digitally sign manifest files for production use.

14. When you get to the point when you want to turn XEP manifest security checking back on, you can use the following .reg file. The only difference is that the *DisableManifestSecurityCheck* value is assigned zero (0) instead of 1:

```
Windows Registry Editor Version 5.00
[HKEY_LOCAL_MACHINE\Software\Microsoft\Office\Common\Smart Tag]
"DisableManifestSecurityCheck"=dword:00000000
```

Testing

1. To test this smart document solution, open Excel 2003. Make sure there is an open workbook with at least one worksheet. Display the task pane if it's not already there (by choosing View | Task Pane). First we need to map the schema to this workbook. Drop down the task pane list box and select XML Source. Then click XML Maps. In the XML Maps dialog box, click Add and browse to the BasicXlSmartDoc.xsd that we created earlier to add this schema to the workbook:

XML Maps			
XML maps in this workbook:			
Name	Root	Namespace	
example_Map	example	urn:schemas-microsoft-com.BasicXlSmartDoc	

Rename... Add... Delete OK Cancel

2. The XML Source task pane should list the structure of this schema, including its two elements. Drag and drop the first (*SomeType*) element onto any cell in the worksheet. Then drag and drop the second (*AnotherType*) element onto any

other cell. This will map those cells to the selected schema elements. You should get a blue border around each mapped cell:

3. From the Excel main menu, go to Data | XML | XML Expansion Packs. This displays the XML Expansion Packs dialog box:

4. Click Add, and browse to the XEP manifest file you created earlier. Click Open. You should get a warning message telling you that XEP security has been disabled and asking whether you want to reenable it. You'll get this warning when you first attempt to attach an expansion pack and every time you update it:

Click No. Then click Attach in the XML Expansion Packs dialog box to attach the expansion pack:

5. Now when you put the cursor on the first mapped cell, you should get the text box control in the Document Actions task pane. When you type something into the text box and then click another cell, you get a message box:

6. When you put the cursor on the second mapped cell, the task pane displays two controls. Note that even though there is a text box, the text box caption is different from when the first mapped cell is active. When you click the button, you get another simple message box.

11.2 Multiple Target Applications

In our first smart document example, we developed a solution that targeted Excel. However, the only piece of our solution that was Excel-specific was the *targetApplication* element in the manifest:

Office 97	
Office 2000	
Office XP	
Office 2003	

```
<targetApplication>Excel.Application.11</targetApplication>
```

Because the solution itself is very generic, we can use it for Word as well as Excel. We'll walk through the steps required to do this in this section. The smart document DLL code itself will not change. We only need to update the XEP manifest and attach it to Word.

> **Note**   The sample solution for this topic can be found in the sample code at <install location>\Code\Office2003\BasicXlSmartDoc_Word. This copy is for convenience only—to keep the material for different examples separate. In fact, because the code is identical to the core solution, there is no real need for a separate copy. Also, because we've moved the location of the solution, we need to update the security policy. If we've used the recommended approach of adding a managed element to the XEP manifest, we won't need to update the registry manually—we just update the XEP from within Word or Excel.

1. The first task is to update the XEP manifest. Add an extra *targetApplication* element for Word, and save the updated file:

    ```
    <targetApplication>Excel.Application.11</targetApplication>
    <targetApplication>Word.Application.11</targetApplication>
    ```

2. Run Word, and create a new document—we need to attach the original XML schema to this document. Word doesn't have a Data menu like Excel does, and it keeps its XML menu options on the Tools menu instead. So, go to Tools | Templates And Add-Ins. Then go to the XML Schema tab. Click Add Schema, and then browse to and select the (unchanged) BasicXlSmartDoc.xsd, and click OK:

3. With the schema attached, we can now type some arbitrary text into the document. Make sure the task pane is visible, and select the XML Structure panel. At arbitrary points, you can drag and drop elements from the schema onto the document, as illustrated below. When you drop schema elements onto the document surface, each element is delimited with pink tags. If you can't see these

pink XML tags, make sure the corresponding check box in the XML Structure task pane is selected:

4. We must now attach the updated XEP to Word. First make sure the security policy and registry information have been correctly set up; otherwise, the operation will fail. To attach the XEP, go to Tools | Templates And Add-Ins. Go to the XML Expansion Packs tab, and click Add. Browse to and select your XEP manifest file. Then click Attach to attach this XEP to Word.

Word does not allow you to attach an XEP if it is considered to be open in more than one document at the same time. So make sure you don't have the manifest open in any other document (not even multiple copies of the same document). Also make sure you don't have the Document Map pane open—if you do, Word regards the manifest as open in two documents at the same time.

5. With the XEP attached, if you put the cursor in any of the mapped schema elements in the document, you can select the Document Actions task pane and it will behave exactly as it did in Excel:

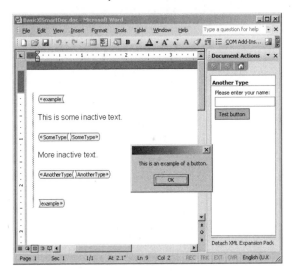

11.3 Smart Documents and PIAs

Office 97   ❌
Office 2000   ❌
Office XP   ❌
Office 2003   ✅

Our first smart document example demonstrated the use of all the major concepts and coding constructs needed to develop a custom smart document DLL. We've also seen that targeting Word or Excel is simply a matter of maintaining the XEP manifest correctly, as long as we keep to generic code. However, if we want to develop code that integrates more closely with either Word or Excel (or both), we need to do a little more work.

In the following exercise, we'll enhance our first example to make explicit use of the Excel object model. To do that, we'll use the Excel PIA, of course. We won't do anything particularly sophisticated—the aim here is to demonstrate the key operations needed to interop with a specific Office object model from within a smart document solution. Many of the techniques explored in other sections of this document can also be used in the context of smart documents.

> **Note**   The sample solution for this topic can be found in the sample code at <install location>\Code\Office2003\BasicXlSmartDoc_ExcelInterop.

1. We'll continue with the BasicXlSmartDoc example. The first change is to add a reference to the Excel 2003 PIAs and an appropriate namespace *using* statement to the code. For the first enhancement, we'll update the *OnTextboxContentChange* method. When the user types some text in the text box in the task pane (and then moves the focus somewhere else), we'll retrieve the text and

place it into the cell that was active at the time. (This will, of course, be a schema-mapped cell.) When the *OnTextboxContentChange* method is called, we're passed a *Target* object that will in fact be the active document element—or, in our case, the active workbook cell:

```
public void OnTextboxContentChange(
    int ControlID, object Target, string Value)
{
    Excel.Range cell = (Excel.Range)Target;

    if (Value.Length > 0)
    {
        //MessageBox.Show("Hello, " + Value);
        cell.Value2 = Value;
    }
}
```

2. For our second example of using the Excel object model, we'll change the button behavior. Now when the user clicks the button, we'll change the color of the active cell. If she clicks it again, we'll change the color again. In fact, we'll cycle through all the 56 possible colors that Excel can display in a cell. First we need a field member to track the current value of the color index:

```
private static int colorIndex = 0;
```

3. Then we'll update the *InvokeControl* method. As with the previous method, we're given the cell as the *Target* parameter. We'll set the color of this cell and increment the color index:

```
public void InvokeControl(int ControlID, string ApplicationName,
    object Target, string Text, string Xml, int LocaleID)
{
    Excel.Range cell = (Excel.Range)Target;

    switch (ControlID)
    {
        case 102:
            //MessageBox.Show("This is an example of a button.");
            cell.Interior.ColorIndex = colorIndex;
            colorIndex = (colorIndex >= 56) ? 0 : ++colorIndex;
            break;
    }
}
```

4. Build and test. This is how the solution should look at runtime:

11.4 Vertigo Managed Smart Documents Wrapper

Office 97	✖
Office 2000	✖
Office XP	✖
Office 2003	✔

Using either managed or unmanaged code, you can develop smart documents by directly implementing the *ISmartDocument* interface. If you've worked through the earlier examples in this chapter, you'll probably agree that the development experience is somewhat painful. The root of the pain is that developing against *ISmartDocu-*

ment directly is not object-oriented: no object contains all the properties and attributes of a given control in a centralized location. Instead, different properties of a single control must be scattered across multiple functions, which is difficult to understand, let alone to maintain. Other features are both irritating and error-prone, such as the need to manually set up unique control IDs and to count the number of controls you have.

Office calls a series of *ISmartDocument* functions in sequence and repeats this for each control you have set up. It works this way because *ISmartDocument* is open-ended, in the sense that it has no foreknowledge of exactly what controls you want to use in your solution. You might even be using custom ActiveX controls, which Office cannot possibly know about in advance. Also, it's up to you to determine how many controls you want to use. The net result is that Office must dynamically walk your collection of controls in a generic manner. Not only must the same function be called several times, but the corollary is that you must code each function to deal with any and all of your control types and control specifics.

Consider ASP.NET Web applications, where you specify the controls and their attributes declaratively in XML and then map their events to handlers in a code-behind assembly. Wouldn't it be nice if we had an object-oriented wrapper to *ISmartDocument* that remapped the procedural *ISmartDocument* interface onto an object-oriented class? Wouldn't it also be nice if we could specify controls declaratively in XML and map to code-behind? Oh, and what about some new Visual Studio project wizards to generate some starter code?

Enter the Vertigo Managed Smart Documents Wrapper, a toolkit that is freely downloadable from *http://www.vertigosoftware.com/*. It hugely simplifies the development of managed smart documents and consists of:

- The *SmartDocumentWrapper* assembly, which contains the *ConfiguredSmartDocument* class, which internally implements *ISmartDocument* and exposes it in an object-oriented manner. Full source code is provided.

- New project templates for Visual Studio for smart document projects using the wrapper, including IntelliSense support in Visual Studio for XEP manifests and the control markup file.

- Documentation, including a sample smart document (document and code) that demonstrates how to use the wrapper.

The *ConfiguredSmartDocument* class uses an XML file to describe the controls in the task pane, using a declarative syntax similar to the markup in an ASP.NET page. The wizard generates a class that derives from *ConfiguredSmartDocument*, in which you write the event handlers. Internally, the *ConfiguredSmartDocument* class maintains a typed dataset that contains information about the controls for the Document Actions task pane. This control information comes from the markup information in the Configuration.xml file. The many benefits of using the wrapper class include:

- Control attributes are centralized in the markup file instead of being scattered across multiple *ISmartDocument* functions. This alone makes it much easier to read, write, and maintain code.

- Pseudo–event handlers are written for each control, so you don't need a single event handler to handle events for all controls of a given type. This simplifies the code and makes it much easier to read and understand.

- The wrapper assigns control IDs, and controls are identified by a friendly name such as "SubmitButton" instead of an integer value. The wrapper also calculates the count of controls you have in your solution.

- The new Visual Studio project wizards automate nearly all of the tedious work of creating a new smart document project, including security configuration, GUID creation, and debugging configuration. The toolkit adds IntelliSense support to Visual Studio for the manifest schema and the declarative configuration XML files, making it much easier to edit these files.

The toolkit includes four new Visual Studio wizards: for Word and Excel and for Visual Basic .NET and C#. They generate seven files, as listed in Table 11-3.

Table 11-3   Files Generated by the Vertigo Managed Smart Documents Wrapper

File	Description
Manifest.xml	The XEP manifest file for the project with the necessary project files included (including DocumentStructure.xsd, Configuration.xml, SmartDocumentWrapper.dll, and the project output assembly). The smart document solution namespace and solutionID are customized and preconfigured.
DocumentStructure.xsd	Defines the logical structure of the document—the XML elements that can be associated with regions or cells in the document. Different sections of the document usually require different sets of controls in the task pane.
Configuration.xml	Defines the controls you are putting on the task pane, including namespaces, sample controls, and comments.
ConfigSecurity.cmd	A command file to configure security for the solution at its current location. This is executed when the project is first created.
<projectname>.doc or *<projectname>*.xls	The solution's document, with comments about how to attach the expansion pack and add logical structure.
OfficeCodeBehind.cs or OfficeCodeBehind.vb	The primary sourcecode file for the solution assembly. Includes a class that derives from *ConfiguredSmartDocument* with a preconfigured event handler for the *SmartDocInitialize* event and sample control event handlers.

The wizards also add all the necessary references for a basic smart document project, including the *SmartDocumentWrapper* assembly, and they configure the solution to open the smart document using Word or Excel when you run it from Visual Studio.

In the following exercise, we'll use the Vertigo wizards and wrapper to build a simple smart document solution that has just enough functionality to illustrate the important features of the wrapper. Before you can build this, you must download and install the Vertigo Managed Smart Documents Wrapper toolkit.

Note   The sample solution for this topic can be found in the sample code at <install location>\Code\Office2003\SimpleVertigo.

The Initial Project

1. Create a new Vertigo Smart Document project for Excel called SimpleVertigo. The wizard offers no choices beyond the language, host application, solution name, and location:

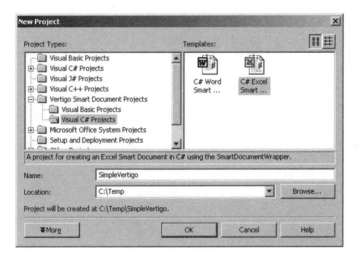

2. After the wizard creates the initial project, look in Solution Explorer at the files and references that have been generated:

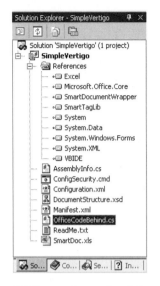

3. We'll examine each of these in turn. ReadMe.txt has some simple instructions for use, as always. AssemblyInfo.cs is completely normal, with the same assembly-level attributes as you would find in many other project types.

4. ConfigureSecurity.cmd contains one CASPol command to set up security policy for the solution and a second command (commented out) to remove policy. The command adds a new code group to the *All_Code* group at the user level, specifying URL evidence for the folder where the solution is, and FullTrust permissions. These two commands are each a single line but are listed word-wrapped in this book:

```
rem  Configure full-trust on the URL to the project's bin folder:

%WINDIR%\Microsoft.NET\Framework\v1.1.4322\caspol -pp off -u -addgroup
"All_Code" -url "file://C:\Temp\SimpleVertigo/bin/*" FullTrust -name
"C:\Temp\SimpleVertigo\bin\*" -description "Auto-
generated Smart Document Wrapper development security. Generated for project 'S
impleVertigo'. In production environments, use strong names for evidence instea
d of URL evidence."

rem  To remove the created code group, uncomment and use the following command:

rem %WINDIR%\Microsoft.NET\Framework\v1.1.4322\caspol -pp off -u -remgroup
"C:\Temp\SimpleVertigo\bin\*"
```

5. As detailed in both Chapter 10, "Visual Studio Tools for Office," and Chapter 12, "Security," URL evidence is fairly weak, and you should not use it in production systems. The ConfigureSecurity.cmd file includes a helpful comment explaining this and advising you to strong-name your assemblies and use strong-name evidence for security policy. For our nonproduction sample, we won't go to these lengths—we'll leave the file unchanged.

6. The manifest is recognizable from our simple early solutions, with some additional elements. Let's take this in sections. (Comments have been removed.)

    At the top is the usual smart documents schema namespace, version number, and update frequency. The *uri* element defines the namespace of the project. It also appears in the DocumentStructure.xsd file and in the *OfficeCodeBehind* class in the call to *LoadConfiguration*. All three instances must be identical, so if you change any one of them, you must change the others in the same way. Also at the top is a fresh GUID for the solutionID, the predefined *smartDocument* type, and a string alias:

    ```
    <?xml version="1.0" encoding="utf-8" ?>
    <SD:manifest xmlns:SD=
        "http://schemas.microsoft.com/office/xmlexpansionpacks/2003">
        <SD:version>1.0</SD:version>
        <SD:updateFrequency>20160</SD:updateFrequency>
        <SD:uri>SimpleVertigo</SD:uri>

        <SD:solution>
            <SD:solutionID>
            57DA38FB-76D9-4CD3-8FE4-C8F07D32125C
        </SD:solutionID>
            <SD:type>smartDocument</SD:type>
            <SD:alias lcid="*">SimpleVertigo Expansion Pack</SD:alias>
    ```

7. Next up is the location of the project output assembly. As before, the *<file>* block includes the path to the assembly, the fully qualified name of the class that implements *ISmartDocument*, and the *<runFromServer>* tag. Of course, our class doesn't implement *ISmartDocument* directly, but it is derived from the wrapper class that does.

    ```
    <SD:file>
        <SD:runFromServer/>
        <SD:type>solutionActionHandler</SD:type>
        <SD:version>1.0</SD:version>
        <SD:filePath>bin\SimpleVertigo.dll</SD:filePath>
        <SD:CLSNAME>SimpleVertigo.OfficeCodeBehind</SD:CLSNAME>
        <SD:managed />
    </SD:file>
    ```

8. The *SmartDocumentWrapper* assembly is described next, with similar tags:

    ```
    <SD:file>
        <SD:runFromServer/>
        <SD:type>other</SD:type>
        <SD:version>1.0</SD:version>
        <SD:filePath>bin\SmartDocumentWrapper.dll</SD:filePath>
    </SD:file>
    ```

9. Next comes the configuration file, which specifies the controls you want to use for the task pane:

    ```
    <SD:file>
        <SD:type>other</SD:type>
    ```

```
            <SD:version>1.0</SD:version>
            <SD:filePath>Configuration.xml</SD:filePath>
        </SD:file>

    </SD:solution>
```

10. The DocumentStructure schema file is the last resource for this solution to be listed in the manifest:

```
<SD:solution>
    <SD:solutionID>
        57DA38FB-76D9-4CD3-8FE4-C8F07D32125C
    </SD:solutionID>
    <SD:type>schema</SD:type>
    <SD:alias lcid="*">SimpleVertigo Schema</SD:alias>
    <SD:file>
        <SD:type>schema</SD:type>
        <SD:version>1.0</SD:version>
        <SD:filePath>DocumentStructure.xsd</SD:filePath>
    </SD:file>
</SD:solution>
</SD:manifest>
```

11. The next file to examine is DocumentStructure.xsd. This is essentially the same kind of schema file that we have used in our non-Vertigo solutions. It is used to determine the logical structure of sections in the Word or Excel document. The DocumentStructure.xsd file defines XML elements that can be associated with regions or cells in the document. When the current selection in the document is in a given section (called a *DocumentAction* section), this determines the current XML element, which in turn determines which set of controls appears in the Document Actions task pane.

    The namespace and target namespace in this file must match the namespace in the *<uri>* element of the Manifest.xml file. Therefore, if you change it here, you must also change it in the manifest file and also in the *OfficeCodeBehind* class in the call to *LoadConfiguration*.

    The wizard inserts two dummy sections, *Section1* and *Section2*, with a comment inviting you to add more sections and/or change the names of (or delete) these dummy sections.

12. Configuration.xml is a new file that is specific to Vertigo-based solutions. It declares the controls you want to use in the task pane for your solution. Controls are declared inside *DocumentAction* sections, which are associated with regions of the Word or Excel document—and here is the connection with DocumentStructure.xsd. Again, the wizard inserts some dummy controls.

    The first control is a button, tagged as *actionPertainsToEntireSchema*—this means that the control will always appear in the pane, regardless of the position in the document. You can remove this, change it, and/or add more controls into this section if you wish.

There is also a second *DocumentAction*, which is linked by an attribute to the section named *Section1* in the schema. This also contains a button. For each section, you can add whatever controls you want. You can also add additional sections, as appropriate for your schema.

This file is validated against its schema when loaded, and this validation includes the XML namespace. So, if you make any changes (as you surely will), you must ensure that the file conforms to the schema in the *SmartDocument-Wrapper* assembly. Visual Studio offers IntelliSense and highlights any errors in the file with a wavy underline.

13. OfficeCodeBehind.cs defines a single class, derived from the *ConfiguredSmart-Document* wrapper class that implements *ISmartDocument*. The class constructor hooks up an event handler for the *SmartDocInitialize* call that Office makes as your solution is loaded. The event handler for this caches references to the host application and document or workbook, and it loads the Configuration.xml file.

```
public sealed class OfficeCodeBehind : ConfiguredSmartDocument
{
    internal Excel.Workbook _workbook;
    internal Excel.Application _application;
    private string _solutionPath;

    public OfficeCodeBehind()
    {
        base.SmartDocInitialize +=
            new SmartDocInitializeEventHandler(
            OfficeCodeBehind_SmartDocInitialize);
    }

    public  void OfficeCodeBehind_SmartDocInitialize(
        object sender, SmartDocInitializeEventArgs e)
    {
        _solutionPath = e.SolutionPath;
        _workbook = (Excel.Workbook) e.Document;
        _application = _workbook.Application;
        LoadConfiguration("SimpleVertigo", "Configuration.xml");
    }
}
```

14. Three pseudo–event handler methods follow. These are not real event handlers, but they have the same standard signature as a .NET event handler (two parameters: an object representing the object that sent the event or made the call and an *EventArgs* derivative containing custom information). The wizard inserts these to illustrate the three pseudo-events that you would normally want to handle for each of your controls: *SetCaption*, *PreRender*, and *Action*. The purpose of *SetCaption* is self-evident, *PreRender* is where you set other display properties of the control, and *Action* is invoked when the user interacts with the control.

15. The final method configures the logging level. It is normal practice to surround critical interop code with structured exception handling (SEH) using *try/catch* blocks. However, we can keep this to a minimum in our solution because the wrapper implements SEH in all its *ISmartDocument* methods. The *ConfigureErrorLogging* method determines how an exception is logged and/or reported, depending on the value assigned to the *ErrorLoggingLevel*. The four possible values range from *NoLogging* to *FullLoggingWithMessageBoxes*. When logging to file is turned on, the output goes to a file named ErrorLog.txt in the smart documents solution folder.

16. If you build and run the solution at this point, it runs Excel and loads the wizard-supplied workbook. If we'd chosen a Word-based solution, this would run Word instead. The workbook (or document) contains comments explaining how to attach the XEP to the workbook and how to map the XML schema. These instructions are the standard ones for setting up any smart document solution. After you've done that, this is how the solution should look (with two cells arbitrarily mapped to the schema and with the cursor in the cell that's mapped to *Section1*):

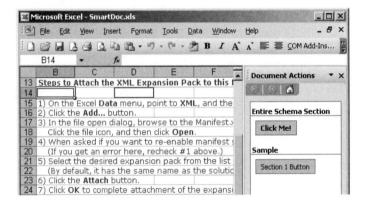

It is safe to delete the explanatory comments when you're done with them. You only need to go through the XEP attach and XML map operations if you change anything in the manifest, the schema, the configuration file, or the policy. If you change only the code, you don't have to redo the setup because the assembly is marked as *<runFromServer>*.

Controls and Behavior

With an understanding of how the Vertigo wrapper works, and with the initial solution functioning correctly, we can now experiment with some alternative controls and behavior.

1. We'll modify our solution to have three different sections. The first section will be mapped to a list box, the second to a combo box, and the third to a calendar

ActiveX control. Let's start at the logical beginning, with the schema. Modify DocumentStructure.xsd to remove the dummy section elements and add our three new sections:

```
<xsd:complexType name="documentSectionType">
  <xsd:all>
    <xsd:element name="fruitSection" type="xsd:string" />
    <xsd:element name="animalSection" type="xsd:string" />
    <xsd:element name="calendarSection" type="xsd:string"/>
  </xsd:all>
</xsd:complexType>
```

2. Change Configuration.xml to match the new schema. First change the *actionPertainsToEntireSchema* element to have a caption (bold, size 16), an image, and a hyperlink. You can use any image you like, and a suitable sample is provided in the sample solution folder. Only the hyperlink element needs to have an *OnAction* attribute, and the plan is that when the user clicks the link, we'll open a browser and navigate to our company Web site. Put a separator line at the bottom to close off the control set for this section:

```
<DocumentAction ActionXmlType="actionPertainsToEntireSchema">
    <Control Name="EverPresentCaption" Type="C_TYPE_LABEL"
        Caption="Contoso Ltd">
        <Property Name="FontWeight">bold</Property>
        <Property Name="FontSize">16</Property>
    </Control>
    <Control Name="EverPresentImage" Type="C_TYPE_IMAGE" >
        <Property Name="ImageSrc">ContosoLogo.jpg</Property>
        <Property Name="W">150</Property>
        <Property Name="H">50</Property>
    </Control>
    <Control Name="EverPresentLink" Type="C_TYPE_LINK"
        Caption="www.contoso.com"
        OnAction="EverPresentLink_Action">
    </Control>
    <Control Name="EverPresentSeparator" Type="C_TYPE_SEPARATOR" />
</DocumentAction>
```

3. Set up the new *fruitSection* with a *Listbox* control. Initialize the list contents statically to some arbitrary string values. Also set up an *OnAction* method. When the user selects an item from the list, we'll copy the selected value into the worksheet:

```
<DocumentAction ActionXmlType="fruitSection"
    PaneCaption="Fruit Section">
    <Control Name="FruitList" Type="C_TYPE_LISTBOX"
        Caption="Select a value:" OnAction="FruitList_Action">
        <Property Name="IsEditable">True</Property>
        <Property Name="ListItem">Apple</Property>
        <Property Name="ListItem">Banana</Property>
        <Property Name="ListItem">Peach</Property>
        <Property Name="ListItem">Strawberry</Property>
        <Property Name="ListItem">Plum</Property>
    </Control>
</DocumentAction>
```

4. The *animalSection* will have a combo box. For this one, we won't set the values statically. Instead, we'll populate the list dynamically, in the *PreRender* method. We'll also provide the caption dynamically in the *OnSetCaption* method. Again, we need an *OnAction* method to respond to the user interacting with the control.

```
<DocumentAction ActionXmlType="animalSection"
    PaneCaption="Animal Section">
    <Control Name="AnimalCombo" Type="C_TYPE_COMBO"
        OnSetCaption="AnimalCombo_SetCaption"
        OnPreRender="AnimalCombo_PreRender"
        OnAction="AnimalCombo_Action">
    </Control>
</DocumentAction>
```

5. The third and final section is for an ActiveX control. There are some particular challenges with ActiveX controls in the task pane, which we shall see shortly. In Configuration.xml, which is used to initialize the task pane for each mapped element, we must specify the CLSID of the control as its *Caption* property. It is also essential to set both the *W* and *H* (width and height) properties of an ActiveX control—otherwise, the control won't be rendered in the pane.

```
<DocumentAction ActionXmlType="calendarSection"
    PaneCaption="Calendar Section">
    <Control Name="Calendar" Type="C_TYPE_ACTIVEX"
        Caption="{8E27C92B-1264-101C-8A2F-040224009C02}">
        <Property Name="W">150</Property>
        <Property Name="H">150</Property>
    </Control>
</DocumentAction>
```

6. If we want to program against the ActiveX control (and assuming we want to avoid late binding), we need an interop assembly (IA) for the control. To get this, add a reference to the Microsoft Calendar Control type library—this will be on the COM tab in the Add Reference dialog box.

7. One last configuration issue before we turn our attention to the code: we need to update the manifest.xml file. We have two additional resources in the solution that are external to the assembly, so they must be listed in the manifest to become part of the deployment:

```
<SD:file>
    <SD:type>other</SD:type>
    <SD:version>1.0</SD:version>
    <SD:filePath>ContosoLogo.jpg</SD:filePath>
</SD:file>
<SD:file>
    <SD:runFromServer/>
    <SD:type>other</SD:type>
    <SD:version>1.0</SD:version>
    <SD:filePath>bin\Interop.MSACAL.dll</SD:filePath>
</SD:file>
```

8. In the *OfficeCodeBehind* class, the *OnSetCaption* method for the combo box is exceedingly simple:

```
private void AnimalCombo_SetCaption(
    string controlName, SetCaptionEventArgs e)
{
    e.Caption = "Pick a pet";
}
```

9. For the *PreRender*, we'll update the list contents each time the control is rendered—just to emphasize when this is happening. The following code uses a *Random* number generator to pick three random strings from a list of 12. (This is very simple—the code doesn't care if the same number gets picked more than once—but you get the idea.)

```
private string[] animals =
    new string[]{
        "Dog", "Cat", "Canary", "Alligator",
        "Tortoise", "Iguana", "Leopard", "Toad",
        "Elephant", "Ant", "Opossum", "Ferret"};

private void AnimalCombo_PreRender(
    string controlName, PreRenderEventArgs e)
{
    Random r = new Random();
    int i = r.Next(0,11);
    int j = r.Next(0,11);
    int k = r.Next(0,11);
    string[] list =
        new string[3]{animals[i], animals[j], animals[k]};
    e.ListItems = list;
    e.ListSelection = 2;
}
```

10. Write stubs for the three *OnAction* methods—we'll finish these off later.

```
private void EverPresentLink_Action(
    string controlName, ActionEventArgs e) {}
private void FruitList_Action(
    string controlName, ActionEventArgs e) {}

private void AnimalCombo_Action(
    string controlName, ActionEventArgs e) {}
```

11. It's worthwhile to build and test the solution at this point. When you run the solution in Visual Studio, it will run Excel and open the workbook. You'll probably get some error messages because we changed most of the solution so it no longer matches the document. To get things back on track, you must go to Data | Xml | Xml Expansion Packs, delete the XEP, and then add it again. Also, go to Data | Xml | Xml Source | XML Maps and delete and then add the schema. Map the three elements to three arbitrary cells.

12.   All of the controls will be displayed, although currently there is no response when the user interacts with any of them because we haven't implemented the three *OnAction* methods yet. When the user clicks our hyperlink, we'll open a browser and navigate to the URL specified in the *Caption* of the control. When the user selects an item from the list box or combo box, we'll copy the selected value into the currently mapped worksheet cell:

```
private void EverPresentLink_Action(
    string controlName, ActionEventArgs e)
{
    System.Diagnostics.Process.Start(e.Caption);
}

private void FruitList_Action(
    string controlName, ActionEventArgs e)
{
    ((Excel.Range)e.Target).Value2 = e.Value;
}

private void AnimalCombo_Action(
    string controlName, ActionEventArgs e)
{
    ((Excel.Range)e.Target).Value2 = e.Value;
}
```

13.   The final control to finish off is the calendar ActiveX control. ActiveX controls need special treatment. By definition, all regular controls are known to Office, and Office knows how to deal with the user interacting with them in a smart document solution. ActiveX controls, on the other hand, are open-ended—there's no way Office can have prior knowledge of the particular ActiveX controls you choose to use in your solution.

Up to now, we've provided enough information for Office to create and render the control. The control itself takes care of its own UI. The only issue is how we program against it. We need to cache a reference to the control object, but we're not in direct control of when the object is created. Instead, we have to wait for Office to create it and then walk the *SmartTags* collection to find it.

In Excel, the *SmartTags* collection is unpopulated unless you have some data in the selected mapped cells. This means you cannot access the *SmartTag* action for a cell until the cell contains some data. So, before attempting to work with the control, open the worksheet and initialize the target cell with a function such as *=TODAY()*. Also, format the cell with a Date format.

1. When the user interacts with a regular control, we use a pseudo-event handler *OnAction* method to code the behavior. Recall that these methods are invoked by the wrapper when Office invokes the *ISmartDocument* functions such as *OnCheckboxChange*, *OnListOrComboSelectChange*, and *InvokeControl*. When the user interacts with an ActiveX control, it will likely fire events (depending on the specifics of how it was designed). We therefore need to hook up event handlers in the standard way—not the pseudo-event handlers used for regular controls. As always, when we hook up an event handler, we must make sure that the object reference that encapsulates the delegate persists across multiple method calls. So, declare a *Calendar* control field at class scope. Also declare an *Excel.Range* field for the target cell:

```
private MSACAL.Calendar calendar;
private Excel.Range dateCell;
```

2. In the *OfficeCodeBehind* constructor, after hooking up the *SmartDocInitialize* event, hook up the *PaneUpdateComplete* event. If you press Tab after typing the new operator, Visual Studio inserts the appropriate delegate type and a stub handler method:

```
base.PaneUpdateComplete +=
    new PaneUpdateCompleteEventHandler(
    OfficeCodeBehind_PaneUpdateComplete);
```

3. In the handler method for this event, cache the reference to the current active cell in our class field and get the *SmartTags* collection. From that, get the *Smart-TagActions* collection from the first (and only) *SmartTag*. From the *SmartTagActions* collection, find a *SmartTagAction* whose name corresponds with the *Calendar* control name. Cast that to a *Calendar* ActiveX control, cache it in our class field, and hook up its *Click* event handler (again using Tab to get the correct type and stubs):

```
private void OfficeCodeBehind_PaneUpdateComplete(
    object sender, PaneUpdateCompleteEventArgs e)
{
    dateCell = _application.ActiveCell;
```

```
Excel.SmartTags tags = dateCell.SmartTags;
if (tags != null && tags.Count >0)
{
    Excel.SmartTagActions actions =
        tags[1].SmartTagActions;
    if (actions != null)
    {
        for (int i = 1; i <= actions.Count; i++)
        {
            Excel.SmartTagAction action = actions[i];
            if (action.Name == "Calendar")
            {
                if (action.PresentInPane)
                {
                    calendar =
                        (MSACAL.Calendar)
                        action.ActiveXControl;
                    calendar.Click += new
                        MSACAL.DCalendarEvents_ClickEventHandler(
                        calendar_Click);
                }
            }
        }
    }
}
```

4. In the *Click* event handler for the calendar control, copy the selected date value into the mapped cell:

```
private void calendar_Click()
{
    dateCell.Value2 = calendar.Value.ToString();
}
```

5. Build and test again.

A Variation for Word

We saw from the first few examples in this chapter that you can develop a smart document solution that will work with both Excel and Word. However, in practice this is restricted to very simple or very generic solutions. Any solution that requires you to develop against the host application's object model becomes difficult to manage if you plan to target more than one host. Some of this pain can be alleviated if you abstract out common functionality to a set of reusable components, and this is generally a good idea. It's no coincidence that the Vertigo toolkit offers you separate wizards for Word and Excel. In the follow-on exercise below, we'll build a smart document solution that is identical in functionality to the SimpleVertigo solution but targets Word. We'll point out only the differences.

1. The Manifest.xml, Configuration.xml, DocumentStructure.xsd and ConfigSecurity.cmd files are identical. The only differences are in the code and (of course)

in the document. The first difference in the code is in the *OnAction* methods for the simple controls. Excel maps complete cells to XML elements, and a cell is essentially discrete. Word, however, maps to arbitrary ranges that can be any size, spanning multiple characters, words, paragraphs, and so on. Therefore, when you assign a value to the mapped range in Word, you must be careful not to overwrite the mapping itself: you should explicitly assign to the *Text* property of the *XMLNode* within the mapped range:

```csharp
private void FruitList_Action(
    string controlName, ActionEventArgs e)
{
    ((Word.Range)e.Target).XMLNodes[1].Text = e.Value;
}

private void AnimalCombo_Action(
    string controlName, ActionEventArgs e)
{
    ((Word.Range)e.Target).XMLNodes[1].Text = e.Value;
}
```

2. For the ActiveX control, the difference in behavior between Word and Excel is more pronounced. First we need a *Word.Selection* reference rather than a *Range* reference, which we can use in the *Click* event handler for the control:

```csharp
private Word.Selection selection;

private void calendar_Click()
{
    selection.Text = calendar.Value.ToString();
}
```

3. Then we need to use a very different mechanism to extract the ActiveX control from the document mapping, using the *Word.XMLNode* object and its collections:

```csharp
private void OfficeCodeBehind_PaneUpdateComplete(
    object sender, PaneUpdateCompleteEventArgs e)
{
    selection = _document.ActiveWindow.Selection;
    Word.XMLNode node = selection.XMLParentNode;

    if (node != null)
    {
        if (node.BaseName == "calendarSection")
        {
            object itemIndex = "Calendar";
            Word.SmartTagAction action =
            node.SmartTag.SmartTagActions.get_Item(
                ref itemIndex);
            if (action.PresentInPane)
            {
                calendar = (MSACAL.Calendar)
                    action.ActiveXControl;
```

```
                          calendar.Click += new
                              MSACAL.DCalendarEvents_ClickEventHandler(
                              calendar_Click);
                    }
              }
          }
      }
```

4. This is how the Word version of the solution looks at runtime:

11.5 Smart Documents and Smart Tags

Office 97	✖
Office 2000	✖
Office XP	✖
Office 2003	✔

You might remember that the smart document object model is closely related to the smart tag object model, and that they're both in the same type library—the Microsoft Smart Tags 2.0 Type Library—and the same PIA. The question is, can you build a solution that offers both smart tags and smart document behavior? If so, can the smart tags and smart document task pane controls work together in an integrated fashion? Is there a formalized channel through which the two technologies can talk to each other? The answers to these questions are Yes, Yes, and No. Even though smart documents and smart tags share a common type library, there is no support in Office for integrating the two in one solution. However, that's not to say it can't be done—it can.

The bigger question is one of design. By their nature, smart tags are open-ended. Although we can predefine the terms that we will recognize and the actions we will take when we do recognize terms, we can't predict whether (or when) any of these terms will be present in any given document (unless we also predefine the document contents, which is sometimes, but rarely, useful). Smart tags are deployed on a per-user basis and are common to multiple applications. More important, they apply to all documents for those applications. Smart documents, on the other hand, are a document-centric technology. The document and the solution code are mapped together via a schema, and elements of the document are mapped to elements of the schema.

Therefore, the assumption is that you do know quite a lot about the document that forms part of the solution, even though you can attach the same smart document solution to multiple documents. In a smart document solution, you know in advance what some of the document contents will be—and you map code against these contents. There might be other arbitrary contents in the document, but in essence you don't care about these because by definition they don't form part of your solution.

So, smart tags and smart documents are designed to meet different business requirements. Does it ever make sense to combine them? One scenario where it does make sense is with document templates. In this scenario, you provide a template for users, from which they produce documents. We can attach a smart document solution to the template to provide additional support during the user's document creation process. At the same time, we can schema-map predefined document contents if we wish. However, we might want to provide an unstructured template without any predefined elements and, therefore, without any elements schema-mapped. In this scenario, the document is a natural environment for smart tags. The idea of combining smart tags and a smart document solution is that the user can enter arbitrary text into the document, some of which we might recognize. If we recognize anything, the associated action could be to update the task pane, with additional information that will help the user to complete the document.

In the following exercise, we'll produce a combined smart tag and smart document solution. The document in the solution will be a Word template, with no initial contents. With no initial contents, we can't schema-map, and indeed we won't even have a schema. The context is a company that produces agricultural machinery. Users can create new documents from the template for any purpose. If they enter agro-machinery terms that we recognize, we'll populate the task pane with further information about that term, including a list of related products that we produce. They can select an item from the list, and we'll insert it into their document for them.

The only technical issue to resolve is how to connect the smart tags with the smart document.

 Note The sample solution for this topic can be found in the sample code at <install location>\Code\Office2003\SmartDocTags.

In the following explanation, only the significant features of this solution are discussed—all the standard features of smart tag and smart document solutions are assumed. You can construct this by implementing *ISmartDocument* directly, but the instructions assume that we're using the Vertigo wrapper. For simplicity, we'll build both the smart tag and the smart document functionality into the same assembly, although this is not required (and for a production system, we'd design it more intelligently).

Smart Tags

Create a new Vertigo solution called SmartDocTags. With the basic project set up, and before working on the smart document, we'll implement the smart tag recognizer and action classes. To do this, we'll add two new classes to the project, *Recognizer* and *Action*.

You can refer back to Chapter 6, "Smart Tags," for details on implementing recognizer and action components. For now, the only significant feature of the recognizer is the list of terms that we'll recognize—everything else is very standard. We'll hardcode an array of three agro-machinery terms:

```
public class Recognizer : SmartTag.ISmartTagRecognizer,
    SmartTag.ISmartTagRecognizer2
{
    private string[] recognizeTerms = {"Harvester", "Hook", "Conveyor"};
```

The action class declares a single string field—this will be used to connect the smart tags with the smart document, and we'll see how shortly:

```
public class Action: SmartTag.ISmartTagAction,
    SmartTag.ISmartTagAction2
{
    private string productName = "ProductName";
```

The action class sets up the shortcut menu in the normal fashion. We have only one action and therefore one item on the menu. For the menu caption, we compose a string that incorporates the recognized term:

```
public string get_VerbCaptionFromID2 (
    int VerbID, string ApplicationName, int LocaleID,
    SmartTag.ISmartTagProperties Properties,
    string Text, string Xml, object Target)
{
    return String.Format("Get details for {0}", Text);
}
```

Create a new class called *Utilities*. This will be shared across the smart tag and smart document parts of the solution. This class will have only two methods, *SetCustomProperty* and *GetCustomProperty*, which will write data into the document's custom properties collection and read it out, respectively. This will form the bridge between the smart tags and the smart document. Using the custom document properties like this is convenient, although not very elegant. Also, for a production system, we'd probably want to use a GUID for the property name, rather than a string—to avoid any possibility of conflict with any custom properties the user might create.

In the smart document piece, we usually know whether we're working with Word or Excel, but this might not always be true. In the smart tag piece, we don't make this assumption. Therefore, the *GetCustomProperty* and *SetCustomProperty* methods use late binding to work with the custom properties. In *SetCustomProperty*, we first try to find the specified custom property in the *CustomDocumentProperties* collection (which is exposed by both Word and Excel). If we find the custom property, we simply over-write its value:

```
public static void SetCustomProperty(
    Word.Document doc, string propertyName, string propertyValue)
{
    try
    {
        object docCustomProps = null;
        Type typeCustomprops = null;

        try
        {
            docCustomProps = doc.CustomDocumentProperties;
            typeCustomprops = docCustomProps.GetType();
            object customProp =
                typeCustomprops.InvokeMember("Item",
                BindingFlags.Default |
                BindingFlags.GetProperty,
                null, docCustomProps,
                new object[]{propertyName});
            string oldPropertyValue = String.Empty;

            if (customProp != null)
            {
                Type typeCustomProp=customProp.GetType();
                typeCustomProp.InvokeMember("Value",
                    BindingFlags.Default |
                    BindingFlags.SetProperty,
                    null, customProp,
                    new object[]{propertyValue});
            }
                return;
        }
```

If we supplied an unknown *propertyName* to index into the collection, we'll get a *TargetInvocationException*, which we'll ignore. With any other exception, we'll rethrow:

```
        catch (TargetInvocationException ex)
        {
            if (!(ex.InnerException is ArgumentException))
            {
                throw ex;
            }
        }
```

If we don't find the property at all, we simply create it from scratch:

```
        object[] args = new object[] {
            propertyName, false,
            Office.MsoDocProperties.msoPropertyTypeString,
```

```
            propertyValue };
        typeCustomprops.InvokeMember("Add",
            BindingFlags.Default |
            BindingFlags.InvokeMethod,
            null, docCustomProps, args);
    }
    catch (Exception ex)
    {
        MessageBox.Show(ex.StackTrace, ex.Message);
    }
}
```

The corresponding *GetCustomProperty* method follows similar lines. We try to find the custom property in the *CustomDocumentProperties* collection, and, if we find it, we read its value:

```
public static void GetCustomProperty(
    Word.Document doc, string propertyName,
    ref string propertyValue)
{
    try
    {
        object docCustomProps =
            doc.CustomDocumentProperties;
        Type typeCustomprops = docCustomProps.GetType();
        object customProp =
            typeCustomprops.InvokeMember("Item",
            BindingFlags.Default |
            BindingFlags.GetProperty,
            null, docCustomProps,
            new object[]{propertyName});

        if (customProp != null)
        {
            Type typeCustomProp = customProp.GetType();
            propertyValue =
                typeCustomProp.InvokeMember("Value",
                BindingFlags.Default |
                BindingFlags.GetProperty,
                null, customProp,
                new object[]{}).ToString();
        }
    }
    catch (TargetInvocationException ex)
    {
        if (!(ex.InnerException is System.ArgumentException))
        {
            throw ex;
        }
    }
}
```

Back in the smart tag action class, the significant piece of code is in the method that is called when the user selects the only option we've provided on the shortcut menu.

What we'll do is write the value of the current recognized term into the document as a custom document property, using the name *ProductName*. Then we'll get hold of the Document Actions task pane and force it to refresh. The idea is that at the other end, in the smart document solution, when the pane is refreshed, we'll fetch this custom property and use it to configure our controls. As part of this operation, we'll call our custom *SetCustomProperty* method:

```
public void InvokeVerb2 ( int VerbID, string ApplicationName,
    object Target, SmartTag.ISmartTagProperties Properties,
    string Text, string Xml, int LocaleID)
{
    Word.Document doc = null;
    try
    {
        doc = ((Word.Range)Target).Document;
        Utilities.SetCustomProperty(doc, productName, Text);
        Office.SmartDocument smartDoc = doc.SmartDocument;
        smartDoc.RefreshPane();
    }
    catch (Exception ex)
    {
        MessageBox.Show(ex.StackTrace, ex.Message);
    }
}
```

That's all the code for the smart tag part of the solution, although we do need to set up registry entries for this. Managed smart document assemblies are loaded by the VSTO loader, and we can ensure that our managed smart tag assembly is also loaded by the VSTO loader if we use the *Managed* value in the registry entry:

```
Windows Registry Editor Version 5.00

[HKEY_CURRENT_USER\Software\Microsoft\Office\Common\Smart Tag\Actions\
SmartDocTags.Action]
"Filename"="C:\\Temp\\SmartDocTags\\bin\\SmartDocTags.dll"
"Managed"=dword:00000001

[HKEY_CURRENT_USER\Software\Microsoft\Office\Common\Smart Tag\Recognizers\
SmartDocTags.Recognizer]
"Filename"="C:\\Temp\\SmartDocTags\\bin\\SmartDocTags.dll"
"Managed"=dword:00000001
```

Smart Document

1. With the smart tag piece done, we can turn to the smart document part of the solution. First, in Configuration.xml, we'll specify the controls for the task pane. We have only one logical section, tagged as *actionPertainsToEntireSchema* so it is always present. We want two controls: an image that corresponds to the current recognized term and a list box for related products:

```xml
<?xml version="1.0" encoding="utf-8" ?>
<SmartDocumentConfiguration
xmlns="http://schemas.vertigosoftware.com/office/2003/smartdocumentwrapper"
    xmlns:xsi="http://www.w3.org/2001/XMLSchema-instance">
    <DocumentAction
        ActionXmlType="actionPertainsToEntireSchema"
        PaneCaption="Contoso Machinery">
        <Control Name="ProductImage" Type="C_TYPE_IMAGE"
            OnPreRender="ProductImage_PreRender">
        </Control>
        <Control Name="ProductList" Type="C_TYPE_LISTBOX"
            OnSetCaption="ProductList_SetCaption"
            OnPreRender="ProductList_PreRender"
            OnAction="ProductList_Action">
        </Control>
    </DocumentAction>
</SmartDocumentConfiguration>
```

2. The manifest.xml file is standard and doesn't need listing here. It specifies the solution assemblies (our assembly and the wrapper assembly), the configuration.xml, and three image resources. It does not list a schema because we don't have one.

3. In the *OfficeCodeBehind* class, we have one string field, which we initialize in the *SmartDocInitialize* event handler to get the current custom document property value—this is one line of code after all the standard work:

```csharp
private string productName = String.Empty;

public void OfficeCodeBehind_SmartDocInitialize(
object sender, SmartDocInitializeEventArgs e)
{
    ConfigureErrorLogging();
    _solutionPath = e.SolutionPath;
    _document = (Word.Document) e.Document;
    _application = _document.Application;
    LoadConfiguration("SmartDocTags", "Configuration.xml");

    Utilities.SetCustomProperty(
        _document, "ProductName", productName);
}
```

4. When the image control needs to be rendered, we refresh our field from the custom document properties and set the image source to a file whose name corresponds to the field. The sample solution has three image files that correspond to the three terms we can recognize in our recognizer class:

```csharp
public void ProductImage_PreRender(
    string controlName, PreRenderEventArgs e)
{
    Utilities.GetCustomProperty(
        _document, "ProductName", ref productName);
    e.ImageUrl = System.IO.Path.Combine(
        _solutionPath, productName +".jpg");
    e.DisplayProps.W = 130;
    e.DisplayProps.H = 110;
}
```

5. For simplicity, this solution hardcodes three string arrays, which simulate the list of related products for the currently recognized term. We use these to populate the list box control in the task pane:

```
private string[] harvesters =
    new string[]{
    "Combine harvester", "Thresher", "Harvester parts"};
private string[] hooks =
    new string[]{
    "Big hooks", "Little hooks", "Fish hooks"};
private string[] conveyors =
    new string[]{
    "Conveyor belts", "Conveyor rollers", "Conveyor motors"};

private void ProductList_PreRender(
    string controlName, PreRenderEventArgs e)
{
    e.DisplayProps.Y = 10;
    e.DisplayProps.FontWeight = "bold";
    switch (productName)
    {
        case "Harvester" :
            e.ListItems = harvesters;
            break;
        case "Hook" :
            e.ListItems = hooks;
            break;
        case "Conveyor" :
            e.ListItems = conveyors;
            break;
    }
}
```

6. Setting the caption for the list box to match the recognized term is trivial:

```
private void ProductList_SetCaption(
    string controlName, SetCaptionEventArgs e)
{
    e.Caption = productName;
}
```

7. Finally, when the user selects an item from the list, we'll insert it at the current cursor location in the document:

```
private void ProductList_Action(
    string controlName, ActionEventArgs e)
{
    _application.Selection.InsertAfter(e.Value);
}
```

8. Build the solution, and register the smart tag. Then open a new Word document, attach the XEP, and save it as a Word template. The user can then create new documents from this template. This is how the solution should look at

runtime, after the user has typed in some arbitrary text that includes one or more of our recognized terms:

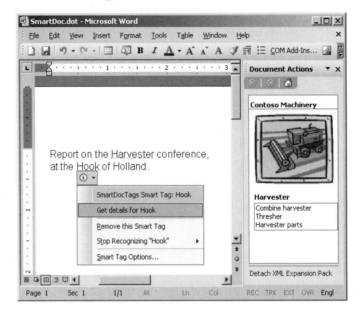

This section has shown that—with a little work—we can make smart tags and smart documents work together to help support a user workflow. The implementation detail of using the custom document properties is inelegant, but the principle is sound. Indeed, the concept is a major factor in the design of the Microsoft Information Bridge Framework (IBF), and you should expect to see further convergence of Office development technologies in the future.

11.6 MOSTL Smart Documents

Office 97	✕
Office 2000	✕
Office XP	✕
Office 2003	✓

You might remember that the smart document object model is closely related to the smart tag object model, and that they're both in the same type library—the Microsoft Smart Tags 2.0 Type Library—and the same PIA. In addition to developing sophisticated smart document solutions with managed or unmanaged DLLs, you can also create simple smart documents using extensions to the Microsoft Office Smart Tag List (MOSTL) file schema. MOSTL-based smart document solutions are limited to hyperlink, separator, button, label, image, and embedded help content only, and buttons are limited to hyperlink actions.

To develop a MOSTL smart document, you need to build three pieces:

- **An XML document schema**   This is no different from the kind of schema you would produce for any Office document XML mapping, including for DLL-based sophisticated smart documents.

- **An XEP manifest file**   This is also no different from a regular smart document manifest file.

- **A MOSTL-conformant XML file**   This is the simple equivalent of the DLL. It's where you specify the controls that you want on the task pane for each logical section of the document.

The same procedure for deployment applies to both MOSTL smart documents and DLL smart documents.

In the following exercise, we'll create a simple MOSTL-based smart document solution, which we'll attach to an Excel template. The idea is that users will use the template to create new worksheets, each of which contains an order for bulk coffee to be delivered by the Fourth Coffee company. The smart document task pane will offer help and guidelines on completing the order form. When the user has completed the order, he clicks a button on the task pane to go to the Fourth Coffee Web site order page, where he can upload the worksheet for processing.

Our solution will not include the server-side work of getting the sheet uploaded, and indeed we won't even build a Web site—we'll just use the standard *www.fourthcoffee.com* site. So, actually, the user's order will never be processed, and he'll never get his coffee. OK, the scenario is a little contrived, but it will do for illustrating the mechanics of a MOSTL smart document. This is how the solution looks after it has been attached to an Excel workbook and the schema has been mapped to cells in the worksheet:

Note   The sample solution for this topic can be found in the sample code at <install location>\Code\Office2003\CoffeeOnline.

1. For convenience in organizing the solution files, create a new blank Visual Studio solution called CoffeeOnline.

2. Add a new schema file to the project called CoffeeOnline.xsd. The user will be prompted to enter his name and telephone number, followed by one or more coffee "order lines." Each order line consists of three fields: the style of coffee, quantity (number of cups), and extras such as sugar, chocolate sprinkles, cinnamon, and so forth. We can model these requirements in our schema with two sections, where the *CoffeeType* element forms a repeating list within the main *CoffeeOrder* section:

```
<xs:schema
    targetNamespace="urn:schemas-xml-office:CoffeeOnline"
    elementFormDefault="qualified"
    xmlns="urn:schemas-xml-office:CoffeeOnline"
    xmlns:xs="http://www.w3.org/2001/XMLSchema">
    <xs:element name="CoffeeOrder" type="CoffeeOrderType" />
    <xs:complexType name="CoffeeOrderType">
        <xs:sequence>
            <xs:element name="Name" type="xs:string" />
            <xs:element name="Tel" type="xs:string" />
            <xs:element name="Coffee" type="CoffeeType"
                minOccurs="0" maxOccurs="unbounded"/>
        </xs:sequence>
    </xs:complexType>
    <xs:complexType name="CoffeeType">
        <xs:sequence>
            <xs:element name="Style" type="xs:decimal" />
            <xs:element name="Quantity" type="xs:decimal" />
            <xs:element name="Extras" type="xs:decimal" />
        </xs:sequence>
    </xs:complexType>
</xs:schema>
```

3. Start Excel and open a new workbook. Type in labels for *Name*, *Tel*, *Style*, *Quantity*, and *Extras*. Then attach the schema and map it to the sheet. Drag and drop the *Name* and *Tel* elements to map to the cells next to the *Name* and *Tel* labels. Then drag and drop the whole *Coffee* element (made up of three subelements) onto the *Style* cell. This will set up a *ListObject* starting at that cell and adopt the existing labels as column headers.

4. Save the book as a template (.xlt) in the CoffeeOnline solution folder, and add it to the solution—this is also just for convenience during development.

5. Add a new XML file to the project, called CoffeeOnlineMOSTL.xml. Some of this will be familiar from the work we did on MOSTL smart tags.

```
<smartTagList
    xmlns="http://schemas.microsoft.com/office/smarttags/2003/mostl">
    <name>CoffeeOnlineMOSTL</name>
    <lcid>*</lcid>
    <description>
        Bulk online coffee orders frome the comfort of your own Excel.
    </description>
```

6. The first difference is that a MOSTL smart document must have a *<smartDoc>* element for each logical section The type attribute of this element maps to an element in the associated schema. In our first section, we'll define four controls (or *action* elements, in this file). The first control is an image file. The second is a *Help* element, with a body defined using standard HTML. The third control is a separator, and the fourth is a hyperlink—this is where the user clicks to upload his coffee order. All of these controls will be present on the task pane when the user is in any of the mapped regions in the worksheet.

```
<smartDoc
    type="urn:schemas-xml-office:CoffeeOnline#CoffeeOrder">
    <caption>Bulk Coffee Order</caption>
    <actions>
        <action id="CoffeeImage">
            <actionType>Image</actionType>
            <caption>Fourth Coffee</caption>
            <imageURL>$solutionPath\Coffee.jpg</imageURL>
        </action>
        <action id="CoffeeOrderHelp">
            <actionType>Help</actionType>
            <caption>How to Order</caption>
            <help><html><body><b><font color="#663333">
                Enter your contact
                details and order.
                <br/><br/>
                Then click below to
                upload your sheet.
            </font></b></body></html></help>
        </action>
        <action id="separator">
            <actionType>Separator</actionType>
        </action>
        <action id="OrderDetailsLink">
            <actionType>Link</actionType>
                <caption>Upload Order Here</caption>
                <url>http://www.fourthcoffee.com</url>
        </action>
    </actions>
</smartDoc>
```

7. For the second logical section in the document schema, we'll have one action element. This will also be a *Help* element, listing the available styles of coffee that the customer can order. This control will be present only on the task pane when the user is in the list section in the worksheet. That means this list of coffee

styles will effectively be additional to the more general help information, the image, and the hyperlink described earlier.

```
<smartDoc type="urn:schemas-xml-office:CoffeeOnline#Coffee">
    <actions>
        <action id="CoffeeStyles">
            <actionType>Help</actionType>
            <caption>Coffee Styles</caption>
            <help><html><body><b><font color="#663333">
            Espresso<br/>Latte<br/>Cappuccino<br/>Ristretto
            </font></b></body></html></help>
        </action>
    </actions>
</smartDoc>


</smartTagList>
```

8. The last XML file to create is the XEP manifest. The general format of this should be familiar from other smart document solutions we've built. A critical difference is that the *<type>* element of the solution file is set to *SolutionList*—not *solutionActionHandler*, as with DLL solutions. Also, the solution *<filePath>* element in this case specifies the CoffeeOnlineMOSTL.xml file instead of an assembly. Of course, we don't need the *<CLSNAME>* or *<managed>* elements at all. The manifest includes a reference to the schema, as normal.

```
<manifest
    xmlns="http://schemas.microsoft.com/office/xmlexpansionpacks/2003">
    <version>1</version>
    <uri>urn:schemas-xml-office:CoffeeOnline</uri>
    <solution>
        <solutionID>
            {4BECA15B-4F26-4b25-871D-F07E35817886}
        </solutionID>
        <alias>CoffeeOnline</alias>
        <type>SmartDocument</type>
        <file>
            <type>SolutionList</type>
            <version>1</version>
            <filePath>CoffeeOnlineMOSTL.xml</filePath>
        </file>
        <file>
            <type>other</type>
            <version>1</version>
            <filePath>Coffee.jpg</filePath>
        </file>
    </solution>
    <solution>
        <solutionID>
            {4BECA15B-4F26-4b25-871D-F07E35817886}
        </solutionID>
        <alias>CoffeeOnline</alias>
        <type>schema</type>
        <file>
            <type>schema</type>
```

```
        <version>1.0</version>
        <filePath>CoffeeOnline.xsd</filePath>
      </file>
    </solution>
  </manifest>
```

9. Save all the files, and test the solution. We've already attached the schema to the Excel template, so we just need to attach the XEP manifest in the usual manner.

Summary

Like add-ins, smart documents are a way of extending the functionality of Office applications to tailor them to meet specific business requirements. Unlike add-ins, smart documents are document-centric rather than application-centric. In this respect, they fall into the same category as Visual Studio Tools for Office solutions: you build a document (or a template) with smart capabilities. In the case of smart documents, the connection between the document and your custom code is established through a common schema, with document elements mapped to schema elements, and schema elements mapped to code elements.

Although very simple, predominantly static smart documents can be constructed using XML files that conform to the MOSTL schema. Most smart documents are built with managed or unmanaged DLLs. Whether you're working in an unmanaged language such as C++ or a managed language such as C#, developing directly against the *ISmartDocument* interface is painful and error-prone. Office uses the interface in a strictly procedural fashion, which is dictated by the open-ended nature of the interface. Office doesn't know what schema you intend to map, and it doesn't know what controls you intend to use for each schema element. Indeed, it is open enough to allow you to use arbitrary ActiveX controls on the task pane. Despite this open-endedness, Office manages to work seamlessly with a well-built smart document solution.

There are several compelling reasons to develop your smart document solutions in managed code—the richness of the .NET Framework and its library being one of them. Another good reason is that in the managed world, you have the option to use the Vertigo Smart Document Wrapper toolkit, which makes smart document development much less painful. *ISmartDocument* is implemented internally and is exposed in an object-oriented manner through a wrapper class. Task pane controls are defined declaratively in simple XML files, and the toolkit is backed up by a set of wizards and IntelliSense support.

Chapter 12

Security

Microsoft Office supports the use of Authenticode technology to enable you to digitally sign a file or a macro project by using a digital certificate. The certificate used to create this signature confirms that the macro or document originated from the signer, and the signature confirms that it has not been altered. When you set the macro security level in Office applications, you can determine whether to run macros, based on whether they are digitally signed by a developer on your list of trusted sources.

Digital signatures are also routinely used to strengthen the security of Microsoft .NET assemblies. Managed assemblies actually support two levels of digital security: strong-naming and digital signing. Strong-naming an assembly provides a unique identity for the assembly and allows the .NET CLR to perform load-time checks to ensure that the assembly hasn't been tampered with. An Authenticode signature verifies that a specific trusted publisher signed the assembly and has not since revoked the certificate associated with the signature. After you've strong-named an assembly, you can also Authenticode-sign it.

Office has long supported configurable security settings aimed at VBA macros, as well as unmanaged add-ins and smart tags. By extension, these settings also apply to managed add-ins and smart tags. The newer Office protocols—Visual Studio Tools for Office (VSTO), smart documents, and VSTO-loaded smart tags—do not use Office macro security. Instead, these protocols use .NET Code Access Security (CAS).

CAS is conceptually similar to traditional role-based security policy, in which specific users and groups are given specific permissions to access machine resources (files, memory, the registry, event logs, and so forth). The significant distinction is that CAS policy applies to code, not to users. As it loads an assembly, the .NET runtime grants that assembly a set of permissions to access resources. The runtime works out what permissions to grant by examining the security policy in force. The policy includes a mapping between assemblies and permissions in the form of code groups.

The default .NET CAS policy grants FullTrust permissions to assemblies installed on the local machine. However, the VSTO loader—used for VSTO solutions, VSTO-loaded smart tags, and managed smart documents—revokes these permissions. As a result, these solutions must be granted explicit permissions before they are allowed to run.

At the same time, you can set the traditional Office macro security level to its most secure.

12.1 Office Macro Security

Office 97	✓
Office 2000	✓
Office XP	✓
Office 2003	✓

Signing documents is a reasonable security strategy regardless of whether the document in question forms part of a programmed solution. The Office macro security settings, on the other hand, apply only to programs. Moreover, they were designed to secure solutions built with traditional tools, such as VBA embedded in a document or workbook, or code written in unmanaged languages such as Visual Basic and C++. These days, the Office macro security settings also apply to managed extensions, including add-ins and smart tags. Only the very newest protocols—that is, VSTO, smart documents, and VSTO-loaded smart tags—do not use Office macro security. These later protocols use CAS instead.

It is normally recommended that you set Office macro security to the highest possible level, not automatically trust installed add-ins and templates, and not trust access to the Visual Basic project. To check your settings, open an Office application and navigate to Tools | Macro | Security. Table 12-1 summarizes all the permutations of settings available for macro security. A blank cell indicates that the value doesn't affect the outcome.

Table 12-1   Office Macro Security Permutations

Security Level	Trust All Installed Add-ins and Templates	Digitally Signed	From a Trusted Publisher	In a Trusted Location	Office's Treatment of Macros	Office's Treatment of Add-Ins
Very High	Y			Y	Enable	Enable
	Y			N	Disable	Enable
	N				Disable	Disable
High	Y			Y	Enable	Enable
	Y			N	Disable	Enable
	N	Y	Y		Enable	Enable
	N	Y	N		Prompt to disable macros or always trust publisher	Prompt to disable add-in or always trust publisher
	N	N	n/a		Disable	Disable

Table 12-1   Office Macro Security Permutations

Security Level	Trust All Installed Add-ins and Templates	Digitally Signed	From a Trusted Publisher	In a Trusted Location	Office's Treatment of Macros	Office's Treatment of Add-Ins
Medium	Y			Y	Enable	Enable
	Y			N	Prompt to disable or enable macro	Enable
	N	Y	Y		Enable	Enable
	N	Y	N		Prompt to disable or enable macro; you can enable the macro for the current session or choose to always trust the publisher	Prompt to disable or enable the add-in; you can enable the macro for the current session or choose to always trust publisher
	N	N	n/a		Prompt to disable or enable macro	Prompt to disable or enable add-in
Low					Enable	Enable

The Very High security level was introduced with Office 2003. Also, there is some minor variation in the security settings that can be applied from one Office application to another. Specifically, Microsoft Outlook, Microsoft Access, and Microsoft Publisher do not allow you to select the Trust Access To Visual Basic Project option. Also, specific Office applications silently load macros only from specific directories. For example, selecting the Trust All Installed Add-Ins And Templates check box allows all macros that are stored in certain personal or workgroup locations that are considered "trusted locations" to run regardless of whether they are code-signed. For example, in Word, to view these locations, you choose Tools | Options, and then click the File locations tab. Also note that not all Office applications support the "trusted locations" option for macros—specifically, Microsoft PowerPoint and Access don't support this option.

In Access, the Very High security level is not available from the macro security dialog box. If you want to set the security level to Very High in Access, you must set a registry key manually. If you do set Access security to Very High, Access cannot open any .adp or .mdb files. However, you can still open Access and go to the Security dialog box, where you will see that none of the three available options is selected. If you select any of the options, the registry key is set to the corresponding 3 (High), 2 (Medium), or 1 (Low) level. You can use the following registry file (SetAccessVeryHighSecurity.reg, available with the sample code) to set the Access security level to Very High:

```
Windows Registry Editor Version 5.00

[HKEY_CURRENT_USER\Software\Microsoft\Office\11.0\Access\Security]
"Level"=dword:00000004
```

Also note that, for Access 2003, in order for the Medium or High macro security levels to function properly, your computer must be configured to run in sandbox mode—this blocks unsafe expressions. Blocking unsafe expressions affects all users on the computer. In sandbox mode, functions that could be exploited by malicious users to access drives, files, or other resources for which they do not have authorization are blocked. Expressions that use these functions will result in an error. Microsoft Jet 4.0 Service Pack 8 or later allows Access 2003 to be fully functional yet still have Jet block unsafe expressions by enabling sandbox mode.

12.2 Code Access Security

Office 97 ✓
Office 2000 ✓
Office XP ✓
Office 2003 ✓

Code Access Security (CAS) is a feature of the .NET Framework that allows you to establish and enforce security restrictions on assemblies and the code within them. As it loads an assembly, the .NET runtime grants that assembly a set of permissions to access system resources, such as the file system, the registry, printers, and the environment table. A group of permissions is called a *permission set*, and these permissions are defined in a *security policy*. There is a standard set of permission sets, and an administrator can create new permission sets. There is also a standard set of code groups, and an administrator can create new code groups. A code group maps assemblies to permission sets.

Evidence

When the runtime loads an assembly, it gathers evidence of the assembly's identity, which can include:

- A strong name (that is, the simple name, version number, and public key)

- The publisher of the assembly (if supplied), as evidenced by its Authenticode signature

- The zone (for example, Local Machine, Local Intranet, or Internet) where the assembly originated

- The location (for example, the file system directory on the local machine or a remote URL) where the assembly originated

Some forms of evidence are more difficult to falsify than others and are therefore considered stronger. Strong evidence includes the cryptographic strong name of an assembly. Weaker evidence includes the URL where the assembly was loaded from because the location might not be secure and might contain assemblies that should not be trusted. Indeed, the URL might even have been falsified. When you, as an administrator, establish a security policy, you can make arbitrary decisions about how to map evidence to permissions, but you should depend more heavily on strong forms of evidence than on weak forms.

Security Policy

The .NET Framework security policy imposes four policy levels: enterprise policy level, machine policy level, user policy level, and an optional AppDomain policy level. Each level consists of a collection of code groups, organized in hierarchies, and each code group has a set of permissions associated with it. A code group at the root level will likely have very limited (or no) permissions associated with it. As you add child code groups, you will likely assign more and more permissions, at the same time requiring stronger and more restricted evidence. In this way, a child code group at the bottom of the hierarchy is likely to offer an extensive set of permissions but also require a narrow set of strong evidence of an assembly before that assembly is granted these permissions. An assembly can match one or more code groups at each policy level.

Permissions

When you establish a set of permissions and configure the security policy to use this set, you must give the set a name and description (using the configuration tool). This becomes a "named" permission set. You can then apply this permission set to any code group or groups you choose. The .NET Framework ships with six predefined permission sets, as described in Table 12-2.

Table 12-2   Predefined Permission Sets

Permission Set	Description
Nothing	No permissions at all: code cannot execute.
Execution	Permits code to execute but grants no other access to resources or protected operations.
Internet	Allows code to execute, to create safe top-level windows and file dialog boxes (but no other user interface elements), to make Web connections to the same site from which the assembly originated, and to use isolated storage with an imposed quota.
LocalIntranet	Allows code to execute, to create user interface elements without restrictions; to make Web connections to the same site from which the assembly originated; to use isolated storage without a quota; to use DNS services; to read the USERNAME, TEMP, and TMP environment variables; and to read files in the same folder as the assembly.
Everything	Grants all standard permissions except the permission to skip verification.
FullTrust	Grants full access to all protected resources.

You cannot modify these predefined permission sets. However, you can create custom permission sets with the same or similar permissions, and then use these as the basis for your security policy.

A code group is a mapping between a set of evidence and a set of permissions. These mappings are entirely arbitrary—you must determine them as an administrative task when you design the overall security policy. When you create a code group, you decide on a set of conditions that an assembly must meet in order to become part of the group. Generally, these conditions will equate to assembly evidence. For example, you might decide that to gain membership of a particular code group, an assembly must have a specific public key or must originate from a particular URL. Any assembly that matches the set of conditions will then be granted the corresponding set of permissions.

Code groups are arranged hierarchically, and the CLR walks the hierarchy when it loads an assembly, to match the assembly evidence with each group in turn. An example of a code group hierarchy at one policy level is shown in Figure 12-1.

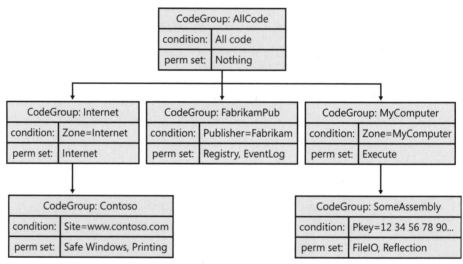

Figure 12-1   A code group hierarchy and permission grants.

Let's say an assembly has the following evidence:

Origin:The local machine

Simple name:SomeAssembly

Version:1.0.0.0

Public key:12 34 56 78 90...

Publisher:(none specified)

Site:(not applicable)

To ascertain what permissions to grant this assembly, given the example code group hierarchy shown above, the runtime would start at the root code group, AllCode, and match the condition against the assembly. In this case, the condition is All Code, so the assembly satisfies the condition and is granted the corresponding permission set—in this case, Nothing. Next, the runtime navigates its way down through the hierarchy. The next code group is Internet, with a membership condition of *Internet Zone*, which this assembly does not match. Therefore, the runtime does not grant the associated permissions, nor does it bother checking any child code groups of this code group. The assembly also doesn't match the membership conditions of the Fabrikam-Pub code group. It does, however, become a member of the MyComputer code group and is granted permission to execute. The runtime navigates to the next level in the code group hierarchy and skips the Contoso code group: only nodes whose parents had their conditions met will be evaluated. The runtime does match the assembly against the SomeAssembly code group, and having matched the public key, it grants File IO and Reflection permissions. The union of the permission sets for the matching code groups is computed—in this case, Nothing Execute FileIO + Reflection = Execute, FileIO, and Reflection.

This process is repeated for each policy level in turn (enterprise, machine, and user). The permission sets computed at each policy level are intersected to compute the final total permissions granted. Let's say that at the next level, the AllCode group offers permission set FullTrust. In this case, the final intersection would be (Execute, FileIO, and Reflection) FullTrust = Execute, FileIO, and Reflection.

12.3 VSTO Security

Office 97	✖
Office 2000	✖
Office XP	✖
Office 2003	✔

VSTO solutions do not use Office macro security. Instead, they incorporate the security features available with the .NET Framework 1.1. VSTO solutions add a custom security restriction of not accepting All Code or Zone-based evidence, which means that they will not run any assemblies that are on the local machine, the network, or the Internet until the assembly is explicitly given security permission.

To deploy and run an Office solution that uses managed code extensions, you must grant FullTrust permissions to the assembly and the document in the security policy of each end user. The required permission set is FullTrust; VSTO solutions do not run assemblies that have partial trust or no trust. The document in the solution must also have full trust. Note that in the default .NET security model, all code on the local computer is automatically fully trusted, but in the VSTO model it is not unless it is explicitly given FullTrust. The VSTO loader performs security checks against policy on both the document and the assembly, as shown in Figure 12-2.

The wizard for creating Word and Excel projects uses URL evidence. This level of security might be sufficient on a development machine, but it poses a security risk on a network because anyone who gains write access to the location can replace the assembly with a malicious one. Before you deploy the assembly, it should be given a stronger form of evidence. The strong name of the assembly is good evidence to use. The wizard can't generate policy for strong-name evidence because the project won't get a strong name until the assembly has been built (using your strong-name key, which the wizard can't possibly know). So, the wizard has to generate some kind of security policy, and it can do so based on URL evidence. The tacit assumption is that you will replace this evidence with something stronger during development.

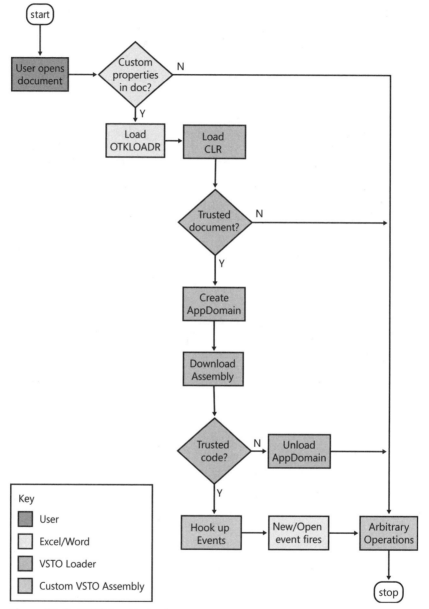

Figure 12-2   VSTO load behavior.

Your solution also takes advantage of the fact that the document itself has location-based evidence, making it harder for malicious users to repurpose trusted code by creating documents that use the code for unintended purposes. If a document that has managed code extensions is not in a fully trusted location, it will not execute the assembly. The relevant permutations of security permissions are summarized in Table 12-3.

Table 12-3   VSTO Document and Assembly Security Permutations

Securable Object	Location	Default Settings	Recommendations
Assembly	The development computer where the project was created	When you create the project, the folder where the assembly is located is granted Execution permissions and the assembly itself is granted FullTrust permissions.	If you move the assembly to a different folder or to a different computer, you must grant it full trust in the new location. If you add a reference to another assembly, the referenced assembly will be copied to the same folder as the main project assembly, where it will have Execution permissions.
	Deployed to a shared network location (HTTP, HTTPS, or UNC)	The location is not trusted, and assemblies have no trust.	The administrator must set up security policy to trust the assembly. Also, you should ensure that only trusted parties have access to modify or replace assemblies on that shared location.
	Deployed to an end-user's computer	*My_Computer_Zone* is likely to have FullTrust permissions, but assemblies have no trust.	The administrator or user must set up security policy to trust the assembly.
Document	The development computer where the project was created	Documents have FullTrust permissions.	No action required.
	Deployed to a shared network location	The location is not trusted, and documents have no trust.	The administrator should set up network security policy that trusts the location or the document. If the share is not locked down, you should set up a custom policy to trust only Office documents.
	Deployed to an end-user's computer	Documents have FullTrust permissions.	No action required.

> **Note**   If the administrator adjusts permissions for a document or assembly, users must quit and then restart all Office applications in order for those changes to be enforced. This also means that any application that is hosting or automating Excel or Word must release its object references—and this might mean closing the application. For example, Outlook is configured by default to use Word, so if you're setting up a Word project, you'll need to close Outlook.

If you are working with a VSTO project that you did not create, you must grant Full-Trust permissions to the assembly before you can use it. If you're building the solution in Microsoft Visual Studio, this policy will be set up for you automatically. If you just want to run a solution that is already built, you must set up policy explicitly. The procedures described next can be used to set up security to mirror the settings that the Visual Studio wizard creates when a project is first created. Note that these default settings are not appropriate for all scenarios.

There are two tools you can use to configure security permissions for folders and assemblies:

- Microsoft .NET Framework Configuration tool (an MMC snap-in, MSCorCfg.msc)

- Command-line Code Access Security Policy tool (CASPol.exe)

> **Note**   The sample code and scripts for this topic can be found in the sample code at <install location>\Code\VSTO\vstoSecurity.

Using MSCorCfg

Go to Control Panel | Administrative Tools | Microsoft .NET Framework 1.1 Configuration. (Note that the .NET Framework 1.1 is the earliest version that works with VSTO; if you have a later version installed, you should use the configuration tool for that instead.)

1. In the treeview on the left side, expand Runtime Security Policy | User | Code Groups | All_Code | Office_Projects. If you have not previously built a VSTO project, you will not have the Office_Projects folder. You can add the new code group to the *All_Code* root node (with a permission set of Nothing).

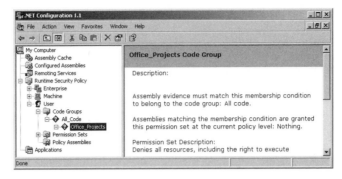

2. In the Tasks section, click Add A Child Code Group to start the Create Code Group Wizard. Select Create A New Code Group, and enter a name and description that will help you identify the project. Click Next.

3. Select URL from the list. Type the path to the bin folder of the project, followed by an asterisk (for example, C:\Temp\ExcelProject1_bin*). Click Next.

4. Select Use Existing Permission Set, and then select Execution from the list. Click Next, and then click Finish.

5. Repeat these steps to add another code group—this time a child of the previous one, specifically for the assembly itself. Set the full path to the DLL, and select FullTrust permissions.

Using CASPol

When you build your first VSTO project, a code group named Office_Projects is added to the All_Code group at the user level on your machine. All subsequent VSTO solutions you create will be given default policy entries under this group. If you need to re-create this group explicitly, you can do so by using this command:

```
caspol -user -addgroup All_Code -allcode Nothing -name Office_Projects
```

To replicate the default policy that is created for an individual VSTO solution, type the following commands in a (Visual Studio .NET) command window, replacing the names and paths to suit your project. There are four CASPol commands: the first to turn off the policy change prompt, the second to set up a code group granting Execution permissions for the folder, the third to set up a child group granting FullTrust for the assembly itself, and the fourth to reset the policy-change prompt:

```
CD %windir%\microsoft.net\framework\v1.1.4322

caspol -polchgprompt off

caspol -user -addgroup Office_Projects -url "C:\Temp\ExcelProject1_bin\*" Execution -
name "ExcelProject1_bin" -description "VSTO Sample #1 folder"

caspol -user -addgroup "ExcelProject1_bin" -url
"C:\Temp\ExcelProject1_bin\ExcelProject1.dll" FullTrust -name "ExcelProject1.dll" -
```

```
description "VSTO Sample #1 assembly"

caspol -polchgprompt on

pause
```

Note that these commands make three assumptions:

- You have extended the PATH in your environment to include the location of CASPol.exe. If not, you must run this from a Visual Studio .NET command prompt or supply the full path to CASPol.exe. This is usually in the Windows root directory structure—that is, somewhere like C:\WINDOWS\Microsoft.NET\ Framework\v1.1.4322.

- You already have the Office_Projects code group (which is created when you build your first VSTO project).

- The policy-change prompt was set to be on to start with. This is a little problematic because the setting persists. The example turns it off at the beginning and on again at the end. However, you should be governed by whatever the normal setting is for your environment instead of arbitrarily changing it.

Whichever tool you use, the results should be the same, and you can use either tool to report the updated status. MSCorCfg doesn't reflect changes made outside the tool—so if you used CASPol, you must close and reopen MSCorCfg for the changes to be recognized.

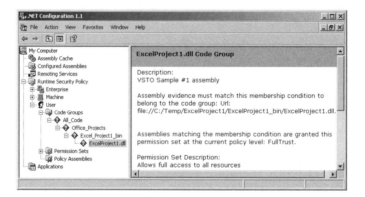

This series of CASPol commands removes the folder code group—and therefore also the child code group for the assembly itself:

```
CD %windir%\microsoft.net\framework\v1.1.4322

caspol -polchgprompt off

caspol -user -remgroup "ExcelProject1_bin"

caspol -polchgprompt on

pause
```

The following JScript script illustrates how you can script CASPol. This takes in a single command-line argument—the absolute path of the assembly, including extension. It parses this argument to determine the folder location of the assembly and to compose arbitrary code group names based on the assembly and folder paths. The script assumes user-level policy and fixed permission sets—Execution for the folder and Full-Trust for the assembly—consistent with the VSTO wizard-generated settings. This script is supplied with the sample code.

```
// SetSecurity.js

if (WScript.Arguments.Length < 1)
{
    WScript.Echo(
        "Usage: SetSecurity <absolute assembly path>\n"
        +"\neg:\n"
        +"     SetSecurity C:\\Temp\\Foo\\Foo_bin\\Foo.dll\n"
        +"\nor (if there are spaces in the path):\n"
        +"     SetSecurity \"C:\\Program Files\\Foo\\Foo_bin\\Foo.dll\"");
    WScript.Quit(1);
}

// Cache the script's command line arguments.
//C:\Temp\Foo\Foo_bin\Foo.dll
var rawPath = WScript.Arguments(0);

// Protect any quotes (") from being interpreted.
var re = /\"/g
var assemblyPath = rawPath.replace(re, "\"")

// Extract the assembly name from the assembly path.
//Foo.dll
var lastSlash = assemblyPath.lastIndexOf("\\");
var assemblyName = assemblyPath.substr(lastSlash+1);

// Extract the folder path from the assembly path.
//C:\Temp\Foo\Foo_bin
var folderPath = assemblyPath.substring(0, lastSlash);

// Extract the folder name from the folder path.
//Foo_bin
lastSlash = folderPath.lastIndexOf("\\");
var folderName = folderPath.substr(lastSlash+1);


// Build the first (folder) code group command.
var folderGroup =
    "caspol -polchgprompt off -user"
    +" -addgroup Office_Projects"
    +" -url \"" +folderPath +"\\*\""
    +" Execution "
    +" -name \"" +folderName +"\"";
```

```
// Build the second (assembly) code group command.
var assemblyGroup =
    "caspol -user"
    +" -addgroup " +folderName
    +" -url \"" +assemblyPath +"\""
    +" FullTrust"
    +" -name " +assemblyName;

// Restore the policy change prompt status.
var ppStatus =
    "caspol -polchgprompt on";


try
{
    var shell = WScript.CreateObject("WScript.Shell");

    shell.Run(folderGroup, 1, true);
    shell.Run(assemblyGroup, 1, true);
    shell.Run(ppStatus, 1, true);

    WScript.Echo(
        "Successfully added " +folderName
        +" and " +assemblyName +" code groups");
}
catch(e)
{
    WScript.Echo("Error:" +e.number + ": " +e.description);
    WScript.Quit(2);
}
```

This registry file adds a command to the Explorer shell shortcut menu to run the foregoing script on the selected DLL. The command is VSTO Add FullTrust.

```
Windows Registry Editor Version 5.00

[HKEY_CLASSES_ROOT\dllfile\shell\VSTO Add FullTrust\command]
@="\"wscript\" \"C:\\Data\\TechEd\\Demos\\SetSecurity.js\" \"%L\""
```

You might wonder why Visual Studio generates default security policy for VSTO solutions at two levels within the file system (folder and DLL). If you were required to give the assembly FullTrust rights in order to run, why does the policy allow other code to run within the same folder? There are two reasons. The first is so that satellite assemblies that might, for example, contain resources such as localized string tables can be loaded. Second, it lets you reference other assemblies within the same folder so that they will at least load and execute. If the separate assemblies try to do anything that requires more than simple execution and you haven't granted them permission via a code group, they will fail. This means that any code you want to use as part of a VSTO solution (except code with the Microsoft or ECMA strong name) must meet the membership condition of some code group (other than the built-in My_Computer_Zone) and that code group must give FullTrust permissions.

Encrypted Office Documents

Recall that when you create a new VSTO project you are given the option to use an existing document or workbook. If you choose to do this, you must be sure to remove the password protection on the document first.

The reason is that the Office password protection feature encrypts a document, including the document properties. The effect of encrypting properties is that they are hidden from non-Office applications such as Visual Studio. Conversely, any properties added to an encrypted file by a non-Office application are not visible to Office once the document is unencrypted. So, once a file has its properties encrypted, Visual Studio cannot be used to change the Assembly Link Location property path. Currently, Visual Studio .NET cannot detect whether a document is encrypted, so you get no errors or warnings. To use encryption on documents that use managed code extensions, you must set all the properties and then encrypt it after all the properties are set.

Information Rights Management

Information Rights Management (IRM) is a new feature in Office 2003 that helps prevent unauthorized people from viewing or altering sensitive information. When IRM is used to restrict permissions to a document or workbook, by default, the VSTO code-behind is not permitted to run.

You can change this so that your managed code extensions can access the object model:

1. Open the document or workbook in Word 2003 or Excel 2003.

2. Choose File | Permission, and in the Permission dialog box select More Options | Additional Permissions For Users.

3. Select the Access Content Programmatically check box to permit programmatic access to the host application's object model.

Note that to make these changes, you must be the author of the document or workbook or have Full Control access.

12.4 Strong-Naming

Office 97	?
Office 2000	?
Office XP	?
Office 2003	✓

You can sign your assembly with a strong name—and most coding standards suggest that you probably should as a matter of course. The core technique explained in this section (strong-naming) can be applied to managed code used with all four versions of Office, and indeed all other managed code, although the example given is a VSTO solution. Strong-naming serves several purposes:

1. It avoids "DLL Hell" by producing unique names for assemblies from different vendors and with different version numbers.

2. It provides a unique identity for each assembly, which can be used not only as a factor in your deployment strategy but also in configurable security (although it should be used to supplement Authenticode rather than replace it).

3. Because the code-signing mechanism is based on public key cryptography, it assures consumers of your assembly of its provenance. A strong name is difficult to falsify.

4. The runtime performs signature verification checks as part of its loading operation, to ensure that the assembly hasn't been tampered with.

Digital signatures are widely used as an important part of many security systems. In the context of Office development, they are used in two main ways: to sign documents and to sign assemblies. A digital signature is a small piece of data—typically a hash—that is encrypted with the owner's private key. A hash—also known as a *digest* or a *checksum*—is a fixed-length number that is computed from a message, a document, an assembly, or any other stream of data. When you hash two different documents or assemblies, the hash will always be different. Even if two assemblies differ by only one bit, the hashes will be different. Using today's technology, it is not feasible to compute a pair of assemblies that translate to the same hash value without breaking the hashing algorithm. This assures users of the integrity of the document. Also, all hashing algorithms are one-way—that is, given a hash, you cannot recompose the original assembly.

Strong-naming your assembly allows you not only to deploy it to the GAC and therefore make it shareable, but also to strengthen the security of your system. This is because a strong name is difficult to spoof—the runtime checks the identity of every assembly it loads, and a strong name is better evidence of identity than a simple name. In addition, the runtime performs checks against security policy, and security policy is strengthened if you use strong names for evidence.

Load-time strong-name verification is not performed for assemblies loaded from the GAC. Instead, the signature and module hashes are verified at the time you install the assembly in the GAC. The GAC is trusted because you have to have administrator rights on the machine to manipulate the GAC. Because strong-name signatures do not need to be verified for GAC assemblies, there is a load-time performance advantage. The procedure for strong-naming an assembly is summarized in Figure 12-3.

The process for generating strong-name keys is simple. To generate the cryptographic keypair, use *SN −k <keyfilename>*. For example, from a command window, you can type this:

```
sn -k ExcelProject1.snk
```

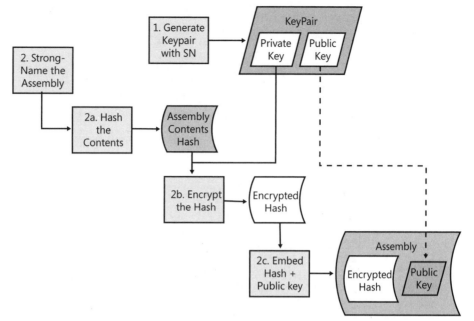

Figure 12-3   Strong-naming an assembly.

Having generated a keypair file, you should keep it safe and give very few people access to it. You should not keep a keypair file in your project folder because this might easily be accessible to others. One simple strategy is to put the keypair file in a folder in your profile, such as C:\Documents and Settings\<*username*>\SomeFolder. This location will normally be accessible only to you and to administrators. Here's an example. (You would substitute <*username*> with an appropriate username.)

```
sn -k "C:\Documents and Settings\<username>\SomeFolder\ExcelProject1.snk"
```

You should also consider using key containers rather than files. More commonly, some designated person holds the key(s) for the organization and delay-signing is used (as described later).

For the purposes of the sample exercises in this book, you can add SN to the Tools menu as an external tool so that you can generate ad-hoc keys for the samples. Note that this is not useful in a production environment, where you will use one key (or a very small number of keys) to sign all your assemblies and where this key will be kept secure. That said, if you want to add SN to the Tools menu, you'll probably want the command-line arguments to include the item directory and target name as the base name for the keyfile—that is, *-k $(ItemDir)$(TargetName).snk*. Note that SN.exe is in the .NET Framework SDK directory structure, not where Visual Studio is installed.

When you run SN.exe, you should get a report like this:

Microsoft (R) .NET Framework Strong Name Utility Version 1.0.3705.0

Copyright (C) Microsoft Corporation 1998-2001. All rights reserved.

Key pair written to C:\Temp\ExcelProject1\ExcelProject1.snk

To incorporate the keypair into the assembly build, you must add this code (as with the version information, either in assemblyinfo.cs or in the main source file):

```
[assembly: AssemblyKeyFile("../../ExcelProject1.snk")]
```

The behavior of the .NET runtime when it loads a strong-named assembly is similar to the procedure for verifying a document signature (as summarized in Figure 12-4).

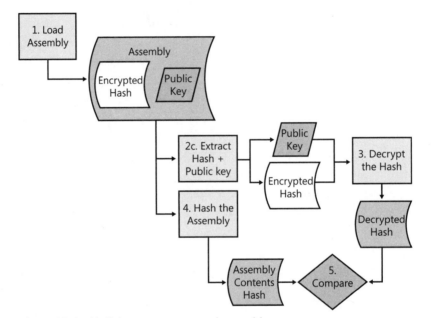

Figure 12-4   Verifying a strong-named assembly.

Delay-Signing

An interesting feature of .NET code signing is the option to delay-sign an assembly. Recall that a cryptographic keypair consists of both a private and a public key. The public key is made publicly available to consuming client applications and is visible in the assembly manifest. On the other hand, the private key is kept very secure. If the security of the private key is compromised, consumers holding the public key can no longer trust an assembly that is correctly verified by the CLR.

Key management should not be taken lightly. In many of the examples in this book, ad hoc keys have been generated to strong-name the assembly, but this should not be taken as normal practice. In the real world (outside this book), you are unlikely to generate ad-hoc keys for a production system. If you're serious about security, you should build a reliable process around the generation, application, and management of strong-name keys.

For this reason, as an added security measure, it is reasonable to withhold the private key from developers until the last possible moment (or altogether). During the development and testing phases of a project, developers are given only the public key. This is needed by client assemblies, so it must be present for building and testing multi-assembly systems. The delay-signing strategy works like this:

The person in the organization who has the appropriate authority generates the key-pair as normal. Typically this is done very infrequently, and the keypair is then kept secure.

She runs SN again on the generated keypair file to extract only the public key, using the −*p* switch. For example:

```
sn -p MyKeyPair.snk MyPublicOnly.snk
```

The public key is distributed to developers in the organization.

To use the public key in place of the full keypair, the code of an assembly must include not only the *AssemblyKeyFile* attribute as normal, but also the *AssemblyDelaySign* attribute. The *AssemblyKeyFile* attribute, of course, specifies the public key file, not the full keypair file. For example:

```
[assembly:AssemblyKeyFile("MyPublicOnly.snk")]
[assembly:AssemblyDelaySign(true)]
```

Alternatively, if you build the assembly with the assembly linker tool (AL.exe), you can use the */delaysign+* and *keyfile:* switches.

A delay-signed assembly does not, of course, have a valid strong-name signature—rather, the compiler reserves space in the assembly for the strong name. So the runtime's loader would reject it during the signature verification stage. For this reason, you can instruct the CLR to skip the verification for this particular assembly on the current machine, using the −*Vr* switch to SN. For example:

```
sn -Vr MyAssembly.dll
```

> **Warning** This is potentially dangerous. You must have a strong developer process around this strategy—that is, a procedure whereby the use of the −*Vr* switch is tracked and monitored. Verification should be turned back on at the earliest opportunity.

Later, when the appropriate product development stage has been reached, the assembly must be properly signed with the full keypair, using the −*R* switch to SN to re-sign a partially signed assembly. Note that this might be a task for the designated security administrator rather than individual developers. The syntax of the command is shown here:

```
sn -R MyAssembly.dll MyKeyPair.snk
```

Signature verification should also be turned back on for the assembly:

```
sn -Vu MyAssembly.dll
```

Note that you do not have to rebuild any clients of the assembly because they had access to the public key when they were built and therefore can create a valid *AssemblyRef* within their own assembly metadata.

In the following exercise, we'll create a new VSTO solution and delay-sign it. We'll configure security policy for the assembly based on the strong name, and then re-sign it as for production.

Note The sample solution for this topic can be found in the sample code at <install location>\Code\VSTO\TestSN. The general techniques discussed in this section are applicable to all versions of Office, although the sample solution is implemented using VSTO (and therefore Office 2003).

Initial Assembly and Delay-Signing

1. Create a new VSTO solution for Excel called TestSN. Accept all defaults. Build (to set up the security policy) and test the generated workbook to ensure that everything works as expected before making any changes.

2. Implement *ThisWorkbook_Open* to put some simple text into the first cell of the active sheet:

```
Excel.Worksheet sheet =
    (Excel.Worksheet)thisApplication.ActiveSheet;
Excel.Range range = (Excel.Range)sheet.Cells[1,1];
range.Value2 = "Hello TestSN";
```

3. Recall that in a production environment you should not normally generate ad hoc keys, and if you do, you should not keep them in the solution folder. That said, for this non-production demonstration sample, we'll do just that. Generate a strong-name keypair file. If you have set up SN.exe as an external tool in the menu, you can simply click the menu item. If not, you must open a Visual Studio .NET command prompt, navigate to the current solution folder, and execute SN.exe on the command line. In this example, we'll create a keypair file called TestSNKeyPair.snk:

```
sn -k TestSNKeyPair.snk
```

4. Run SN again on the generated keypair file to extract only the public key, using the –*p* switch:

```
sn -p TestSNKeyPair.snk TestSNPublicKey.snk
```

5. Apply the public key to the assembly—in Visual Studio .NET, open the assembly-info.cs file and modify the *AssemblyKeyFile* attribute to specify the (relative or absolute) path to the public key file. Also specify delay-signing, and make sure you have an explicit version number:

```
[assembly: AssemblyVersion("1.0.0.0")]
[assembly: AssemblyDelaySign(true)]
[assembly: AssemblyKeyFile("../../TestSNPublicKey.snk")]
```

6. Rebuild the assembly, and test to see if it works by double-clicking on the .xls file in Explorer. This step simulates the ongoing development stage of the project. You should find that it fails to load—because the assembly is delay-signed. So, instruct the CLR to skip its usual load-time verification for now:

```
sn -Vr TestSN_bin/TestSN.dll
```

This should produce a confirmation message like this one:

> *Microsoft (R) .NET Framework Strong Name Utility Version 1.1.4322.573*
>
> *Copyright (C) Microsoft Corporation 1998–2002. All rights reserved.*
>
> *Verification entry added for assembly 'TestSN,FB44155EE6576F81'*

7. Test again, and the assembly should load.

Strong-Name Security Evidence

Moving on to deployment, we'll now configure the security policy for this assembly. Recall that you can use either CASPol.exe or MSCorCfg.msc. If you're not familiar with the tools, you should use MSCorCfg.msc because then you're less likely to cause accidental damage. For real development, you're more likely to use CASPol.exe because it can be scripted.

1. Open the MSCorCfg MMC snap-in, and delete the default wizard-generated policy entry for this assembly. This will be a child node under Runtime Security Policy | User | Code Groups | All_Code | Office_Projects.

2. Recall that the wizard-generated policy uses URL evidence, which is not very strong. We'll set up a new policy for this assembly using the strong name as evidence. However, at this point the assembly is only partially signed. Re-sign the assembly with the full keypair:

```
sn -R TestSN_bin/TestSN.dll TestSNKeyPair.snk
```

3. Back in MSCorCfg, navigate to the *Office_Projects* node under User policy, right-click, and add a new child code group. Give it the name *TestSN* and whatever description you like.

4. On the Choose A Condition Type tab, select Strong Name from the list and click Import. Navigate to TestSN_bin/TestSN.dll and click OK. This imports the public key from the strong-named assembly to use as evidence. It also ensures that only assemblies with the specified public key are granted permissions. In production systems, this public key is used to sign many assemblies, so this provides for a consistent security policy.

   If you want to ensure that only a specific assembly is granted permissions, you can also select the Name check box. You probably don't want to select the Version check box because that would significantly increase your deployment burden—every time you changed the assembly version, you'd have to redeploy policy:

5. On the Assign A Permission Set tab, select FullTrust, and finish the wizard. Finally, turn on CLR load verification again:

   ```
   sn -Vu TestSN_bin/TestSN.dll
   ```

6. Now when you double-click the .xls in Explorer, it should load the trusted code-behind assembly correctly. (If it doesn't, and if you've completed all the steps correctly, the shadow copy in the download cache—the one that was only partially signed—is probably being used.). Clear the cache and try again:

   ```
   gacutil /cdl
   ```

   If you want to achieve the same results with CASPol instead of MSCorCfg, you can use a command file like this (in this example, specifying the Name and Version):

   ```
   CD %windir%\microsoft.net\framework\v1.1.4322

   caspol -polchgprompt off

   caspol -user -addgroup Office_Projects -strong -file
   "C:\Temp\TestSN\TestSN_bin\TestSN.dll" TestSN 1.0.0.0 FullTrust -name TestSN

   caspol -polchgprompt on

   pause
   ```

GAC-Deploying Code-Behind Assemblies

It is also possible to deploy VSTO code-behind assemblies into the GAC. Since we have already strong-named our assembly, we can install it into the GAC without any further work.

1. The simplest way is to open Windows Explorer and then drag and drop the assembly into C:\windows\assembly (or C:\winnt\assembly). Alternatively, you can open a Visual Studio .NET command window and use the GACUtil.exe tool from the command line (using *i* for install):

```
gacutil /i TestSN.dll
```

Of course, the drag-and-drop option is useful only on the development machine, not for deployment. Indeed, the GACUtil.exe tool might not be available on the end users' machines either. So, for a production system, you'll probably want to deploy via an MSI.

2. Next, open the .xls and modify the custom properties. When it loads a strong-named assembly, the CLR will search the GAC early in the probing (search) algorithm. Therefore, we'd ideally delete the *_AssemblyLocation0* property altogether because we don't need it. However, the VSTO assembly loader will fail if this property is not present. Instead, we'll change it to any arbitrary text (such as C:\). Don't forget to click Modify.

3. The important property is *_AssemblyName0*. Change this to the strong name of the assembly. You can get the strong name using GACUtil.exe (with *l* for list):

```
gacutil /l TestSN
```

This should produce a report like the following:

> *The Global Assembly Cache contains the following assemblies:*
>
> *TestSN, Version=1.0.0.0, Culture=neutral, PublicKeyToken=fb44155ee6576f81, Custom=null*
>
> *The cache of ngen files contains the following entries:*
>
> *Number of items = 1*

4. As an alternative to GACUtil, you can use the GetSN tool provided in the sample code. The GetSN tool is simple: it takes the assembly name as its only argument and outputs the strong name in exactly the right format for the *_AssemblyName0* property. You can either use this at the command line or merge this .reg file into the registry and then use it from the Windows Explorer shortcut menu:

```
Windows Registry Editor Version 5.00

[HKEY_CLASSES_ROOT\dllfile\shell\GetSN\command]
@="C:\\Data\\Utils\\GetSN\\GetSN.exe \"%L\""
```

5. Whichever tool you use, copy the strong name from the command window and paste it into the _AssemblyName0_ custom property field in the .xls. Again, remember to click Modify. We only need the simple name, the version, the culture, and the public key token:

```
TestSN, Version=1.0.0.0, Culture=neutral, PublicKeyToken=fb44155ee6576f81
```

Note that if this strong-name string is more than 255 characters, you must split it up. In this case, you should use the _Persistence_ control to do the job for you instead of manually editing the property. (See Chapter 10, "Visual Studio Tools for Office.")

6. Clear the assembly download cache (gacutil /cdl), and double-click the .xls to test the solution. It should load correctly. If you have a utility such as Process Explorer (freeware from *www.sysinternals.com*), you can double-check that the code-behind assembly is indeed being loaded from the GAC.

Strong-Naming an ActiveX Control

In the OfficeDocumentBrowser solution presented in Chapter 4, "Integrating Managed Code," we had a custom managed assembly and an imported ActiveX control. We used the ActiveX control through an interop assembly (IA) that was generated automatically when we added the control to the Visual Studio Toolbox. This is the standard approach to importing ActiveX controls into a managed project.

If you use the Toolbox Wizard to import an ActiveX control into your managed project, the wizard will use the AxImp tool under the covers. Using this approach is obviously very convenient. However, it doesn't give you the opportunity to fine-tune the AxImp behavior—specifically, in the current context, it doesn't give you the opportunity to tell AxImp to strong-name the IA that it generates. Therefore, if you need to strong-name your IA, you must use the AxImp command-line tool directly.

To do this, first strong-name your custom assembly in the usual way, by applying a strong-name keypair with the *AssemblyKeyFile* attribute:

```
[assembly: AssemblyKeyFile("../../OfficeDocumentBrowser.snk")]
```

Open a Visual Studio command window (or any command window, if you have the Visual Studio tools folders in the path), and enter the command to generate an IA from the Microsoft WebBrowser ActiveX control, and sign it with your strong-name keypair:

```
aximp C:\windows\system32\SHDocVw.dll /keyfile:OfficeDocumentBrowser.snk /
out:AxInterop.SHDocVw.sn.dll
```

If you don't have the AxImp.exe tool in the path, you can fully qualify its name instead:

```
"C:\Program Files\Microsoft Visual Studio .NET\FrameworkSDK\Bin\aximp"
C:\windows\system32\SHDocVw.dll /keyfile:OfficeDocumentBrowser.snk /
out:AxInterop.SHDocVw.sn.dll
```

This generates two IAs:

SHDocVw.dll   The CLR proxy for COM types—the conventional IA that equates to the COM type library.

AxInterop.SHDocVw.sn.dll   The Windows Forms proxy for the ActiveX control, which is loaded at runtime.

Finally, add references to both these assemblies in your project.

12.5 Authenticode Certificates

Office 97
Office 2000
Office XP
Office 2003

Strong-naming an assembly with SN.exe provides a unique identity for the assembly and allows the CLR to perform load-time checks to ensure that the assembly hasn't been tampered with. SN builds into the assembly a cryptographic hash of the contents of the assembly, signed with a particular cryptographic keypair. So, if the private key has been kept secure, you can be sure of which keypair the assembly was signed with and that the assembly has not been tampered with since.

You can also use Authenticode in addition to strong-name code signing. An Authenticode signature verifies that a specific trusted publisher signed the assembly and has not subsequently revoked the certificate associated with the signature. Authenticode and .NET code signing serve two different purposes but are entirely complementary. The Authenticode signature must be applied after the strong-name signature because strong-naming modifies the bits that Authenticode tries to sign (hence, the assembly will appear to be "tampered with" by Authenticode if you strong-name afterward).

A certificate is different from a strong-name keypair because a keypair is basically just a couple of numbers, whereas a certificate contains the keypair along with information about who it was issued to, who issued it, when it expires, and what purposes it is valid for (e-mail signing, code signing, etc.). Also, while anyone can use SN.exe to generate a keypair, you typically obtain a certificate from an internal or external certification authority. The certification authority verifies your credentials before issuing you a certificate. You can also self-generate certificates, but they will not be trustable by end users until they install them; this strategy is mainly used for testing purposes during development.

Authenticode can be tied to an identity with a higher degree of certainty than is possible with strong names alone. Authenticode uses a hierarchical system of trusted authorities to verify that someone who claims to be the publisher of a given file is indeed its publisher. In particular, Authenticode implies a level of trust associated with a software publisher, while strong names do not. Also, with Authenticode you can take advantage of such features as a certificate revocation list (CRL) if a certificate has been revoked. Unlike certificates, strong-name keys don't expire. Also, if a strong-name key is compromised, the only recourse you have is to set up .NET security policy to not trust that key.

During development, you might not have access to the Authenticode certificates used in your organization. For this reason, the .NET Framework ships with a tool for generating X.509 test certificates, MakeCert.exe. You should convert your test certificate into a Software Publisher Certificate by using Cert2Spc.exe. (Note that test certificates generated in this way should be used only for testing during development, not for final production.)

Once you have received or generated a certificate, you must sign your assembly with it. To do this, you use the SignCode.exe tool, which ships with Visual Studio .NET.

> **Note**   Under Windows 2000 and Windows XP without SP1, you also need to run SetReg.exe with the appropriate option to configure the computer to trust the test root certification authority. If you don't do this, your test certificate will not be trusted. Under Windows XP SP1, this is not required. The appropriate command line is:
>
> ```
> setreg 1 true
> ```

In the following exercise, we'll create a simple VSTO solution, strong-name it, and sign it with an Authenticode signature. The core technique explained in this section (Authenticode) can be applied to all four versions of Office, although the example used to illustrate the technique is a VSTO solution.

> **Note**   The sample solution for this topic can be found in the sample code at <install location>\Code\VSTO\TestSigs. The general techniques discussed in this section are applicable to all versions of Office, although the sample solution is implemented using VSTO (and therefore Office 2003).

Strong-Naming

1. Create a new VSTO solution for Excel called TestSigs. Accept all defaults. Build (to set up the security policy) and test the generated workbook to ensure that everything works as expected before making any changes.

2. Implement *ThisWorkbook_Open* to put some simple text into the first cell of the active sheet:

```
Excel.Worksheet sheet =
    (Excel.Worksheet)thisApplication.ActiveSheet;
Excel.Range range = (Excel.Range)sheet.Cells[1,1];
range.Value2 = "Hello TestSigs";
```

3. Generate a strong-name keypair file (bearing in mind the earlier caveat that you would not do this for a production system). If you have set up SN.exe as an external tool in the menu, you can simply click the command. If not, you must open a Visual Studio .NET command prompt, navigate to the current solution folder, and execute SN.exe on the command line. In this example, we'll create a keypair file called TestSigs.snk:

```
sn -k TestSigs.snk
```

4. Now apply the strong name to the assembly—in Visual Studio .NET, open the assemblyinfo.cs file and modify the *AssemblyKeyFile* attribute to specify the (relative or absolute) path to the keypair file:

```
[assembly: AssemblyKeyFile("..\\..\\TestSigs.snk")]
```

5. Rebuild the assembly.

Authenticode Signatures

1. Now we'll create a test certificate. Open a Visual Studio .NET command prompt, and run MakeCert.exe to generate an X.509 certificate signed by the test root. Specify options to provide an arbitrary certificate name (which should be prefixed with *CN=*), to store the private key in a key container location with a suitable name (which will be created if it doesn't already exist), and to write it to a file called TestSigs.cer.

```
makecert -n "CN=Contoso" -sk MyContainer TestSigs.cer
```

Just for curiosity, you can open the TestSigs.cer file in Visual Studio (use Open with Binary Editor). You'll see your chosen certificate name embedded in the file. Note that if you don't specify a certificate name, test certificates are nominally published by Joe's-Software-Emporium.

2. Create a test Software Publisher Certificate from the X.509 certificate:

```
cert2spc TestSigs.cer TestSigs.spc
```

3. Finally, sign the assembly with the Authenticode test certificate, using Sign-Code.exe:

```
signcode -spc TestSigs.spc -k MyContainer TestSigs_bin/TestSigs.dll
```

> **Note** You can double-check to verify that the publisher certificate has been embedded at the end of the assembly file by opening the signed DLL in the Binary Editor in Visual Studio.

The Publisher Code Group

1. The final step is to configure the security policy to allow the assembly to run. The default VSTO security policy is suitable for development but is inherently

weak because it is based on URL evidence. Strong-name evidence or publisher certificate evidence is far stronger.

2. First remove the default developer policy for this solution, using either CASPol.exe or MSCorCfg.msc. To do this, go to Control Panel | Administrative Tools | Microsoft .NET Framework 1.1 Configuration. Expand the Runtime Security Policy node and go to User | Code Groups | All_Code | Office_Projects. Select and delete the node for the TestSigs solution. Then verify that the VSTO assembly no longer has security permission to execute, by loading TestSigs.xls again.

3. Back in MSCorCfg, go to the User Level policy node, and select the Add A Child Group link in the right-hand pane. Specify the name *ContosoPublisher*. Click Next.

4. On the Choose A Condition Type tab, select Publisher from the list, and click Import From Certificate File. Navigate to your TestSigs.cer file, and click OK:

5. On the Permission Set tab, select Execution from the list, and click Next and then Finish.

6. Now create a child code group of the new publisher group you've just added. Give this child group a suitable name (such as TestSigs). On the Choose A Condition tab, select Strong Name from the list, click Import, and select .\TestSigs_bin\TestSigs.dll. On the Permission Set tab, select FullTrust from the list, and click Next and then Finish.

7. Before final testing, you should clear the assembly cache:

    ```
    gacutil /cdl
    ```

12.6 VSTO Deployment Options

Office 97   ⊗
Office 2000   ⊗
Office XP   ⊗
Office 2003   ✔

In essence, VSTO solutions consist of two logical parts: an Office document or workbook, and a .NET assembly. The .NET assembly might consist of multiple physical files, and it might have dependent assemblies. Dependent assemblies must be deployed in the same folder as the main assembly or in the GAC (and must be explicitly given the security permissions they need). So, in the context of deployment, the .NET assembly or assemblies can be treated as one logical part.

The "logical" assembly and the document or workbook that together form the solution can be deployed either together or separately, and there are three possible models for VSTO solution deployment, described in Table 12-4.

Table 12-4   Alternative VSTO Solution Deployment Models

Office Document	.NET Assembly	Benefits	Limitations
Local	Local	No server access required, therefore supports offline use. You don't need to be admin to change policy, so an end user can run a batch file, use setup.exe, or use a logon script.	Difficult to deploy updates to the document or the assembly.
Local	Network	Easy to update the assembly. The assembly can assume it has access to server resources.	Difficult to deploy updates to the document. The assembly is not accessible offline (unless it's in the download cache, governed by Internet Explorer cache size limitations).
Network	Network	Easy to update the document or the assembly. The assembly can assume it has access to server resources.	The user experience is downgraded—as if the user were using a dumb terminal instead of a PC. The assembly is not accessible offline (unless it's in the download cache, governed by Internet Explorer cache size limitations).

In the following exercise, we'll explore some of the deployment options for code-behind projects, including setting up security policy.

Note   The sample solution for this topic can be found in the sample code at <install location>\Code\VSTO\vstoSecurity.

Local Deployment Changes

1. First make sure you have a simple code-behind solution working. The ExcelProject1 solution will do fine, as long as it has its original security policy (that is based on URL evidence, not on a strong name).

2. Move ExcelProject1.xls and ExcelProject1.dll to a new location on your machine—say, C:\Temp\NewLocation. When you try to open the workbook, you'll get an error indicating that the code-behind assembly could not be found. (This won't happen if you move the entire folder because the link is relative.) To fix this, first change the _AssemblyLocation0_ custom property to specify the new location.

3. When you try to open the workbook, the code-behind assembly will be found but not executed because security policy prevents it from being loaded. You must therefore set up security at the user policy level to grant FullTrust permissions to the assembly. You can use either MSCorCfg or CASPol to achieve this, as described earlier.

When you open the workbook now, it should successfully load and execute the code-behind assembly.

Assembly Deployed to a Network Share

1. Suppose we now have the workbook file on our local machine but the code-behind assembly is deployed to a network share. If you have access to another machine on the network, you can try the following exercise.

2. Move the assembly to some network share. Also update the custom _AssemblyLocation0_ property in the workbook to match the new location. When you try to open the workbook now, you'll get another security error. But this time, you must change security at the *machine* policy level. Apart from the change in policy level, all other security settings can be the same (bearing in mind, of course, that URL evidence is even less secure at the machine level than it is at the user level). For example, you can use the following CASPol commands. (Note: There is unlikely to be an Office_Projects code group under *All_Code* at the machine policy level, so you must add this first (with a permission set of Nothing). The crucial difference is that we specify *–machine* instead of *–user* in this command:

```
caspol -polchgprompt off -machine -addgroup Office_Projects -
url \\servername\Share\ExcelProject1_RemoteAssembly\* Execution -name
```

```
"Remote ExcelProject1_bin" -description "VSTO remote network folder"

caspol -machine -addgroup "Remote ExcelProject1_bin" -
url \\servername\Share\ExcelProject1_RemoteAssembly\ExcelProject1.dll FullTrust
 -name "Remote ExcelProject1.dll" -description "VSTO remote assembly"

caspol -polchgprompt on
```

If you're doing this on your normal development machine, you might well have admin rights, so it won't be apparent that you need admin rights to change machine-level policy.

The solution should now work.

Workbook Deployed to a Network Share

1. Suppose we want to deploy both the code-behind assembly and the workbook file itself to a network share and then have the user open it from there. Try this: move the workbook file to some network share (either the same one as the code-behind assembly or a different one). Then, from the local machine, try to open the workbook on the network share. You'll get another security error.

2. To fix this, you need to grant FullTrust permissions to the workbook file on the network share, at machine level:

```
caspol -polchgprompt off -machine -addgroup "Remote ExcelProject1_bin" -
url \\servername\Share \ExcelProject1_RemoteAssembly\ExcelProject1_RemoteAssemb
ly.xls FullTrust -name "Remote ExcelProject1_RemoteAssembly.xls" -description
"VSTO remote workbook"
caspol -polchgprompt on
```

This should now work. Bear in mind that you've just given FullTrust permissions to a document on a network share. The security implication is that anyone who has write permission on that network share can now replace your fully trusted document with another one of the same name, yet it will still have FullTrust permissions.

Assembly Deployed to a Web Site

1. Instead of deploying to a network share, we can deploy to a Web site. This is a reasonable strategy for the code-behind assembly (although it's less useful for the workbook itself). To set up this exercise, make a copy of the ExcelProject1.dll code-behind assembly in a new folder on a machine running a Web server (such as Microsoft Internet Information Services). Expose that folder as a new virtual directory.

2. Make another copy of the workbook file on the local machine, and set its *_AssemblyLocation0* custom property to point to the virtual directory on the Web server:

```
http://webserver/ExcelProject1_Website
```

3. Of course, you must set up security for this location—and because it's not local, you must do this at the machine policy level:

```
caspol -polchgprompt off -machine -addgroup Office_Projects -url http://
servername/ExcelProject1_Website/* Execution -name "Web ExcelProject1_bin" -
description "VSTO web folder"
```

```
caspol -machine -addgroup "Web ExcelProject1_bin" -url http://servername/
ExcelProject1_Website/ExcelProject1.dll FullTrust -name "Web ExcelProject1.dll"
-description "VSTO web assembly"
```

```
caspol -polchgprompt on
```

Strictly speaking, we can simply trust the assembly for this example because there is only one assembly involved—we don't have to trust the folder as well.

4. Test to make sure this works as expected. As with other .NET assemblies, the VSTO solution assembly will be downloaded from the server, placed in the user's download cache, and run from there. This cache is a subfolder of the user's profile.

There are no guarantees about how long an assembly (or any dependent files) will live in the download cache. There is a default 50-MB quota for the cache, and once the quota is exceeded, bits can be scavenged on a least-recently-used basis. By definition, simply named assemblies do not have strong names, so they can be updated in place at any time. For this reason, they are always re-downloaded from the server. Strong-named assemblies can be reused from the download cache if the URL where the loader will probe for the assembly matches the URL of the cached bits (and the assemblies have the same strong identity). If these conditions are met, no request is issued to the server.

Updating VSTO Solutions

One of the strengths of the code-behind architecture is loose coupling: the document or workbook and the .NET assembly can be developed largely independently. You can easily update either the document or the assembly, or both, as required. If you only need to update the assembly, updating the entire solution is just a question of redeploying the updated assembly to the same location as the original.

The approach to updating the document in a VSTO solution depends on the mode of deployment.

- If the document is on a network share, updating is simply a matter of overwriting the original document with the updated one.

- If the document is local and the assembly is also local, updating requires redeploying using the standard deployment mechanism (such as Systems Management Server).

If the document is local and the assembly is on the network, you have the option to update the document via a notification assembly.

A *notification assembly* is an assembly that notifies the user that an updated version of the document is available. In fact, the third option applies to any deployment mode where the assembly is on a network share. However, it is generally useful only if the document is deployed locally and the assembly is on the network. The basic steps are:

1. Build an updated version of the document, and deploy it somewhere suitable on the network.

2. Move the original code-behind assembly to a different network location than the original location (possibly the same location as the new document, but this is not essential).

3. Build a notification assembly with the same name and code-behind class type as the original assembly. In the *ThisWorkbook_Open* handler, write code to notify the user that an updated document is available for download. This assembly needs to contain only this notification code, but it can also contain some or all of the functionality of the original code-behind assembly for the solution. (Your decision will depend on whether you want to allow users to continue working with the original functionality at this point, or whether you want to force them to download the new document before they can continue.)

4. Deploy this notification assembly to the location where documents expect to find the original code-behind assembly. Because this notification assembly has the same name, you'll be replacing the original assembly. The next time a user opens his local document, he'll load the notification assembly instead of the original assembly.

5. The updated version of the document should refer to the original version of the assembly, in its new location. It can refer to an updated version if you wish, but not to the notification assembly.

OfficeDocumentMembershipCondition

Another variation on the option of deploying to a network location is to constrain security to grant permissions only to Office workbooks or documents in the share, rather than to all content. You do this by using the predefined *OfficeDocumentMembershipCondition* security evidence. When you use this evidence, only Office documents are trusted; assemblies and executables are not granted permission to be run from the share. The basic steps are as follows:

- Add MSOSec.dll to the GAC. This assembly implements *Microsoft.Office.Security.Policy.OfficeDocumentMembershipCondition*, which is used to identify documents and workbooks.

- Create a code group that has restricted permissions for the server or specific folder.

- Create a second code group underneath the first that grants FullTrust permissions to Office documents.

You can do this using either MSCorCfg or CASPol.

First add MSOSec.dll to the GAC. By default, you'll find this assembly under the install location for Office: C:\Program Files\Microsoft Office\Office11\Addins\Msosec.dll.

Create a code group with restricted permissions for the server or folder. Using MSCorCfg, you expand Runtime Security Policy | Machine | Code Groups | All_Code. Right-click LocalIntranet_Zone, and then click New. This step assumes that the server is in the Local Intranet zone. If it has been added to the Trusted Sites zone in Internet Explorer, right-click Trusted_Zone instead.

Supply a suitable name for the code group, say *MyServerName*. This code group does not grant any permissions to the folder; it is just a container for the next code group. Specify URL in the Choose The Condition Type For This Code Group list, and in the URL text box, type the path to the shared folder (for example, *ServerName**ShareName**). The asterisk on the end is important because it applies the permissions to all files and subfolders in this folder.

Select Nothing in the Use Existing Permission Set list. The default value is FullTrust. You must change this to Nothing to avoid granting full permissions to all files in the specified location.

Now create a code group granting FullTrust permissions to Office documents. Right-click the folder code group you've just added, and then click New. Give the new code group a suitable name—say, MyOfficeDocuments.

Select (Custom) in the Choose The Condition Type For This Code Group list. Click Import, and then navigate to MSOSec.xml in the Office installation folder (for example, C:\Program Files\Microsoft Office\Office11\Addins\Msosec.xml). This is a simple XML file that specifies MSOSec.dll, where *OfficeDocumentMembershipCondition* is defined:

```
<IMembershipCondition class="Microsoft.Office.Security.Policy.OfficeDocumentMembersh
ipCondition, msosec, Version=7.0.5000.0, Culture=neutral, PublicKeyToken=b03f5f7f11d
50a3a" />
```

Select MSOSec.xml, and then click Open to import the XML custom code condition:

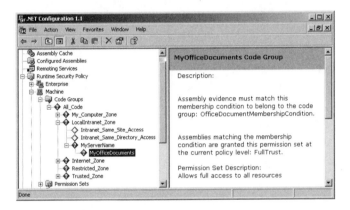

Select FullTrust in the Use Existing Permission Set list. You should end up with a new code group that grants FullTrust only to Office workbooks or documents.

> **Caution**   If you create a policy that includes any custom membership condition, you must make sure that the assembly that implements the condition tests is always available to the runtime (that is, it is installed in the GAC). If the runtime cannot find the assembly, it must fail to load *any* managed code because the assembly it can't find to perform the custom membership condition tests might be denying permissions to some assembly. The runtime defaults to a secure position—that is, it doesn't load anything. So, for example, if you create such a custom policy and then remove the assembly from the GAC, you have no option but to reset all policy using this command:
>
> ```
> caspol -all -rs
> ```

As with any other deployment, it is important to test your installation/deployment strategy and try to mimic your end users' computing environment as much as possible. For example, you can run your installation package on a machine that does not have Visual Studio .NET installed (only the .NET Framework) or that has a custom installation of Office. (Remember that the Office 2003 PIAs are not installed with a typical install of Office.)

12.7 Smart Document Security

Office 97	✖
Office 2000	✖
Office XP	✖
Office 2003	✔

Recall that it is possible to produce smart document solutions using simple MOSTL-conformant XML files with no associated code. It is also possible to produce smart document solutions using unmanaged COM components. Simple MOSTL XML smart documents require minimal security configuration because they are restricted to static text—there is no associated code that could cause a security problem. They do, however, require the XEP manifest to be signed. Because COM smart document solutions use unmanaged code, they cannot leverage .NET security. Therefore, only managed smart document DLL-based solutions can use (and can be constrained by) .NET security.

Best practice suggests the following general security recommendations:

Configure client computers with the strongest security settings available.   Office macro security set at High or Very High, with the Trust All Installed Add-Ins And Templates check box cleared. This ensures that security decisions are not left to an end user who might not have the knowledge required to protect her computer.

Code-sign all the files.   You should strong-name all assemblies, sign them using Authenticode, and sign XEP manifest files (as described later).

Do not disable XML expansion pack security.   Production computers should always have security checking enabled to ensure that untrusted manifest files are not loaded. You should disable security only on development computers during the development phase of the project to simplify debugging.

Manage privacy.   If you are distributing a smart document solution outside your organization, you should consider detaching the manifest file unless you want external users to have access to the deployed solution files.

Host smart document solutions within firewalls.   This reduces the number of sites that users need to trust and reduces the risk of network attacks.

Recall that code that runs from the VSTO loader is not subject to standard Office security levels but is controlled by the VSTO security checks. VSTO loader security is based on the .NET security model, but it enforces stricter rules. Most importantly, in the default .NET security policy, all code on the local machine is trusted by default. In the VSTO loader, it is not; it must be explicitly granted FullTrust permissions under a security policy. Managed smart document DLL solutions are also loaded by the VSTO loader, so the same CAS policy requirements apply.

In addition to the CAS policy requirements, a smart document manifest goes through security checks. When a user opens a document with a smart document solution attached or tries to attach a solution, the first thing to happen is that the XEP manifest file is accessed to discover the files that the solution uses. Office 2003 performs a series of security checks before allowing the file to be downloaded and read. (See Figure 12-5.)

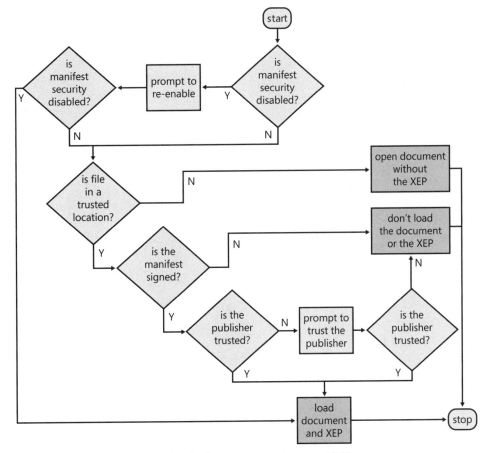

Figure 12-5   Load-time security checks on a smart document XEP.

So far, we've disabled the manifest security checks. In this section, we'll re-enable them and secure our solution instead. Here are the three basic steps:

- Acquire a digital certificate, or create a test certificate by using MakeCert.
- Sign the XEP manifest file with the digital certificate by using XMLSign.
- Deploy the XEP manifest file to a trusted location.

> **Note**   The sample solution for this topic can be found in the sample code at
> <install location>\Code\Office2003\BasicXLSmartDoc_Secure.

1. The first step is to strong-name our assembly. Use *sn −k <keyfilename>.snk* to generate a keyfile, and attach it to the assembly by updating the assembly attribute. Also set a specific version number. For example:

```
[assembly: AssemblyKeyFile("../../BasicXlSmartDoc.snk")]
[assembly: AssemblyVersion("1.0.0.3")]
```

2. Next we'll create a test certificate (for the purposes of this exercise only, not for production solutions). Open a Visual Studio .NET command prompt, and navigate to the SDK bin folder, which will be somewhere like this: C:\Program Files\Microsoft Visual Studio .NET 2003\SDK\v 1.1\bin folder. Execute the following MakeCert command (all on one line):

```
makecert -sk myKeyContainer -r -n "CN=myName" -ss
 myStore C:\Temp\BasicXlSmartDoc_Secure\myCert.cer
```

   This command specifies creating a new certificate called myCert.cer in a key container called myKeyContainer (which will be created if it doesn't already exist). It also stores the certificate in a store called myStore. The name of the publisher's certificate will be myName, and it will be self-signed.

3. You should get a confirmation message from the command, and if you want to manage this certificate later, you can use the Certificates MMC snap-in. To run this, go to Start | Run. Type **MMC**. When the MMC runs, go to File | Add/ Remove Snap-in. In the Add/Remove Snap-in dialog box, click Add, and select Certificates from the list.

4. Once you have a certificate, you can use the XMLSign.exe utility to sign the manifest file with that certificate. This tool ships with the Microsoft Office 2003 Smart Document SDK. Start XMLSign.exe, which will be located in the Office 2003 Smart Document SDK folder structure; you should also find a shortcut to it on the Start menu. Click the browse (...) button next to the XML File box, and locate the manifest file that you want to sign. Click Load XML. This loads the manifest and represents the elements as a tree.

5. In the Stores list, select the certificate store holding your certificate—for example, myStore. In the Certificate list, select the appropriate certificate—for example, myName. In the document tree, right-click Manifest, and choose Append Signature To This Node:

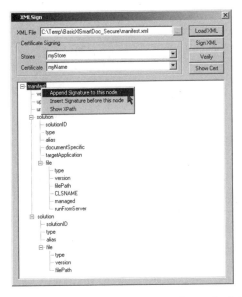

This appends the signature to the end of the manifest and displays an updated tree:

6. Click Sign XML. Specify a location to store the new signed manifest file, and then click Save. By default, it will be saved as *<original manifest name>*_signed.xml, so in our example, this will be *manifest_signed.xml*. You'll get a message asking if you want to view the associated certificate chain. If you click Yes, you'll be shown the certificate information. You should see a final confirmation message, after which you can close XMLSign.

7. The final step is to deploy the signed manifest in a trusted location. A trusted location is any site listed in Internet Explorer's Security lists. To examine these, run Internet Explorer, and go to Tools | Internet Options | Security. By default, the Local Intranet Zone trusts all network paths. For our purposes, we can deploy the solution to somewhere on the local machine (assuming that .NET CAS security has been set up to give the DLL FullTrust permissions in this location).

8. Now run Excel, and either create a new workbook, attach the original XML schema and map some cells, or use a previously saved workbook with cells already mapped. The important step at this point is to attach the new signed XEP manifest file. If you have a previous version of this manifest already attached, detach it now. Then attach the new signed one. To do this, go to Data | XML | XML Expansion Packs. Click Add, and browse to and select the signed manifest file.

The first time you do this, you will see a security warning. If you are happy with all the details offered by this dialog box, you can select the Always Trust Macros From This Publisher check box and click Enable Macros. Everything should then work correctly.

Summary

In developing Office 2003, Microsoft incorporated the new processes and principles inspired by the Trustworthy Computing initiative and created a product that is more secure by design, more secure by default, and more secure in deployment than previous versions of Office. As evidence, consider that all the new Office development protocols allow you to lock down your Office macro security completely and force you to apply explicit CAS policy.

This is evidence of an increasing trend toward making Office more and more secure. Every developer who builds solutions that work with Office is responsible for ensuring that his solution does not pose a security risk. Several techniques and tools are available to support this initiative, including strong-naming, digital signing, and CAS.

Another way that Office 2003 strengthens the security of Office solutions is through the architectural trend away from macro code embedded in a document and toward code-behind assemblies. VBA macro code itself is not a security problem—the problem is that people don't manage documents that contain VBA in a strict enough manner because they don't realize that documents pose the same risk as code. The VSTO model makes a clear separation between document and code, and both are subject to security constraints. VSTO goes even further by revoking all default permissions on the assemblies it loads and by granting only permissions that have been explicitly set up in policy.

Index

Practical strategies
and proven techniques for building
secure applications
in a networked world

U.S.A. **$39.99**
Canada $57.99
ISBN: 0-7356-1588-8

Hackers cost businesses countless dollars and cause developers endless worry every year as they attack networked applications, steal credit-card numbers, deface Web sites, hide back doors and worms, and slow network traffic to a crawl. Keep the bad guys at bay with the tips and techniques in this entertaining, eye-opening book. You'll learn how to padlock your applications throughout the entire development process—from designing secure applications, to writing robust code that can withstand repeated attacks, to testing applications for security flaws. The authors—two battle-scarred veterans who have solved some of the toughest security problems in the industry—give you sample code in numerous languages to demonstrate the specifics of secure development. If you build networked applications and you care about the security of your product, you need this book.

microsoft.com/mspress

Microsoft Press

Work smarter—conquer your software from the inside out!

Microsoft® Windows®
XP Inside Out, Second
Edition
ISBN: 0-7356-2044-X
U.S.A. $44.99
Canada $64.99

Microsoft Office
System Inside Out—
2003 Edition
ISBN: 0-7356-1512-8
U.S.A. $49.99
Canada $72.99

Microsoft Office
Access
2003 Inside Out
ISBN: 0-7356-1513-6
U.S.A. $49.99
Canada $72.99

Microsoft Office
FrontPage® 2003
Inside Out
ISBN: 0-7356-1510-1
U.S.A. $49.99
Canada $72.99

Hey, you know your way around a desktop. Now dig into the new Microsoft Office products and the Windows XP operating system and *really* put your PC to work! These supremely organized software reference titles pack hundreds of timesaving solutions, troubleshooting tips and tricks, and handy workarounds into a concise, fast-answer format. They're all muscle and no fluff. All this comprehensive information goes deep into the nooks and crannies of each Office application and Windows XP feature. And every INSIDE OUT title includes a CD-ROM packed with bonus content such as tools and utilities, demo programs, sample scripts, batch programs, an eBook containing the book's complete text, and more! Discover the best and fastest ways to perform everyday tasks, and challenge yourself to new levels of software mastery!

Microsoft Press has other INSIDE OUT titles to help you get the job done every day:

Microsoft Office Excel 2003 Programming Inside Out
ISBN: 0-7356-1985-9

Microsoft Office Word 2003 Inside Out
ISBN: 0-7356-1515-2

Microsoft Office Excel 2003 Inside Out
ISBN: 0-7356-1511-X

Microsoft Office Outlook 2003® Inside Out
ISBN: 0-7356-1514-4

Microsoft Office Project 2003 Inside Out
ISBN: 0-7356-1958-1

Microsoft Office Visio® 2003 Inside Out
ISBN: 0-7356-1516-0

Microsoft Windows XP Networking Inside Out
ISBN: 0-7356-1652-3

Microsoft Windows Security Inside Out
for Windows XP and Windows 2000
ISBN: 0-7356-1632-9

To learn more about the full line of Microsoft Press® products, please visit us at:

microsoft.com/mspress

Microsoft Press products are available worldwide wherever quality computer books are sold. For more information, contact your book or computer retailer, software reseller, or local Microsoft Sales Office, or visit our Web site at **microsoft.com/mspress**. To locate your nearest source for Microsoft Press products, or to order directly, call 1-800-MSPRESS in the United States. (In Canada, call 1-800-268-2222).

Andrew Whitechapel

Andrew spent many years in the wilderness, writing inventory control systems in COBOL and UNIX kernel extensions in C, before discovering Microsoft Windows and C++. After an enjoyable 12-year relationship with MFC, ATL, and COM, he turned to .NET and pastures green and has been living in a hybrid managed-unmanaged world for several years now. When he's not architecting enterprise systems or bashing in code, Andrew runs (slowly) around a rugby field for Battersea Ironsides.

What do you think of this book? We want to hear from you!

Do you have a few minutes to participate in a brief online survey? Microsoft is interested in hearing your feedback about this publication so that we can continually improve our books and learning resources for you.

To participate in our survey, please visit:

www.microsoft.com/learning/booksurvey

And enter this book's ISBN, 0-7356-2132-2. As a thank-you to survey participants in the United States and Canada, each month we'll randomly select five respondents to win one of five $100 gift certificates from a leading online merchant.* At the conclusion of the survey, you can enter the drawing by providing your e-mail address, which will be used for prize notification *only*.

Thanks in advance for your input. Your opinion counts!

Sincerely,

Microsoft Learning

Microsoft | Learning

Learn More. Go Further.